PRESIDENTS AND THEIR GENERALS

PRESIDENTS AND THEIR GENERALS

AN AMERICAN HISTORY OF COMMAND IN WAR

Matthew Moten

THE BELKNAP PRESS OF HARVARD UNIVERSITY PRESS

Cambridge, Massachusetts, & London, England
2014

First Printing

Library of Congress Cataloging-in-Publication Data
Moten, Matthew, 1960–
Presidents and their generals : an American history of command in war /
Matthew Moten.
pages cm
Includes bibliographical references and index.
ISBN 978-0-674-05814-9 (alkaline paper) 1. Presidents—United States—
History. 2. Generals—United States—History. 3. Command of troops—History.
4. Civil-military relations—United States—History. 5. United States—History,
Military. 6. United States—Military policy. 7. United States—Politics and
government. I. Title.
E176.1.M93 2014
355.0092'2—dc23
[B]   2014009057

For Stephanie and Marshall

One a civilian, one a soldier,
both beloved

CONTENTS

A few months after 9/11, I was at a dinner party with my neighbors in Fairfax, Virginia. I worked at the Pentagon, and had been there on the day of the attack. I was long accustomed to fielding questions from my friends about foreign policy and military strategy. Now, the voices were more anxious and the questions more urgent than in the past. The Bush administration was not yet clear about its strategic direction, or at least if it was, it wasn't saying. One friend, Mark, pointedly asked me why the generals didn't just tell the administration what to do and how to do it. With a Wharton MBA and a software company that he later sold for a tidy sum, Mark was nobody's fool. I tried to tell him that we don't make policy that way in this country, but he insisted that we were under attack, and it was a cop-out for the generals not to take charge. I was appalled and concerned. Bright, outgoing, honest, articulate, Mark is a good man and a good friend. Yet I felt that he ought to understand more about how his government and its military work together to protect the country. His insistence that the generals take charge was not only ludicrous but dangerous. As a historian who has been studying political-military issues for twenty-five years and as an army officer who has worked at the highest levels in the Pentagon, I wrote *Presidents and Their Generals* for Mark and Americans like him—smart people who make this country and its economy run—to explain why they should be knowledgeable about the roles and responsibilities of civilian and military leaders, and why the relationships between them are vitally important to the outcomes of the decisions they make.

I want to thank a number of people who helped make this book possible. Joe Glatthaar, Ira Gruber, Dick Kohn, Wayne Lee, Alex Roland, and Geoffrey Ward read and offered insightful criticism on various chapters. Jenny Boyle was my able research assistant during the first year of this enterprise. Her enthusiasm and expertise kept me going in the early stages. Lance Betros, my boss during most of this writing, gave me unstinting support in more ways than I can count. Pete Maslowski and Roger Spiller read every word and saved me from many egregious errors. Roger offered support and encouragement when it was most needed. Thanks to my editor, Joyce Seltzer, and her assistant, Brian Distelberg, for their belief in the project and their assistance throughout the publishing process. Working with them has been a joy. Finally, I want to thank my wife, Margaret, who has lived with this project for five years and has ever been its biggest champion.

PRESIDENTS AND THEIR GENERALS

John Trumbull, *General George Washington Resigning His Commission to Congress as Commander in Chief of the Army at Annapolis, Maryland, December 23d, 1783*. Oil on canvas. Courtesy of the Architect of the Capitol.

In the Rotunda of the Capitol, the physical center of American government, hang eight immense oil paintings. Commissioned in the early nineteenth century, these grand canvases depict signal events in the life of the nation, including Columbus's arrival in the New World, the embarkation of the Pilgrims, Cornwallis's surrender at Yorktown, and the signing of the Declaration of Independence.[1] Among them is a John Trumbull portrait of the Continental Congress on December 23, 1783. At center stands General George Washington, commander of the Continental Army, his left hand resting on the hilt of a sheathed sword, his officers gathered reverently behind him. With his outstretched right arm Washington tenders to the seated legislators a parchment, the commission they had given him eight years before, authorizing him to take command of a fledgling army in defense of the rebelling colonies. His mission accomplished, Washington is surrendering his military authority to his political masters and asking leave to retire. It is a moving scene, at once triumphant and poignant.

The literal and figurative centrality of this portrait says a great deal about the way Americans see themselves, or at least about the way early national leaders wanted to see their country. The portrait propounds a cherished trope. The British foe has been vanquished and the nation is whole, independent, and at peace. The congressmen appear sober, affluent, and wise. The leader of the army, an institution so long feared on both sides of the Atlantic, stands strong yet subordinate before them, requesting his own relief and, by extension, the dissolution of that army. He yields not to a king or another general, but to the assembled representatives of the people. Republican government had called an army into being, wielded that military power in pursuit of its ends, and accomplished an almost impossible task—gaining independence from the greatest empire on earth—all the while maintaining control of the lethal sword. The danger gone, the nation returns to peace, and its soldiers repair to their homes and civilian pursuits. The trust that Congress had reposed in Washington had been well placed.

For most of their history Americans gave little systematic thought to the relations between the government and its armed forces. The prevailing view was that large standing armies were dangers to liberty—their soldiers licentious and their commanders ambitious. If an emergency made force necessary, citizen-soldiers—militia or volunteers—were best, as they could be expected to return to the plow or the factory as soon as peace would allow. Yet a willingness to follow the colors in wartime was a mark of patriotism. Former citizen-soldiers often became political leaders. Generals always bore close watching, for few could be expected to emulate Washington either in competence or self-abnegation. Paradoxically, to the extent that they came close, they were elected president. In brief, the consensus held that the military should be kept as small as possible in peacetime, expanded when threats emerged, then contracted again as quickly as possible at war's end. Most of all, it should be controlled.

Before the 1950s, scholars, like most Americans, rarely addressed the topic of the military as an institution or its relation to the broader government. Then the Cold War demonstrated that the old myth that Trumbull portrayed bore little resemblance to current reality. A global state of conflict was permanent and a shooting war continuously imminent. The armed forces remained large by historical peacetime standards, their prowess enhanced by a growing nuclear arsenal. In 1957 Samuel Huntington explored a topic that he termed "civil-military relations." He looked at the military in American history and compared its place in American society with armies, governments, and populations overseas. *The Soldier and the State* posited competing imperatives in national security: the need to balance effective military force with civilian control of that force. He concluded, *contra* Clemenceau, that war was too important to be left to the generals or the politicians. Maintaining a professional military carefully overseen by competent civilian authority was the only way to guarantee the security of the state.

Morris Janowitz soon followed with a sociological study of military elites in *The Professional Soldier* (1960). His title stipulated the existence of a military profession, and he categorized officers into three archetypes—heroic leaders, managers, and technologists—according to their social origins, political ideologies, strategic beliefs, and career motivations.

Together, these works spawned a new interdisciplinary field of study, civil-military relations. In 1974 Janowitz founded *Armed Forces and Society*, a journal devoted to the field. Over the past four decades, most of the studies in civil-military relations, like that of Huntington and Janowitz, have been theoretical works in sociology and political science.

Historians have looked at specific historical eras and episodes, but none has satisfactorily approached the long historical development of American civil-military relations since Huntington. This work focuses on specific and representative personal relationships at the highest levels of civil-military relations during wartime over three centuries. For that reason, it will employ the term "political-military relations" to distinguish it from the broader study of "civil-military relations," which includes interactions between the military and society.

Why should Americans be interested in the relationships between soldiers and statesmen? What is important about the roles and responsibilities of civilian and military leaders? How do those relationships affect the outcomes of the decisions they make?

The relationship between a president and his military commanders and advisers is never as simple as the Trumbull tableau would have us believe. No wall separates the making of policy from the prosecution of war. Political-military relations do not begin and end with the president giving orders and the general dutifully carrying them out, although that should and does occur. Instead, that interaction occurs after a process of intense and often contentious negotiation over the aims of policy, the forms of strategy to be used, the resources to be employed, and the timing of execution, to name only the most major considerations. Once execution of strategy begins, policy usually changes along with evolving circumstances, causing the process of negotiation to be constant and continuous.

The premise of this book is that these negotiations materially affect the making of national security policy and military strategy. The outcomes of the decisions taken matter in the lives of every American. Therefore, the relationships between the soldiers and statesmen who make difficult decisions and momentous decisions are vitally important. As concerned and conscientious citizens, we need to understand better the dynamics of their working relationships.

Presidents and Their Generals attempts to explain those relationships through narrative history, setting up negotiations among soldiers and statesmen who have flesh and bone and warts. Some protagonists will be familiar to readers; others will need more introduction. Occasionally, bit

3

players in one chapter will become protagonists in the next. The give-and-take illuminates issues in political-military relations. Some chapters examine conclusive solutions to problems. Others narrate unfortunate and destructive events that left bitter legacies. Throughout the American experience political and military leaders continually negotiated with one another, especially in time of war, and, in so doing, continually shaped and reshaped the political, social, legal, and military parameters of political-military relations in American history.

The principal elements of the political-military negotiation are authority and responsibility for determining policy and strategy. The authority and responsibility that each party to the negotiation exercises derive from the Constitution and the law. Of course, interpretations of the Constitution evolve and vary, and the law continually shifts with circumstances. Presidents draw political authority from the electorate, to whom they are, in turn, responsible under the Constitution for faithful execution of the law. Politicians gain or lose political authority as the voters register their assessment of performance in office. Politicians tend the electoral garden constantly in order to retain the political authority to govern in peacetime and in war.

Military authority derives from a commission, proffered by the president and approved by the United States Senate. At the highest levels, that commission confers an office with specific authority—to command armed forces, to superintend the military services, or to render professional advice, to name a few. Ultimately, military officers are responsible to civilian society as well, but they exercise that responsibility through a chain of command that extends through the secretary of defense to the president of the United States. In practice, the extent of military authority varies depending upon how presidents choose to exercise their role as commander in chief of the armed forces, as well as how much trust and confidence they retain in the military profession itself and its incumbent leaders.

The environment in which the relationship occurs has changed dramatically over American history as political and military institutions—the president, Congress, the War Department and the Department of Defense, the Joint Chiefs of Staff, and the military services—have evolved. The elements of authority and responsibility that operate in this swiftly changing environment of political and military power relations and negotiation are critical to an effective national security. The personal and institutional give-and-take between politicians and senior officers yields national policy and the strategies to carry it out. Generals often find themselves confronting political issues, and presidents of necessity delve into strategy. The continuous negotiation involves collaboration and competition among politicians and soldiers, a dialogue or conflict that results in creative or destructive tension, and often a mixture of both. Personalities and vested interests matter when choices are made, and fateful consequences follow.

In these relations, military leaders surrender some control over military matters—strategy, operations, force structure—in exchange for a seat at the table from which to offer professional advice on decisions that they judge to be the most effective and least costly. Civilian leaders, too, cede some authority—control of information, political maneuvering room—in order to obtain professional advice on how best to implement policy, and to get competent and subordinate military leadership that will execute strategy. A high degree of mutual trust is important, if not essential, in successful partnerships. Too much sympathy with the other's views can generate an unwillingness to test assumptions, while too much suspicion can disastrously impede communication. In the most effective political-military relations, such as the Lincoln-Grant collaboration and the FDR-Marshall partnership, mutual trust was born of candor, respect, demonstrated competence, a shared worldview, and an expectation that each partner would take responsibility for the decisions made. In the least effective relationships, such as Lincoln-McClellan and Truman-MacArthur, few if any of those traits were present. Political and military institutions undergird personal relationships. The more stable, secure, and supportive they are, the more likely their leaders will act with conviction and commitment. The dynamics of such institutions must be understood, nurtured, and reformed when necessary, both from within and without. The personal relationships among presidents and generals rest upon those foundations, and the firmer and more transparent their norms, the greater the likelihood that they will lead to effective decision making.

Society delegates to professionals jurisdiction over complex and important areas of human life. The essential responsibility that any individual professional owes is to society as a whole, but in most professions practitioners exercise that responsibility with one client at a time. A doctor treats one patient, a lawyer tries one case, a clergyman counsels one layman. The trust that society reposes in professions and professionals allows these interactions to occur routinely and effectively, and society as a whole benefits from the exchange. Yet each practitioner must repay and re-earn society's trust daily by ministering to each client with expert and ethical practice.

Conversely, most members of the military profession have no such individual interaction with their clients; they practice as part of a hierarchical federal organization, ministering to and for the entire nation as the government directs. Thus, most military officers cannot reinforce society's trust through continual personal interaction. Instead, they must rely on the profession's institutional reputation and credibility to retain the public's trust. They do that through well-honed expertise and adherence to ethical and disciplined behavior. They commit themselves to act in the way that society expects, which is under the control of duly constituted governmental authority—civilian control of the military.

Only at the highest levels do military professionals treat with individual clients who stand in for society—elected and appointed officials: the president, secretary of defense, members of Congress, and other high-level political leaders. At this level, personal relationships between civilian and military leaders are determinative. If there are honest, emotionally healthy adults with a penchant for goodwill on both sides of the relationship, good things will likely ensue. Of course, more than a modicum of political talent on one side and mature professionalism on the other are indispensable. Tensions will still exist, because the demands of policy and strategy often tug in different directions. Yet adults who trust and respect each other can work through the knottiest of problems, which are the kind that war and national security present. Such people, when committed to the national welfare, can make the tension creative and constructive, with good results for both policy and strategy.

Yet political-military conflicts are both natural and inherent in the structure of our government. They derive from mixing together the leaders of two distinct national institutions. Such leaders are likely to be powerful, ambitious, and strong-willed advocates of their unique perspectives and experiences who must work closely on solving the pressing and demanding problems of armed conflict. When political-military tension fosters informed decision making, it can be productive of effective policy and strategy. Unfortunately, history does not always place forthright, well-meaning, talented, and stable people at the political-military nexus. It puts a Lincoln on one side and a McClellan on the other, and the result is strategic stasis compounded by repeated embarrassment at the hands of the enemy. When Grant replaces McClellan, the new combination wins the Civil War with relentless campaigning in little more than a year. Tragedy substitutes Andrew Johnson for an assassinated Lincoln, and a dysfunctional relationship with military leaders in the occupied South results in a crippled presidency and three years of failed Reconstruction, the ramifications of which we have yet to overcome.

Presidents and Their Generals explores these unpredictable relationships over three distinct eras. The first period, from the Revolution through the first half of the Civil War, established the principle of military subordination to civil government, witnessed the beginnings of a professional military, and provided opportunities for the presidency to articulate its constitutional powers as commander in chief. At the beginning of this period, military and civilian were hardly separate spheres of operation. By the Civil War, there was a clear sense that professional officers had first claim on military leadership, even if their soldiers were still largely citizens in arms. The national government and the military establishment grew up together, and the relations between presidents and generals matured apace.

From Lincoln's administration to FDR's the power of the presidency came into full maturity with the professional military its (usually) reliable servant. The peacetime military establishment remained a small burden on the economy and the body politic, but it mushroomed to gargantuan proportions in wartime. The latter parts of the Civil War and World War II provided the high points in effective political-military relations, largely because presidents and their generals worked through early setbacks to attain mutual trust and common aims. Over this same period the military became fully professionalized and almost entirely nonpartisan, even if the enlisted soldiers and junior officers necessary for nationwide mobilization were part-timers. After World War II, the emerging national security state codified FDR's idiosyncratic military administration even as the presidency and the military arm each gained ever greater governmental power, largely at the expense of Congress.

With the advent of the bipolar Cold War, soon compounded by fear of nuclear Armageddon, presidents accrued unprecedented sway over national security matters that Congress could scarcely contest. Concurrently, the hero-generals and -admirals of World War II gained suzerainty over burgeoning armies and fleets and their attendant budgets, placing them and their successors near the apex of the Washington power structure. The newly powerful military bureaucracy ever more carefully groomed officers to take on institutional values. General Douglas MacArthur's insubordination to President Harry Truman in the Korean War testified to the personal power of a military hero and put future presidents on notice that generals warrant close scrutiny. Beginning with Eisenhower, a former general himself, presidents tried to corral the top brass, but chafed at the military chiefs' increasing concern with the growth and promotion of their own branches of service. Presidents came to mistrust the professional assembly line. Given that the major conflicts of the late twentieth and early twenty-first centuries were wars of choice, commanders in chief felt a need for publicly voiced support from their uniformed counselors, and they began to buck the profession by selecting generals who would provide partisan support. In Vietnam, Desert Storm, and the wars in Iraq and Afghanistan, the principal military leaders—Taylor, Powell, Franks—responded by allying themselves politically with the (first) administrations they served, rather than offering critically nonpartisan counsel. The results in each case were amicable relations between presidents and generals, but less satisfactory military and national security results for the nation. In each case, succeeding chief executives had reason to doubt the loyalty of those generals and their successors.

Presidents and Their Generals is not a continuous narrative through American history. Instead, it focuses on twelve wartime episodes when political-military relations were most important to the republic, and perhaps when conflict or collaboration were most acute. On the political side, presidents get the spotlight, but sometimes their secretaries of war, state, or defense play major roles. Key members of Congress walk on and off the stage. On the military side, army generals dominate the dramatis personae. When sailors, marines, and airmen have important roles to play, they get their due, but thus far in American wartime, for better and worse, the dominant military leaders have been army generals.

This book aims to provide a deeper understanding of the discussions between political and military leaders, to show how the negotiation does and does not work effectively, and to give the reader an appreciation for the decisions that flow from these interactions and their critical importance to the nation, to their own lives, and to posterity.

I

SETTING

PRECEDENTS

★ When the American Revolution began, a dearth of national precedents, either for the government or the military, complicated the new nation's existential challenges. George Washington established the principle of civilian control of the military by consistently subordinating himself to the Continental Congress despite enormous pressures and temptations to seize greater power. After the war a new Constitution codified roles for the executive and legislative branches in the control of the sword, but those powers placed the two branches in conflict and the military uncomfortably subordinate to both. Early national administrations sparred over those roles, especially that of the president as commander in chief. Building the military apparatus was a long test by trial and error. The lack of clearly separate spheres of military and civilian life complicated those negotiations through the War of 1812. After near disaster, the military began to professionalize and become a more reliable servant of the state.

Under Andrew Jackson the presidency attained energy and authority at the expense of Congress. The War and Navy Departments gained institutional coherence, as did the services they oversaw. President James K. Polk both used and disdained these military instruments in his expeditionary war against Mexico. His legacy was that of an energetic commander in chief who did not yet trust the military to do the executive's bidding.

Abraham Lincoln's election as president brought on the nation's greatest crisis. The new president had almost no military or executive experience, but he quickly grew into the job while raising an army to quash a rebellion. By 1861 there was a clear sense that professional officers had first claim on military leadership, even if their soldiers were still citizens in arms. Lincoln learned to employ the powers of his office while searching for generals who would follow his lead and convert his policies into successful strategy. He became a commander in chief who fully grasped the need to think of his generals as implements of his policy, even as he changed his policy to transform the war and the nation.

1

GEORGE WASHINGTON

AND THE CONTINENTAL CONGRESS

They called it the Temple of Virtue. Standing majestically upon a hill, it commanded the New Windsor cantonment of the Continental Army. Constructed of stone and timber like the six hundred soldiers' huts that surrounded it, the meeting hall covered some thirty-three hundred square feet, with a large central hall warmed by a number of fireplaces. Three months after its construction it was still redolent of fresh-cut green timbers.

The temple's builders were part of an army seven thousand strong then at the height of its prestige. Many soldiers sported new chevrons on their sleeves denoting the years they had bravely and patriotically served their country. The speed with which they had built such a sturdy and comfortable encampment was a testament to their discipline and training. Proud of their Revolutionary virtue and a bit cocky about their victory over the British regulars, they looked forward to the announcement of a peace treaty and a joyous, triumphant return to their homes.

Within a few hours, a bitter clash would determine whether the temple's name was a tribute to its builders or a stain upon their character.

A few miles away at his Newburgh headquarters, their commander in chief shared many of their emotions. George Washington had served with this army for eight long years with scarcely a break and, at his own insistence, no salary. He had built the Continental Army from a ragtag assortment of New England militia in 1775 into a formidable fighting army. He had led it in defeat at Brooklyn and Brandywine and Germantown and in victory at Trenton and Princeton and Yorktown. He had shared its hardships in winters at Valley Forge and Morristown. He had fought with these soldiers against the British and for them in a years-long struggle with his political masters—their capricious financiers, clothiers, and commissariat—the Continental Congress. He was unreservedly proud of this army—this regular army—that he had worked so hard to raise, and so much harder against the individualistic nature of his soldiers and the democratic nature of his people to whip into shape. Now, after all that effort and all that they had accomplished, everything they had fought for seemed at risk. Still, he had been in many tough scrapes. He walked outside and mounted his awaiting horse for a brisk winter morning's ride through new-fallen snow to the temple.

He had fought with Congress, to be sure, but he could not judge its members too harshly. He, more than anyone, understood their trials and obstacles. He had worked with them as closely as anyone in the army. Besides, eight years earlier he had served alongside them.

General Washington's political-military relations with the Congress—and the states—went through four broad stages during the war, as the Congress and the army learned and matured. The first phase came with Washington's selection as commanding general and continued through the siege of Boston as he built the Continental Army. This Congress, delegate for delegate the most talented, acted with resolve to organize the colonies for war. Yet the delegates were not sure whether they sought reconciliation with or independence from the mother country. Washington actively subordinated himself to Congress to strengthen it and give it confidence. And in 1775 when the British evacuated Boston under his guns on Dorchester Heights, his army's accomplishments fostered in Congress the fortitude to declare independence.

The second stage coincided with a series of battlefield defeats as the British forced Washington into retreat through southern New York, across New Jersey, and into Pennsylvania. In response, Congress granted Washington extraordinary powers to prosecute the war. While remaining subordinate, Washington took a harder line with this Congress, demanding everything in its power to support his army and assure victory. He soon ended his string of losses and recovered his reputation with brilliant victories at Trenton and Princeton. Having declared war in pursuit of independence, Congress began to feel the inadequacy of its legal writ vis-à-vis the states. The delegates understood that the war's outcome would brand them as traitors or anoint them as founders. Anything short of victory was unacceptable, and they began to consider the ramifications of governmental disorganization and weakness.

A third and most difficult stage came in 1777–78 when Washington's operational failures caused the evacuation of Congress from Philadelphia even as his subordinate general, Horatio Gates, was forcing the surrender of a British army at Saratoga. The Valley Forge winter that followed was one of reassessment, rebuilding, and reform. This Congress, having evacuated Philadelphia for a second time in the face of a British offensive, started to lose confidence in Washington, but in so doing, gained confidence in itself as a governing body. It insisted on greater supervision of the war effort. Congress labored unsuccessfully to bring forth a better system of government and a better means of supervising its army. Washington's position in command was precarious for a time, but he responded to Congress's concerns and outmaneuvered his adversaries, emerging more firmly in control of the army and more secure than ever in his relations with Congress.

In the final stage, having regained a measure of trust in the army, Congress and the nation plunged into one of the darkest times of the war. The government was bankrupt and the economy in collapse. Soldiers were mutinying in the middle states, and armies were surrendering in the South. The country turned toward nationalist politicians to strengthen Congress and win the war. Those leaders also began to look toward the postwar nation, attempting in wartime to shape the government and the people that they would become. Congress reorganized under the newly ratified Articles of Confederation, instituted executive departments, and declared its authority to levy taxes. On the operational front, this stage encompassed three years of mostly desultory maneuvering in the middle states, two years of losing, then winning by Washington's subordinates in the South, and the victory at Yorktown followed by two years of waiting for a peace treaty. It ended with the greatest trial of political-military relations in American history, the Newburgh Conspiracy. During that episode, Washington became the bulwark and symbol of an emerging American system of political-military relations. He retained control of the army while insisting upon his own and the army's subordination to political authority—despite enormous pressure and temptation to throw off his fetters—and established a tradition that would echo through American political and military history.

Maintaining this attitude of subordination was infinitely more difficult than it would be for any of his successors under the Constitution of the United States, for political authority was doubly diffused. The Continental Congress was a legislative body acting with ill-defined executive authority. Over eight years Washington reported to eight successive presidents of the Congress, as well as dozens of committees. Congress was also politically weak, existing at the sufferance of the several colonies, with only limited ability to tax or raise other revenues to fund a government, much less support an army. Real political power lay with the thirteen colonies, all of whom were experimenting with new forms of republican government and all of whom had to be placated and motivated to remain in the fold and support the war effort. Washington's task was to buttress the Continental Congress and coordinate with an unwieldy coalition of semiautonomous states even as he attempted to build a national army and win a war.

In April 1775, delegates to the Second Continental Congress were preparing to converge on Philadelphia when word swept through the colonies of the battles at Lexington and Concord. A political dispute with Parliament, complicated by British occupation of Boston and suspension of the Massachusetts assembly, now exploded into the possibility of war. The second Congress would spend weeks considering "the state of America," an all-encompassing debate about first principles. Were the colonies' relationships with Great Britain irreparable? Should the colonies unite? What powers should their government have? If armed conflict were unavoidable, how should Americans fight? Should the colonies rely on their militias? Should they put aside their long-held hatred of standing armies? Had Congress the authority to call an army into being? If so, how would the army be recruited, fed, and supported? How would it be controlled? Who should command? All of these questions demanded answers from delegates who were not even sure that they had authority to make such decisions.

George Washington, a Virginia delegate, left his Mount Vernon home on the fourth of May sure that war loomed. He had been inspecting local militia companies and meeting with former soldiers to prepare the colony for defense. In his baggage was a buff and blue uniform that he had designed for the Virginia militia, which he resolved to wear at the continental assembly to demonstrate Virginia's readiness to support its New England brethren. A few days after arriving in Philadelphia, he lamented to an old friend, "Unhappy it is though to reflect, that a Brother's Sword has been sheathed in a Brother's breast, and that, the once happy and peaceful plains of America are either to be drenched with Blood, or Inhabited by Slaves. Sad alternative! But can a virtuous Man hesitate in his choice?" Virginia's most distinguished soldier probably expected to return home after Congress adjourned to command its local forces.[1]

For three weeks the Continental Congress deliberated on organizing the colonies' defenses. The American seizure of Fort Ticonderoga aroused rejoicing, while arbitrating disputes between colonies caused vexation. A committee wrote to America's Canadian neighbors attempting to enlist them in the fight with Great Britain. Then, on June 2, Dr. Benjamin Church arrived from Boston carrying a plaintive missive from the Massachusetts Provincial Congress. After listing British depredations upon their lives, liberties, and property, leaders of the Bay Colony had concluded that they were "now compelled to raise an Army.... But as the sword should in all free states be subservient to the civil powers ... we tremble at having an army (although consisting of our countrymen) established here without a civil power to provide for and controul them." They asked for the Continental Congress's "most explicit advice" and pronounced themselves ready to "submit to such a general plan as you may direct for the colonies ... as shall not only promote our advantage but the union and interest of all America." Specifically, and lest Congress miss the main point, they noted that the army gathering in Massachusetts came from several colonies "for the general defence of the right of America" and they begged "leave to suggest to yr. consideration the propriety of yr. taking the regulation and general direction of it, that the operations may more effectually answer the purposes designed."[2]

The Massachusetts letter helped Congress to resolve a number of questions. A colony under British invasion was asking for assistance and direction from a central government. Over the next several days, the Congress took action to impede the British invasion, to borrow money and raise other revenues, to draft letters to the king and to the people of Great Britain, and to gather provisions and war matériel and speed them to Massachusetts.[3] For all that has been written about the ineptitude of the Continental Congress, in these early days it was energetic and willing to accept responsibility. On June 14, 1775, Congress resolved to raise an army.[4]

Who would command it?

Even before the Second Continental Congress convened, Washington's selection as commander in chief might have been a foregone conclusion. The Massachusetts delegation had already resolved to nominate him. Washington later insisted that he had not wanted or expected the post, but his attendance in Congress in military uniform attested to his availability.[5]

George Washington had gained his colleagues' trust and respect as a founding member of the First Continental Congress. Tall, taciturn, dignified, he looked the part of a soldier, and his record in the French and Indian War, including his command of the First Virginia Regiment, was well known throughout the colonies. One Philadelphian enthused that he "has so much martial dignity in his deportment that would distinguish him to be a general and a soldier from among ten thousand people. There is not a king in Europe that would not look like a valet de chambre by his side." Members of the first Congress had sought his counsel on military matters, most of all on the question of whether a war with England was feasible. They had taken his measure, and found him calm, disciplined, and reliable.[6]

Yet his military experience worried his contemporaries as much as it reassured them. The fear of standing armies was an Anglo-American tradition that stretched back to Cromwell's time. Washington's record as a military commander could easily have caused his colleagues to fear him as a potential Caesar, who once in possession of an army would use it to depose Congress and seize political control.

However, in addition to his military experience, Washington had spent fifteen years in the Virginia House of Burgesses. The once impetuous young soldier had matured over those years, coming to comprehend the slow, often frustrating give-and-take of legislative bodies. He understood the need for compromise and the importance of building consensus. His soldierly qualities earned him respect. His grasp of the nature of Congress earned him their trust.[7]

Political concerns as much as military ones determined Washington's selection. A loose confederation of militias from four New England colonies faced the British army in Boston. New England, especially Massachusetts, needed the rest of the colonies to commit to repelling the British. That meant gaining the support of and superintendence from the Continental Congress. If the middle and southern colonies remained aloof, the British might be able to subdue the rebellion piecemeal. John Adams knew that selecting a Virginian, representing the largest southern colony, to command would symbolically unite the colonies and the Congress behind the war. The most experienced and trustworthy Virginian was sitting across the room.[8]

The day after it authorized the Continental Army, Congress unanimously chose Washington "to command all the continental forces, raised, or to be raised, for the defence of American liberty." Accepting the appointment and thanking Congress for its approbation, he confessed that he felt "great distress, from a consciousness that my abilities and military experience may not be equal to the extensive and important Trust." This was more than mere politesse. Washington had never commanded more than a regiment; now, the weight of an army, a war, and a country rested on his shoulders. Patrick Henry later recalled that Washington told him with tears in his eyes, "Remember, Mr. Henry, what I now tell you. From the day I enter upon the command of the American armies, I date my fall and the ruin of my reputation."[9]

His charge from the Congress was vague: to establish order and discipline. Congress did not expressly declare war on England. More than a year would pass before it would declare independence. American strategy was murky, thus far limited to defending American liberty and "repelling every hostile invasion thereof." To that end, Congress vested Washington with "full power and authority to act as you shall think for the good and welfare of the service."[10]

Congress was taking a large step toward expanding its authority by creating an army, commissioning officers, and ordering Washington to take command of the forces outside Boston. Nonetheless, its authority was tenuous. It was an extralegal body fomenting rebellion against a Crown that had ruled on the continent for the better part of two centuries. In that moment no outcome was certain. Washington later said that "we all fought with halters around our necks."[11]

Washington quickly became the preeminent leader in America, the embodiment of the rebellion. Everything depended on his leadership. He was in many ways uniquely qualified for the task. He was thoroughly dedicated to the cause and indefatigable in his pursuit of victory. He was dignified, and he inspired great confidence. As taciturn as he was in person, he was an eloquent and prolific correspondent, sending thousands of letters to Congress, to governors, and to other leaders around the country. He was adept at explaining the army and its needs to Congress, the states, and the public, as well as explaining the challenges of Congress and the states to the army. He fully grasped the colonial fear of standing armies, and understood that in popular Whig thought, control of the military meant legislative, not executive control. However, at this point he was militarily unqualified for supreme command. He was occasionally indecisive, and he made major tactical and strategic errors. Fortunately, he was capable of learning from those mistakes. He prized his personal reputation highly and was exceptionally sensitive to any criticism. He could be vindictive toward those who he came to believe were his enemies. Yet he was exceptionally skilled in the arts of politics—so skilled, in fact, that historian John Ferling has written that "he alone of all of America's public officials in the past two centuries succeeded in convincing others that he was not a politician."[12]

As he began his career in command, Washington set to work on four fronts, not least of which was the very real one, the British army occupying Boston. At the same time, he began corresponding continually with Congress and the provincial governments of New England to keep his army supplied and manned, quickly appreciating the diffuseness of political power in the colonies and how much the colonists cherished the newfound autonomy of their legislatures. He also commenced a charm offensive with the local elites in Massachusetts, knowing that he needed to demonstrate a sharp contrast with the behavior of the British invaders. Immediately, however, he began to discipline and organize the army.

Washington made an excellent start, born of his keen understanding of his countrymen—he had traveled more broadly in America than almost any Revolutionary leader. He refused a salary, asking Congress only to defray his expenses. With this gesture he ran the risk of portraying aristocratic arrogance, but many looked upon it as republican self-abnegation, and frugal New Englanders seemed especially gratified. When he stopped in New York en route to Boston, he shrewdly attempted to allay fears of a large standing army and, especially, its commander. He told a gathering that "when we assumed the soldier, we did not lay aside the citizen." Rather than claim limitless powers, he willingly obeyed political authority.[13]

When Washington arrived at the camp outside Boston, he soon grasped why Congress had charged him first with establishing order and discipline. Militiamen were famously independent, coming and going as they pleased. Moreover, still basking in the glory of their successes at Lexington, Concord, and Bunker Hill, many soldiers considered the prevailing standards of discipline more than adequate. There were, in fact, four colonial forces in camp, forming a loose coalition rather than an army. When Washington asked for an accounting of how many men he commanded, it took a week to get the returns. The supply system was haphazard, almost nonexistent, and dependent upon the patriotism and generosity of several New England colonial legislatures. Yet the effort to establish discipline carried risks, as New Englanders were highly suspicious of regular armies, not just for ideological reasons but because decades of interaction between their own militias and British regulars during the colonial wars had created bad blood. Washington, a southern outsider, needed to gain their trust. He recognized the need to lead these soldiers, not just to command them.[14]

Washington initiated a series of inspections, both to understand the challenges he was facing and to demonstrate his concern for the men's health and welfare. He reorganized the army along the British model with which he was familiar, forming regiments and brigades, giving regularity to the chain of command. He created a military structure that he would build upon continually through the war.[15]

One of his greatest challenges was dealing with the poorly disciplined New England militia, a hodgepodge of local institutions as old as the colonies themselves. Based on the principles of local defense and universal manhood military obligation, the militia was interwoven with New England society politically and culturally. Local elites both recruited and commanded their soldiers, contracting with them for a specified period of service. The contract was a covenant between officers and men with the full force of the community behind it. When the contract was broken or expired, militia soldiers felt well within their rights as free men to return home. Washington found contracts expiring and militia units dissolving as soon as he arrived. He faced the real prospect that his new command might simply walk away. At its peak the army surrounding Boston numbered twenty-three thousand men. By the end of 1775, only four thousand of those had reenlisted, and entire units began marching for home. Yet, rather than repeating British mistakes of the French and Indian War—abrogating the contracts, enforcing the harsh discipline customary with European conscripts, and then treating American militia as inferiors—Washington showed restraint, diligently working with Congress, governors, and legislatures to send more troops.[16]

Yet, in a private letter, he railed against New England soldiery, suggesting that their reputation after Bunker Hill was much better than they deserved: "Their Officers generally speaking are the most indifferent kind of People I ever saw. I have already broke one Colo. and five Captains for cowardice, & for drawing more Pay & Provisions than they had Men in their Companies. There is two more Colos. now under arrest. . . . I daresay the Men would fight very well (if properly Officered), although they are an exceedingly dirty & nasty people." Unfortunately, the letter leaked, and his thoughts soon found their way to Philadelphia, causing an uproar among the New England delegations, and creating a touchy political problem.[17]

The damage was done. Washington sought to undo it in the best way he knew—by writing more letters. During his nine months in Cambridge, the general wrote fifty-one letters to the president of Congress, thirty-four to the Massachusetts Provincial Congress, forty to the governor of Connecticut, and thirty to the governor of Rhode Island. His letters to John Hancock, president of the Continental Congress, were lengthy reports, detailing his tactical situation, his personnel strength, and his supply difficulties. When faced with problems, such as the commissioning of general officers, an authority Congress had retained for itself, he was correctly subordinate but forthright in urging further action. His correspondence showed assiduous attention to Congress's authority: its right to commission officers, its strategic designs, and its orders about the organization of the army.[18]

Washington quickly felt a need to communicate with local governors and legislatures in order to gain their support for the army. He was respectful in those letters, deferring to local authorities and acknowledging their prerogatives. But he was not subordinate, instead writing to colonial leaders as an equal, all the while reminding them of the army's needs of men, supplies, uniforms, ammunition, guns, and cannon. His correspondence with Governor John Trumbull of Connecticut, for example, was remarkable for its frequency and businesslike character. These two men, both bearing enormous burdens but with quite different responsibilities, wrote frankly to one another. When some Connecticut militiamen left camp before their enlistments had expired, Washington remonstrated with Trumbull to take action against them. Trumbull assured him that he would do so and would ask the General Assembly to make up the shortfall. He also apologetically suggested "that the conduct of our Troops is not a rule whereby to judge of the Temper and Spirit of the Colony." Sometimes, the two leaders felt comfortable enough to quarrel with each other, but they patched things up quickly and moved on to other matters. Corresponding with so many governments consumed enormous time and the efforts of several Washington aides. Moreover, the need for so much correspondence points up the diffuseness of governmental power during the Revolution, and thus the need for continuous negotiation. Washington would wrestle with those two problems for the rest of the war.[19]

Chosen to provide geographic political balance as much as for his competence, Washington recognized that he needed not only to lead New England soldiers, but to win the trust of civilian leaders as well. While reforming the army, he had to instill discipline without harshness. The Revolution was a triangular conflict in which the British and American armies competed for the allegiance of the people. Washington determined to show deference to the colonial leadership, while building and maintaining an army. He grasped the need to provide a clear contrast with the imperiousness of the British Crown by showing respect for the populace if he were to win the hearts and minds of Americans and to build an army.[20]

Washington courted local leaders, inviting them to his camp and dining with them when he had the opportunity. Soon after his arrival he charmed Abigail Adams, who chided her husband, John, that while he had prepared her to have a favorable opinion of Washington, "I thought the one half was not told me," and quoted romantic verse to describe the general. The local clergy, which had fretted about the potential vices of twenty thousand young men gathered closely together, appreciated his establishing discipline among the soldiers. The Reverend William Gordon noted that before Washington arrived, "there was little emulation among the officers: and the soldiers were lazy, disorderly, and dirty," unknowingly voicing Washington's own private complaints. "The freedom to which the New Englanders have always been accustomed makes them impatient of control," he said, but now "every officer and private begin to know his place and duty." When the army left Massachusetts following the British evacuation of Boston, the General Court thanked Washington for his service and for their deliverance, but especially praised "the Mild, yet strict Government of the Army, your Attention to the Civil Constitution of this colony, the regard you have, at all times, shewn for the lives and health of those under your Command, the Fatigues you have with chearfulness endured, the regard you have shewn for the preservation of our Metropolis." In his reply, Washington thanked them for noting his attention to their liberties, saying, "A regard to every provincial institution, where not incompatible with the common Interest, I hold a principle of duty, & of policy, and shall ever form a part of my conduct." He had won the campaign for local opinion.[21]

All of these efforts, however, were merely ancillary to the mission of expelling the British army from Boston. Naturally aggressive, Washington wanted to attack the British garrison as soon as the state of his army would allow. Yet Congress had also enjoined Washington to consult with his general officers, and they, in council of war, repeatedly advised against attack. In October 1775, Congress sent a committee, including Benjamin Franklin, to inspect the army and consult with Washington about numerous matters. They also delivered a message that Congress desired the general to consider an attack on the British garrison. Despite his own preferences, Washington presented the committee with the advice of his general officers, laying before them the probability of Boston's destruction by artillery bombardment in the attack. The committee demurred, as the "Matter [was] of too much Consequence to be determined by them therefore refer it to the Hon. Congress." Washington had neatly finessed the issue, offering the committee members the opportunity to share in the responsibilities of wartime command, an honor they quickly declined. Five months later, when the American army placed cannon atop Dorchester Heights, the British army evacuated Boston and set sail for Halifax. Unbeknownst to the Americans, the British had decided to change their strategy, leave Boston, and continue the campaign in New York. Still, Washington's army appeared to have scored an almost bloodless victory, providing a boost of confidence to the Continental Congress, which was deliberating a declaration of independence from Great Britain.[22]

Nine months later, the situation looked far different. After the war shifted to New York, the British inflicted a series of tactical defeats as they forced Washington and his army off Long Island and Manhattan and into retreat through southern New York, across New Jersey, and into Pennsylvania. On December 18, 1776, Washington wrote his brother that "the game is pretty near up.... No man, I believe, ever had a greater choice of difficulties and less means to extricate himself from them."[23] He was not exaggerating.

After the British left Boston, Washington redeployed his forces to New York in anticipation of the next British offensive. New York was a bustling city and a strategically important port. At the mouth of the Hudson River, the area was the key to the defense of the middle states. If the British could gain control of the Hudson, they might split New England from the middle and southern states, dealing a deadly blow to the Revolution. Washington soon discovered that the region—three large islands at the confluence of two major rivers, numerous bays, and Long Island Sound—posed almost insuperable problems for his army of twenty thousand men forced to defend against the British army and navy. The British first encamped on Staten Island. Yet when they attacked, they threw away their operational advantage by landing directly in front of Washington's forces on Long Island, rather than bypassing his forward defenses with an assault on northern Manhattan. Nonetheless, the British rapidly turned Washington's flank on Brooklyn Heights and threatened to crush his army. The only bright spot in the battle of Long Island was a nighttime evacuation that saved the army from capture and a capitulation that might have ended the Revolution.

With wide latitude from Congress, Washington resolved to adopt a "Fabian strategy" or a "war of posts," defending ground as long as he would not be decisively engaged, then falling back with his army intact to fight another day. However, he then made a politically sensible but operationally hopeless effort to defend Manhattan. Only General William Howe's strategy saved the Continental Army from a rout. Following a traditional and methodical eighteenth-century conception of warfare, General Howe decided to land on Manhattan, pushing the Americans north rather than cutting them off and trapping them on the island. Howe harried Washington into Westchester County, bloodied him at White Plains, and separated the field army from its two strongholds on either side of the Hudson—Fort Lee in New Jersey and Fort Washington on the northern end of Manhattan. Although his announced strategy should have dictated evacuation of both garrisons weeks earlier, Washington continued to hold them in mid-November. Fort Washington fell to the British on November 18, with a loss of almost three thousand prisoners. Three days later, the British took Fort Lee as well, along with thirty cannon and tons of irreplaceable supplies. Washington retreated with a dwindling army of five thousand across New Jersey, leaving another eight thousand in the Hudson Highlands. Adding insult to injury, the British captured one of his senior commanders, Charles Lee, in a compromising position in a Brunswick boardinghouse. Indeed, the game did seem to be pretty near up. The crisis moved Tom Paine to lament, "These are the times that try men's souls."[24]

Unsurprisingly, Washington's prosecution of the war came under criticism. Members of Congress began to grumble. John Adams pithily explained the Long Island defeat: "In general, our Generals were out generalled." The misgivings also extended into the army. Washington accidentally intercepted a letter from General Lee to Joseph Reed, a Washington aide, that alluded to a shared opinion about the dangers of a "fatal indecision of mind," a phrase clearly meant to describe their commander. Yet Congress had too much invested in its commander in chief, and too much residual respect for his abilities, to abandon him, especially at this critical moment. As the British closed in on the Delaware, Congress fled Philadelphia. As it decamped, the panicking Congress voted to grant Washington extraordinary power: "to order and direct all things relative to the department, and to the operations of war" until it ordered otherwise.[25]

Washington appreciated the vote of confidence, but as soon as had he received his enhanced authority, he asked for even more: "It may be said that this is an application for powers, that are too dangerous to be intrusted. I can only add that desperate diseases, require desperate remedies." Congress, packing for Baltimore, all but abdicated to Washington, giving him all that he requested, as much as was in its power to give. He was almost a Caesar, and it was a measure of the trust that Congress had in his character that they had delegated such sweeping authority. The congressional resolution reposed these powers in George Washington by name—not by title as commanding general. "Happy it is for this country that the general of their forces can safely be entrusted with the most unlimited power," gushed the letter accompanying the resolution, "and neither personal security, liberty, or property be in the least degree endangered thereby." Washington further reassured Congress, promising "to constantly bear in mind that, as the sword was the last resort for the preservation of our liberties, so it ought to be the first thing laid aside when those liberties are firmly established." He did not abuse Congress's trust, but neither did he hesitate to use his new powers to put the army and the war effort on a sounder footing.[26]

Since the early months of his command, Washington had gently, later more insistently, advocated for long-term enlistments, a precursor to a permanent force, a standing army in the parlance of the day. Washington felt it critical to recruit soldiers for the Continental Army for periods of time long enough so that they could be trained, disciplined, and accustomed to the rigors of war. His service in the French and Indian War had convinced him of the folly of relying too heavily on militia. His command of American forces against the British had solidified that view. He was not universally hostile to militia, understanding both the political value they possessed for the states and their role as an adjunct to regular forces, especially in their own locales. Yet, in his view, regulars were the soul of an army. He gingerly approached the matter with Congress, knowing that his thinking contrasted sharply with that of many political leaders and with American colonial traditions and ideology. Although Samuel Adams snorted that "standing armies are always dangerous to the liberties of the people," Congress had approved one-year enlistments at the end of 1775. After the evacuation from Long Island, Washington used the impending crisis in New York to renew his call, becoming ever more insistent and ever more dire in his predictions if Congress failed to act. Once again, his army was evaporating as whole regiments left the city. Finally, in September 1776, Congress approved enlistments for three years or the duration of the war and a total of eighty-eight Continental battalions. Furthermore, they strengthened the Articles of War, delegating power to Washington and his commanders for stiffer, European-style punishments as a means of instilling the kind of "standing army" discipline that many republicans feared. These authorizations, the foundation for a regular force, marked a new departure in American commitment to victory and, more broadly, in America's relations to its military forces.[27]

With a fleeing Congress's resolution in his breast pocket, Washington proposed to go further. With a more imperious tone than he had taken theretofore, he wrote John Hancock that he had "waited with much impatience to know the determinations of Congress" in regard to his request that they create an engineer and an artillery corps. Now, he was going ahead with organization of three artillery battalions and placing General Henry Knox in command of them. He intended to add twenty-two regular regiments to the eighty-eight Congress had authorized in September. He lectured his former colleague, saying, "It is needless to add, that short inlistments, and a mistaken dependence upon Militia, have been the Origin of all our misfortunes, and the great accumulation of our Debt." The New Jersey militia had failed to answer the call when Howe was marching across their state:

> Could anything but the River Delaware have saved Philadelphia? Can any thing . . . be more destructive to the recruiting service, than giving Ten dollars bounty for Six weeks of service of the Militia, who come in, you cannot tell how—go, you cannot tell when—and act, you cannot tell where—consume your provisions—exhaust your stores, and leave you at last at a critical moment. These Sir, are the men, I am to depend upon, Ten days hence. This is the Basis on which your Cause will and must forever depend, until you get a large standing Army, sufficient of itself to oppose the Enemy.

Washington clearly intended to lay a solid foundation for a permanent, regular army. He also cagily noted that "if any good Officers offer to raise men upon Continental pay and establishment in this Quarter, I shall encourage them to do so, & regiment them when they have done it." Having officers recruit Continental soldiers would allow him to bypass the states, eliminating mountains of political difficulty for himself. In a sign of his changed relations with Congress, he gave them an opportunity to veto, not to approve his action: "If Congress disapprove of this proceeding, they will please to signify it, as I mean it for the best." Congress ratified all his requests and extended his extraordinary writ for six months.[28]

Newfound authority seemed to energize Washington. He personally inspired battalions of soldiers whose enlistments were due to expire at the end of the year to stay with him and the Revolutionary cause a few weeks more, giving him six thousand men to lead back across the Delaware on Christmas Day, 1776. The brilliant victories at Trenton and Princeton ended his string of battlefield defeats, restored his reputation, and breathed new life into the Revolution. Shortly thereafter, Howe withdrew through New Jersey back into his New York City garrison.[29]

Congress met in Baltimore until the end of February 1777 when Howe's withdrawal to New York made a return to Philadelphia prudent. In the meantime, it accomplished a great deal, as the forced move seemed to focus its energies. The major legislative issue before it in 1777 was fundamental—designing and agreeing to articles of confederation for the American government. The states held a great deal of political power—as well as manpower, finances, and other resources—that they were loath to entrust to Congress. Still, the loss of New York City made it obvious that the war was not going well, the army needed better support, and the nation might well lose its independence. Congress resolved the issues and approved the Articles of Confederation in November, but more than three years passed before all of the states ratified them. Yet the Continental Congress remained an extralegal body in dangerous rebellion against the British Crown—the halters weighed heavily on their necks.[30]

Congress's other major problem was financing the operations of government, especially recruitment, payment, and supply of 110 infantry battalions that Washington had insisted upon as essential to the war effort. Although the army never came close to raising the full complement, the fiscal burden on Congress grew with each Continental soldier. With almost no authority to tax, Congress had to look for other sources of revenue. There was some good news. France and to a lesser extent Spain had provided secret aid since the beginning of the war. Early in 1777 France sent two hundred brass cannon, one hundred tons of gunpowder, clothing for thirty thousand men, and mountains of ammunition. The government also secured loans from France and Spain, as well as issuing and selling credit certificates at home. There was no American banking system from which to borrow. Another option was to place levies on the states to support the army with food, clothing, blankets, and ammunition, but the states responded sporadically and unreliably. The primary source of revenue, however, came from printing paper money. With too little hard specie in the treasury to back them, the value of "continentals," as the currency became known, soon became so inflated that the term became a synonym for worthlessness. The problems of supporting the war would only get worse.[31]

British strategy in 1777 was a muddle. General John Burgoyne had prevailed upon Lord George Germain to allow him to attack south from Canada and down the Hudson, where he expected that Howe would support him. When their forces joined, they would have separated New England from the rest of the states. But Burgoyne underestimated both the operational challenge he faced on his campaign and his American enemy. Unlike their New Jersey brethren the year before, the New York and New Hampshire militia flocked to assist the Continentals under General Horatio Gates. The battles of Freeman's Farm and Bemis Heights enabled one of the greatest strategic victories in the history of American arms, forcing Burgoyne to surrender his entire army at Saratoga on October 17. The triumph fostered rejoicing across the continent and was the proximate cause of France's decision to ally with the Americans against Great Britain the next year. General Gates became a national hero overnight.

Part of Burgoyne's problem was that he got no support from Howe. A combination of professional jealousy, poor communication, and weak coordination allowed Howe to ignore Burgoyne's plan, instead embarking his army on his brother's fleet into the Atlantic and sailing south for a campaign against Washington's army in Pennsylvania. The British fleet bypassed the nearer Delaware estuary in favor of the Chesapeake and landed the army at Head of Elk, fifty-seven miles southwest of Philadelphia. When Howe began to march on September 7, Washington was there to meet him. Yet Washington lost a battle at Brandywine Creek in

Pennsylvania, largely owing to his own tactical mistakes. Howe then out-maneuvered him to threaten Philadelphia, forcing the Congress to de-camp for Lancaster and then York. In early October Washington lost another battle at Germantown, allowing Howe to settle into comfortable winter quarters in the Philadelphia lodgings many members of Congress had so recently vacated. Washington took his wounded and hungry army to a woebegone camp at Valley Forge. Washington's star, at its zenith in January, fell to its nadir in October.

Comparisons between Gates and Washington were inevitable, as were questions about whether the right general was in overall command. As early as February, some members of Congress had voiced concern that they had delegated too much authority to the commander in chief. John Adams worried about the "superstitious veneration that is sometimes paid to General Washington." After Brandywine, a quiet season of letter-writing against Washington commenced in Congress, although no one took the floor to air his criticisms. New Jersey delegate Jonathan Ser-geant disparaged Washington and decried "such blunders as might have disgraced the soldier of three months' standing." In a letter to Adams, Benjamin Rush directly compared Gates's army to Washington's. The former was "a well-regulated family" and the latter "an unformed mob." He went on to compare the two generals' characters: Gates was at "the pinnacle of military glory, exulting in the success of schemes planned with wisdom and executed with vigor and bravery." Washington, on the other hand, was "outgeneralled and twice beaten, obliged to witness the march of the body of men only half their number through 140 miles of a thick-settled country, forced to give up a city the capital of the state." He called for a congressional inquiry. Not willing to go quite so far, even in private, John Adams nonetheless wrote Abigail about Washington's dimin-ished stature, "Now We can allow a certain Citizen to be wise, virtuous, and good, without thinking him a Deity or a saviour."[32]

Washington had made serious mistakes. In two years he had lost New York City and all of New Jersey, and then Philadelphia. Congress had been forced to vacate the capital twice and was well within its rights to question his abilities. Washington also suffered from his proximity to Congress, just as Gates benefited from his distance. Yet no other general on either side of the war, or perhaps in any war, could have compiled Washington's record and escaped criticism. Still, General Howe, sitting in Philadelphia in the winter of 1777, was no closer to winning the war than he had been sitting in Boston in 1775. The cities of New York and

Philadelphia—and even Boston, for that matter—were clearly not the keys to victory. Washington, though naturally aggressive, had learned to restrain his impulses and to accept what he called a war of posts, which, while losing ground, kept the Continental Army intact and the Continental Congress protected. The members of Congress clamoring for a more aggressive strategy were upset at having been displaced, and also inconsistent, inasmuch as they had counseled caution before. Some wanted Washington to attack Howe in Philadelphia and bring the war to a quick end. Others went further, suggesting that Washington was cautious because he favored a long war that would enhance the stature of his standing army. The criticism, almost all of it private, pointed in every direction. General Nathanael Greene, a calmer head on whom Washington was coming to rely, advised his chief to ignore the criticism, avoid decisive battle, and keep the army intact. It was sound counsel and Washington followed it, to the chagrin of his detractors.[33]

In its frustration, Congress became far less deferential to Washington than it had been at the beginning of the year. In October Washington learned that Congress had appointed another foreigner, Thomas Conway, a Frenchman of Irish extraction, to major general. To this point in the war Washington had patiently accepted Congress's insistence on retaining the authority to commission general officers, partly because of his principled deference to civilian control of the army, and partly because the arrangement shielded him from the political heat that naturally accompanied such appointments. The Conway matter was different. Conway was no stranger to Washington, having commanded a brigade with some distinction at Brandywine Creek and later at Germantown. Yet he was an arrogant and voluble officer who never allowed an opinion to go unexpressed. Furthermore, his view of his commander's abilities was not flattering, especially after Washington spurned his advice in general officer councils. Conway was not only a foreigner whose elevation would rankle American officers, but he was junior to most other brigadiers. Washington knew that his promotion would likely prompt many of them to resign. He wrote a letter to Congressman Richard Henry Lee calling the Conway promotion "as unfortunate a measure, as ever was adopted." Washington then hinted at the possibility of his own resignation if the matter were not reconsidered: "To sum up the whole, I have been a Slave to the service: I have undergone more than most men are aware of, to harmonize so many discordant parts but it will be impossible for me to be of any further survice if such insuperable difficulties are thrown in my way." This implied threat shows not only Washington's frustration over Conway's elevation, but a growing concern over his ability to manage the war with dwindling support and confidence from Congress.[34]

As he took the army into winter quarters at Valley Forge, his relations with his political masters were at ebb tide. Congress admonished Washington to restore discipline and to quell discontent, especially among the officers. They officially criticized him for army supply shortages at Valley Forge, problems that were largely of their own making. Ironically, they upbraided him for not foraging more aggressively, for not demanding more food and fodder from the farmers of Pennsylvania. Washington protested that he had meant to be more scrupulous of American liberties. Never before had Congress questioned his actions so minutely.[35]

In November Congress decided that Washington needed closer supervision. The previous year it had created a Board of War to relieve Washington of the complexity of treating with several congressional committees. (Nonetheless, they continued to send numerous committees to his camps.) With John Adams, the prickly, brilliant workhorse of Congress, as chairman, the board had cooperated with Washington to find solutions to the myriad problems of governing, supplying, equipping, and manning the army, albeit with limited success. Later, Congress created commissary, clothier, and quartermaster departments, although these performed poorly, partly because of weak organization and congressional micromanagement, and partly because they lacked adequate funding.[36]

When Adams left for Paris in November, Congress reconstituted the Board of War with General Gates in its chair and Thomas Mifflin, a former Washington aide turned critic, as one of its members. Gates, whose relations with Washington had soured as his own reputation grew, retained his commission as a major general, ostensibly overseeing the army commander to whom he reported.[37]

Congress was under pressure to respond to the British occupation of the capital. It dispatched a committee to Washington's headquarters to urge an attack on Philadelphia. A council of Washington's generals disabused it of the operation's practicality.[38] A month later, a group of Pennsylvania officials visited the camp to question Washington about his plans to protect New Jersey and Pennsylvania from British attack. Washington thought that they had seen the ragged condition of his army and gone away convinced that he needed considerable help to clothe and feed them before they could undertake a winter campaign. Incensed when he

32

learned that they had sent a "remonstrance" to Congress, urging a campaign, Washington sent this blistering response: "I am now convinced beyond a doubt, that unless some great and capital change takes place . . . that this Army must inevitably be reduced to one or other of these three things. Starve—dissolve—or disperse." After detailing the deficiencies of the commissary, quartermaster, and clothier departments in support of the fact that his soldiers were naked, cold, and starving, he turned his fire on the Pennsylvania delegation. "These very Gentlemen, who were well apprized of the nakedness of the Troops," had advised him to postpone military operations until they could secure clothing for the men, which they assured him would be done in ten days, "(not one article of which, by the bye, is yet come to hand)." How could they imagine that "a Winters Campaign . . . [to be] so easy and practicable a business?" Washington was fed up:

> I can assure those Gentlemen, that it is a much easier and less distressing thing, to draw Remonstrances in a comfortable room by a good fire side, than to occupy a cold, bleak hill, and sleep under frost & snow without Cloaths or Blankets: However, although they seem to have little feeling for the naked and distressed Soldier, I feel superabundantly for them, and from my soul pity those miseries, which it is neither in my power to releive or prevent.[39]

The sense of cooperation between Congress and Washington that had obtained in 1775 was almost gone. Nerves were strained. Howe was in the capital and Congress was on the lam. Washington's army was immobile at Valley Forge, and rumors were about that Gates would be a more effective commander in chief. Washington was under closer scrutiny from Congress than at any time in the war, and it took little imagination to see the hand of the newly reconstituted Board of War behind these inquiries. To make matters worse, on the same day that Washington sent his furious letter, Congress approved a Board of War recommendation to make Thomas Conway a major general and inspector general of the Continental Army. He would oversee the restoration of discipline and improvement of training. The Conway appointment was a vote of no confidence in Washington's command of the army.[40]

At this point, Washington demonstrated two characteristics: his hypersensitivity to criticism and his skill as a political infighter. In early November as the new Board of War was just being organized, Washington learned of a letter from General Conway to General Gates that contained a disparaging comment about Washington himself. Seizing an opportunity, the commanding general sent a curt missive to Conway:

> Sir: a letter I receivd last night containd the following, paragraph. In a letter from Genl Conway to Genl Gates, he says—"Heaven has been determind to save your country, or a weak General and bad Councilors would have ruined it."
> I am Sir Yr Hble Servt,
>
> George Washington[41]

Before long, both Conway and Gates were frantically trying to determine who might have leaked their private correspondence. Both apologized to Washington, although insisting upon their innocence and absence of bad intent. They snarled at each other over the position in which they both found themselves. Conway wrote to Gates, lamenting that he had been accused of "intriguing at Congress with General Mifflin and you in order to remove General Washington," indicating that he might have been an unwitting pawn. In short, Washington had his adversaries fighting with each other. When Conway reported to Valley Forge as inspector general, Washington gave him a frosty reception and refused to deal with him until Conway produced a set of orders from the Board of War.[42]

Over the winter, Washington heard several rumors of plots in Congress and at the Board of War to remove him as commanding general. Henry Laurens, president of Congress and a Washington devotee, forwarded him an anonymous pamphlet, titled "Thoughts of a Freeman," that had literally been dropped on the doorstep of Congress. This voluminous screed rehearsed the well-known criticisms of Washington, who handled the situation perfectly, saying, "why should I expect to be exempt from censure; the unfailing lot of an elevated station?" He insisted that his only concern was for the public good: "The anonymous paper handed you exhibits many serious charges, and it is my wish that it should be submitted to Congress." It was not. No investigation took place. Furthermore, Washington was learning from Laurens and other friends that there was no support in Congress for replacing him.[43]

Nonetheless, Washington was not finished with his adversaries. When Conway wrote characteristically sarcastic letters—one snidely compared Washington to Frederick the Great—complaining of the commander in chief's refusal to recognize Conway's authority as inspector general, Washington calmly forwarded them to Congress. When Conway complained to Congress and offered to resign, he was much surprised to find his offer quickly accepted. Conway was out of the army, having destroyed himself.[44]

Washington was still convinced that a plot existed to relieve him, with Gates as its ringleader and Mifflin a key confederate. Gates now repeatedly professed his loyalty to Washington, assuring him that he had never entertained any but the kindest thoughts. Washington doubted Gates's veracity and forced him to continue to plead his innocence in the matter until Gates disavowed Conway altogether. Meanwhile, Congress launched an investigation of Mifflin's control of finances during his earlier tenure as quartermaster general. The inquiry came to nothing, but it consumed more than a year.[45]

By the spring of 1778, if any conspirators against Washington remained, they were in full flight. He had maneuvered his detractors into several corners, separating them from one another. He had neutered the Board of War, at least as a body that might have controlled the commander in chief. Washington's handling of the entire matter was extraordinary testament to his political skill. However precarious his position at the end of 1777, he emerged from the ordeal more firmly in control of the army and more secure in his relations with Congress than ever. His authority as commander in chief never faced another congressional challenge for the rest of the war.

But had Washington really been challenged? Some historians have portrayed the affair as the Conway cabal, and viewed it as near treason, as if any assault on the man who would become the "Father of his Country" were inexcusable. More recent historical studies have agreed that the cabal was probably a myth, existing mostly in the minds of Washington and his supporters. Yet it is beyond question Washington believed a plot existed and that he and his staff labored to crush it. As he mentioned to Patrick Henry at the start of his command, his jealous regard of his honor and reputation were almost equal to his devotion to the Revolutionary cause.[46]

Washington was vulnerable at the end of 1777, and Congress was right to give him more scrutiny. Civilian authority has a right and a duty to replace generals who fail to perform and to replace them with others who have shown their mettle. In late 1777, Washington seemed to be the former and Gates the latter. Yet Washington possessed an uncanny ability to respond effectively to adversity. He examined Congress's misgivings and set about to reform the army. He did many things well that winter. With the help of Conway's replacement as inspector general, Baron von

Steuben, he trained and drilled the army until it became the disciplined force of regulars he had always wanted. Despite some bad blood, he coordinated with Congress on strategy—eventually convincing them to give up the campaign into Canada—and on methods to improve supply and pay for his soldiers. He presented Congress with a thirty-eight-page treatise on army reform, proposing a remodeling of the supply system, establishment of a military police corps, a regular system for officer promotions, a formal sanctioning of conscription, and a pension of half-pay for life for Continental officers. Congress approved almost every request. The army that marched out of Valley Forge was a match for any equal-size force of British redcoats.[47]

The economic situation continued to worsen. In January 1779, $1 in specie was worth $6.84 in continental paper. Over the next year Congress printed paper ostensibly worth $124 million. By December, it took $42.20 in continentals to buy the same $1 coin. In December 1780, the figure was $99.54. "Worthless as a continental" was more than a slogan. Public credit collapsed, people refused to be paid in continentals, and the army could scarcely feed itself. In September 1779, Congress decided to stop printing money when the amount in circulation reached $200 million, a ceiling that was quickly reached. Six months later, Congress repudiated the continental, in essence declaring bankruptcy, by announcing that it would retire its bills at a ratio of forty to one. Its $200 million debt was reduced to $5 million in one stroke, but the economy was in collapse.[48]

In December 1779 Congress decided to reduce operations of the national government by stripping its logistical departments of personnel and shifting responsibility for supplying the army to the states. Of course, the states were also suffering from economic collapse, and ever more mindful of their own concerns, they gave scant attention to the needs of the Continental Army.[49]

Financial collapse and devaluation of the continental created special hardships for the army. Soldiers were not just poorly clad, shod, fed, and armed—they were also broke. Their salaries, paid in continentals, were worthless. Thousands deserted. The Continental Army that Washington had built with the authorizations of 1776 withered from twenty-six thousand men to fewer than fifteen thousand from July 1779 to July

1780. Weak morale changed to indiscipline in May 1779 when officers of the New Jersey line petitioned their state legislature for redress and threatened to resign en masse if their concerns went unanswered. The legislators met enough of their demands to mollify them, and the officers returned to duty. Nevertheless, Washington was appalled, accurately predicting that "this cannot fail to operate as a bad precedent." Over the next year, enlisted soldiers from Rhode Island and Connecticut mutinied in three separate incidents. They were barely contained by their officers and, on one occasion, by another regiment. On January 1, 1781, veterans in the Pennsylvania line mutinied against their officers, killing three of them, and marched toward Philadelphia. Representatives of Congress and the Pennsylvania legislature were forced to negotiate, offering back pay, clothing, and immunity from court-martial. Most of the soldiers returned to duty, but the impact of their indiscipline was profound, especially when it was discovered that two British spies had infiltrated the Pennsylvania regiment for the purpose of monitoring the disorder for their commanders. Days later, New Jersey soldiers mutinied and also threatened to march on Congress. Washington responded by deploying a loyal regiment to surround and subdue them. The next day, two of the ringleaders were executed by a firing squad of their peers. Washington's harsh and rapid action, perhaps combined with improving war news and a subsequent march to Yorktown, ended the uprisings, but echoes of mutiny resonated around the country, instilling fear in the people, Congress, and the army.[50]

In the midst of the army mutinies and economic collapse, three stunning events shocked the nation, awakening it to the possibility that the war could yet be lost. In May 1780 General Benjamin Lincoln, commanding a Continental Army at Charleston, surrendered the city and his force of more than three thousand after a six-week British siege. Three months later, Horatio Gates, hero of Saratoga and rival of Washington, suffered a humiliating defeat at Camden, South Carolina, and most of his army was captured. The southern states seemed near capitulation. Then, in September 1780, partly motivated by disillusionment over the state of the army and his own finances, Benedict Arnold attempted to sell West Point to the British. The potential loss of that critical strategic garrison on the Hudson was alarming, but the treason of such a famously valiant general shook the country. A recognition that all these events were related to the financial crisis and the failure to support the army galvanized Americans and started a movement to strengthen the national government. This nationalist feeling was widespread and popular, and even leaders of state governments, contrary to their prior attitudes, supported it. The states began returning to Congress men of political talent who had previously shunned tedious, bootless, and thankless service in Congress, preferring private life or service in state government. Now such men as Philip Schuyler and Robert Livingston of New York, James Madison and Joseph Jones of Virginia, agreed to serve in Congress in order to reform it. Alexander Hamilton, a former Continental officer and longtime trusted aide to Washington, joined them in November 1782.[51]

As might be expected of strong personalities, the nationalist delegates disagreed among themselves at first about their goals and how to attain them. In general, however, they all aimed to strengthen the central government, reform its organization, and support the army. Over time, recognizing the power of the purse—the government's ability to finance itself—as paramount in their efforts, they seized on the need to service the growing debt as a means of accomplishing those goals.[52]

Shortly after the mutinous Pennsylvania line appeared in the capital, Congress began to act. Within a matter of weeks it created secretaries of foreign affairs, war, and marine, and a superintendent of finance. These positions replaced various committees, such as the Board of War, in hopes that single executives vested with authority would exercise genius that committees could not. After some delay, Congress appointed Robert Livingston secretary of foreign affairs; General Benjamin Lincoln, paroled after his surrender in Charleston, became secretary at war; and Robert Morris was superintendent of finance and acting secretary of marine. After the British capitulation at Yorktown, Washington spent four months in Philadelphia, meeting with these three executives weekly. He was pleased with the new arrangement, a situation that greatly eased his burdens of communication with the Confederation government.[53]

Morris's position as head of finance was the most important and most difficult in Philadelphia. A wealthy and self-made businessman, Morris was an administrative, managerial, and financial genius. He set three simple and ambitious goals for himself: raising revenues, controlling costs, and restoring public credit. Earning the moniker "the Financier," Morris became the preeminent leader of the nationalist faction in government. A partial solution to the fiscal crisis was a 5 percent tax on imports, called the impost, which Congress had passed early in 1781. Although it did little to decrease the debt, the impost was politically important because it established Congress's willingness and authority to levy taxes. However, all thirteen states had to ratify the measure as an amendment to the Articles. Rhode Island balked, and the impost died.[54] Morris complained that the Articles of Confederation (ratified in March) gave Congress "the privilege of asking for everything" and the states "the prerogative of granting nothing." He prevailed upon Congress to assess $8 million in levies on the states in October 1781, but the state legislatures again refused to tax their citizens to meet Continental obligations. The states were "deaf to the calls of Congress, to the clamors of the public creditors, to the just demands of a suffering army, and even to the reproaches of the enemy," who scoffed at the Continental Army as a ward of France. By September 1, 1782, Congress had collected only $125,000.[55]

The reverberations of mutiny returned in 1782. The army was starving and had not been paid in months. With peace negotiations beginning, Continental officers feared that Congress would renege on its promises and abrogate its commitment to half-pay pensions, leaving them destitute. They had sacrificed a great deal during the course of the war, including the best years of their productive lives, and felt that the country owed them recompense. They predicted that when the war ended Congress would disband the army, and once it had disbanded, their claims would be easy to ignore. In December, General Alexander McDougall led a delegation of Continental officers to deliver a petition to Congress. "We have borne all that men can bear—our property is expended—our private resources are at an end, and our friends are wearied out and disgusted with our incessant applications." The officers offered a commutation of the pensions to lump-sum payments, but warned that their patience was at an end: "further experiments . . . may have fatal results."[56]

Nationalist leaders seized on McDougall's petition as a way out of the fiscal morass. The pension issue created more demand for national funds, and for a purpose that was morally and politically difficult to deny—the relief of soldiers who had fought the Revolution. The McDougall delegation helped the nationalists make arguments for the pensions, which the nationalists then tied to the need for an impost. There matters took a more sinister turn.

The nationalists suggested to McDougall that a demonstration of the army's willingness to use force to coerce Congress into action would be politically invaluable. McDougall wrote to General Henry Knox, a trusted Washington subordinate, of the importance of combining "the influence of Congress with that of the Army and the public Creditors to obtain permanent funds for the United States." Morris, Hamilton, and assistant finance superintendent Gouverneur Morris (no relation) hoped that Knox could induce all Continental officers in New Windsor to make a statement in support of the commutation of pensions and the impost. In the following days, while conferring with nationalist leaders, the Mc-Dougall delegation predicted a mutiny if the army were not paid and the pensions not guaranteed. Congress met to discuss the matters and agreed that the crisis demanded action, but refused to approve the officers' pensions. More important, it refused to consider commutation, which would immediately bind Congress to more debt, as well as benefiting speculators who might attempt to buy the government bonds that commutation would have generated.[57]

In February, as McDougall and the nationalists awaited an answer from Knox, a still darker scheme emerged. Robert Morris knew of a discontented group of young officers in camp who chafed at Washington's perceived moderation. This faction was ostensibly loyal to Gates, who had returned from South Carolina to be Washington's second in command. They might be encouraged not only to support the nationalists, but to mutiny against Washington in a much more dangerous plan. Gouverneur Morris hinted at the potential in a letter to John Jay: "The army have swords in their hands. You know enough of the history of mankind to know much more than I have said and possibly more than they themselves think of."[58]

At this point, Alexander Hamilton began manipulating both Washington and Congress. Hamilton had served as Washington's closest aide, a de facto chief of staff, for more than four years. Now he traded on that relationship to advance the nationalist agenda. On February 13 he lamented to Washington that Congress, "not governed by reason," would likely not act to secure the country's financial health. He warned Washington of his officers' discontent over the commutation issue and advised him to get ahead of the problem: "The difficulty will be to keep a *complaining* and *suffering army* within the bounds of moderation. This Your Excellency's influence must effect . . . to take direction of them . . . to guide the torrent, and bring order and perhaps even good, out of confusion." He coyly confided to his former chief that a feeling was abroad in the army that Washington was not forceful enough in his advocacy for the army, that a certain "delicacy carried to an extreme prevents your espousing its interests with sufficient warmth." Of course, Hamilton protested, he never believed such falsehoods.[59]

A week later, Hamilton was advising Congress "that it was certain that the army had secretly determined not to lay down their arms" until the pay and pension issues were addressed. Washington was "extremely unpopular," and certain characters were manipulating that situation and might even move to displace him. "Hamilton said that he knew Genl. Washington intimately and perfectly, that his extreme reserve, mixed sometimes with a degree of asperity of temper both of which were said to have increased of late, had contributed to the decline of his popularity." He also knew that Washington would never be involved in any disloyalty, and that he, Hamilton, had written to His Excellency advising that he take the lead in presenting the officers' concerns to Congress.[60] Hamilton was careful enough with his language to Washington and the Congress to shield himself from accusations of double-dealing, although the tones of his messages were strikingly different.

Washington, probably unaware of Hamilton's remarks in Congress, was nonetheless growing concerned. He agonized that "the predicament in which I stand as Citizen and Soldier is as critical and delicate as can well be conceived. . . . The sufferings of a complaining army on one hand, and the inability of Congress and tardiness of the states on the other, are the forebodings of evil." Still, he trusted his army and his conviction that his officers fully understood the extent of his efforts on their behalf. They would trust him in return. He chided Hamilton that he was "under no great apprehension of [the army's] exceeding the bounds of reason and moderation."[61]

By the end of February, the nationalists' legislative ambitions were in dire trouble. General Knox answered McDougall's request with an inspiring testament to the army's integrity: "I consider the reputation of the American Army as one of the most immaculate things on earth. . . . We should even suffer wrongs and injuries to the utmost verge of toleration rather than sully it in the least degree."[62] Neither Hamilton and the Morrises nor McDougall and his officers could expect any help from Knox or Washington.

At that point, Hamilton and company determined to employ their last resort and sent an emissary, Colonel Walter Stewart, to Gates in New Windsor. No record of their conversation survives, but shortly thereafter disgruntled officers in camp put a plan in motion. In early March, Gates's aide, Major John Armstrong, wrote two anonymous letters that came to be known as the Newburgh addresses. With inflammatory rhetoric, the first demanded redress of the officers' grievances and suggested that if the war continued the army might move westward and leave Congress and the country to the mercies of the British. If the war ended, the army might refuse to disband until its demands were met. The letter called for a meeting on March 11, when the officers would discuss the wording of a petition that they might deliver to Congress. The commander in chief, who was disparaged in the letter, was not invited.[63]

By this time, Washington had determined that Philadelphia, not New Windsor, was the origin of these treasonous ideas, although he seems not to have suspected Hamilton. To nationalist delegate Joseph Jones he confided that the camp had been quiet until four days earlier, when reports arrived "propagated in Philadelphia that dangerous combinations were forming in the Army; and this at a time when there was not a syllable of the kind in agitation in Camp." Washington concluded that some of his officers were pawns in a dangerous "Scheme [that] was not only planned, but also digested and matured in Philadelphia; and that some people have been playing a double game; spreading at the Camp and in Philadelphia Reports and raising jealousies equally void of Foundation." Still, he pressed Jones to encourage Congress to act on the officers' pensions to avoid "ineffable horrors."[64]

On the morning of the scheduled assembly, Washington moved deftly to regain the initiative. He promulgated a general order, expressing his "disapprobation of such disorderly proceedings," and canceled the meeting. Instead he scheduled his own officers' conference for March 15, which would hear a report from a congressional committee and deliberate on how to proceed. Washington gave the impression that he would not attend, and ordered the senior officer present, presumably Gates, to preside and report back to him on the results. He also wrote letters to the president and other members of Congress, apprising them of the situation and warning of its dangers. Meanwhile, Major Armstrong wrote a second letter that attempted to deflect the sting of Washington's rebuke by saying that his order "sanctified" their purposes and that an assembly with his imprimatur would "give system" to the meeting. The plotters hoped that with Gates in the chair, the meeting might yet bear fruit.[65]

On Saturday morning, March 15, 1783, as Washington rode through the snow to New Windsor, he was facing a challenge as daunting as any he had encountered in the war. In his mind, it was his task "to arrest on the spot, the foot that stood wavering on a tremendous precipice . . . to rescue [the officers] from plunging themselves into a gulph of Civil horror."[66]

Nervous, angry, and agitated, the Continental officers gathered at the Temple of Virtue. At the stroke of noon, General Gates was standing at the head table about to call the meeting to order when Washington opened a side door and strode in. The commander in chief took center stage and began to speak. He condemned the author of the anonymous addresses as "unmilitary" and "subversive." "Can he be a friend to the Army? Can he be a friend to this Country? Rather, is he not an insidious Foe? Some Emissary, perhaps, from [the British army in] New York, plotting ruin of both, by sowing the seeds of discord and seperation between the Civil and Military powers of the Continent?" The "anonymous Addresser" had offered a "dreadful alternative, of either deserting our Country in the extremest hour of her distress, or turning our Arms against it . . . something so shocking . . . that humanity revolts at the idea."

Instead, Washington appealed to the officers' reason and patriotism. He also asked them to remember their trust in him:

> I was among the first who embarked in the cause of our common Country. As I have never left your side one moment, but when called from you on public duty. As I have been the constant companion and witness of your Distresses, and not among the last to feel, and acknowledge your Merits. As I have ever considered my own Military reputation as inseperably connected with that of the Army. As my Heart has ever expanded with joy, when I heard its praises, and my indignation has arisen, when the mouth of detraction has been opened against it, it can scarcely be supposed, at this late stage of the War, that I am indifferent to its interests.

He promised to continue his advocacy for them with Congress, and, as they trusted him, he asked that they also trust the government under which they had fought so long. He reminded them of the difficulties under which Congress labored, but asked that they have patience and confidence that the good men in Philadelphia would not forget all that the army had done for the country.[67]

It was a noble and eloquent speech, but when it ended, Washington had not convinced his audience, who remained sullen and unmoved.[68]

Then he drew from his coat pocket a letter from Joseph Jones that promised action on the officers' concerns. He began to read it and stumbled over the first sentence. He tried again with no greater success. Then he reached into his pocket for his reading glasses, which none but his most intimate aides had ever seen him wear. He paused, looked out over the assembly, and said, "Gentlemen, you will permit me to put on my spectacles, for I have not only grown gray, but almost blind, in the service of my country." That gesture and statement did all that his rhetoric could not. Brave and battle-scarred men wept openly. Washington finished the letter, turned on his heel, and marched quickly out the door. It was a bravura performance. In the half hour that followed, the officers repudiated any thoughts of breaching the covenant that bound them to the government. Henry Knox took control of the proceedings, led the officers in a motion to thank Washington for his speech, and became chair of a committee to draft a message of loyalty to Congress. Washington had averted the crisis. The great hall remained a Temple of Virtue.[69]

In one sense, the nationalists' plot had worked. The Hamilton-Morris double game—employing Gates and his acolytes as would-be mutineers while relying on Washington, Knox, et al. to restrain them—seems to have gone as planned. In response to the Newburgh episode, Congress acted in the following weeks to approve commutation and pass a variant of the impost, steps that it had been debating for more than two years. Congress even found funds to pay the soldiers; unfortunately, the notes arrived in camp six days after they were furloughed.[70]

In the end, the Continental officers saw themselves as patriots, authors of victory and trustees of Revolutionary virtue. Their men, equally proud of their accomplishments and their Revolutionary credentials, and with little to gain and much to lose, had little interest in mutiny. Henry Knox touched on these issues in his own written reply to the Newburgh addresses, which matched them in eloquence and fury. Challenging the anonymous plotters directly, he asked, "And when the Soldiery forsake you, what will be your situation? *despised* and *insulted*, by an *enraged* populace, *exposed* to the *revenging* hand of *justice*—You will then flee to *Caves* and *Dens* to hide yourselves from the *face* of *day,* and of Man." Forfeiting the legacy of noble sacrifice for the obloquy of mutiny and treason was to swap a cherished identity for infamy.[71]

The importance of the Newburgh Conspiracy lies in its failure. For once an army has risen up against its government, the people can never fully trust it again. That is especially true when an army rebels *under the command of its officers.* In earlier incidents, enlisted men mutinied against their officers. In one instance, officers petitioned the New Jersey legislature and threatened mass resignation. The Newburgh Conspiracy was far more menacing because the officer corps threatened to lead the army into mutiny. The importance of that day in the temple was that the army and the officer corps retained their virtue, and did not act against Congress or the people. They did not create a precedent for military intervention in political affairs. They did not break the bond of trust between the people and their army.[72]

At the end of the war, Washington responded to a congressional request for his views on a peacetime defense force. His "Sentiments on a Peace Establishment" acknowledged the need to reduce the size of the regular army, but insisted that a small permanent force would be necessary. He argued for several garrisons, arsenals, and one or more military academies "to preserve the knowledge which has been acquired thro' the various Stages of a long and arduous service." He acknowledged that militia would continue to have a central place in the American system of defense. Toward that end, he advocated a universal manhood obligation for militia service and national government control over the discipline and training of militia forces. Congress did little to act on his suggestions. The nation would have no permanent army worthy of the name for another forty years. However, most of his ideas eventually came to fruition, even if they took a long time to do so.[73]

As he prepared to retire, Washington offered his views on the future of the national government in his final "Circular to the States." He regretted that some might think that "I am stepping out of my proper line of duty," but he assured them of his good intent and his resolve to leave public service soon. He told the state governors that the country had a stark political choice to make, either to have a strong, respectable federal government or a weak and ineffectual one. He advocated the former, founded on four principles: an "indissoluble Union of the States under one Federal Head"; regard for "Public Justice"; a "Peace Establishment"; and a spirit of community within the nation, wherein all sacrificed for the good of the whole. As he explained his views, it became clear that he had taken up the nationalist program, insisting that a strong union entailed a vigorous central government to which the states would delegate more power than they had so far done. Without such political strength the Union would fail and the gains of the Revolution would be lost. Public justice demanded that the states pay their debts to Congress, and that soldiers and officers receive their pay and commutations as they had been promised. The people should not think of these as entitlements, but as "a debt of honour." He reiterated the call for a strong national defense that he had made in "Sentiments on a Peace Establishment." Then, in closing, he argued that the war could have been won "in less time and with much less expence . . . if the resources of the Continent could have been properly drawn forth." The fault lay not with "a deficiency of means," but "from the want of an adequate authority in the Supreme Power, from a partial compliance with the Requisitions of Congress in some of the States, and from a failure in punctuality in others." If the army had been "less patient, less virtuous, and less persevering," it might have dissolved and the war might have been lost. This final "Circular" is a powerful sermon to a people blessed with natural abundance. It is all the more remarkable as a political tract from the nation's first military leader on the need to preserve the Union.

Political-military relations during the Revolution were more complex and contentious than they have ever been in American history. The reasons were simple and profound. This was a revolutionary war fought against a despotic, too-powerful monarchy. As Americans struggled to govern themselves, they wrestled with questions of how much authority to grant to a central government, lest it oppress them just as the old one had done. Yet a weak government would not have the wherewithal to lead them to independence, so a balance had to be struck. The states had autonomy, but a lack of responsibility, which frequently hampered the war effort and the Congress. Furthermore, while large portions of the populace supported the rebellion, many others remained neutral, loyal to the British Crown, or vacillated with the vicissitudes of war. The nature of government and the war effort itself had to take these groups into account. Finally, the stress of fighting in one's homeland for years complicated all questions political and military.

The most elemental challenge for the new United States was that there were no national precedents, either for the government or the army. Thirteen states and a new nation, all of whom had been subjects of a British king and vassals of royal governors for almost two centuries, now found themselves experimenting with governance. The rebellion's motivating grievance was a lack of political representation in Parliament. The one thing certain as Americans began to govern themselves was that they would be sensitive to issues of representation. They determined to have a republican government, not a monarchy. Thus, executive authority in the Confederation government was weak and diffuse. The states guarded their prerogatives jealously.

Likewise, there was no precedent for a national army, except the repellent one of the British redcoats who had occupied their homes and oppressed the people. Fear of a standing army was an old and oft-reinforced tradition. Thus, Americans slowly and reluctantly took the decision to build the Continental Army. Washington's role was essential, both in overcoming old fears and in convincing Americans that their traditional reliance on militia would not suffice in a war of survival against Great Britain.

He did so by establishing trust with the people, insisting that he would remain a citizen although he was the new nation's top soldier. He provided discipline and organization to the New England militiamen who constituted his new army. He quickly learned that sustaining them in the field required more than simply stating his requirements to Congress. A longtime legislator as well as a colonial officer, Washington comprehended the diffusion of political authority in the colonies and negotiated continually with governors and legislatures to keep his army manned and supplied. Recognizing that fighting a revolutionary war depended upon the support of the people, he acted responsibly to build rapport with local leaders, addressing their concerns, and above all, manifesting a distinct contrast in the behavior of his army with that of the British invaders. As the war continued, Washington showed that he was sometimes more sensitive to American civil liberties than were his political superiors.

Among his most important contributions was establishing a relationship of principled subordination to the Continental Congress. When he accepted his commission, Washington humbly and sincerely deprecated his own abilities and experience. Still, he demonstrated remarkable energy and character, as well as superb political and organizational skills. Although he was never shy about expressing the army's needs, Washington deferred to Congress's authority and obeyed its orders. He took responsibility and acted through subordination to give Congress confidence and thus strengthened its resolve. However, if Washington was unfailingly subordinate, he was not subservient. He negotiated continuously with his civilian masters and hectored them on every matter relating to the war and the Continental Army. He rendered his advice in unmistakable terms, frequently warning them that their failure to respond to his requests might mean losing the war. Thus, candor in his dealings with Congress is another of his political-military legacies.

A theme that emerged during the war—one that would echo through American history—was the importance of a nexus among the government, the army, and the power of the purse. Military expenditures easily dwarfed all other government requirements. Supporting the army thus became one of the principal responsibilities of the fledgling government. Yet the authorities to tax and to write government debt were fraught with the potential for political mischief and aggrandizement, if not corruption. Some politicians proved more than willing to manipulate the army and its generals for reasons that had nothing to do with strategy. Of course, it must be said, generals were also willing to play the game of politics, angling for preferment or promotion with little thought to the best interests of the service.

Washington was not wholly above such dealing; witness his ruthless crushing of the Conway cabal. Yet more often he employed his understanding of the legislature and the army to explain each to the other to the betterment of both. During the Newburgh Conspiracy, he even protected Congress from itself. When the nationalist faction of Hamilton and the Morrises acted irresponsibly to strengthen the central government in a rash and complex manipulation of the national debt, public creditors, and the army, Washington stood at center stage and arrested the plot. Hamilton later admitted that he was trying to use the army for political purposes, although he denied involvement in a coup. The Newburgh Conspiracy did not plunge the country over the political-military abyss, thanks in giant measure to Washington's character and skill.[74]

It is too much to say that he constructed the edifice of political-military relations in the United States, but he certainly laid the cornerstones of the foundation upon which his successors, both civilian and military, might build. Washington became the bulwark and symbol of an emerging American system of political-military relations, establishing a tradition of civilian control that would echo through American history. He reinforced that principle at the end of the war when he voluntarily stepped down and surrendered his commission to Congress.

In the days before Christmas 1783, George Washington advanced on the national capital. Anything, any office, any power he might have wished was his for the taking. Many times during his command of the army, leaders of various stripes had suggested that he become the first American king. Washington would have none of it.

Congress had moved once again, this time to Annapolis. Scarcely twenty members, far less than a quorum, were present. Constitutionally weak in any case, they currently had no power to act in the nation's interest. Washington took no notice of this institutional frailty, but labored, as he had for eight years, to build up the Congress as a national symbol of unity and strength. He entered the hall, bowed, and paid his respects to the president of Congress, his erstwhile aide and sometime adversary, Thomas Mifflin. With a trembling hand, he read a short address, thanking the Congress, his countrymen, and Providence. When he expressed his gratitude to his officers, many of whom were standing behind him, his voice faltered and he felt it necessary to steady the trembling parchment with both hands. Then he commended "the interests of our dearest country to the protection of Almighty God." There was not a stray sound or a dry eye in the chamber. Washington paused to gather his voice, then closed his remarks and his career in the army: "Having now finished the work assigned me, I retire from the great Theatre of action, and, bidding an affectionate farewell to this august body, under whose orders I have so long acted, I here offer my commission, and take my leave of all the employments of public life." Thomas Mifflin expressed the thanks of the nation, saying, "You have conducted the great military contest with wisdom and fortitude invariably regarding the civil power and through all disasters and changes." Thomas Jefferson expressed the sentiment more forcefully and eloquently when he wrote "that the moderation and virtue of a single character has probably prevented this revolution from being closed as most others have been by a subversion of that liberty it was intended to establish."[75]

After accepting the thanks of Congress, Washington stepped outside, mounted his horse, and rode home to Mount Vernon.

2

At the end of the eighteenth century two of the most influential founders, John Adams and Alexander Hamilton, engaged in a rivalry that ripened into a titanic feud at once political and personal. Each man believed that he had the best interests of the country in mind, but Hamilton doubted Adams's competence, and Adams questioned Hamilton's motives. Though he held no political office, Hamilton frequently exercised more control over Adams's cabinet, the Congress, and the army than the president. Their conflict took on critical importance immediately after Adams's inauguration, when a long-simmering dispute with France threatened to erupt into war. Fifteen months later, Hamilton maneuvered Adams into appointing him de facto commander of a new army to meet that threat. Over time, mistrust grew into enmity and hatred. By the end of Adams's term, Hamilton publicly called the president's fitness for office into issue, questioning his psychological stability. Adams vilified Hamilton's character, parentage, and sexual morality, calling him "the bastard brat of a Scotch pedlar." Yet the vitriol of their dispute had far larger significance than simple discord between eminent historical figures. In the face of a major international crisis and fears of internal unrest, Adams and Hamilton contested the control of the government, the command of the army, and the constitutional principle of the president's role as commander in chief. At stake during the Quasi-War with France was not only war and peace, but fundamental questions about the military's place in the American polity and the very nature of the presidency.[1]

On Inauguration Day, 1797, John Adams presented an almost comical contrast with his distinguished predecessor. For most of the preceding twenty-two years, George Washington had been the first man in America, commander of the Continental Army, president of the Constitutional Convention, and first president of the United States. Beside this tall, dignified icon, the diminutive but portly new president cut an unpromising figure.[2]

Nevertheless, Adams had a great deal to recommend him for his new post. He started in Massachusetts politics by leading that colony's opposition to the Stamp Act in 1765. An accomplished and skillful lawyer, he demonstrated integrity, courage, and grace when he successfully defended the British soldiers charged in the Boston Massacre. One of the country's foremost political thinkers, Adams had a keen sense of history and a clear vision of the future—he was usually far ahead of his colleagues in seeing both problems and opportunities.[3] He was among the first and most influential members of the Continental Congress, serving on over thirty committees. He chaired the committee that wrote the Declaration of Independence. He drafted the Plan of Treaties in July 1776, the framework for an alliance with France. Later he became head of the Board of War and Ordnance, working eighteen-hour days to oversee Continental Army administration for over a year. When he left Congress in 1777, one colleague said it was "the opinion of every man in the house that he possesses the clearest head and firmest heart of any man in the Congress." Then he began a career as a diplomat, serving for ten years as minister plenipotentiary to France, Holland, and Great Britain and (with Benjamin Franklin and John Jay) negotiating the treaties that secured victory and independence. Finally, he had spent the past eight years as the nation's first vice president. Brilliant, prolific, and hardworking, Adams would stand in the front rank of the founders even if he had never reached the presidency.[4]

Following Washington into the presidency was destined to be one of the most thankless second acts in political history. Adams's personality suited him poorly for the role; he was vain, sensitive, stubborn, querulous, and paranoid. He disdained ceremony and political hobnobbing, but could talk for hours in Congress, or, worse yet, from his chair as Senate president. When his wife and closest political counselor, Abigail, was with him, she could curb his excesses. When she was not, he was often adrift and depressed. Franklin, his longtime colleague, aptly summed up the Adams character: "He means well for his Country, is always an honest Man, often a Wise One, but sometimes, and in some things, absolutely out of his Senses."[5]

Moreover, despite his long and distinguished career, Adams was assuming executive power for the first time. His initial decisions betrayed that inexperience. In a bid to emphasize continuity (when taking steps in a new direction might have been politically more prudent), Adams retained every member of Washington's cabinet. These men were third-rate functionaries whom Washington himself had been loath to appoint. Secretary of the Treasury Oliver Wolcott Jr. had been Hamilton's loyal assistant at Treasury. James McHenry was the fourth man Washington asked to replace Henry Knox at the War Department. Timothy Pickering was Washington's sixth and bitterly regretted choice to fill the post at State.[6] Adams had not played an important policy role as vice president, and none of these old ministers was beholden to him. What was worse, all three were acolytes of Adams's adversary, Alexander Hamilton. It was not long before the president had reason to suspect their loyalty.[7]

Adams followed Washington's example of principled aloofness from partisanship, refusing to act as leader of the Federalists. He truly believed that maintaining a centrist position would better allow him to exercise national leadership, bridge the partisan divide, and borrow from both sides to craft policy. In time, Adams's independence allowed him to lead the country away from a potentially debilitating war with France, but at the cost of his political support and, ultimately, his office.[8]

Hamilton was only too happy to fill the void as party leader, controlling Adams's cabinet and a large coalition of Federalists in Congress. On the other side of the political divide, Vice President Thomas Jefferson was acknowledged leader of the Republicans. For the first and only time in American governance, the country had elected both partisan rivals in the presidential contest. Yet Adams and Jefferson were also longtime friends and colleagues, and Adams reached out to Jefferson after the election, offering him an important role in the new government, in a kind of national coalition that would rise above parties. Jefferson seemed receptive for a while, even warning Adams to be wary of "the tricks of your archfriend from New York [Hamilton] . . . who most probably will be disappointed as to you." But Jefferson decided to spurn Adams's gesture in favor of partisanship. Soon after the inauguration, president and vice president fell out over the future course of the country and worked at cross-purposes for their entire term. Thus, the new president was at loggerheads with both party leaders, who were relentlessly promoting their own agendas and thwarting his own.[9]

Adams compounded these difficulties throughout his term by moving home to Quincy for months at a time, usually when Congress was not in session. He insisted that he could work as well in Massachusetts as he could in Philadelphia, but the more important truth was that he needed desperately to be near Abigail, who hated the capital. Yet mail delivery between the two places required at least a week, and receiving replies to important state questions could easily double that. Under the sway of Hamilton, the cabinet officers could and did engage in much mischief when the chief magistrate was away. This relaxed attitude toward presidential management was to be the source of endless trouble.[10]

Adams had good reason to suspect Hamilton, who had worked against him in the elections of 1788 and 1796. Before Adams's inauguration, Hamilton was already conspiring with his Federalist clique, describing Adams as "a man of great vanity . . . and of far less real abilities than he believes he possesses." The president spewed forth his own contempt to Abigail: "Hamilton I know to be a proud Spirited, conceited, aspiring Mortal always pretending to Morality, with as debauched Morals as . . . any one I know. As great an Hypocrite as any in the U.S." Abigail returned the sentiment, warning about "that spair Cassius . . . that cock sparrow. O I have read his Heart in his wicked Eyes many a time. The very devil is in them. They are laciviousness itself, or I have no skill in Physiognomy." Adams admitted that Hamilton possessed many talents, "but I dread none of them. I shall take no notice of his Puppy head but retain the same Opinion of him I always had and maintain the same Conduct towards him I always did, that is keep him at a distance." He would find that easier said than done.[11]

Hamilton was one of the most complex and fascinating characters among the founders.[12] Born into poverty and illegitimacy in the Caribbean, he made his way to New York through striving, self-promotion, and genius. After two years at King's College (later Columbia) he gained a commission as captain of artillery in the Continental Army, fighting under Washington in the 1776 campaign in New York and through the long retreat across New Jersey. He distinguished himself at Trenton and Princeton, after which Washington selected him as aide-de-camp, a position that soon had him drafting hundreds of the general's letters. Over time he became the closest and most trusted of Washington's men, a de facto chief of staff. Washington made him a battalion commander at Yorktown, where Hamilton led the storming of a key redoubt, the capture of which led to the British surrender. Soon thereafter, he left the army staff following a personal disagreement with the general. When next they spoke a year later, Hamilton was a nationalist delegate in Congress pressuring Washington during the Newburgh Conspiracy. Hamilton acquired and discarded patrons as they suited his needs. His intermittent relationship with Washington was only the most notable of several.

As soon as he arrived in Congress, Hamilton became a leader of the nationalist faction. Through his marriage into New York's powerful Schuyler clan, he became a key delegate to the Constitutional Convention, pushing for a strong central government with a powerful Senate and an "elective monarch," both serving for life "on good behavior." Critics labeled him a monarchist who would have been happy to return the country to British rule.[13] During the campaign to ratify the Constitution, Hamilton teamed with James Madison and John Jay to write a series of essays explaining the document's provisions and arguing why they were necessary for the American future. *The Federalist* is Hamilton's best-known contribution to the founding era, with a continuing place in American curricula and jurisprudence today. Hamilton's essays on the Constitution's military powers emphasized the necessity of regular forces and the propriety of controlling them at the national level.[14]

Hamilton's management of national finances as the first treasury secretary left an equally profound legacy. With a deep understanding of economics, consummate political skill, a genius for public administration, and unmatched personal energy, Hamilton—under Washington's tutelage—forged the strong executive that the Constitution promised in theory. Hamilton had learned from Robert Morris how control of taxes and debt, maintenance of a strong military, and development of an effective bureaucracy could combine to strengthen government. Through masterly control of national debt and advocacy for revenues to service it, he fortified the federal government at the expense of the states. His grasp on the federal purse gained him influence over other departments, and his tentacles stretched into every corner of government. His reach was so extensive that many thought of him as Washington's chief minister.[15]

Hamilton spent six years at the Treasury, after which he continued to offer advice to the president in lengthy missives on a variety of topics. By this time, he also enjoyed considerable influence over the second cohort of Washington's cabinet secretaries, the men that Adams felt compelled to retain when he ascended to the presidency.[16]

Hamilton had a knack for turning rivals into enemies. The list comprises a veritable "who's who" of the founding generation—Adams, Jefferson, Madison, Monroe, and Burr were only the most famous of the lot. The factionalism that fast became partisanship owed as much to the personal animus between Hamilton on the one hand and Jefferson on the other as it did to ideological struggles over the reach of the national government or whether to ally with Great Britain or France. Hamilton's enemies envied his influence in the Washington administration and his success in enacting his vigorous programs. They pilloried him in the increasingly partisan press, investigated him in Congress, and whispered about his character.

Scandal also enlivened the Adams-Hamilton rivalry. In the early 1790s, Hamilton had conducted a torrid affair with Mrs. Maria Reynolds, after which her husband extorted hush money from the treasury secretary for a number of months. Soon after Adams assumed the presidency, a Republican gazetteer with ties to Jefferson exposed the affair, alleging that as Hamilton surely would not have been foolish enough to be blackmailed over sexual indiscretion, he must have engaged in official financial improprieties. Hamilton *was* foolish enough to rebut the charges in his own widely printed pamphlet, denying official misconduct but confessing in embarrassing detail to the affair and the blackmail. Any hope that Hamilton had of gaining elective office vanished with the printing of that tract. He would have to employ his manifest genius and satisfy his considerable ambitions by other means.[17]

It is impossible to understand the politics of the Federalist period without recognizing the intensely personal relationships among the leading actors. These men, a small political elite, had known each other intimately for decades in a time of revolutionary upheaval. Personal reputation and honor carried immense weight in this rarefied culture, especially for men like Hamilton and Adams, who had been born into relatively obscure, although radically different, circumstances.[18]

John Adams took the ship of state during a typhoon of political instability. The country was in a quiet war with France and an uneasy peace with Great Britain. His predecessor had defined the captaincy, and no one could imagine anyone else in command. Americans harbored real fears for the survival of their republic, fears that were based in an understanding of history, recent experience with internal rebellion, and evidence that the French were attempting to interfere in American government and politics. American leaders were ill-equipped to mediate these problems, shackled with a political lexicon that turned adversaries into traitors and buffeted by vitriolic public calumnies that took little notice of gentlemanly sensibilities. Adams spent his presidency attempting to navigate through that storm.

By Adams's inauguration France and the United States were already engaged in an undeclared naval war. The French had seized more than three hundred American ships. These hostilities marked a dramatic change, given American gratitude for the French alliance and its importance in the success of the American rebellion. After the war, U.S. ties to France remained strong, just as relations with Great Britain were further strained when the British failed to keep promises to withdraw their forces from the American frontier. That situation slowly changed after the French Revolution and especially after the execution of Louis XVI. When revolutionary France went to war with Great Britain, the United States declared its neutrality, essentially abrogating its long-term alliance with France. Washington argued that the 1778 treaty with the Bourbon monarchy was invalid following Louis's overthrow. The administration concluded the Jay Treaty with Britain, which cleared up boundary disputes and established a trade pact, but the French revolutionary government railed against what it saw as an Anglo-American alliance, and refused to recognize Washington's new minister to France. Word of this effective withdrawal of diplomatic recognition—a traditional prelude to a declaration of war—reached the United States just weeks before Adams's inauguration. Adams thus entered office with a very real prospect that the Quasi-War might explode into a conflict much more serious.[19]

Adams was also ascending to the presidency at a time of virulent political strife. He had been elected in the first truly contested presidential election in American history, but his problems did not end there. Americans of the Revolutionary generation wanted to think of themselves as above political striving. Washington had set himself above partisanship and enjoined other leaders to follow his example for the sake of the Union. That stance was either naïve or disingenuous: by the end of his presidency Washington was clearly understood to be the Federalist leader. Worse yet, it left his successors without a lexicon or framework for principled, legitimate political discourse. Consequently, the Hamiltonian Federalists and the Jeffersonian Republicans considered each other politically illegitimate.[20]

Political discourse in late eighteenth-century America had become poisonous. In a few years the body politic had plummeted from an idealistic perch in which the very notion "faction" was anathema to an abyss in which rival parties saw one another as illegitimate governors. Republicans and Federalists each thought of themselves as legitimate heirs to the Revolutionary legacy. Republicans emphasized the liberties they had fought for and won against an oppressive government. Federalists extolled the national unity—with its central government and national army—that had made independence possible. When Federalists spoke of a system of government, they looked to Great Britain as the model. Republicans looked to the French, who were not only America's wartime allies, but now its revolutionary successors carrying forward the spirit of '76. To Federalists, the Republicans were "Jacobins" or the "French party." Federalists, in Republican eyes, were "monarchists" or "Tories" in thrall to Great Britain. Neither saw the other as fit to govern. Each saw the other as potential traitors. To lose political power, then, was to invite civil rebellion and perhaps to forfeit the future of America itself.[21]

Historical and contemporary reasons for such fears abounded. No republic in history had long endured without descending into either chaos or despotism. America itself had been born in a violent revolution that was still a vivid memory for every political leader of that generation. The Declaration of Independence had propounded the right of the people to rise up and overthrow despotic government. Did that sacred text not assert the right of posterity to revolt again? And at that moment an even bloodier revolution was ongoing in France, its head count climbing and its trajectory unknown. Moreover, homegrown insurgencies had threatened civil order twice since the Revolution. Daniel Shays led a rebellion in Massachusetts in 1786 that gave impetus for strengthening the Confederation government, eventually leading to the Constitutional Convention. Pennsylvania distillers and farmers rose up against a whiskey tax in 1794, compelling President Washington to call out and personally lead state militias to disperse them. Although both rebellions were quickly put down, subsequent rhetoric about the dangers of violent internal uprisings was more than mere political posturing. The fear was real.[22]

Two days before his inauguration, Adams learned that the French Directory had issued a decree annulling the principle of free ships, free goods. That action essentially authorized French vessels to seize any American or other neutral ship or sailor. Adams called a special session of Congress for the middle of May. He proposed a policy of both arrows and olive branches: a naval buildup along with negotiations. Two months later he sent a three-member peace commission to Paris.[23]

Unsurprisingly, deep political divisions greeted Adams's decisions. The Federalist press hailed the president's statesmanship and strength. Even Hamilton applauded, and secretly influenced the cabinet to support the peace commission. Republicans called Adams a warmonger and a British toady. Vice President Jefferson muted his public criticism, but worked behind the scenes to undermine the Adams policy. He secretly met four times with the French chargé d'affaires in Philadelphia, urging the French to declare war on England. As for the American embassy to Paris, Jefferson counseled the French to "listen to them and then drag out the negotiations at length." Exposure of the Hamilton-Reynolds affair— for which Hamilton blamed Republican James Monroe—and Hamilton's embarrassing response dismayed his friends and heartened Republicans. In the midst of this turmoil, Adams quit Philadelphia with its July heat and annual yellow fever outbreak and decamped to Quincy for a four-month stay.[24]

Americans anxiously and angrily awaited news from the peace mission through the summer, fall, and winter. Congress and the president returned to the capital in November as divided as they had been in July. Rumors circulated that the peace mission had failed and war was in the offing. In a speech to Congress, Adams acknowledged that he had no word from the commissioners, that he saw no near-term prospect for "permanent tranquility and order," and that the defense measures already taken remained necessary. This moderate address did nothing to quell concerns and divisiveness. Jefferson noted the tense atmosphere in Philadelphia: "Men who have been intimate all their lives cross the streets to avoid meeting and turn their heads another way, lest they should be obliged to touch their hats." The waiting was taking its toll.[25]

The peace commission arrived in Paris in late September. General Bonaparte's recent lightning conquest of Italy and subsequent dictation of peace terms to the Austrians had emboldened the Directory, which staged the coup of 18 Fructidor (September 4, 1797), closed down dozens of newspapers, and arrested and deported political moderates favorable to the United States. In this atmosphere Foreign Minister Charles Talleyrand refused to see the commissioners officially, but quietly sent insulting demands, including a $10 million American loan to the French government and, most galling of all, a $250,000 personal bribe. The American delegation refused to meet any of these demands, although one commissioner, Elbridge Gerry, began to meet with Talleyrand and his agents privately. The commission broke up after six frustrating months, but Gerry stayed behind in hopes of reaching an agreement.[26]

Adams received official word of the embassy's failure on March 4, 1798, one year into his presidency. The delegation had sent coded reports detailing the French ultimata and Talleyrand's artifice, avarice, and arrogance. The president sent an anodyne message to Congress, saying only that the mission had failed and that the country should prepare for what might ensue. Republicans, sure that the administration was covering up the reasons for its failure, and Hamiltonian Federalists (who had garnered intelligence about the reports' damning contents) combined to pass a House resolution demanding release of the commission's letters to Congress. Adams complied, disguising the foreign minister's agents as X, Y, and Z, but the House was wholly unprepared for what it read. Three days later the Senate reviewed the reports as well, causing Abigail Adams to crow, "The Jacobins in the Senate and House were struck dumb." Indeed, the Republicans were in disarray, scarcely believing the French actions and trying to lay blame on the administration. The Federalists knew that they had stolen a march, and when the XYZ papers were published a few weeks later, the party rode a wave of patriotism and francophobia that promised to propel the country headlong into war.[27]

President Adams was soon at the height of his popularity, reveling in his escape from his predecessor's shadow. During the Revolution, Adams had lamented not being a soldier—now he had his chance. Caught up in war fever, he exhorted his admirers to take on a "warlike character." On at least one formal occasion he appeared in military dress, affecting an officer's sword. Patriotic groups around the country sent him formal "addresses" of support, which were widely published along with Adams's triumphant and bellicose replies. Gangs of war supporters, sporting black cockades on their hats, and war opponents, wearing the French tricolor cockade, clashed violently in the streets of Philadelphia, causing the governor to call out cavalry to disperse them. Responding to the president's call to action, Congress appropriated almost $1 million for cannon foundries, coastal fortifications, and naval vessels. A new Department of the Navy was established. In a three-month legislative frenzy Congress enacted twenty war measures. Jefferson referred to the militant atmosphere as a "reign of witches."[28]

Opposed in principle to standing armies and firm in his belief in the protective prowess of an effective navy, Adams had not asked for an army bill, but he got one just the same. Although the United States Army today traces its lineage to 1775, the historical truth is that for four decades following the Revolution the nation maintained no true standing army—only the shell of one—occasionally raising a force of militia or volunteers in response to a frontier crisis or an internal rebellion. In the spring of 1798, the United States scattered a total of thirty-five hundred men under arms along its western borders. The war scare impelled Congress to approve a "provisional army" of ten thousand soldiers in April. Yet the bill was far weaker than the Hamiltonian Federalists wanted. The army was truly provisional: the president could call it up only after a declaration of war or if the country were under imminent threat of invasion.

Hamilton wrote a series of seven newspaper articles called "The Stand," detailing French perfidy, advocating an immediate expansion of the army, and chastising the "Jacobin" Republicans: "Such men merit all the detestation of their fellow citizens and there is no doubt that with time and opportunity they will merit much more from the offended justice of the laws." His aim, as always, was a permanent army financed by federal debt and serviced by federal taxes that would enable a robust central government to grow as the precursor to a great fiscal-military state. Through the spring of 1798, Federalists whipped the army proposal in Congress, arguing alternatively that an army was necessary as a deterrent, that an invasion was imminent, or that the country was already at war. The argument that they eschewed in public was the one that animated them in private caucuses: the need for an army to put down a potential Republican insurrection, especially one that might be coupled with a French invasion. The Republicans were alive to the unspoken motive, anxiously pondering what "much more from the offended justice of the laws" might entail, and clearly understanding that an administration wary of domestic upheaval would find a permanent army a ready instrument for targeting political opponents."[29]

In an atmosphere in which the opposing parties saw one another as illegitimate, the Federalists were raising an army that most Republicans feared as a wholly partisan stalking horse for a military state. The Constitution itself seemed to hang in the balance.

The Federalists then gave Republicans more substantiation for their fears. During the early summer, while Congress was adding another dozen regiments to be recruited immediately—twelve thousand men in what was termed the "New Army"—it also passed four of the most reprehensible bills in American political history, the Alien and Sedition Acts. During the "reign of witches" that spring, the Republicans and their supporters overreacted as badly as the Federalists, starting riots, raising invective in the press, and appearing to send their own emissary to France. Jefferson continued to undermine Adams in secret meetings with the French chargé d'affaires in which he urged the Directory to stall negotiations. The Federalists answered with three acts directed against foreign nationals, of whom there were between twenty-five and thirty thousand living in the United States, giving the president expeditious power to deport or imprison them on suspicion of being "dangerous." These Alien Acts spurred an exodus of expatriates, many of whom were refugees from the French Revolution and presumably the sort of Frenchmen most disposed to supporting America against the Directory. Congress also passed the Sedition Act, which prohibited any public assembly manifesting opposition to the government, or the utterance or publication of any statement opposing the government deemed to be "false, scandalous, or malicious." Adams had not asked for these powers, but he did nothing to oppose their passage and quickly signed them into law. His approval remains the blackest mark on his historical legacy. Moreover, aside from jailing a number of hostile editors and frightening immigrants, their primary effect was to galvanize and unite the Republican opposition against the oppressive but splintered Federalists.[30]

Riding the crest of a breaking wave of nativism, Adams signed a law in early July abrogating American treaties with France. He weighed the option of asking Congress for a declaration of war, but refrained because, not knowing if the peace commissioners were still in France, he feared for their safety. In the summer of 1798 the first of several naval battles between French and American forces heightened war hysteria, but the country remained bitterly divided, and most members of Congress were not yet ready to declare war. Though no one recognized it at that moment, the war fever had peaked.[31]

After he left the Treasury, Alexander Hamilton had continued to advise President Washington and the cabinet secretaries he had dominated when in government. Soon after Adams assumed the presidency, Hamilton sent him the same sort of long advisory paper he was accustomed to providing Washington, but Adams rebuffed him. Hamilton pivoted cleanly, continuing to correspond with Secretary of State Pickering, Secretary of the Treasury Wolcott, and Secretary of War McHenry just as effectively as he had done before. When Adams asked his cabinet for advice, they routinely forwarded the questions to Hamilton, ensconced in his law offices in New York. He never failed to answer in lucid, extensive missives, employing his formidable grasp of politics, economics, and diplomacy. The secretaries often parroted Hamilton's precise verbiage in their subsequent responses to the president. When Adams read his cabinet's reports, they formed a remarkable synergy, as well they might, having emanated from a single intellect.[32]

For all his faults, Adams was nobody's fool (save his own). Within months of taking office, he recognized that his cabinet was loyal to Washington and, more importantly, to Hamilton, rather than to him. Furthermore, he grasped the influence that Hamilton had over the secretaries and the degree to which their advice was his. In letters to Wolcott, Pickering, and McHenry, Hamilton betrayed the hubris at the core of his character when he referred to the "*actual* administration" that was "not much adverse to war with France." The "*actual* administration" (italics his) of course meant his control of the machinery of government in contrast to Adams's own presumed impotence. It is difficult to fathom why Adams did not ease these men out of office and replace them with trustworthy advisers.[33]

Just as he controlled the cabinet, Hamilton guided his partisans in Congress. As party leader, Hamilton wielded enormous influence over the Federalists in both houses. Given that he held no office, that was no small political feat. Adams was no advocate of a standing army, but Hamilton plumped for one after the provisional army passed, and within a couple of months, the Federalists approved the New Army—twelve infantry regiments and six troops of dragoons. Adams later groused that Hamilton had embarrassed him with more troops than he wanted, "without any recommendation from the president," and he was right. Not quite the force of fifty thousand men that Hamilton desired, it was nonetheless a building block for a man with great aspirations and no future in elective politics. Adams saw the New Army as a vehicle for Hamilton's ambition: "The army of fifty thousand men . . . appeared to me to be one of the wildest extravagances of a knight errant. . . . Hamilton knew no more of the sentiments and feelings of the people of America, than he did of . . . the inhabitants of one of the planets." Adams intended that Hamilton would never wield power over a standing army.[34]

With that negative intention perhaps too firmly in mind, Adams seems to have given too little consideration to the choice of an army commander. He ended by making perhaps the worst possible choice for the country, his office, and himself.

On May 19, 1798, Hamilton wrote to George Washington, then in retirement at Mount Vernon, apprising him of the gathering war clouds, his belief that the Republicans were in cahoots with the French, and a concern that the southern states might be vulnerable to invasion and insurrection. He also sounded his old chief out on the possibility that "the public voice will again call you to command the Armies of your country." Washington did not close the door on the idea, but suggested that many others could serve as well as he, expressing the hope that the command might devolve upon "a man more in his prime." Writing to Hamilton, Washington asked whether, if he were to take the post, his old aide-de-camp would be disposed to serve alongside him. Hamilton rushed into the opening, expressing his "great satisfaction" and the sentiment that "no one but yourself . . . could unite the public confidence in such an emergency." The country's desire for Washington's service would be "*ardent* and *universal*." For his part, Hamilton announced his willingness to serve as "Inspector General with a command in the line"—in other words, as second in command. He took it "for granted" that Washington would have authority to recommend his subordinates and "that your choice would regulate the Executive," that is, President Adams. All this correspondence transpired more than a month before Congress approved the New Army.[35]

Near the end of June, Adams wrote Washington alluding to the tensions with France. Speaking of his burdens and responsibilities, he confessed that he had "no qualifications for the martial part of it, which is likely to be most essential." He flattered Washington that the country would be better off if Washington could return to the presidency. As for forming an army, he admitted to being "at an immense Loss whether to call out all the old Generals, or to appoint a young sett. . . . I must tap you, Sometimes for Advice. We must have your Name, if you, in any case will permit Us to Use it. There will be more efficacy in it, than in many an Army."[36]

Washington answered on Independence Day, more than twenty-three years after he had taken command of the Continental Army, assuring the president "that as far as it is in my power to support your Administration, and to render it easy, happy & honorable, you may command me without reserve." Neither of them had yet mentioned the army command, but both seemed to understand that the offer was implicit. Washington went on at some length discussing the selection of officers, suggesting that "the *old set* of Generals" might no longer be up to the task. Instead, they should select the best available talent from "the late Army; without respect to Grade." He had no list in mind, but he gave it as his "decided opinion" that the general staff—the inspector general, quartermaster general, adjutant general, and commanding general of artillery and engineers—must be men in whom the commander in chief, "be him whom he will," could repose his complete confidence. He implied that the selection of those general officers should, therefore, be the prerogative of the commander in chief. Tellingly, Washington confused the constitutional term for the president in his command of the army and navy with the connotation of a commanding general of the army.[37] In a letter to Secretary of War McHenry the following day, he was more explicit, but his explanation compounded the mistake:

> The President's letter to me, though not so expressed in terms, is, nevertheless strongly indicative of a wish that I should take cha[rge] of the Military force of this Country; and if I take his meaning right, to aid also in the Selection of the General Officers. The appointment of these are *important;* but those of the General Staff, are *all important;* insomuch that if I am looked to as the Commander in Chief, I must be allowed to chuse such as will be agreeable to me.[38]

Washington did not know as he was writing those lines that the president had already nominated him, and that the Senate had confirmed him as lieutenant general in command of the army.

With the best of intentions, both Adams and Washington made serious mistakes. Still awkwardly emerging from Washington's eclipsing shadow, Adams needed to help the country to separate its conception of national leadership from its hero-worship of Washington. Returning to him in the first emergency of his post-presidency undercut not only Adams's own public stature, but the republican principles of the Revolution. Delegating military command to his president-general predecessor undermined the most important constitutional function of the presidency by implicitly saying that Washington was indispensable, that no one else was fit to command. Yet Americans had already demonstrated remarkable resilience and stamina in self-defense during an eight-year revolution. Moreover, many other potential commanders were near at hand, including Knox, Gates, Lincoln, and Pinckney, as well as dozens of the "younger set" whom Washington professed to prefer, who were in good health and had earlier served with distinction.[39] Adams's nomination of Washington sacrificed a number of principles worth preserving or establishing.

No one should have understood those imperatives better than Washington. He had been the army's first commanding general and the nation's first president and commander in chief under the Constitution. He had shown immeasurable selflessness and insight in both roles, carefully establishing precedents that would well serve his successors, most notably stepping down from both positions voluntarily to demonstrate the principle of continuity of the office and the institution, rather than the tenure of the incumbent—a government of laws and institutions, not of men. By agreeing to return, he lent credence to the myth of his own indispensability, diminishing the institutional authority of both the president and the commanding general. By placing conditions on his acceptance—insisting on naming his general officers—Washington further undermined the president as commander in chief. Under the Constitution he had done so much to bring into existence and whose principles he had nurtured and matured as president, Washington asked Adams to forfeit a presidential prerogative that was clearly codified in Article II, Section 2, the power to appoint officers of the government. The unerring judgment that the country had come to prize seems to have abandoned Washington in this moment. Washington was right; he was no longer in his prime.

Secretary of War McHenry traveled to Mount Vernon to confer with his new subordinate, carrying Washington's commission and a packet of letters in his pouch. Adams sent a note explaining McHenry's visit, apologizing to Washington—whether for nominating him without his consent or simply for intruding on his retirement is not clear—and asking Washington to serve. Secretary of State Pickering wrote to say how important it was for Hamilton to be named inspector general. He related that Adams was opposed to commissioning Hamilton and that Washington's influence would be necessary to change the president's mind. It would be difficult to gather more incontrovertible evidence of where the cabinet's loyalties lay. In reply, Washington agreed with Hamilton's indispensability: "I think as you do; and that his Services ought to be secured at *almost* any price." McHenry also carried a letter from Hamilton himself, who was in Philadelphia. Hamilton was shocked that Washington had been nominated "without any previous consultation." He urged Washington to accept his commission for all the reasons he had earlier given and because "the President has no *relative* ideas & his prepossessions on military subjects in reference to such a point are of the wrong sort." Washington and McHenry discussed the New Army's organization and the selection of officers for three days. Before McHenry departed, Washington wrote to Adams expressing his gratitude "at this New proof of public confidence." Yet having earlier promised that Adams could command him "without reserve," Washington placed another condition on his acceptance, namely "that I shall not be called into the field until the Army is in a Situation to require my presence, or it becomes indispensible by the urgency of circumstances."[40]

As he considered selection of his subordinates, Washington clearly wanted to name Hamilton inspector general. Since he also intended to remain at Mount Vernon until some crisis demanded his presence, Hamilton would effectively command the army. Yet Washington showed sensitivity to political concerns. Charles C. Pinckney, on his way back from France after the failed peace mission, was a respected Revolutionary general, a well-connected southerner—therefore representing a region thought to be the target of a potential French invasion—and now a highly popular statesman in the wake of his performance in the face of French boorishness. Washington wanted Pinckney on the general staff, but was concerned that he might not serve in a position subordinate to Hamilton. He expressed the same concern about Henry Knox, artillery commander during the Revolution and the first secretary of war under Washington. However, when he composed a list of prospective officers for the New Army he set aside those reservations, recommending Hamilton as inspector general, followed by Pinckney and Knox. It is interesting to note that he placed two of the "old Generals" he had suggested might be past their prime beneath one of the "younger set." Still, he maintained his rule that he should have general staff officers in whom he had total trust and confidence. The question was whether the president shared that esteem for his choices.[41]

He did not. Adams became agitated when he saw Hamilton at the top of Washington's list. Yet the president was now in a self-made trap. Having appointed Washington without his consent, he now found himself with a prestigious army commander, confirmed by the Senate, who had placed two conditions on his acceptance of the post—the right to name his own generals and leave to remain at home until an emergency required him to join his army in the field. Adams submitted Washington's list to the Senate, which approved the major generals' commissions of Hamilton, Pinckney, and Knox, in that order. Shortly thereafter Adams quit the capital for Quincy, where he remained for seven months. He had signed none of the major generals' commissions.[42]

With the president in Massachusetts, his secretaries of state and war in Philadelphia, the army commander in chief in Virginia, and Hamilton in New York, organizing the New Army was troublesome to say the least. Dozens of letters circulated among those principals.[43] McHenry and Pickering fed Washington and Hamilton information about discussions and correspondence with the president. Washington and Hamilton routinely exchanged intelligence relating to the inspector generalship, the need to mollify Knox, and the political value of Pinckney. Washington attempted in vain to assuage the feelings of his old comrade-in-arms, Knox. The president compounded the trouble by declaring that the order of names in the Senate confirmation had no bearing on seniority, and that he intended Knox to be second-in-command, with Hamilton ranking fourth behind Pinckney. Adams felt that if he appointed Hamilton as second-in-command, he would "consider it as the most [ir]responsible action of my whole life, and the most difficult to justify." Hamilton had only been a lieutenant colonel in the Revolution, and Adams considered him a foreigner.

Sensing the dénouement, Hamilton told McHenry that he would not serve under Knox or Pinckney. Knox angrily told both McHenry and Washington that he would not serve under Pinckney or Hamilton, citing his higher rank in the Revolution.[44] With uncharacteristic understatement, Adams complained in an August 29 letter to McHenry that "there has been too much intrigue in this business." The president mistakenly believed that Washington was blameless, having acted "with perfect honour and consistency." Adams reiterated that he would accept the responsibilities of his office. "The power and authority is in the President. I am willing to exert this authority at this moment & to be responsable for the exercise of it." Adams was drawing himself up to his full height, such as it was, and growing into the presidency.[45]

Adams was right on two counts: the responsibility and authority for these matters rested with the president, and there had been a great deal of intrigue, much of it orchestrated by his own cabinet. McHenry immediately divulged the text of this Adams letter to Washington, a remarkable breach of trust between a president and his war secretary. And on

September 1, Secretary of State Pickering sent Washington a "private" letter to inform him that the president intended to reverse the order of the major generals, going into some detail to impeach the president's reasoning. That note spurred another flurry of letters to and from Mount Vernon.[46]

Washington decided that a confrontation could wait no longer. On September 25, he wrote directly to Adams, first reminding him of the great respect he had for the president's "public station" and "private character," then apologizing in advance for the "candour" that was to follow. The subject of the letter was "the change which you have directed to be made in the relative rank of the Major Generals," as well as more minor matters relating to the selection of officers. He reminded Adams that he had appointed Washington "without any previous consultation of my sentiments," placing him in a "delicate situation." Had Adams awaited his assent, he would have learned "on what terms I would have consented to the nomination; you would then have been enabled to decide whether they were admissible, or not." Nonetheless, after his Senate confirmation, Washington had told Adams how important it was "that the General Officers, and General staff of the Army should not be appointed without my concurrence." Washington asserted that he had made no other stipulations, which conveniently overlooked his insistence on staying at Mount Vernon until some emergency should call him forth to the army. He had even told McHenry to return his commission to Adams until the president understood and concurred with those conditions, but the secretary had assured him that such a formality was unnecessary. Getting to the sticking point, he told Adams that he had been surprised to learn of his decision concerning the major generals: "you have been pleased to order the last to be first, and the first to be last." He explained at some length why he had ordered his list as he had, condescendingly reminding Adams of the vast experience he had "both in the Civil & Military administration of the Affairs of this Country [that] enabled me to form as correct an opinion of them as any other could do." Washington obliquely echoed the contingent language of his earlier letter to Adams, referring in the third person to "the Commander in Chief of the Armies (be him whom he may)." It was not a resignation threat, but it was close. In closing, he directly requested "to be informed whether your determination to reverse the order of the three Major Generals is final." That Washington would have a decision of his own to make based upon that information was unstated, but clear.[47]

Adams could not afford to let Washington resign; the political cost would be too great. He informed Washington that he had signed all three commissions on the same date, hoping that "an amicable Adjustment or Acquiescence might take place among the Gentlemen themselves." If not, he said, they might appeal to Washington for adjudication, and Adams would support his commander's decisions. Essentially, Adams delegated his authority to Washington, although, almost as an aside, he noted "that by the present Constitution of the United States, the President has Authority to determine the Rank of officers." Hamilton would be second-in-command with Pinckney ranking below him. Knox, the general who had commended Captain Hamilton to Washington after the victories at Trenton and Princeton, bitterly declined his commission. Wrangling over relative seniority among three major generals had delayed the New Army's organization for three precious months.[48]

Adams knew by this time that his cabinet was conspiring with Hamilton against him. Given Washington's desire to elevate Hamilton, it was reasonable to assume that the former president, now "commander in chief" of the army, was informed by those circles as well, as in fact he was. Adams later lamented his plight: "With all my ministers against me, a great majority of the Senate and of the House of Representatives, I was no more at liberty than a man in prison, chained to the floor and bound hand and foot." Fate gave Adams a way out of his dilemma in the forlorn figure of Elbridge Gerry, just arrived in Boston after a circuitous journey from Paris. Gerry, who had not been in the president's good graces for having overstayed his colleagues' welcome in France, nonetheless visited Adams in Quincy on October 4. During a long conversation, Gerry confirmed what his fellow peace commissioner John Marshall had said when he returned in July: the French wanted no war. Indeed, Gerry confided, Talleyrand was ready to discuss peace. Here lay a way for Adams to cut the Gordian knot, to emasculate Hamilton, and to regain control of the army and his government. He would have to bide his time, but time began to work in his favor.[49]

Having pledged on retirement never to travel ten miles from Mount Vernon, Washington rode through adoring throngs when he returned to Philadelphia as commanding general in early November, 1798. He plunged into the details of organizing the New Army, the first of which was recruitment of officers. In meetings with Hamilton and Pinckney, Washington insisted on excluding Republicans from the officer corps. In his first memorandum after his appointment in July, Washington followed a list of requested appointments with a warning: "There may be among the foregoing some of bad political principles, and others whose true characters I have mistaken—and the whole of them require to be investigated." Washington later heard that "Brawlers against Governmental measures" were angling for commissions, with the intent "to divide, & contaminate the Army, by artful & Seditious discourses; and perhaps at a critical moment, bring on confusion." Washington's fear of this conspiracy was informed by his now entrenched partisanship. He gave his opinion "that you could as soon scrub the blackamore white, as to change the principles of a profest [Republican]; and that he will leave nothing unattempted to overturn the Government of this Country." For his part, Hamilton seems to have followed, rather than led, this attempt to politicize the army. In pages of charts he had submitted in August 1798 recommending men for commissions, he mentioned party affiliation only occasionally, and then sometimes to recommend an officer in spite of Republican leanings. The recommendations that came out of the weeks of Washington-Hamilton-Pinckney conferences seem to have been much more partisan—few Republicans were on the list. Hamilton regretted that "Antifœderalism has been carried so far. . . . We were very attentive to the importance of appointing friends of the Govern[men]t." Yet they had given a few commissions to deserving Republicans at lower grades so as not "to give to appointments too absolute a party feature." After all, as he explained to McHenry, they were building a government as well as an army: "Military situations, on young minds particularly, are of all others best calculated to inspire a zeal for the service and the cause in which the Incumbants are employed." Hamilton was less zealous a partisan than Washington or the Federalists in Congress, at least when it came to commissioning officers. He seems to have understood the problems of a too partisan officer corps, although, in the end, his concerns were a matter of degree, not absolute objection. Adams asked his cabinet and party leaders in Congress to review the list. No suitable Federalists could be found in five southern states until Pinckney traveled south to consult with leaders there. Until then, Adams refused to submit a partial list, one more dilatory tactic that postponed army organization by yet another three months.[50]

Their time in the capital served to confirm Washington's and Hamilton's suspicions that their old friend McHenry was unsuited to his role as secretary of war in a time of incipient crisis. Hamilton had earlier confided to Washington that McHenry was "wholly insufficient for his place, with the additional misfortune of not having himself the least suspicion of the fact!" Washington concurred, regretting "that these opinions are so well founded." Their assessment was unfair, given that McHenry had labored for months to recruit and supply an army while the appointments of his immediate subordinates were up in the air and while dealing with vexing delays awaiting replies from Adams, Washington, and Hamilton, who were not only at odds but spread from Massachusetts to Virginia. Moreover, there was a real question about who was ordering whom. Nominally superior to Washington and Hamilton, McHenry was inferior to both in experience and from past subordination to them. McHenry found himself dominated by both these generals, Pinckney when he returned from France, the president, and the secretary of state into the bargain. With all these bosses and the distances that divided them, it is hard to see how McHenry might have done better. To make matters worse, his constitutional superior, Adams, was obviously delaying army organization through willful inattention. "At present there is no more prospect of seeing a French army here," Adams wrote to McHenry, "than there is in Heaven." Having been outmaneuvered on the ranking of generals, Adams was content to allow military confusion to fester as a way of thwarting Hamilton's designs.[51]

After several weeks in the capital, Washington returned to Mount Vernon and took little further part in organizing the army. He left Pinckney in command of forces in the South, Hamilton of those in the North. Yet Hamilton's position as inspector general, his indefatigable energy, his relative proximity to the capital, and McHenry's troubled management combined to place him effectively in charge of the whole. From that point forward, Hamilton was in de facto control if not command, making all plans, developing army organization, even drafting legislation and advising congressional committees to put his designs into effect.[52]

Hamilton had grand plans for the New Army, which he intended to be a strong and permanent force, the keystone in the arch of a strong, centralized federal government. His allies in Congress pressed for five-year enlistments and approved an "Eventual Army" of thirty thousand more men. The enlistment legislation never passed, and the Eventual Army never came into being, but both initiatives clearly showed plans for a permanent military force. With characteristic attention to detail, Hamilton drafted regulations to govern every aspect of the army, from

71

uniforms and drill manuals to the design of huts and hospitals. He aimed for the New Army to be capable of meeting an invading French army, cowing potential insurgents, or even mounting offensive operations in the southwest or overseas.[53]

Domestic use of the army became especially controversial, not only in the wake of the partisan officer appointments, but also in response to Republican political actions. In November and December 1798, the state legislatures of Virginia and Kentucky passed resolutions that declared the Alien and Sedition Acts unconstitutional and declared a right to obstruct their enforcement. Although it was not known at the time, Jefferson had secretly drafted the Kentucky bill, and Madison had done the same in Virginia. These resolutions struck the Federalists as not only unconstitutional themselves, but probable preludes to rebellion. Hamilton referred to "the tendency of the doctrines advanced by Virginia and Kentucke to destroy the Constitution of the United States" and "the full evidence which they afford of a regular conspiracy to overturn the government." He planned to combine congressional pressure with a show of force by the New Army to intimidate potential rebels. When German farmers and tradesmen in Pennsylvania rioted against federal taxes in March 1799, Hamilton sent New Army companies and local volunteers to suppress them, far more than were necessary for the task. He explained to McHenry, "Beware, my Dear Sir, of magnifying a riot into an insurrection, by employing in the first instance an inadequate force. 'Tis better far to err on the other side. Whenever the Government appears in arms it ought to appear like a Hercules, and inspire respect by the display of strength." Critics ranging from Abigail Adams to Thomas Jefferson began comparing Hamilton to Bonaparte.[54]

They were probably unaware how apt the comparison was. Hamilton dreamed of building an offensive, even expeditionary, capability—a fifty-thousand-man army that would be able to invade the Floridas or Louisiana and take possession of them. In his wildest flights of fancy, he discussed adventures into Mexico or South America. Approached by a South American freebooter and onetime French lieutenant general, Francisco de Miranda, Hamilton became involved in a plot to liberate Venezuela from the Spanish. He secretly wrote to Miranda of using a British fleet to deploy the New Army overseas: "I shall be happy in my official station to be an instrument of so good a work." Hamilton also apprised Representative Harrison Gray Otis of his plans, couching them in terms of thwarting the growth of the French empire: "What can tend to defeat the purpose better than to detach South America from Spain, which is only the channel th[r]ough which the riches of *Mexico* and *Peru* are conveyed to France?"[55]

Adams would never have countenanced Hamilton's grandiose plans. The two men were at polar extremes in their conceptions of the purposes and, therefore, the proper composition of the nation's forces, especially in the crisis with France: "I have always cried Ships! Ships! Hamilton's hobby horse was Troops! Troops! . . . With all the vanity and timidity of Cicero, all the debauchery of Marc Anthony and all the ambition of Caesar. . . . His object was the command of fifty thousand men. My object was the defense of my country, and that alone, which I knew could only be affected by a navy."[56]

When Adams got wind of Hamilton's expeditionary schemes for the army, he did "not know whether to laugh or weep. . . . Miranda's project is as visionary, though far less innocent, than . . . an excursion to the moon in a cart drawn by geese." Adams railed to Elbridge Gerry "that he thought Hamilton and a Party were endeavoring to get an army on foot to give Hamilton the command of it & then to proclaim a Regal Government, place Hamilton at the Head of it & prepare the way for a Province of Great Britain." Clearly, Adams could engage in flights of fancy himself, but he had resolved to stop Hamilton.[57]

Despite enormous pressure to do so, Adams never asked for a declaration of war against France. Adams gave a speech to Congress in December 1798 with Generals Washington, Hamilton, and Pinckney near him in the chamber. As was by now characteristic of Adams, his message was too bellicose for the Republicans, too pacific for the Federalists. He held the door slightly open for further negotiations, and again postponed a declaration of war.[58]

Time and again, reliable envoys counseled that war was avoidable. John Marshall returned from his humiliating experience in Paris to a hero's welcome in the summer of 1798. Nonetheless, he disappointed hawkish Federalists when he told them that peace was yet attainable. Elbridge Gerry reinforced that view with Adams when he returned in October. Then in January, Adams's son, Thomas, returned from a four-year absence in Europe where he had served as secretary to his elder brother, John Quincy, then the most gifted of American diplomats. Thomas bore a message from his brother—the French were ready to negotiate.[59]

On February 18, 1799, Adams sent a brief message to the Senate, which Vice President Jefferson read aloud from the chair. Having consulted no one, especially not the cabinet that he had come to distrust profoundly, Adams was nominating William Vans Murray to be minister plenipotentiary to the French Republic. In two paragraphs, Adams jerked the props from beneath the Federalist argument for a standing army—that war with France was imminent. Republicans were astonished, but gratified. The Federalists were irreparably split; many would refuse to support Adams for reelection. Secretary Pickering was "thunderstruck," saying that Adams had made the nomination "without any *consultation with any member of the government* and for a reason *truly remarkable—because he knew we should all be opposed to the measure!*" Although it took several months for Murray, and two more delegates that the Federalists forced on Adams, to arrive in Paris, the mere fact of impending negotiations stilled the war ardor.[60]

For the rest of 1799, the New Army died a slow death. Top-heavy with Federalist officers, it never approached half its authorized strength of twelve thousand. A land tax assessed to pay for it became increasingly unpopular, and was the proximate cause of Fries's Rebellion in northeastern Pennsylvania. George Washington lost interest in the army—"or more properly the Embryo of one," as he dejectedly put it—and refused to issue any further orders. Hamilton continued manically with his plans, frequently upbraiding McHenry about his management and failure to obtain sufficient funding, and railing about Adams's willful delays. At one point, he told McHenry to move forward with their plans if the president was "too desultory."[61]

Hamilton accosted Adams for one final interview in October. The president had returned from another seven-month stay in Quincy to temporary quarters in Trenton, where the government was waiting out Philadelphia's annual yellow fever epidemic. In a stormy cabinet session, Adams had made a final decision to dispatch the peace commission. Hamilton determined to try to change his mind, arriving unannounced at the president's boardinghouse. Accounts of the meeting differ starkly, but the encounter went on for hours, with each man rehearsing years of grievances against the other. Adams asserted that Hamilton was enraged while he remained calm: "His eloquence and vehemence wrought the little man up to a degree of heat and effervescence. . . . I heard him with perfect good humor, though never in my life did I hear a man talk more like a fool." While it is hard to imagine Adams responding with such equanimity under provocation, whatever relationship the two men had ended when Hamilton departed. They were mortal enemies ever afterward.[62]

Washington died in December, and was eulogized from one end of the country to the other. Adams refused to fill his vacant command or to promote Hamilton. While peace negotiations continued, Congress initially decided against disbanding the army, but agreed not to enlist any more troops. Yet the expense of maintaining the army was becoming a political issue. Federalists moved a bill to disband in May, largely to deprive the Republicans of credit for doing so. Adams pounced and ordered the army disbanded immediately. He darkly joked that if he had given Hamilton free rein, a second army would have been needed to disband the first one.[63] The Republicans used the army as a campaign cudgel throughout the election of 1800. Prospects for peace allowed them to denounce Federalist militarism, taxes, debt, war policy, a supposed British alliance, and the threat to employ a standing army against the American people. In May Adams fired McHenry and Pickering—dismissals long overdue—in large part to distance himself from the unpopularity of the army, the war, and the taxes needed to fund them.[64]

Seething from the loss of his cherished army and the end of his quest for martial glory, Hamilton carried out a vendetta against the president who had thwarted him by pursuing peace. In October 1800 he published another of the petulant pamphlets that had become one of his signature traits, a screed titled *A Letter from Alexander Hamilton, concerning the Public Conduct and Character of John Adams, Esq. President of the United States*. Adams, wrote Hamilton, "does not possess the talents adapted to the *Administration* of Government." His main defect was an "ungovernable temper" that gave vent to "gusts of passion." Adams was devoid of self-control: "he is often liable to paroxisms of anger, which deprive him of self command, and produce very outrageous behaviour to those who approach him." The source of these outbursts was to be found in the president's character: "the disgusting egotism, the distempered jealousy, and the ungovernable indiscretion." In sum, Adams, who was even then seeking reelection, was "unfit for the office of Chief Magistrate." The essay embarrassed both men, reinforcing Hamilton's reputation for recklessness and helping to cement a historical consensus about Adams's personal instability. When Adams lost the presidential election, Hamilton received a generous portion of the blame for electing his greater enemy Jefferson and for hobbling the Federalist Party.[65]

Long after he left the presidency and Hamilton was dead at the hand of Aaron Burr, Adams acidly reviewed his enemy's entire life and character: "Hamilton had great disadvantages. His origin was infamous; his place of birth and education were foreign countries; his fortune was poverty itself; the profligacy of his life—his fornications, adulteries, and his incests—were propagated far and wide." Hamilton, Adams slandered, had "a superabundance of secretions which he could not find whores enough to draw off." Adams's hatred of Hamilton remained unabated to the end of his long life.[66]

Too late to affect the outcome of the election, word arrived in November of a peace treaty with France, the Convention of Mortfontaine. Adams had preserved the peace at the price of his presidency. As he prepared to leave office, Adams spoke of his journey to his son: "My little bark has been overset in a squall of thunder & lightning & hail attended with a strong smell of sulphur. . . . I feel my shoulders relieved from a burden."[67]

Ever since 1780, one of the low points of the Revolution, when a group of nationalist congressmen led by Alexander Hamilton created a coalition in favor of a vigorous central government, a strong defense establishment had been the centerpiece of their program. When Washington retired from command of the Continental Army in 1783, he offered the nation his considered thoughts on a future "peace establishment." Careful not to call it a standing army, he cautiously advocated a small constabulary with fortresses along the frontier, arsenals and magazines at strategic locations, a system of coastal fortifications protected by a small but expansible navy, and a military academy to propagate professional education for officers. Over two decades, Washington and the nationalists, then the Federalists, used one emergency after another to build this establishment, pulling along public sentiment and even the Jeffersonian opposition in an incremental coalescence of national consensus for their program. After Shays's Rebellion, nationalists demanded reforms to the Articles of Confederation to strengthen the government and its defense capability. Those demands led to the Constitutional Convention. Hamilton carried the argument for the Constitution's military clauses in *The Federalist* and as secretary of the treasury almost single-handedly built the fiscal-military apparatus that allowed the central government to prosper. In crisis after crisis during the Washington administration, militia proved inadequate to the challenge of defending the frontier, and the government raised emergency forces to face the threats. When Washington left office, the Federalists had erected a peace establishment, including an institutionally maturing War Department, with everything they had advocated save a military academy and everything they wanted except a standing army.

Then they overreached, inflating fear in a crisis and forcing a regular army on a reluctant president and a divided body politic, half of whom dreaded this new army as a threat to their liberties.

Adams deserves credit for pursuing peace with France throughout his presidency, especially his decision to send a second commission to Paris after the first had been so badly treated. At the same time, he kept Great Britain at arm's length. He effectively implemented the foreign policy prescription of Washington's Farewell Address, to maintain peace with European powers without allying with any of them. With difficulty, Adams kept the United States neutral in the growing European wars in order to focus on national consolidation and growth.

Although he made mistakes in his first year or more as president, most notably the Alien and Sedition Acts, Adams grew in the job. Losing control of his administration concentrated his mind on the task of regaining it. While not always as vigorous in that pursuit as he might have been—witness his sojourns in Quincy—Adams bided his time and prepared for opportune moments, such as his surprise announcement of Murray's mission to France.

Far too late Adams sacked two of his troublesome ministers, McHenry and Pickering, regaining full control over foreign and military policy with two quick blows. When Congress moved to disband the New Army, Adams quickly approved the measure and tried to accelerate the timetable. With that he toppled Hamilton as well.

Before he stepped aside in favor of Hamilton, Washington feverishly worked to recruit Federalists and exclude Republicans from the army officer corps. To be sure, men with commissioned experience were more likely to be Federalists, but Washington made no pretense toward even-handedness. Even Hamilton, the most partisan of men, was surprised at how one-sided the officer corps had become. This sustained act of partisan recruitment seems quite out of character for Washington, who had long bemoaned the spirit of party and who had condemned it in his Farewell Address. The impulses that led Washington to recruit the only completely partisan army in American history are especially damning in a man who, more than anyone, ought to have known the dangers to the army and to the country. Years later, when retirement afforded him lei-sure to reflect, Adams confided to a correspondent that "Washington ought either to have never gone out of public life, or he ought never to have come in again." Although Adams conveniently overlooked his own agency in the matter, especially the act of nominating Washington with-out his assent, his judgment was nonetheless correct.[68]

Throughout his extraordinary career Alexander Hamilton did as much as anyone to create a national military establishment. He helped establish the nationalist political coalition that adopted a coherent mili-tary program and pursued it for a generation. He supported the military clauses of the Constitution in the Convention and developed an ideologi-cal structure tying them closely to a strong central government in *The Federalist.* As secretary of the treasury he was the energy and the genius behind the birth and growth of a fiscal program to support a military establishment. He assisted and mentored James McHenry in rationaliz-ing procedures and institutionalizing a War Department bureaucracy. Yet during that long career, Hamilton manifested a tin ear for traditional American fears of the military. He acted irresponsibly, with too few concerns about the threat that an army could pose to the Republic, and thought far too little about the need to build broad political consensus for military policy. Indeed, his partisanship contributed as much as any single factor to the political controversies over military policy in the Fed-eralist era. During the Adams administration Hamilton, having little prospect for feeding his enormous ambition for power otherwise, came to personify militarism—the man on horseback.

Hamilton lusted for military glory. He encouraged Washington's de facto abdication of command and leapt at the opportunity to seize au-thority that rightly belonged to the president. He labored with his cus-tomary energy and brilliance to expand the army further, to accomplish the Federalist's long-cherished goal of a permanent national army, with himself at its head. He foolishly, perhaps treasonously, plotted using that army against internal political opponents and outlined operations into the Floridas, Louisiana, Mexico, and South America. To be sure, none of those grandiose plans ever came close to realization, partly because the New Army never achieved half its authorized strength, but largely be-cause President Adams would never have allowed them to proceed, and even Hamilton was not willing to challenge the president's constitutional authority directly. Nonetheless, the New Army had never been a national institution, but a partisan one in both its composition and its contemplated purposes. In order to regain his constitutional authority and save his presidency, Adams was forced to neutralize Hamilton by acting with Congress to disband the New Army. Yet the political damage was done, and the controversy over military policy became the defining issue of the 1800 election, enabling the Jeffersonians to gain power for the first time and eventually to eliminate the Federalist Party as a force in American politics. Even the Alien and Sedition Acts begot one salutary effect: in opposing them the Republicans articulated an American conception of freedom of speech much different from the British model, enhancing First Amendment protections for generations of political minorities and antigovernment protesters yet to come. Fittingly, Hamilton finished his military career and limped off the national stage a defeated, bitter, and angry man.[69]

The interpenetration of military officership and political leadership explains some of the problematic issues that arose during the Quasi-War with France. Officers did not yet see military service as a lifelong professional calling for the simple reason that the United States did not yet have a regular army, aside from a small frontier constabulary. Reacting to one crisis after another, the government raised small forces to contend with each emergency. As a result, there was no continuity in the army officer corps. When it came to naming major generals, Henry Knox could point to his Revolutionary War service in that rank, and former lieutenant colonel Hamilton to his distinguished civilian service—neither of them having served in uniform for more than a decade. If a regular army as a going concern had existed, there would have been no need to appoint new generals. Instead, one would simply have assigned the most deserving senior officers on active duty. The same logic holds true for inferior ranks. Rather than creating a controversy by appointing officers on the basis of impeccable Federalist credentials, with a standing force the government could have rewarded the experience of those who had pursued officership as a professional livelihood and the merit of those who had done it well. An aversion to a standing army left the nation with a dearth of military expertise, signified by long service and personal identification with commissioned service.

Rows over officer appointments, coupled with Hamilton's schemes for employing the army, and especially the widely feared threat that he might use it against the "Jacobin" opposition, reinforced mistrust of standing armies. The threat was hardly realistic, but the fear and anger that the New Army engendered were real. By demonstrating a clear contrast between the small but effective frontier constabulary and a New Army raised for presumed political purposes, Hamilton's overreaching served to increase acceptance across the political spectrum of the former as the "right kind" of standing army. Hamilton and the New Army retarded development of a true regular force, one capable of more than western border defense, led by long-service leaders who would one day be known as professional officers.

On the other side of the political-military divide, Adams's actions manifest surprising growth during his presidency, not just personally but for the office of the president and its constitutional authority as commander in chief. Adams entered office in a weak position vis-à-vis his predecessor and in his political relations with his cabinet, the Congress, and Hamilton. At the moment of greatest perceived danger—the prospect of war with France—Adams realized both his greatest political popularity and sowed the seeds for his loss of presidential control. Within six months, he had an army and civil liberties restrictions he had not asked for, a conflict with his larger-than-life predecessor, and a de facto army commander whom he distrusted. The height of political prestige had presaged his fall. Then, the nadir of political authority pressed the wily Adams into calculating, careful action to restore his presidency. By maintaining a policy of international neutrality and pursuing peace with France rather than declaring a full-scale war that would surely have been destructive regardless of its outcome, Adams had laid the groundwork for his revival. By naming a second peace commission and seeing it through, by firing his disloyal cabinet officers, and by disbanding the New Army and crippling Hamilton, Adams ended by strengthening the presidency itself. These actions, along with the peace treaty with France, came too late to secure his reelection, but in the long course of American political history, Adams's failure to retain his office pales beside his contributions to the office of the president itself.

Adams later said that he wanted his tombstone to say only that he had kept the peace with France. Yet his accomplishments in life were far more extensive, and even his presidential legacy was more profound. He not only avoided a war, but saved the presidency and the army as institutions, reasserting his primacy as chief diplomat and as commander in chief, albeit by the negative act of disbanding the army. He saved the army from Washington's and Hamilton's perfidious politicization, allowing his rival-successor, Jefferson, to reform the army as a responsible instrument of government. The great irony of this most partisan time is that Adams trusted his sworn political enemy, Jefferson, to assume the preserved presidency in its role as commander in chief, and perpetuate a military that might serve the nation, not a party.

John Adams's final presidential legacy was equally profound and much misunderstood. Adams surrendered the presidency to his rival after a bitter election contest ultimately decided in the House of Representatives. That peaceful transfer of power in perhaps the most rancorous political atmosphere in American history, save the Civil War, marked a momentous milestone in the life of the American system of government. Stepping down, Adams set an important example of constitutional responsibility, demonstrating that the republic could survive a political transition, that the opposition could be trusted to govern, and that the military would obey a new president of a different party.

Ironically, Republican Jefferson co-opted the Federalist national defense agenda, dismantling none of its achievements, and even accomplished a long-cherished Federalist goal by establishing a national military academy one year after taking office. He was the first, but assuredly not the last, president to knead the opposition's program into his own executive agenda. Jefferson called it "a chaste reformation" of the army, but to be sure, he had no better conception of a nonpartisan army than did Hamilton. Yet over the following three decades the Military Academy at West Point fitfully matured and spawned a national officer corps that disdained partisanship as a principle of professional military service. The nation was a long way from accepting a "standing army," but it had taken the first steps.

3

In late 1811 Governor William Henry Harrison of the Indiana Territory had taken the field in command of a small army of regulars and volunteers just outside a Shawnee camp called Prophetstown near the mouth of the Tippecanoe River. Because Harrison had been forcing treaties on the Indians that squeezed them into ever smaller parcels of land, the Shawnee and their tribal allies became increasingly militant. They raided white settlements, sometimes with British assistance. The Indians saw Harrison's advance as yet another provocation. Just before dawn on November 7 they attacked Harrison's bivouac and inflicted heavy casualties. Harrison regrouped and counterattacked, driving the Indians from the field. The Indians suffered about one hundred casualties, Harrison's forces double that number. The next day Harrison burned Prophetstown along with the Indians' winter provisions.[1]

In many respects the battle of Tippecanoe foreshadowed the War of 1812 to come. A U.S. regional commander, who alternated effortlessly between political and military leadership, operated with little communication, support, or strategic guidance from Washington. He commanded a hastily assembled force too small and poorly trained for the mission. And he gained a limited victory that he trumpeted as a triumph of American arms, although he had gained nothing worthwhile by his efforts. And at the end of the day, little of strategic consequence had changed for the Americans.

Although considered a Republican radical, President Thomas Jefferson largely continued Federalist foreign policies, especially eschewing foreign alliances. The Jefferson administration came to power as the Napoleonic

Wars were raging in Europe, and Jefferson pursued a military policy that was almost entirely defensive. He left the Federalist military establishment in place, but spent little on its upkeep and reduced the regulars. Jefferson preferred to rely upon the more republican militia as the primary line of defense, to hold back any likely invader and buy "time for raising regular forces after the necessity of them shall become certain." He pared the Adams navy from the Quasi-War, and placed his stock in a brown-water gunboat fleet to defend the American coast. On the other hand, he was capable of violating his own small-government principles, sending a small flotilla to the Mediterranean to defend American shipping. Jefferson likewise signed legislation founding the United States Military Academy at West Point, but his purpose was to create a national scientific university and to politically reform the army rather than to create a professional officer corps. Furthermore, he ostentatiously purchased the Louisiana Territory in 1803, thereby doubling the territory of the United States.[2]

Britain and France engaged in more or less continual conflict for a decade after 1805. In that year Napoleon announced the Berlin Decree, an attempt to close all European ports to British goods, and Great Britain responded with Orders in Council blocking all oceangoing trade with France. Both measures hurt American commerce, and both nations added insult to injury by boarding American commercial vessels and impressing U.S. sailors for their own fleets. But because Great Britain was so much more powerful at sea, and because of traditional Republican antipathy toward the British, their depredations rankled far more deeply than those of the French. Jefferson's responses, such as imposing an embargo on American trade with the Europeans, were largely ineffectual and indeed harmful to the U.S. economy, especially in New England, where they were most unpopular. The country he left to his successor was twice as large, but divided and vulnerable to European mischief.[3]

Taking office in 1809, James Madison was a weak president, both personally and as a matter of principle. Article I, Section 1, of the Constitution established the authority of the legislative branch, and it was an article of Republican orthodoxy to respect Congress's primacy in government. Madison continued his predecessor's policies, adhering strictly to Republican principles, which called for limited government, little taxation, and minuscule military forces. Jefferson had wielded much influence by controlling the Republicans in Congress, but Madison had no such charisma or political skill. Although he possessed one of the finest political minds in American history, Madison had no inclination to dominate other men. Reserved and often overshadowed by his vivacious wife, Dolley, the diminutive (five-foot-four) Madison acted as though he expected the force of his arguments to substitute for vigorous leadership. As the war drums began to sound, Treasury official Richard Rush described Madison as "a little commander-in-chief, with his little round hat and huge cockade." He was an unlikely war president.[4]

A year into Madison's term many Americans were fed up with an international situation that crippled the U.S. economy and embarrassed American sovereignty. Moreover, as the populace expanded toward the western frontier, settlers came ever more frequently into contact with Indians in the Indiana and Michigan Territories. British settlers and the British army were none too secretive about their assistance to tribes that contested American expansion. Thus, the rallying cry in the elections of 1810 was for war with Great Britain. In 1811 sixty-three new representatives joined the 142-seat House, many of them southern and western Republicans describing themselves as "War Hawks." That bellicose caucus elected first-term congressman Henry Clay of Kentucky Speaker of the House, but the Federalists and moderate Republicans were not intimidated, and the Twelfth Congress became one of the most fractious in history.[5]

Even the War Hawks were still Republicans, and if they were to support a war it would be fought upon Republican principles. Treasury Secretary Albert Gallatin argued for war without "the evils inseparable from it . . . debt, perpetual taxation, military establishments, and other corrupting or anti-republican habits or institutions." For most of 1811 Republicans in Congress showed themselves willing to plump for war even as they opposed strengthening the army and navy to prepare for it. They refused to increase naval shipbuilding, lest "a permanent Naval Establishment become a powerful engine in the hands of an ambitious Executive." Congress even voted on, but defeated, a measure to abolish the army outright. Raising taxes to support the war was anathema, so it would have to be fought with borrowed money.[6]

Nonetheless, in January 1812 Congress, anticipating war, began approving measures to increase the regular army to thirty-five thousand men and to authorize the president to raise fifty thousand volunteers and call one hundred thousand militiamen into federal service. But by the middle of the year, the regular strength stood at barely twelve thousand,

and the administration was finding it difficult to raise volunteers and militia as well. Nonetheless, Clay and the War Hawks were demanding a war message from the president. On June 1 Madison satisfied them by asking Congress for a declaration of war for three ostensible purposes: to stop British impressment of American sailors; to protect American shipping from the Royal Navy; and to break up the British alliance with Indians on American soil. Then the president raised the real question near the end of his war message: "whether the United States shall continue passive under these progressive usurpations, and these accumulating wrongs, or, oppos[e] force to force in defence of their natural rights." It was a matter of "National character and Independence" and whether the first generation of heirs to the Revolution had the "will & power to maintain" them. The question for many was whether the fledgling nation would fight to survive, or slide into submission under British intimidation. A majority in Congress and the president agreed: war with Great Britain was a question of honor.[7]

The war measure was hotly debated. Federalists and traditional Republicans, especially those from New England, led the opposition. Every Federalist in Congress voted no. Notwithstanding England's abuse of American shipping and sailors, a New England economic interest, the Federalists maintained their tradition of supporting the British over the French, and stoutly opposed Republican anti-British measures such as the embargo. For them the vote against war with England was ideologically consistent. New England would drag its feet throughout the war. Yet the War Hawks forced through the declaration of war on the closest of such votes in American history—79 to 49 in the House; 19 to 13 in the Senate. Just as the measure was passing, the British government removed the primary casus belli, repealing the Orders in Council. Word arrived too late in Washington to avert an unnecessary war.[8]

Although maritime issues were the main causes of war, the conflict occurred mostly along the U.S.-Canadian border. Partly because the United States assumed it could not compete with the Royal Navy on the high seas (the navy had no ships of the line and had gained no new frigates since the Adams administration), conquering Canada became the Americans' strategic focus. As Henry Clay put it, "Canada was not the end but the means, the object of the War being the redress of injuries and Canada being the instrument by which that redress was to be obtained." In that day, just as the United States was only beginning to encroach on the Mississippi, Canada as a geographic expression extended from Halifax on the Atlantic coast up the Saint Lawrence River to the Great Lakes. Its population numbered but half a million, compared to almost eight million Americans. The watershed defined Canada in two parts: Upper Canada (modern Ontario), and Lower Canada (modern Quebec). From a strategic standpoint, the Saint Lawrence was the essential line of communication for British forces in Upper Canada; thus, if Americans could gain control of the river, perhaps at Montreal or Quebec, the British would be at a desperate disadvantage. Indeed, the Americans seem to have been overconfident about their prospects for doing so. Thomas Jefferson predicted that the conquest of Lower Canada would be "a mere matter of marching." Yet the United States had neither the sea power to control the Saint Lawrence nor yet the army to seize Montreal, and the Madison administration lacked the professional military counsel to apprise it of the import of those facts. Thus, the administration determined to focus its efforts on Upper Canada.[9]

A dozen years of Republican rule had had little positive effect on the War Department. Secretary of War William Eustis was a reliable Republican politician, but he was no administrator. With no army general staff and but eleven inexperienced clerks to assist him, Eustis attempted to function as the army's commander, operations officer, and quartermaster. He had seen service in the Revolution as a regimental surgeon, but he was incapable of running a department that was attempting to add thousands of soldiers and the matériel to equip them for an offensive war. He soon found himself mired in detail and neglecting larger strategic decisions. Eustis was "a dead weight in our hands," lamented a congressman. "His unfitness is apparent to every body but himself."[10]

The army officer corps was no better. The senior general was James Wilkinson, a Revolutionary War veteran who had interspersed his service with sidelines as a Kentucky merchant and land speculator, governor of the Louisiana Territory, Aaron Burr's coconspirator in southwestern imperial schemes, and a twenty-year career as Agent 13, a spy on the Spanish payroll. Winfield Scott, who later became one of the young heroes of the war, was once court-martialed for calling Wilkinson a traitor, a liar, and a scoundrel, and averring that serving under him was as dishonorable as being married to a prostitute. The garrulous Scott had nothing

but disdain for most other army officers of the day, calling them "swag-
gerers, dependents, decayed gentlemen . . . *utterly unfit for any military
purpose whatever.*"[11]

Inheriting such a sorry lot, Madison determined to name other men
from civilian life to high command, usually on the strength of their
Republican credentials, regional political influence, or both. Henry
Dearborn, another veteran of the Revolution, became major general
and senior officer in the army in January 1812. Dearborn's principal
qualification lay in his service as Jefferson's secretary of war, when he
carried out Republican policies to reduce the army's ranks and funding.
At sixty-one, he was old, obese, overcautious, and overwrought about
the prospects of a Federalist revolt in his native New England. For that
reason he preferred to stay in Boston rather than either of the two places
he might have gone, either to the front to command in person, or to
Washington, where he might have provided military advice to an administration that badly needed it. Unfortunately, he was incapable of performing well in either place.[12]

In yet another example of fighting a "Republican war," Madison decided upon a three-pronged strategy focused on Upper Canada, although
the army was scarcely large enough for one offensive. Hoping to please
northeastern Republicans, including New York governor Daniel D.
Tompkins, the president ordered a thrust up the Lake Champlain corri-
dor toward the Saint Lawrence and Montreal. Quebec City was the key
to the river, but it was heavily defended, well supplied by the Royal Navy,
and too far north of New England to entice militiamen to tramp across
northern woodlands to fight. The middle offensive, centered on the Niagara Valley between Lakes Erie and Ontario, was intended to placate
western New York Republicans, especially War Hawk congressman Peter
B. Porter. The western prong, planned for the benefit of Clay and his acolytes, focused on Lake Erie and the Michigan Territory around Detroit.[13]

Another reason for three offensives was that regional concerns often
trumped national strategy. The nation's strategic objective was to conquer Canada and force Britain to negotiate. Yet Madison felt the need to
garner local support from Republicans Tompkins and Porter and Clay, as
noted above. Likewise, the Indian confederacy under Tecumseh seemed
to pose a large threat in the Northwest, just as the Creek Indians did in
the Southwest. It was far easier to raise volunteers and militia to fight
against regional enemies than to entice men to deploy from Tennessee to
the Saint Lawrence in pursuit of national objectives. Furthermore, the

primitive state of transportation and communication enhanced local control and detracted from strategic coordination from Washington. Although regional campaigns did not usually support one another, neither did losses in one place spell defeat in another.[14]

Henry Clay had boasted that "the militia of Kentucky are alone competent to place Montreal and Upper Canada at your feet." Clay's prediction proved optimistic. To command the western offensive the administration selected William Hull, yet another exemplar of the porous boundary between political and military leadership. Governor of the Michigan Territory, Hull was a fifty-nine-year-old Revolutionary War veteran who had been slowed by a recent stroke. His men referred to him as "the Old Lady," and he earned the moniker with a halting offensive into Canada that a British force of regulars, militia, and Indians easily repulsed. Hull retreated back across the Detroit River, holed up in Fort Detroit, and soon surrendered without firing a shot. A court-martial sentenced him to death for his cowardly performance, but Madison remitted the punishment. The western offensive of 1812 was a catastrophe.[15]

Even before the war started the administration had prodded Dearborn to take command of the two offensives in the Lake Champlain and Niagara regions, but the accident-prone general had taken a fall that confined him to his Boston home for several months. Tired of waiting, Governor Tompkins appointed wealthy Federalist Stephen Van Rensselaer to command the New York militia and the Niagara front. Tompkins hoped thereby to blunt Federalist opposition to the war and to occupy his principal rival for reelection, but Rensselaer was a poor choice on two counts. He was a vocal partisan implacably opposed to Madison's war, and he had no military experience or skill. He socialized with his aristocratic British opponents under flags of truce while his mostly Republican enlisted men seethed with resentment. Hull's failure had put a great deal of pressure on Rensselaer to advance, so in October he ordered an attack across the Niagara at Queenston Heights. The initial assault succeeded, killing a popular British general and routing enemy forces there. But when he tried to consolidate his position, Rensselaer found that many of his militia refused to leave American soil, partly on constitutional scruples,[16] but largely because their general declined to lead them in person. The British counterattacked, forcing the Americans on the Canadian shore to surrender a thousand troops. Rensselaer abruptly resigned his command.[17]

In July 1812 Dearborn went to Albany, where he waited another four months to start deploying toward Montreal. This was a month after Rensselaer's disaster, long after the offensives might have supported one another. Dearborn's six thousand regulars and militia desultorily marched north until they reached the Saint Lawrence, where the militia refused to cross into Canada. Dearborn retired southward, never having met the enemy.[18]

At the end of 1812 Albert Gallatin summed up the Upper Canada campaigns as a "series of misfortunes" exceeding the expectations of "those who had the least confidence in our inexperienced officers and undisciplined men." The *Philadelphia Aurora* blamed Republican neglect of the military: "The degraded state in which the military institutions have been retained comes upon us with a dismal sentence of retribution."[19] Three piecemeal offensives had failed for lack of men, communications, mutual support, and effective leadership. The administration's strategy lay in tatters.

Unlike their army counterparts, the officers and men of the United States Navy were skilled veterans, many of them having fought in the Quasi-War (1798–1800) and the Tripolitan War (1801–5). While it was true that the bulk of the Royal Navy was busy with the war against France, the seventeen American warships that remained from the Adams naval buildup showed admirable aggressiveness against their British foes. In June the USS *Constitution* earned the nickname "Old Ironsides" in a victory over the *Guerriere*. Four months later the *United States* defeated and captured HMS *Macedonian,* bringing the prize home to Newport. In December the *Constitution* won another single-ship engagement over the *Java*. These victories over a Royal Navy that had suffered only one loss to the French in two decades of warfare gave a tremendous boost to American morale, a lift badly needed after the poor showing in Canada.[20]

Naval victories were not enough to conceal the administration's embarrassment at the mismanagement of the land campaigns on the Canadian border. The losses reflected failures of planning, mobilization, transportation, communication, and leadership at all levels, setbacks that were especially hard to take in light of the overweening optimism with which the war had begun. Scarcely six months later it was hard to see how the United States could hope to prevail.

These failures played on concerns about "Little Jemmy" Madison's weakness. Henry Clay pronounced him "wholly unfit for the storms of War. Nature has cast him in too benevolent a mould." Nevertheless, Madison managed reelection largely on the feebleness of the Federalist Party, which declined to name a candidate, and the tardiness of his Republican rival, DeWitt Clinton, in mounting a credible campaign. Madison's victory meant that the war would continue. The question was how.[21]

Madison began by replacing his secretaries of war and navy. His cabinet had been remarkably fractious, and he had thus far done little to rein them in. Moreover, Eustis could largely be blamed for the army's failures, and no one credited Secretary of the Navy Paul Hamilton with the navy's maritime successes. The new navy secretary, William Jones, brought far more order to the fleet, but finding a new secretary of war proved more difficult. Secretary of State James Monroe temporarily added the War Department to his portfolio, but he was hoping to be relieved of both positions to take a high command as a lieutenant general. Madison denied his request, suspecting that Monroe was simply attempting to burnish his presidential credentials. Instead, the Department of War went to John Armstrong of New York, the same Major Armstrong who had authored the Newburgh Addresses. Armstrong soon lived up to his well-deserved reputation as an intriguer. He, too, was hoping to be elected president and soon alienated the rest of the cabinet and many in Congress. Nonetheless, he took the reins of his department far more forcefully than his predecessor.[22]

By the spring of 1813 the army had thirty thousand men under arms. Armstrong divided the country into nine military districts, with a regular officer in charge of each. No general commanded the whole, but Armstrong largely took on that role himself, although he still had no general staff. He proposed to focus on controlling Lakes Erie and Ontario in 1813, preparatory to an offensive downriver on Montreal. Once again, poor execution stymied American plans. On a brighter note, on September 10, 1813, Oliver Hazard Perry, although outnumbered by the British, won a brilliant naval victory on Lake Erie. His dispatch, "We have met the enemy and they are ours; two ships, two brigs, one schooner and one sloop," was an accurate masterpiece of naval brevity. Yet the Americans were no closer to victory at the end of 1813 than at the start. Moreover, the administration again neglected Lower Canada, which is to say an attack on the Saint Lawrence, control of which might have starved British forces on the lakes.[23] The reason for this strange oversight lay in finance and politics.

Refusing to raise taxes to support the war, the administration was forced to borrow $40 million. The bulk of American wealth resided in New York and New England, bastions of Federalism and war opposition. Men of means could scarcely be induced to fund a war they opposed; New England supplied but $3 million of the total needed. Strapped for cash, Treasury Secretary Albert Gallatin at last found a potential lender in David Parish, who owned two hundred thousand acres in the Saint Lawrence Valley. Much of Parish's revenue derived from a brisk smuggling business with Canada. He offered to front $7.5 million, most of the country's near-term need, in exchange for a hands-off policy along the Saint Lawrence near the towns of Prescott and Ogdensburg, the natural route of advance on Montreal from Lake Ontario. Astoundingly, the administration agreed.[24] If war is an extension of politics, then politics (and money) can and did act to shape strategy.

The campaigns of 1812 and 1813 had at least seasoned the soldiers and their officers. As men such as Hull, Rensselaer, Dearborn, and Wilkinson stumbled and stepped aside, younger officers were proving their mettle in combat and moving up the ranks. These included Edmund Gaines, Alexander Macomb, Jacob Brown, Winfield Scott, and Andrew Jackson, all of whom gave good accounts of themselves in 1813, even if the general strategy bore no fruit. For example, Andrew Jackson and southwestern militia and volunteers opened a new regional front against the Creek Indians in the South and crushed them in three separate offensives. Jackson acted largely on his own initiative in accord with no larger strategy and brooked no interference from Washington, showing once again the regional nature of the war and the weakness of administration control of military affairs during the War of 1812.

At the end of March 1814 the defense of France collapsed and the Allies entered Paris, forcing Napoleon to abdicate. Europe was at peace for the first time in a decade. Britain now could turn its full attention to the war in North America. The Royal Navy arrived in force, driving American ships into port, and landing soldiers for their own version of a three-prong offensive. The British commenced a campaign south along the Richelieu River and Lake Champlain, another up the Chesapeake, and a third to conquer New Orleans. The redcoats marauded through the Chesapeake Valley, scattering American soldiers before them, sacking Washington and burning the Capitol and the White House. They advanced as far as Baltimore, where a spirited militia defense and the walls of Fort McHenry stopped their assault and compelled them to retire down the Chesapeake Bay. Armstrong resigned in disgrace after the campaign. Monroe once again acted as both secretary of state and secretary of war.[25]

In late September 1814 a doughty American flotilla under Captain Thomas Macdonough destroyed the Royal Navy squadron on Lake Champlain in a battle near Plattsburgh, killing the British advance into New York—a naval Saratoga. News of that victory and the British retirement down the Chesapeake arrived at roughly the same time at Ghent, where American negotiators had been stalling for months in the face of insulting British demands. Now the tables turned. Two British offensives that were meant to end the war quickly had been blunted. By Christmas the delegations agreed to a peace treaty that reestablished the status quo antebellum. In other words, two and a half years of war had ostensibly yielded nothing for either side.[26]

That disappointing result might have defined the War of 1812 for Americans but for the pace of early nineteenth-century communications and news of two other events that reached Washington at the same time as announcement of the treaty. Despairing of peace or victory, Federalists in New England had convened in Hartford in December 1814 to discuss the possibility of secession. They stopped short of treason, but word of their gathering made the party an object of ridicule, leading to its quick demise in national politics. The other news brought tidings of Andrew Jackson's stunning victory over the British at New Orleans. Jackson's combined force of regulars, militiamen (including two brigades of free black men), volunteers, a number of Indians, and eight hundred pirates had routed the redcoats in January, well after the Treaty of Ghent had been signed, so their triumph had no official effect on the outcome of the war. Yet in the popular imagination, the common American man, answering his nation's call in its hour of need, had beaten those hated oppressors of liberty, the British regulars. Rather than simply ending a pointless war, these near-simultaneous announcements allowed

America to believe that it had redeemed its honor and salvaged its independence.

Thus, the United States went to war in 1812 with a weak executive, a divided Congress, an unprepared military, an incoherent strategy, an overweening sense of grievance, and abundant national confidence. Three years later, having gained nothing tangible, it nevertheless emerged a stronger and more united nation ready to welcome unprecedented prosperity and growth.

National institutions both military and political were still in their infancy during the War of 1812. Presidential authority and responsibility remained weak. Madison reserved the veto for measures he felt truly unconstitutional, rather than those he simply opposed. The cabinet was a policy council of semiautonomous secretaries whose capacities for administration and wise counsel varied widely from one incumbent to the next. Madison confined his annual message to Congress to laying out the problems he felt the nation faced, then letting the legislature decide whether and how to address them. He laid out no plan of action.

Congress, on the other hand, was a wild and unruly child, accurately reflecting the political passions of the day. The War Hawks entered a House in 1811 after a 44 percent turnover in membership, and they promptly elected a first-termer their speaker. The pace was fast, the committees ad hoc, and the factions fluid—excitement reigned on Capitol Hill. A dearth of a sense of responsibility allowed Congress to play at government when so many new Republicans could both demand an unnecessary war with Britain and refuse to vote for increases to the army and navy.

Military institutions were adolescent as well. Republican thrift with military spending had not been accidental; it was studied and principled. That armies and navies were dangerous to liberty was an article of Jeffersonian faith. The navy remained in fighting trim better than its landward brother, because it had been practicing its maritime craft in peace and war, especially in the Tripolitan War of 1801–5. Officers and sailors were experienced in seamanship and gunnery, although there was no naval high command that had learned strategy and how to advise its civilian superiors. The army was in far worse shape. Emblematic was Jefferson's retention of the execrable James Wilkinson as senior army general long after his treason with Aaron Burr and spying for the Spanish Crown were widely known, if not legally proven. And even Wilkinson was merely senior, not responsible as the commanding general of the army (the position did not yet exist), not summoned to Washington to provide strategic counsel to the government. The army was small and its soldiers ill-paid, ill-trained, and ill-disciplined. Congress exemplified the Republican attitude toward the regular army in January 1812 when it authorized raising almost five times as many militia and volunteers as regulars.

Indeed, on the eve of war Americans scarcely had a lexicon to distinguish military from civilian. For example, Secretary of State James Monroe retained the honorific of "Colonel" three decades after his service in the Revolution. He angled for a commission as a general officer before and after he took the portfolio at State, assuming that he, as a man of affairs, was as qualified as any other to aspire to high command. And in this period before a professional officer corps, perhaps he was. Certainly Andrew Jackson, a man without formal military training, showed that natural aptitude for leadership could go a long way in making a successful commander. Monroe was undoubtedly intrepid. When the British were advancing on Washington in 1814, Monroe saddled up and deployed into Maryland as a volunteer cavalry scout rather than attending to the business of state in the threatened capital. Likewise, Secretary of War John Armstrong left Washington in 1814 to take the field in New York, where he attempted to coordinate operations between two feuding generals, one of whom, of course, was Wilkinson. In these and myriad other ways, the line between military and civilian was blurred.

Officers did not see themselves in a lifelong professional pursuit, or sometimes even in a full-time and stable position. The army scarcely controlled standards of entry and promotion within the officer corps. No special training or education was required for a commission at any rank. The army as a corporate body scarcely existed, and it certainly did not enjoy the trust of society that would have extended autonomy and deference to its professional authority. The army of the War of 1812 possessed none of the traditional attributes of professions.[27]

The administration's early selection of generals reinforced an unfortunate trait of partisanship. As we have seen, Washington and Hamilton recruited an almost entirely Federalist officer corps during the Quasi-War. Jefferson put the army through "a chaste reformation," preferring to commission his own partisans. In the War of 1812 Harrison and Hull gained their commands on the strength of regional political office. Dearborn was a Republican stalwart in Federalist New England. Governor Tompkins bypassed the administration to give Federalist Rensselaer command of the Niagara theater, but his motives were cynically partisan, and Rensselaer answered in kind during his brief tenure. None of these generals gained command on the basis of demonstrated ability, and all but Harrison amply manifested the opposite.

Yet warfare tends to punish incompetence. As the war progressed those generals left the scene for a younger set of self-taught officers who worked their way up the ranks to more responsible commands. Brown, Gaines, Jackson, Macomb, and Scott all proved themselves as trainers and combat commanders, building a small army that could stand against British regulars by the end of the war. These same men dominated a burgeoning profession for the next generation.

One among many bitter fruits of the Republicans' administration of the military establishment was that no officers had matured over a long career to arrive at a competency to provide useful strategic counsel at the highest levels. General Dearborn briefly pretended to such a role, but none too ably and only insofar as it did not inconvenience him. No respected military leader could privately ask the president to articulate the designs of his policy. It might have been helpful, shortly after the declaration of war in June 1812, when the British rescinded the Orders in Council and eased the impressments of American sailors, to have an able soldier close at hand to ask, "What now, sir, is our policy aim? Why are we going to war?" Absent such questions, Madison and his cabinet failed to reckon with their neglect of Lower Canada, and allowed war aims to drift unhelpfully toward the Great Lakes. Moreover, confused policy begat confusing strategy, and the weakness of executive authority, along with primitive communications and transportation systems, allowed regional chieftains to intuit their own strategies, else why spread U.S. forces across three autonomous theaters on the Canadian frontier?

Despite these debilities, the United States eked out a peace treaty codifying the status quo antebellum. Many basked in Jackson's victory at New Orleans, the narrative of the triumph of the common American over the hirelings of Britain. Yet quietly, more thoughtful observers recognized that the outcome of the war had been a near-run thing. John C. Calhoun, a War Hawk from South Carolina and in those days an ardent nationalist, became secretary of war in the Monroe administration. With help from Winfield Scott and others, he began to reform the army, promulgating regulations and publishing training manuals. He built upon an

1813 law that established a bureau system, with offices for an army quartermaster, a chief engineer, and a chief of ordnance, to name a few. Not quite a general staff, this establishment, headquartered in Washington with the Department of War, was still a vast improvement over the eleven inexperienced clerks that Eustis supervised in 1812. To the bureaus Calhoun added a commanding general to supervise all the line regiments of the army. This solution was not perfect, as overlapping authorities and responsibilities between the commanding general and the secretary of war caused no end of controversy over the coming decades. Yet it gave the army at least a titular head. Most important, Calhoun thought deeply about what a standing army should mean to the people and the government, about how to raise and support an army that would not be a menace to liberty. His most profound pronouncement, that the purpose of the peacetime army is to prepare for war, sounds commonplace today, but it was novel at the time in America. Calhoun pointed toward a professional army: "War is an art," he wrote, "to attain perfection in which, much time and experience, particularly among the officers, are necessary." Officers would need to begin to think of the military as a full-time career.[28]

Simultaneously, and with Calhoun's enthusiastic blessing and assistance, West Point underwent a reformation under the tutelage of Colonel Sylvanus Thayer, who established academic and military standards for cadets, including a four-year curriculum focused on military engineering to prepare officers for the lifelong calling Calhoun envisioned. It would take years for these reforms to bear fruit, but the seeds of a military profession were planted by Calhoun, Scott, Thayer, and others in the years after the war.

The presidency, however, remained a weak and limited institution under its next two incumbents. It required a political reformation, the advent of the age of mass politics, to give energy to the executive. Andrew Jackson created a populist movement that swept him into office and remade American politics. He expanded the office of the president by wielding its constitutional authority with far less constraint and leveraging his power as leader of the first broad-based political party in U.S. history. His heirs would build upon his legacy to enlarge the role of the commander in chief.

4

Soldiers of the honor guard wept as they presented arms in honor of their departing general. The old man, all three hundred pounds of him, painfully mounted the pitiful carriage—drawn by mules and driven by a disabled veteran—that would take him to Veracruz for the voyage home. He had mobilized, organized, equipped, and commanded this victorious army. He had planned the first major amphibious operation in American history and executed it without the loss of a single life. He had led these soldiers on a brilliant campaign into the interior of Mexico, never losing a battle, seizing the capital, and conquering the nation. One of his greatest difficulties had been to foster creation of a new Mexican government that could treat for peace. Now, as he put it, "My poor services with this most gallant army are at length to be requited as I have long been led to expect they would be." The president had unceremoniously relieved him of command in his moment of triumph and called him to answer charges before a military court of inquiry. The army was outraged at the shabby treatment of the man who had accomplished so much while being so stingy with their blood. He had requested a quiet departure, but his soldiers gathered in the plaza for the send-off, and thirty officers accompanied him out of the city until he begged them to return. They all insisted upon a handshake and a few words of personal farewell before allowing their commanding general to depart.[1]

Largely forgotten by Americans today, the Mexican War of 1846–48 was among the most controversial and consequential events in American history. From the outset war hawks charged that Mexico had forced the conflict on the United States, which was only defending its sovereignty over the new state of Texas. Opponents insisted that the Polk administration had manufactured the Mexican provocation in order to wage an offensive war for territorial conquest and the expansion of slavery. Despite the discord, less than eighteen months after hostilities commenced, American forces occupied Mexico City and dictated terms of a peace treaty that increased the territory of the United States by one-third, an expansion that rivaled the Louisiana Purchase. However, as many critics had warned, the addition of new territories reignited the sectional strife over the future of chattel slavery, a virulent political conflict that ended in civil war.

The war covered a broad expanse of territory, involving tens of thousands of combatants on both sides in complex operations. Mexican and American forces fought in four distinct theaters in California, New Mexico, Texas, and northern Mexico, and central Mexico from the Gulf coast to Mexico City. The U.S. Navy maintained a blockade against Mexican ports, transported the U.S. Army, and supported army operations in California and an amphibious operation at Veracruz.

American political-military relations were equally complex and controversial. Although the telegraph and railroad were recent innovations, neither yet had the strategic reach necessary to assist communications from Washington to forces in Mexico. Weeks and months passed between the issuance of orders and the receipt of reports from operational commanders. As a result, the president and his cabinet in Washington and commanders in the field experienced prolonged frustration. Time refused to stand still in either place, causing the administration to make decisions in ignorance of recent operational events and commanders to operate under political guidance that often changed before they had a chance to act on it. Under the best of situations, these vexations would have caused both generals and politicians to question the actions, if not the competence and the motives, of the other.[2]

The three principal American actors in the drama of the Mexican War were President James K. Polk and his most senior generals, Winfield Scott and Zachary Taylor. As different from one another as three men could be, each possessed towering strengths and enormous flaws. Conflict among three such men engaged in a great enterprise seems almost foreordained. These Mexican War relationships present a peculiar challenge. On the one hand, rancor, mistrust, manipulation, and enmity marked interactions among Polk, Taylor, and Scott. On the other lies the unalloyed strategic success of American arms. How do we reconcile this record of discordant political-military relations with the outcome of rapid military victory?

During the Jacksonian era, America was growing geographically and demographically, but in many ways it was becoming smaller culturally as transportation and communications became more efficient. A market revolution made the nation less rural and less fragmented. National institutions of government—Congress, the presidency, and the departments of the executive branch, including the army and the navy—began to grow from childhood to adolescence. The Military Academy at West Point was among those evolving institutions. Evangelical churches and mass-based political parties also grew and began to mature during these decades.

If the fractious relations among President Polk and his senior generals were not dysfunctional, part of the explanation lies in the maturation of three of these national institutions, specifically the presidency, the army, and political parties. Largely through the ministrations of Andrew Jackson, the presidency had become a powerful office by the 1840s, wielding initiative in legislative matters and foreign affairs, dispensing patronage through thousands of appointments, and carrying out the functions of executive governance through several departments and their bureaucracies. Perhaps as important as any of those functions was the president's recognized leadership of his party. Political parties had come to shape public life in America, and partisanship was an accepted norm, for better or worse. Participation in elections was high among those favored with the franchise, and voters tended to identify with one of the two major parties. Partisanship offered a sense of predictable stability in terms of programs and policies and promoted discipline among legislators, but it also fostered prejudice and competition for competition's sake, sometimes to the detriment of the national interest. Finally, the regular army, which earlier generations had feared as a standing army, was a small but widely accepted fixture of American life. Its officer corps had a developed a sense of long-term national service, a body of governing regulations, a shared history of achievement, and a sense of fraternity. Still, American partisanship extended into the army officer corps, at least into the cohort of Scott and Taylor, the founding generation of this professional army, men who may be considered fathers and forerunners of it, but not fully professional in the manner of the West Point–trained officers who followed and served under them. These three energetic, clumsy, adolescent institutions established the parameters within which flawed leaders—

Polk, Scott, and Taylor—acted to achieve political and strategic aims during the Mexican War.

James K. Polk was an unlikely president. A lifelong politician, Polk was a protégé of Andrew Jackson, an association that earned him the sobriquet "Young Hickory." He represented Tennessee in Congress for seven terms, the last two as Speaker of the House, before returning home in 1839 to run for governor. He won, but served only one term and was twice defeated for reelection. As the 1844 presidential campaign approached, former president Martin Van Buren was a prohibitive favorite to regain the Democratic Party nomination. With Jackson's help Polk was angling to resurrect his faltering career and become Van Buren's running mate. Then, Van Buren and his likely Whig opponent, Henry Clay, both repudiated plans for annexation of Texas into the Union. Van Buren's support plummeted. In the middle of a deadlocked Democratic Convention, party elders hatched Polk's presidential candidacy, and newspapers coined the political term "dark horse" to describe it. Polk seized the Democratic nomination and handily defeated Clay, largely on the Texas issue.

Many historical figures are endlessly complex, frustrating efforts to explain them, but Jim Polk's character was transparently manifest. A primitive gallstone removal had left him sterile and probably impotent at the age of seventeen. Dour, even puritan, he was single-minded in his pursuit of political power, and driven in his pursuit of political objectives once in office. Spiteful and humorless, Polk had little interest in anything outside politics and governing. In those arenas, however, he was a fiercely partisan Democrat, distrustful of rivals to the point of paranoia. Never doubting his own beliefs, he could be cunning, sly, and deceitful in dogged pursuit of his aims. Polk fixed on "four great measures" for his presidency: tariff reduction, establishing an independent treasury, settling the Oregon boundary dispute with Great Britain, and acquiring California. Having pledged to serve only one term, Polk drove the executive with punishing energy through long hours six days a week to accomplish those objectives. In a radical change, he required his cabinet secretaries to remain in Washington year round, rather than take customary long vacations during congressional recesses. Even so, he personally oversaw details of departmental administration with a demanding punctiliousness. Through dint of effort and an iron will, Polk achieved all four of his goals and more, but literally worked himself to death in the process, dropping dead at fifty-three a few months after leaving office.[3]

Polk's dearest presidential ambition, and the one that consumed his term, was to accelerate the territorial expansion of the United States. In public pronouncements Polk spoke boldly of securing the Oregon territory from the British and of "reannexing" Texas, a contrived formulation with no legal or diplomatic foundation. Privately, he also hoped to gain territory west of Texas all the way to the Pacific, including present-day New Mexico, Arizona, and the great prize, California, whose fine harbors offered a gateway to the Pacific. A few days before Polk's inauguration, President John Tyler approved the Texas annexation, a move that was controversial in the United States and anathema in Mexico. The Texas government accepted the offer in June 1845, and President Polk ordered an "army of occupation" under Brigadier General Zachary Taylor into south Texas to defend the new territory. The Mexicans began mobilizing a few days later.[4] The yawning chasm between Polk's expressed policy of defending Texas and his sub rosa intent to conquer and retain northern Mexican territory from the Gulf to the Pacific fostered strategic complications and political embarrassment throughout the war.

Zachary Taylor looked more like an impoverished farmer than a commanding general. Famously careless of his appearance, he was rarely found in a complete uniform. He preferred a straw hat when on campaign, and his own troops often mistook him for a private soldier. However, his unaffected air made him a favorite with his men, who sensed correctly that he had their interests, although not necessarily their discipline, at heart. He had earned the nickname "Old Rough and Ready," but many soldiers referred to him affectionately as "Ol' Zach."

Appearances are sometimes deceiving. At sixty-one, Taylor had served in the army for most of four decades. He had fought in the War of 1812 and distinguished himself in the Black Hawk War twenty years later, where he personally accepted Chief Black Hawk's surrender. He earned a brevet to brigadier general in 1837 during the Seminole War, and was one of the few commanders to emerge from that conflict with his reputation intact. His long, continuous service marked him as one of the first generation of American officers who looked upon military service as a lifelong occupation. Taylor had learned his craft on the job, guarding the western frontier and battling Indians. By 1845 he was a thoroughly experienced soldier in the first generation of American officers who had begun to think of themselves as members of a profession.[5]

For Taylor, however, as for many of his contemporaries, a claim of professionalism rested entirely on experience, long service, and dedication to national service. Yet as Frederick the Great said of Prince Eugene's mule, having been on twenty campaigns had taught him nothing of the art of war. Taylor's formal education ended long before he entered the army, and he seldom bothered to study military history or theory. Winfield Scott assessed Taylor's mind as well as anyone, noting that he had an abundance of common sense, but that "his mind had not been enlarged and refreshed by reading, or much converse with the world." A lifetime confined to frontier posts had left him "quite ignorant, for his rank, and quite bigoted in his ignorance." Among his biases was a vigorous anti-intellectualism: "Any allusion to literature much beyond good old Dilworth's Spelling Book, on the part of one wearing a sword, was evidence . . . of utter unfitness for heavy marchings and combats. In short, few men have ever had a more comfortable, labor-saving contempt for learning of every kind."[6] That ignorance extended into the corpus of military knowledge, especially at its higher reaches. Taylor was a competent administrator and an effective trainer, skills that could be learned on the job. But he was an artless tactician, a careless logistician, and an inadequate strategist. His battles tended to be needlessly bloody affairs that relied heavily on the skill of his officers and the superiority of his artillery to rescue his unimaginative tactics. His plodding operational maneuvers often forced him into unnecessary battlefield crises. He was utterly lost as a strategist, incapable of linking his operations to administration policy.

Taylor established a small camp for fifteen hundred men that summer of 1845 near Corpus Christi, just south of the Nueces River. Quickly, that number grew almost to four thousand, about half the regular army with more volunteers, mostly from southern states, mustering behind them. The camp's position was strategically trivial, but politically provocative. The Republic of Texas had claimed the Rio Grande as its southern and western border, although the United States had never recognized that boundary, accepting the Nueces as the international line. Mexico, never having accepted Texas's independence, nonetheless observed the Nueces as a provincial border. Now, claiming Texas, Polk went one step further, insisting for the first time that the Rio Grande was the border between the United States and Mexico. Thus, south of the Nueces but north of the Rio Grande, Taylor's camp was on contested soil. In August, Secretary of War William Marcy sent Taylor an ambiguous order to "approach as near the boundary line—the Rio Grande—as prudence will dictate. . . . The President desires that your position . . . should be near the river Nueces." Those instructions fudged a gap of 120 miles, leaving Taylor with the responsibility for provoking war, as Polk and Marcy no doubt intended. Taylor interpreted his orders cautiously and remained at Corpus Christi for the next several months.[7]

During those months, when the slogan of "manifest destiny" was gaining popular currency, the Polk administration engaged in ham-fisted negotiations to buy California and New Mexico from the Mexicans. Arrogantly, Polk instructed his envoy to insist on Mexican recognition of the Texas annexation as a precondition, a concession no Mexican government could make and hope to remain in power. The talks went nowhere. In January 1846, when he confirmed that the embassy had failed, Polk ordered Taylor to advance to the Rio Grande. The general made a leisurely advance, taking almost two months to establish a new camp across the river from Matamoros, where a watchful Mexican army that outnumbered his own was regularly receiving reinforcements.[8]

Lieutenant Colonel Ethan Allen Hitchcock, a regimental commander in Taylor's army, penned a bitter note in his diary: "It looks as if the government sent a small force on purpose to bring on a war, so as to have a pretext for taking California and as much of this country as it chooses." In a memoir published years later, Second Lieutenant U.S. Grant echoed Hitchcock's resentment: "We were sent to provoke a fight, but it was essential that Mexico should commence it. It was very doubtful whether Congress would declare war; but if Mexico should attack our troops, The Executive could announce, 'Whereas, war exists by the acts of, etc.,' . . . Mexico showing no willingness to come to the Nueces to drive the invaders from her soil, it became necessary for the 'invaders' to approach to within a convenient distance to be struck." Senator Thomas Hart Benton, a sometime Polk ally who had reservations about launching an offensive war, later remembered that the president "wanted a small war, just large enough to require a treaty of peace, and not large enough to make military reputations, dangerous for the presidency."[9]

Polk got his war. Mexican cavalry ambushed a U.S. dragoon detachment on April 24, 1846, killing eleven, wounding a half dozen, and capturing most of the rest. Taylor's report to Washington laconically noted: "Hostilities may now be considered as commenced." The president's war message to Congress was more passionate: Mexico had repeatedly rebuffed all attempts at a peaceful redress of grievances and had threatened invasion of the United States. "The cup of forbearance had been exhausted even before the recent reports from the frontier," Polk lamented. Then, he declared a casus belli that was accurate only because he had chosen to define it so: "Mexico has passed the boundary of the United States, has invaded our territory and shed American blood upon American soil." Polk asked Congress to recognize that a state of war already existed, and he pledged to bring the conflict to a speedy end. His message was silent on the subject of how he intended to accomplish that aim. Despite the reservations of leading senators such as Benton and John C. Calhoun and most Whigs in both houses, Polk's Democratic allies pushed a declaration of war with appeals to patriotism and plaintive cries to support the troops in the field. Within two days Congress passed the legislation by overwhelming margins. They further appropriated $10 million and authorized the president to enlist fifty thousand volunteers. Calhoun, who had abstained, expressed revulsion: "Never was so momentous a measure adopted with so much precipitancy; so little thought; or forced through by such objectionable means." He feared that Congress had set a dangerous precedent of ceding its war powers to the president.[10]

Calhoun had a point. A thorough congressional debate might have raised important questions, such as what the president's war aims were and how he intended to accomplish them. Polk's message to Congress asserted the right to defend Texas and negotiate with Mexico to right historic wrongs. All that might have been accomplished by leaving Taylor on the Rio Grande and reopening diplomatic communications. Although he never said so publicly, Polk intended (as some hoped and most suspected) to redraw the border with Mexico from the Gulf to the Pacific. When Secretary of State James Buchanan drafted a communiqué explaining the war measure to European governments, he included a passage abjuring any ambition to seize territory, including vast provinces of New Mexico and California. Angrily insisting that he would not have his hands tied, Polk excised that sentence in his own hand. By May 30 Polk had confided to the cabinet his intention of "acquiring California, New Mexico, and perhaps some others of the Northern Provinces of Mexico." He made plans to send forces into New Mexico and California.[11] Polk had wanted and provoked a war. He demanded that Congress acknowledge the existence of war. Congress declared war, and now Polk intended to wage war for his own expansionist objectives. Calhoun's warning was prescient. Polk set an example of a unified executive under a vigorous commander in chief leading a divided Congress and nation into war. He thereby established a precedent that effectively allowed the executive branch to neuter the legislature's war-making power under the Constitution. Never again has Congress vigorously asserted its constitutional power to declare war (or to refuse to do so) in opposition to a determined president.

Moments after he signed the declaration of war, Polk asked Major General Winfield Scott to command the army in Mexico. Polk had reservations about him, but Scott was commanding general of the army, and "his position entitled him to it if he desired it." After a long conference the next day in which they spelled out a plan to invade northern Mexico, Polk told his diary that "General Scott did not impress me as a military man. He has had experience in his profession, but I thought was rather scientific and visionary in his views." Scott asked for twenty thousand volunteers for his campaign, which Polk thought excessive, "but I did not express this opinion, not being willing to take the responsibility of any failure of the campaign by refusing to grant General Scott all he asked." Neither man knew it at the time, but their relationship had just reached its peak of mutual understanding and trust.[12]

Winfield Scott had been in uniform for thirty-eight years, thirty-one of them as a general officer. At six feet, four inches and over three hundred pounds, the sixty-year-old was a mountain of a man and a legend in the army. Commissioned as a captain in 1808, Scott got off to a rough start when he was tried by court-martial and suspended from service for a year for financial irregularities and for telling General James Wilkinson to his face that he was a liar, a scoundrel, and a traitor—a remark that had the distinction of being both accurate and insubordinate. Scott recovered and made his name in the War of 1812 as the heroic commander of American regulars in the battles of Chippewa and Lundy's Lane. After the war, he stood among a handful of young, new generals of demonstrated competence, whose willingness to remain in a peacetime army was harbinger of a new departure in thinking about national defense: the bankrupt American reliance on militia had to give way to an acceptance of a standing army as the first line of defense if the nation expected to take a respectable place on the world stage. Scott embraced a new ethos of professionalism, reified at West Point, though he was not an alumnus. He saw the graduates of the Military Academy as the infant progenitors of a new American military; he nurtured both academy and graduates as the pod and seeds of a future profession. For his own part, Scott traveled abroad to study the armies of Europe, compiled forty years of congressional legislation appertaining to the army in a single accessible volume, and authored regulations that governed army administration and a system of tactics that guided army training for decades to come. All the while, he commanded large portions of the peacetime army. More than any single person, Scott systematized the American military profession. In addition to his command responsibilities, during the 1830s he became a politico-military troubleshooter for the government, playing key roles in boundary disputes, Indian relocation, and the South Carolina nullification crisis. In 1841 he became the army's commanding general.[13]

For all his accomplishments, Scott was not without fault. He was arrogant, vainglorious, insecure, thin-skinned, disputatious, and, compounding all—verbose. As a result, he made enemies as quickly as he gained admirers. His love of martial ceremony and every accoutrement of military haberdashery earned him the dubious nom de guerre "Old Fuss and Feathers." He quarreled with every general officer of his generation, bludgeoning his foes with turgid, pedantic letters that read like legal briefs. Chief among his rivals was Andrew Jackson, the famously self-made militia hero of the battle of New Orleans, who disdained Scott's regulars and thought little of the need for military discipline, military training, or military thought. The notions of a regular army or of a military academy to educate and commission regular officers were foolish anathema to Jackson. Scott's feud with Old Hickory began shortly after the War of 1812, when a shrinking army was no longer large enough for two such enormous egos. Scott found himself on the outs when Jackson ascended to the presidency and remade American politics in a populist, small-government, anti-intellectual, and anti-professional fashion. His personal antipathy for Jackson and principled opposition to Jackson's policies pushed Scott into the Whig camp. Military professionalism did not yet encompass nonpartisanship, and Scott allowed his name to be placed in nomination for the presidency at the Whig convention in 1840. The Whig affiliation would complicate his relations with Democratic presidents for the next twenty years.

Although Polk had not applied the adjectives "scientific" and "visionary" as compliments, Scott was both in the best senses of the terms. He studied military history and theory assiduously, becoming a self-taught master of pre-Clausewitzian military thought. This expertise informed his tactical and organizational reform of the army, which was, on the eve of the Mexican War, an organization that clearly bore his intellectual and professional stamp.

That imprint failed to impress the president. For a man bent on war, Polk made no secret of his disdain for the regular army. Ever the protégé of Old Hickory, Polk uncritically accepted Jackson's critique of regulars. "It has never been our policy to maintain large standing armies in time of peace," he asserted before the war. "They are contrary to the genius of our free institutions, would impose heavy burdens on the people and be dangerous to public liberty. Our reliance for protection and defense on the land must be mainly on our citizen soldiers, who will be ever ready, as they have been ever ready in times past, to rush with alacrity, at the call of their country to her defense."[14] If the conflict between regulars and militia was receding into history, a new rivalry between regulars and volunteers was taking its place.

Polk extended his contempt for regulars without reservation to the army's officers, and especially its generals. A fiercely partisan Democrat, Polk regarded the army officer corps not as a professional body, but as a bastion of Whiggism: "These officers are all Whigs and violent partisans," he complained, "and not having the success of my administration at heart seem disposed to throw every obstacle in the way of my prosecuting the Mexican War successfully. An end must be speedily put to this state of things." Party allegiances, usually Whig, among many officers gave Polk reason for his suspicions. Although he could not know it at the time, Taylor and Scott were to be, respectively, the next two Whig nominees for the presidency. What Polk had in mind was commissioning his own generals to command new units that would soon be forming, partly as a means of dampening political aspirations among Whig generals. Thus, to Polk and other anti-professionals, army commissions were extensions of political patronage rather than recognitions of competent professional service. Polk sent a bill to Congress to create two new major generals and four brigadiers in the regular army, as well as eight more of volunteers. Scott, as the army's only major general, "smelt the rat," seeing in the proposal a plan to push him and other regulars aside in favor of presidential cronies. He felt the bill was not only a personal affront, but an attempt to dismantle the professional army he had labored for decades to create. The Senate passed the bill, but the House cut the number of regular commissions in half, and all those stars fell on regulars' shoulders. However, as Scott suspected, all eight volunteer commissions went to loyal Democrats with slim military résumés, including Gideon J. Pillow, whose qualifications consisted of having been the president's law partner and engineer of his improbable presidential nomination.[15]

Polk's assumptions about the volunteers' ready martial prowess caused him to disparage Scott's preparations for the coming campaign. When Scott detailed for the president the complexities of mustering, organizing, equipping, and training twenty thousand volunteers, the logistics of transporting them to the front and supplying them, Polk was unmoved. When Scott explained that he did not expect to be ready to deploy to the theater of operations until at least September, four months hence, Polk was sure that the general was dragging his feet. Polk told Secretary of War William L. Marcy that he would relieve Scott if the general did not quickly leave for the front.[16]

To give Polk his due, he knew that he was waging a controversial war, one that he had forced upon the Whig opposition. The president needed a quick end to the conflict before national sentiment turned against him. At best, President Polk believed that Scott the soldier failed to understand political imperatives. At worst, Democrat Polk suspected that Scott the Whig might be sabotaging the war effort. Scott soon gave the president cause for his suspicions.

The army's rapid expansion created hundreds of officer positions to be filled. Polk, Marcy, and Scott were all soon awash in applications, each accompanied by earnest recommendations from elected officials. Scott declined to act on one such request, telling his correspondent that the candidate lacked the requisite political connections to be considered by this administration: "Not an eastern man, not a graduate of the Military Academy and certainly not a whig would obtain a place under such proscriptive circumstances." That observation was probably accurate, albeit impolitic. Polk's partisanship and anti-professionalism were well established, and Secretary Marcy was originator of the nineteenth-century political maxim "to the victor belong the spoils." Unfortunately, Scott's letter soon fell into Polk's hands. The president was incensed at Scott's "highly unjust and disrespectful" sentiments. "The letter was of a partisan character," Polk wrote, "wholly unbecoming to the commander-in-chief of the army, and highly exceptionable in its tenor and language towards the President. It proved to me that General Scott was not only hostile, but recklessly vindictive in his feelings towards my administration." Polk lost confidence in Scott's abilities to carry out administration policies.[17]

Later that same day, Scott gave the president an official reason to sack him. After the president's threat to relieve Scott, Marcy had visited the general's office to prod him along. Scott was offended by the foot-dragging accusation and angrily told Marcy so. Then, characteristically and unwisely, Scott penned an eight-page treatise on mobilization and logistics for the military education of his neophyte superiors. A superb administrator, Scott had commenced a herculean effort to enlarge and organize the army for an expeditionary campaign. He had issued a blizzard of orders to the army's bureau chiefs. Again, he explained, the army could not possibly be ready to fight in Mexico until September, and until then, his place was in Washington, supervising the preparations. To go forward now would leave much important work undone. To arrive in Mexico without significant reinforcements would displace and embarrass General Taylor. Moreover, Scott sensed political shenanigans afoot:

> I am too old a soldier and have had too much *special* experience, not to feel the infinite importance of securing myself against danger (ill will or pre-condemnation) in my rear, before advancing upon the public enemy. . . . Whoever may be designated for the high command in question—there can be no reliance . . . other than the active, candid, & steady support of his government. If I cannot have that sure basis, to rest upon, it will be infinitely better for the country (not to speak of my personal security) that some other commander . . . should be selected. . . . My explicit meaning is—that I do not desire to place myself in the most perilous of all positions—*a fire upon my rear from Washington, and the fire, in front, from the Mexicans.*[18]

Polk consulted his cabinet, read them Scott's letter to Marcy, and relieved Scott of operational command the following Monday, less than two weeks after appointing him.[19]

That evening Marcy personally carried the president's order of relief to Scott's office, but learning that the general had gone out to eat, had it forwarded to him at a local restaurant. Scott read the letter, rushed back to his office, and scribbled another ill-considered reply. He had been working grueling hours for days to prepare the army, he said, and had only stepped away from his desk "to take a hasty plate of soup." He denied insulting the president and obsequiously attempted to flatter Polk for all his fine qualities. Within days, Scott became the butt of jokes around the country, most of which focused on the "fire upon my rear" and the cartoonish notion of the gargantuan general eating "a hasty plate of soup." Wags began calling Scott "Marshal Tureen," a pun on the name of a seventeenth-century French commander. Worse, Polk refused to reinstate him, although Scott remained commanding general of the army in

Washington, dutifully working to prepare forces to deploy without him. One pundit remarked that the general had "committed suicide with a goose quill."[20]

From a professional military point of view, Scott was right—it was unreasonable, perhaps unconscionable, to send untrained, poorly organized, and ill-equipped men into battle. Moreover, Scott's work to harmonize the efforts of the army's staff bureaus was masterly and indispensable. He needed several months to complete that task, and it is doubtful that anyone without Scott's encyclopedic understanding of the army could have done it. Yet Scott failed to understand the political imperative. Polk needed a quick end to a war that he had commenced by steamrolling the partisan opposition, before political controversy grew into nationwide unpopularity forcing him to stop before he realized his true objective, the conquest and acquisition of millions of square miles of Mexican territory. For that he needed a reliable commander at the front.

While the Scott drama was unfolding in Washington, word arrived that Taylor had given the administration just what it needed, twin victories on May 8 and 9 at Palo Alto and Resaca de la Palma, just north of the Rio Grande. Taylor then languidly followed the retreating Mexicans across the river and took the city of Matamoros. Polk nominated Taylor for brevet major general, and Congress voted to strike a gold medal in his honor. In June Taylor received the kind of letter from Secretary Marcy that any theater commander would love to receive: he was being promoted, retained in command, and given reinforcements. Marcy presumed that the general knew best about operational matters in his theater. In fact, the president solicited Taylor's strategic advice, although administration policy remained amorphous—to "dispose the enemy to desire an end to the war." There was no mention of territorial expansion. Marcy requested Taylor's opinion whether operations in northern Mexico would suffice, or if an offensive toward Mexico City would be necessary. What support would be required in either case? A month later, having heard nothing from Taylor—not surprising, given that it took a month for his letters to get to Taylor—Marcy wrote confidentially but pointedly to ask whether the general thought it better to commence operations on Mexico City from the Gulf coast at Veracruz. He also offered detailed advice on lenient treatment of the Mexican people and frequent communication with Mexican commanders in order to induce peace negotiations. With less patience this time, Marcy directed Taylor to send his reply directly to the president. Here was Taylor's chance to write his own mission and secure the resources to accomplish it.[21]

Taylor flubbed the opportunity. Slow to respond, he complained of supply and transportation problems, as well as finding fault with the volunteers they had sent him—their behavior was uncontrollable and their numbers too great. He might be able to move as far south as Monterrey if all conditions were right—weather, availability of foodstuffs, performance of the soldiers—but that was unlikely. Probing farther into the interior, he feared, depended upon too many unknown variables. He refused to hazard a guess about the efficacy of a potential campaign from Veracruz. Polk was disappointed in this counsel and began to suspect that Taylor was not the right man for the job: "He is brave but he does not seem to have resources or grasp of mind enough to conduct such a campaign. . . . He seems ready to obey orders, but appears to be unwilling to express any opinion or take any responsibility on himself." Although Taylor seemed "a good subordinate officer," Polk thought him "unfit for the chief command." Taylor had failed his first test as a commander and strategist.[22]

By late September Taylor had advanced to Monterrey and bested the Mexican army in a violent, but poorly controlled five-day battle. On the twenty-fourth he granted his defeated foe an eight-week armistice, partly because American forces were too weak to continue the offensive without resupply and reinforcement. Moreover, Taylor reasoned that a cease-fire might induce the Mexicans to negotiate, in accord with the administration's vague policy guidance. But political changes in Mexico—the dashing and bellicose Antonio López de Santa Anna had returned to power—had made negotiations unlikely and, from the president's perspective, undesirable, a policy shift the administration had not bothered to relay to Taylor. Thus, when Polk learned of the armistice, he angrily countermanded it and ordered Taylor to resume the attack.[23]

Over the next several weeks, the administration debated a new offensive to commence at Veracruz and sent Taylor a series of contradictory orders—to take the port of Tampico on the Mexican coast, to advance to San Luis Potosí, and finally, to remain at Monterrey. As always, part of the difficulty lay in the six- to eight-week round trip from Washington to northern Mexico. Nonetheless, Taylor was by turns confused, frustrated, and angry. In violation of express orders, he advanced southwest to

Saltillo, as he felt it offered better defensive terrain until matters were sorted out in Washington.[24]

Polk deemed Taylor's actions insubordinate and inexcusable. Compounding his doubts about Taylor was the general's rising popularity. Soon after Taylor's success on the Rio Grande, Whig party activists began promoting him for the presidency. Ever the partisan, Polk began to find political motives behind Taylor's every action. The armistice in Monterrey fueled his suspicions. By November, Taylor's failure to take Tampico and his advance to Saltillo solidified Polk's assessment: "He is evidently a weak man and has been made giddy with the idea of the presidency.... I have promoted him, as I now think, beyond his deserts, and without reference to his politics. I am now satisfied that he is a narrow-minded, bigoted partisan, without resources and wholly unqualified for the command he holds." The president had now lost confidence in both his senior generals, and began to search for alternatives.[25]

By this time, Polk had decided that negotiating with the Mexicans would be useless and determined to land a force at Veracruz for an invasion toward Mexico City. The overriding concern was to find a suitable commander, and the administration was fast running out of acceptable candidates. Taylor and Scott were both suspect, and their subordinates were deemed incapable. Senator Benton wanted the job, but he would need to rank those two to gain the command, and it was unlikely that the Senate would approve such a proposal. Moreover, in the six months since his relief, Scott had behaved relatively well, holding his tongue and working prodigiously to support Taylor, to advise Marcy and Polk, and to plan an amphibious landing near Veracruz. Much as he disliked and distrusted Scott, Polk was out of options. Still, the president hesitated to install him in command for fear that a successful campaign would make Scott a military hero and a presidential prospect. The canny Marcy advised Polk to "let him go to Mexico and get affairs in train, and before the war is ended we can easily take the wind out of his sails—he is sure to give us the opportunity." Reassured, the president summoned the general to the White House on November 19 and offered him the command. Reminding Scott of his past transgressions, Polk "was willing that bygones should be bygones." He gained Scott's tearful gratitude and fealty. Scott swore off politics, putting partisanship aside, at least for the time being: "I laid down *whiggism,* without taking up *democracy,* but without reference to party or politics, I have felt very much like a Polk-man. At least the President has all my personal respect, sympathy and esteem." Pitifully gratified at his redemption, Scott demonstrated an incapacity for professional detachment in service to the government. He was either a "Polkman" or an enemy. He quickly came to rue his newfound loyalty.[26]

During the summer Senator Benton, knowing that Polk was looking for a way to avoid "entrusting the chief command of the Army to a general in whom I have no confidence," had proposed to sponsor a bill to revive the rank of lieutenant general, dormant since Washington's retirement. Once the bill passed Congress, the president could then appoint a commander of his choosing. Benton, whose massive ego allowed him to overlook his own scant military record, suggested that he might be the nominee. Polk told Benton that he thought such legislation would have little chance in Congress, but, needing Benton's political goodwill, did not say no. The legislation languished for a few months, until the decision for a Veracruz operation brought matters to a head. Polk told Benton to revive the bill and promised to nominate him lieutenant general and commander of American forces if it passed. The legislation passed the House, but it failed in the Senate. Scott learned of these machinations during a stop in New Orleans on his way to Mexico, declaring that "a grosser abuse of human confidence is nowhere recorded." Scott decided that Polk was "an enemy more to be dreaded than Santa Anna." The army commander had basked in the president's confidence for a matter of days.[27]

Scott's selection was also a vote of no confidence in Taylor, who felt that he had done everything that had been asked of him. Bitter and angry, Taylor penned a vitriolic attack on the administration in a private letter to Brigadier General Edmund Gaines. He rehearsed his grievances against Marcy and Polk before going on to question the administration's entire policy and rationale for the war. Gaines circulated the letter among friends, who persuaded him to have it printed. The administration reprimanded Gaines for printing the letter and Taylor for providing information on government plans that would soon be read by the enemy. Polk then published a bulging file of correspondence between Taylor and the War Department "for the vindication of the truth and the good of the service." The break between the administration and its commander in northern Mexico was now painfully public.[28]

After his reinstatement, Scott had wasted no time in getting to Mexico. He attempted to soften the blow for Taylor, assuring him that he came not to supersede him, but to open a new front, although he would have to take most of Taylor's troops, leaving him with only enough to remain on the defensive. In fact, Scott regretted the need to take any of Taylor's forces. With more troops, Taylor might have presented a credible threat from the north while Scott invaded from the east, but the army did not have the strength to do both. Scott's message accomplished quite the opposite of his intent, making Taylor as suspicious of Scott as he was of Polk.[29]

When Scott arrived in Mexico, Taylor refused to meet with him to discuss future operations, curtly sending a message that he would, of course, obey all Scott's orders. Instead, he failed to relay movement instructions to his subordinates and refused Scott's most important directive, to withdraw to Monterrey and remain on the defensive, unless he was "positively ordered to fall back by the government at Washington." As a result, Taylor fought and won one more costly battle at Buena Vista, but it had little effect on the war's outcome. Polk criticized the battle as unnecessary, which it certainly was, and, in another presidential slap at the notion of a professional army, insisted that no credit was due to Taylor, as "our troops, regulars and volunteers, will obtain victories wherever they meet the enemy. This they would do if they were without officers to command them higher in rank than lieutenants." Taylor decided that "Polk, Marcy, and Co." had become political enemies more than superiors, and had "been more anxious to break me down than to defeat Santa Anna." To be sure, there was blame to go around, but Taylor was effectively sidelined, and soon took a leave of absence to focus on his political fortunes.[30]

In April, after an unopposed coastal assault and a brief siege, Winfield Scott entered the gates of Veracruz at the head of his conquering army, radically altering the course of the war. Scott had planned, coordinated, and executed the expedition, the first major amphibious operation in American history, requiring extraordinary army-navy cooperation, and it had come off without a hitch. Veracruz fell within a few days, and the National Road to Mexico City beckoned invasion.[31]

Scott understood that strategy serves policy. Although Polk's policy remained vague, Scott planned a campaign meant to produce political results. His aim was to stay on the offensive, moving into the Mexican interior to threaten the capital and to persuade the Mexicans to sue for peace. He imposed a discipline on his troops and a martial regime on captured territory that sought to encourage the Mexicans to respect his army, not to interfere with its progress, and to desire peace. Taking the capital was not a crucial part of his plan, unless it contributed to a peace settlement. Sparing the lives of his small army was essential. In sharp contrast with Taylor, Scott, always outnumbered, won a series of battles with careful reconnaissance and tactical finesse that relied on attacking the enemy's flanks rather than his frontal strength. Then, halfway to the capital, Scott faced a dilemma. Several thousand of his volunteers' enlistments were about to expire. Scott determined that they would create more difficulty for him if they remained with the army, but outside military discipline, than if he sent them home under command of their officers. He ordered them back to Veracruz. As the volunteers marched east, Scott moved west to Puebla, where he awaited reinforcements. When they arrived, he severed his line of communications with the coast, confident that his nimble army could subsist on the Mexican economy, and advanced toward Mexico City. In six months Scott patiently advanced along the National Road, never losing a battle, always sustaining fewer casualties than the defending enemy, and finally capturing the capital. It was among the most brilliant campaigns in American military history.[32]

Scott wanted power to negotiate a peace when the force of arms made it possible. Instead, Polk dispatched the chief clerk of the State Department, Nicholas Trist, with a secret charter to claim Texas to the Rio Grande and all territory from the southeastern boundary of New Mexico to the Pacific. Trist was authorized to offer as much as $30 million to consummate the deal. He was an ambitious Virginia aristocrat who thought highly of his abilities, an assessment he rarely made about others. A protégé of both Presidents Jefferson and Jackson, he was well connected in Washington and the Democratic Party. Eight years as U.S. consul in Havana had polished his skills as a diplomat and his facility with Spanish. He shared many character traits with Winfield Scott—pomposity, bullheadedness, verbosity, self-righteousness, but also moral rectitude, idealism, and an abiding sense of duty. Their similarities offered little promise for a fruitful partnership between the two men.[33]

When Trist arrived at Veracruz in May, he and Scott immediately had trouble. Rather than paying Scott a courtesy visit, the diplomat sent him a peremptory note with a sealed message for the Mexican government, instructing Scott to convey it to them. Scott haughtily refused, and a war of words began that rivaled the clash of arms. Scott interpreted a vaguely worded letter from Marcy to indicate that Trist was authorized to order him to suspend military operations in order to treat with the Mexicans. He told Trist that "the Secretary of War proposes to degrade me, by requiring that I, the commander of this army, shall defer to you, the chief clerk of the Department of State the question of continuing or discontinuing hostilities." He would have none of it. Scott remonstrated with Marcy, demanding "to be spared the personal dishonor" of subordination to a State Department clerk and asking to be relieved as soon as his replacement could arrive. Trist complained to Secretary of State James Buchanan that Scott was undermining his embassy. Salvoes of letters flew from the prolix pens of Scott and Trist, aimed at one another and at their superiors in Washington. Marcy expressed his "fear that Trist and Scott have got to writing. If so, all is lost!" The entire affair was an embarrassment to both men and their government. Polk and his cabinet debated recalling them both. Polk decided to reprimand both men, but could not afford the political cost of relieving them, so they stayed in place—for the time being.[34]

As their official rebukes were making the month-long voyage to Mexico, Scott and Trist reconciled. Trist had taken it upon himself to communicate with the Mexican government, employing British colleagues as intermediaries. The British embassy informed Trist that the Mexicans would consider talks, and Trist penned a note informing Scott. Shortly thereafter, Trist fell ill, and Scott thoughtfully sent him a get-well note along with box of guava marmalade, not knowing that it was the envoy's favorite from his time in Cuba. The two men met for the first time, found a common enemy in Polk, and became fast friends and collaborators.[35]

Santa Anna sent word through the British that his government might be willing to consider peace talks if an inducement of $1 million were quietly tendered. The British assured Trist that such was the nature of diplomacy in Mexico. Trist consulted Scott, who conferred with a council of his generals, and they agreed to the bribe on the grounds that it might hasten the end of the war. Scott forwarded a down payment of $10,000 out of army funds, only to have Santa Anna renege on the deal and pocket the stipend. The administration did not learn of this scheme or Scott's involvement in it until months after Mexico City had fallen. Nonetheless, the matter became part of the rationale for Scott's eventual dismissal.[36]

Scott never believed the capture of Mexico City was necessary to his mission. Indeed, he thought that threatening it while leaving a viable Mexican government in place might be a shorter path to peace. Accordingly, when Mexican officials approached American forces under a flag of truce south of the city, Scott quickly acceded to an armistice. Trist got nowhere with subsequent negotiations, and, true to form, Santa Anna violated the cease-fire terms by reinforcing the city. Vexed, Scott canceled the armistice after two weeks and resumed the offensive. The battles necessary to take the city were the costliest of the campaign.[37]

As Scott feared, the Mexican government fell with its capital, and two precious months passed before a successor regime took over. The policies of military discipline and lenience with civilians that had worked so well along the National Road now prevented a nascent insurgency from burgeoning into civil war. By this time, Polk had learned of the Scott-Trist rapprochement, causing him to mistrust his envoy as much as he did his commander. Moreover, convinced that occupying Mexico City strengthened his hand, the president began to hope for greater territorial concessions. He decided to broaden the war, occupying more cities and ports until the Mexicans begged for peace. Soon, Polk was telling Congress that the United States should seize California and New Mexico as indemnity for the cost of the war—such cessions would not be part of any peace negotiations. Early in October Polk directed Secretary of State Buchanan to recall Trist. Trist received the orders revoking his authority just as he was preparing for talks with the fragile, new government. Scott, ignorant of Polk's plan to continue the fighting, assured the diplomat that Polk would not have called him home if he knew how close Trist was to a treaty. Trist agreed, ignored the recall order, recommenced negotiations, and concluded the Treaty of Guadalupe Hidalgo, firmly along the lines of his original charter, on February 2, 1848.[38]

Polk raged about Trist's insubordination, but he could hardly denounce a treaty that had been worked out along terms he had dictated. Naturally, he blamed Scott for Trist's perfidy: Trist "has become the perfect tool of Scott. . . . He seems to have entered into all Scott's hatred of the administration, and to be lending himself to all Scott's evil purposes." Always distrustful of subordinates and compulsively managing every detail, Polk could not comprehend that events moved forward in Mexico just as they did in Washington in the two months required to exchange communications. His enmity toward Scott only intensified.[39]

In the weeks after the capital fell, boredom, the ancient seed of military indiscipline, infected the army. Scott's generals, anxious for glory, began to write their campaign reports, improving on the truth as they polished their prose. General Gideon Pillow, Polk's former law partner, architect of his surprise nomination for president, and now a spy in Scott's camp, was more creative than most. He submitted a report to Scott that inflated his slight battlefield accomplishments and denigrated those of his fellow officers. Scott, who had thus far treated the president's crony with kid gloves, quietly directed Pillow to tone down his verbiage and resubmit the dispatch. Soon, a scarcely edited version of the same account appeared in a New Orleans newspaper, lauding Pillow's "masterly military genius and profound knowledge of the science of war, which has astonished so much the mere martinets of the profession." Scott exploded in rage. The article was not just an affront to him, but a slur on the military profession that he had spent his career trying to build: "False credit may, no doubt, be obtained at home, by such despicable self-puffings and malignant exclusion of others; but at the expense of the just esteem and consideration of all honorable officers, who love their country, their profession, and the truth of history." Scott promulgated an order reminding his officers of a regulation forbidding unauthorized correspondence. He arrested and preferred charges on Pillow and two other officers who had committed similar infractions, and directed courts-martial to try them.[40]

Pillow quickly availed himself of his presidential connection, playing on Polk's prejudices against Scott and arguing that he was being unfairly treated by a man who lusted for military glory. He detailed the $1 million bribery scheme of the previous summer, conveniently overlooking the fact that he had supported it in a council of war. For Polk the courts-martial constituted the final straw. He was convinced that Scott had duped Trist into undermining his policy and was now persecuting General Pillow "for no other known reason than that he is a Democrat in his politics and was supposed to be my personal and political friend." Polk ordered Scott relieved of command—Marcy insisted that he was only acceding to Scott's request for relief from the previous spring—and convened a court of inquiry into his behavior. Despite his earlier rebuke of Taylor and Gaines for the same offense, Polk reduced Pillow's and the other courts-martial to courts of inquiry.[41]

The army was outraged. Junior officers such as Captains Robert E. Lee and Ulysses S. Grant wrote of their support for their commander. Lieutenant George B. McClellan described a brigade parading past Scott's house "as the fine old soldier came out on his balcony. The noble old fellow must have felt that even if the administration has relieved him from command, they could not weaken the hold that he has upon the respect and affection of every man in the army. I for one will never say another word against General Scott." Lieutenant William T. Sherman vilified Pillow as "a mass of vanity, conceit, ignorance, ambition and want of truth." Daniel H. Hill railed in his diary against "the intrigues of that arch-scoundrel Pillow. . . . That an idiot monkey could cause the greatest Captain of the age to be disgraced upon the very theater of his glory will not be credited by posterity. The whole Army is indignant." Nicholas Trist, now a committed supporter of Scott, told his wife "that a baser villain and dirtier scoundrel does not exist out of the penitentiary or in than Genl Pillow." For his part, Pillow gloried in the coming inquiry: "I will blow him higher & kill him deader than did the 'hasty plate of soup' letter or 'the fire in front & fire in rear.' " Scott, angered, then depressed, and finally resigned, sat for months in Mexico while a court of subordinate officers debated his fate. The court eventually exonerated him, but not before the excesses of his character were paraded in the national press. Pillow, who successfully whitewashed his record before a court stacked in his favor, received a White House welcome and a promotion to major general.[42]

With ill grace Polk sent the treaty to the Senate, which ratified it March 10, 1848. A month later the Mexican Congress followed suit, and the war was over.

By that time the presidential contest of 1848 was well under way. A year earlier when news arrived in New Orleans that Scott had only lost one hundred men taking Veracruz, one leather-lunged observer shouted, "That won't do. Taylor always loses thousands. He's the man for my money." Indeed, the hard-fighting man-of-the-people had caught the popular imagination, and Whig kingmakers saw him as their best chance for taking back the White House. Polk's earlier denunciation of Taylor as a "bigoted partisan" was tested against the reality that as a candidate Taylor had little interest in or knowledge of Whig policy or ideology. Indeed, for a while he attempted to win the presidency with no partisan affiliation whatever, until friends and advisers tutored him in the ways of Jacksonian politics—such independence was no longer possible if one hoped to win. Taylor was elected and inherited the problems that Polk's war had bred, namely, determining how far the institution of slavery would be allowed to extend into the new territories. Taylor fought against the expansion of slavery and the first halting steps toward disunion during the fifteen months he served as president before dying of complications from dysentery in July 1850.[43]

Although a mediocre commander and an indifferent strategist, Taylor did win all his battles and followed the administration's uncertain strategy as well as he could. By the time Polk decided upon the Veracruz operation, Taylor's army and other forces in New Mexico and California had achieved all of the president's policy aims, inasmuch as they held all the territory from Texas to the Pacific, as well as enough of the Mexican interior to gain leverage in negotiations. Polk calculated that Santa Anna's return to power would make those talks fruitless, so he determined to widen the war, but that was no fault of Taylor's. Afterward, Old Rough and Ready petulantly disobeyed operational orders and refused to work effectively with Scott, and for those lapses he deserves censure. By that time, he felt that the Polk administration was treating him, as it certainly was, as a political rival rather than a military subordinate. Politicians who deal in such fashion with generals, especially generals whom the public views as successful, should not be surprised when those officers meet their expectations. Such behavior—on both sides—is not conducive to military professionalism or to effective political-military relations, but it is not unusual or surprising.

Winfield Scott was among the ablest generals in American history, and his own worst enemy. In May 1845, after Polk had relieved him of command, Scott dutifully labored at his post in Washington to mobilize, equip, and train the army. Those efforts provided the foundation of Taylor's success and later Scott's, a fact the administration failed to appreciate. Administration policy was purposely ambiguous when Scott commenced his Mexico City campaign, consisting only of the nebulous formulation "to conquer a peace." Scott held up his end of the bargain, devising an operational plan flexible enough to achieve almost any strategic objective or political aim that the administration might desire. An almost flawless campaign achieved everything Polk had ordered, including dissolution of the Mexican army, successful peace negotiations, and an end to the war. Then, when Scott and his army had done all that had been asked of them and more, Polk expanded his aims once again, demanding a broader war. When Trist foiled Polk's scheme by violating orders and securing a peace agreement, Polk found a pretext to relieve Scott and disgrace him professionally and cripple him politically.

Thus, two American generals had carried out strategically offensive campaigns into a neighboring country, performed acceptably well in one case and brilliantly in the other. They had done so in spite of ambiguous policy direction and shifting political aims. The regulars constituted the base and the military expertise of these forces, although large numbers of volunteer soldiers and officers augmented them. Both Taylor and Scott complained about the indiscipline and fecklessness of the volunteers. Scott even chose to send several of their regiments home rather than continuing on to Mexico City with them. He determined that his regulars would be more effective without the volunteers, and the results bore him out. These achievements testify to the capabilities of Scott, Taylor, and the generation of officers who molded the hodgepodge army of the War of 1812 into the regular force that won the Mexican War. Scott and many historians have likewise lauded the professionalism of the next generation, educated and trained at West Point, reared in the army of the frontier and coastal fortresses, who provided the junior officer and field-grade leadership of regular formations. Despite Andrew Jackson's disdain for regular soldiers and West Pointers in particular, despite James Polk's antiprofessional bias, the record of Military Academy graduates in the Mexican War spoke for itself. Many of the lieutenants and captains in Mexico would command far larger forces in the American Civil War. West Point, the professional foundation of the United States Army, was well established, and now its progeny had been proven in combat.[44]

Still, the army was far from perfect, as the spotted record of political-military relations in the war had shown. If Polk and Marcy failed to trust army officers as apolitical servants of the government, their attitude was due in part to officers' partisanship. Apolitical service was not yet part of the professional ethos. As one historian has observed, the army of the Mexican War was "a creature of politics."[45] Scott, Taylor, and their peers thought little of openly affiliating with a political party, and seem not to have thought at all about the threat that such partisanship would pose to their civilian superiors, especially those on the other side of the political divide. Their West Point subordinates observed this behavior, and most disdained it, at least in terms of overt partisanship. However, as the coming sectional crisis and Civil War would show, when profound political issues were at stake, such as union or secession, an alarming number of West Pointers would choose to abrogate their oaths to the Constitution.

War presents the most challenging test of presidential leadership. The president's responsibility is to recognize a threat and marshal the resources of government to meet it. He must explain the threat to the public, and articulate a policy to meet and defeat it that will win their support. He must work to maintain the public trust, and that of Congress, throughout the war in order to gain the money, weapons, food and clothing, and manpower necessary to be successful. At the beginning of almost every American war, the general consensus born of hope has been that war would be short and that the soldiers would return quickly, covered with laurels. In almost every American war, those hopes and beliefs have been quickly dashed. Then, the challenge of presidential leadership is to rally the public for a conflict of indeterminate duration, and prepare the people for the trials that lie ahead. When bad news comes, as it inevitably does, the president must convince the people that the sacrifice is worthwhile, and that more sacrifice will be necessary.

President Polk's challenge was especially difficult, as he chose an aggressive war that did not have to be fought. One could argue that the defense of Texas, even to the Rio Grande, was necessary, but once Taylor had repulsed the Mexican army, he could easily have stood on the defensive and attained that goal. Rather than rallying all the people to his side with an openly declared policy, Polk leveraged a Democratic majority in Congress to declare a war to defend American soil, knowing that he intended to invade his neighbor to conquer and seize millions of square miles of its territory. The Whig opposition saw through his deceit but was powerless to stop it. Polk opted to gain the support of only a partisan majority of the public for purposes he refused to acknowledge openly, but he was politically canny enough to know that he could not ride that tiger far, and he drove his government and army to achieve a quick victory.

While he obfuscated in public, Polk adopted no greater clarity when expressing strategic aims to his generals. He claimed a desire "to conquer a peace." He enjoined Taylor to "dispose the enemy to desire an end to the war." Militarily naïve, Polk disdained the abilities of professional officers, appointing political hacks such as Gideon Pillow. He never appreciated the martial expertise necessary to carry out his aims, although he was careful to keep regular officers in the highest commands. He never explicitly told his commanders that he intended to take Mexican territory from the mouth of the Rio Grande to the southern tip of California, leaving it to them to interpret his hidden policy. Thus, he negotiated for himself maximum political flexibility, which he continually abused, while leaving the responsibility for failure with his generals. Scott used a felicitous phrase in a different and more personal context, but "a grosser abuse of human confidence is nowhere recorded." In the continuous negotiation, political leaders naturally desire such ambiguity so as to respond to political pressures, just as it is human nature for military commanders to ask for clear and precise objectives so as to argue for resources to accomplish assigned missions. Yet without such precision the army gave Polk the object of his ambition, the northern third of Mexico, the fruit of manifest destiny. After his commanders succeeded, despite his failures of political leadership and abuse of their professional trust, Polk discarded them so as to damage their future political prospects. All the while he railed against the generals who won his war, faulting them for their incompetence, their partisanship, and their hatred for his administration. Nonetheless, he was able to convince his diary that "I have myself been wholly uninfluenced by any references to the political opinions of the officers of the Army in the conduct of the war." Arrogant, mendacious, and paranoid, he pitifully complained that no one understood the cares that he bore. He embraced what one writer has called "the martyrdom of duty." And yet, despite this sorry record, James Polk achieved everything he cunningly sought from his invasion of Mexico.[46]

Three contemporary observers may represent the many who recorded this historical injustice. An obscure Whig congressman from Illinois introduced a number of resolutions in 1848 to embarrass the Polk administration for its deceptive argument for the original declaration of war. These measures, known as the "spot resolutions," were intended to force the president to name the precise spot where "American blood [had been] shed upon American soil." For his pains their author, Representative Abraham Lincoln, lost his bid for reelection. Lieutenant George Gordon Meade, later commanding general of the Army of the Potomac and victor at Gettysburg, confessed, "Well may we be grateful that we are at war with Mexico! Were it any other power our gross follies would surely have been punished before now." Captain Ulysses S. Grant, who would likewise attain a degree of success in the Civil War, later acknowledged that he considered the Mexican War "one of the most unjust ever waged by a stronger against a weaker nation. It was an instance of a republic following the bad example of European monarchies, in not considering justice in their desire to acquire additional territory. . . . The Southern rebellion was largely the outgrowth of the Mexican war. Nations, like individuals, are punished for their transgressions. We got our punishment in the most sanguinary and expensive war of modern times."[47]

5

EXECUTIVE MANSION, *Washington, D.C., January* 26, 1863.

Major-General HOOKER:

GENERAL: I have placed you at the head of the Army of the Potomac. Of course I have done this upon what appears to me to be sufficient reasons, and yet I think it best for you to know that there are some things in regard to which I am not quite satisfied with you. I believe you to be a brave and skillful soldier, which, of course, I like. I also believe you do not mix politics with your profession, in which you are right. You have confidence in yourself, which is a valuable, if not an indispensable, quality. You are ambitious, which, within reasonable bounds, does good rather than harm; but I think that during General Burnside's command of the army you have taken counsel of your ambition, and thwarted him as much as you could, in which you did a great wrong to the country and to a most meritorious and honorable brother officer. I have heard, in such a way as to believe it, of your recently saying that both the Army and the Government needed a dictator. Of course, it was not for this, but in spite of it, that I have given you the command. Only those generals who gain successes can set up dictators. What I now ask of you is military success, and I will risk the dictatorship. The Government will support you to the utmost of its ability, which is neither more nor less than it has done and will do for all commanders. I much fear that the spirit which you have aided to infuse into the army, of criticising their commander and withholding confidence from him, will now turn upon you. I shall assist you as far as I can to put it down. Neither you nor Napoleon, if he were alive again, could get any good out of an army while such a spirit prevails in it. And now beware of rashness. Beware of rashness, but with energy and sleepless vigilance go forward and give us victories.

Yours, very truly,
A. LINCOLN.[1]

It was early October 1862, two weeks after the bloodiest day of the Civil War. Robert E. Lee and the Army of Northern Virginia had retreated south across the Potomac. The Army of the Potomac was still encamped near Sharpsburg, Maryland, its commanding general, George B. McClellan, fearful of another Confederate offensive. The president had daily been urging the general to move, to pursue the rebel forces while they were still relatively close at hand and suffering from their losses at Antietam. Now he had come to army headquarters, and had pressed his case in person all the previous day and long into the night.

The president left his tent early that morning for a stroll around the camp with his old friend Ozias M. Hatch. The president spoke little and seemed to be in a serious mood. Upon reaching the top of a hill that gave a commanding view of the bivouac for a hundred thousand soldiers stretching miles around them, the president stood in deep contemplation. After a few moments, he turned and leaned down to his friend and asked in a stage whisper, "Hatch, Hatch, what is all this?"

His friend was surprised and not a little worried at the question. The president could get mystical at times. "Why, Mr. Lincoln, this is the Army of the Potomac," he responded.

The tall, sad president straightened up, slowly shook his head, and intoned, "No, Hatch, no. So it is called, but that is a mistake; it is only McClellan's bodyguard."[2]

Lincoln had traveled seventeen months to gain that perspective. Taking office during the gravest crisis in American history, he was by his own admission unfamiliar with the duties of the president, let alone those of commander in chief. Yet he brought on his journey great natural gifts, including patience, a sense of humor, abundant common sense, and a deep understanding of people. To these he added a creative mind developed by a prodigious capacity for learning and a ferocious ambition to do so. Most important of all Lincoln's traits was the strength of character that steadied him against pressure, doubt, and disappointment. All these tools gave him a store of self-confidence to face the unprecedented challenges that lay ahead.

Lincoln grew into his office, and the office grew with him. Initially underestimated by most observers, he quickly showed his ability to lead with political deftness and the courage to take responsibility for decisions with existential consequences for the nation. He radically expanded the size and reach of the federal government to meet the demands of war, sometimes eliding constitutional strictures in doing so. Recognizing his own ignorance of military affairs, he worked sedulously to gain strategic expertise, finally surpassing many of his generals in their own field of knowledge. Except for Winfield Scott, still general-in-chief of the army a dozen years after the Mexican War, those generals were all alike in their total inexperience commanding large bodies of soldiers. Lincoln was responsible for selecting men to command his armies, and for a while he tried to shoulder the task of developing the highest among them, especially George McClellan, for their duties. Through hard knocks Lincoln came to realize that, try as he might, he could not make generals. The war itself would do that. It was his job to recognize talent and reward it, to see incompetence for what it was and penalize it. After two frustrating years, Lincoln had learned what he needed in his commanders and became unstinting in his attempts to get it. He also understood where those generals stood in relation to their government and president, and was now confident enough in his office to demand their loyalty and support of his policy. The president's letter to General Joseph Hooker above stands as a pithy encapsulation of all he had learned.

Lincoln's first crisis awaited him on Inauguration Day, March 4, 1861. Seven states had seceded and formed a Confederate government; more threatened to follow. Two small U.S. forces retained possession of Fort Sumter in Charleston harbor and Fort Pickens off Pensacola on the Gulf coast, but their supplies were dwindling, and Confederates were massing in Charleston. Lincoln promised in his inaugural address to hold the Union together and, more specifically, to "hold, occupy, and possess" all federal properties. Nevertheless, General-in-Chief Winfield Scott told the president that he needed twenty-five thousand troops to reinforce Sumter and six months' time to prepare them for the operation, or the fort's surrender was inevitable. That assessment was similar to the counsel he had given Polk fifteen years earlier, but the government had neither the troops nor the months. Two weeks later Scott recommended abandoning both fortresses, a course that "would instantly soothe and give confidence to the eight remaining slave-holding States, and render their cordial adherence to this Union perpetual." The cabinet was almost unanimous in advocating evacuation of Sumter, hoping that conciliation might avert war. William H. Seward, Lincoln's secretary of state and former political rival, used the crisis to promote his own ends in a wide-ranging policy memo for his far less experienced president. After a month in office, Seward scolded, the administration still had no coherent policy. He advised reinforcement of Pickens but surrendering Sumter, a course that would, somehow, change the national issue from slavery to union. Then, the United States should provoke a confrontation with a European power, several of whom had interests in the Caribbean or Mexico, thus uniting the country against a common foe. Expecting to become Lincoln's de facto premier, Seward counseled that "whatever policy we adopt . . . either the President must do it himself . . . or DEVOLVE it on some other member of his Cabinet. . . . It is not in my especial province. But I neither seek to evade nor assume responsibility."[3]

From the Sumter crisis, which Lincoln later described as the worst of his presidency, Lincoln learned several things. He had a clear policy, to maintain the Union, but he needed to articulate it and stand behind it forcefully. While he made himself accessible to several advisers, it was his job to sift their counsel, making sure that it adhered to and supported his policy. His advisers might be giving him similar recommendations, but that consistency didn't necessarily make them right. Finally, the president and no one else could make policy for the government, and it was the president's responsibility to see that his policies were carried out.

The president was also concerned that his general-in-chief was coloring his professional military judgment with political advice. Lincoln summoned the eighty-four-year-old Scott into his office and told him that abandoning his inaugural pledge would put his administration and the Union at risk. Further, if General Scott "could not carry out his views, some other person might." He ordered Scott "to make short, comprehensive daily reports to me of what occurs in his Department, including movements by himself, and under his orders, and the receipt of intelligence." Scott got the message and fell in with Lincoln's policy, rendering much valuable service to the administration during the time he remained general-in-chief, and continued as an informal adviser to

Lincoln thereafter. Lincoln had established his control over a man who had been a general almost as long as Lincoln had been alive, and who had been general-in-chief of the army for two decades.[4]

Lincoln drafted a reply to Seward's memorandum, but he never sent it. Nonetheless, probably in a private conversation, Lincoln drilled through the logical inconsistencies in the secretary's arguments. Did the secretary not understand administration policy? How did the circumstances for reinforcing Sumter differ from those for Pickens? How would reinforcing Pickens change the national issue at stake? Most important, whatever course the government took, "I must do it." Chastened, Seward grasped the president's clear meaning. The secretary of state thereafter became one of Lincoln's most loyal, trusted, and effective lieutenants.[5]

Lincoln sought advice from military and naval officers about reinforcing or resupplying Fort Sumter. While the task would be risky, some advocated a nighttime resupply of the island garrison. The president decided to resupply Sumter, but not reinforce it with men and ammunition. He then sent a message to the governor of South Carolina (*not* to Jefferson Davis) informing him of this intent, thereby leaving it to the rebel forces to determine whether they wanted to fire upon U.S. vessels on a routine mission. The ploy neatly placed the onus for war on Davis without recognizing his rebellious government. Davis ordered Confederate artillery to fire on Fort Sumter on April 12, 1861. Lincoln condemned the unprovoked assault, and announced that he was expanding his policy. Not only would he "possess, occupy, and hold" federal property, but he would "repossess" any places that had already been seized by the states attempting to secede. War fever seized the North, and with public support Lincoln called for approximately 150,000 recruits over the next several weeks.[6]

The president reached another conclusion: he could make strategy as well as the experts.

In May Scott proposed a war plan for bringing gradual but unprovocative pressure on the South. In what reporters soon derided as the "Anaconda plan," the general planned to surround the seceded states, blockade their ports, cut off their access to the Mississippi, and allow economic and political forces to squeeze the South until its populace demanded peace. However, Lincoln was under tremendous pressure from northern press and politicians to act decisively and to attack the growing Confederate army, pressure that only increased when southerners moved their national capital to Richmond. Once again, Lincoln overruled his general-in-chief, directing General Irvin McDowell to launch an offensive on southern forces near Manassas Junction in northern Virginia. McDowell asked for more time to train, but Lincoln demanded immediate action: "You are green, it is true, but they are green also; you are all green alike." McDowell dutifully complied, and developed a plan of attack that might have worked with seasoned veterans. As it turned out, a Confederate counterattack routed McDowell's army, exciting despair in the same northern voices that had so recently been chanting "On to Richmond."[7]

Lincoln and Scott had each been half right. Surrounding the Confederacy and choking it to death was how the Union eventually won the war. But choking required squeezing by huge military forces, applying pressure at as many points as possible, defeating Confederate armies and seizing southern territory, rather than simply surrounding the South and waiting for the enemy to capitulate. Lincoln understood that to maintain public support for the war, he had to keep the public engaged and involved. In this instance, having lost some confidence in his military advisers, the president acted too hastily and suffered an important setback. He refined his earlier conclusion: if he were to make strategy as well as the experts, he would have to study the art of war.

George McClellan arrived in Washington on the heels of the Bull Run debacle in July 1861. Having won a minor battle in western Virginia, he was about the only successful general Lincoln had at that moment. Lincoln rewarded his perceived aggressiveness with command of the army defending the capital.

McClellan was accustomed to being the smartest boy in class. Son of a Philadelphia ophthalmologist, he entered the University of Pennsylvania at thirteen and moved on to West Point at fifteen. Graduating second in his class of 1846 (he always blamed faculty bias for his second-place finish), he took a commission in the engineers and soon found himself in Mexico serving under Taylor, then Scott, and for a time under Gideon Pillow. He took part in every major action of the war, served ably and courageously, and was brevetted twice. Along the way he developed a disdain for volunteer soldiers and politically appointed officers. He later served on a topographical expedition in Texas before taking command of an expedition to survey a proposed transcontinental rail route through the Oregon Territory. In 1855, he received a plum assignment as one of three officers on an American commission to cross the Atlantic to study European military establishments and to observe the Crimean War. His selection marked McClellan as one of the finest young officers in the army. He spent a year abroad, rubbing elbows with European officers, diplomats, nobles, and heads of state and gaining a perspective on foreign militaries that few Americans could claim. He returned home, as one friend said, "chock full of big war science." Within three months of his return, he taught himself enough Russian to translate a Cossack cavalry manual for use in the U.S. Army.[8]

While writing a report on his European ventures, McClellan manifested a trait that dogged him all his life—an inability to abide any superior. He had quarreled with a senior member of the commission for a year. Now he entered into a dispute with Secretary of War Jefferson Davis. Its precise nature is lost, but McClellan thought it substantial enough to resign his commission. He left the army in early 1857 and embarked on a railroad career, first as a chief engineer and then vice president of one line before jumping to become superintendent of another. He had left a bright future in the army for an equally promising and far more lucrative career in railroads. Still, he continued to clash with his superiors and began to pine for the army. The outbreak of civil war gave him his wish. The governor of Ohio made him a major general and gave him command of the state's growing numbers of volunteers. McClellan was thirty-four.[9]

For all of his obvious brilliance, George Brinton McClellan possessed glaring personal flaws, among them overwhelming arrogance, as well as bigotry, obstinacy, paranoia, and narcissism. Worse yet for an army commander, he had an abiding fear of failure, an unwillingness to shoulder responsibility, a maddening tendency to overestimate his enemy, a fixation on his own theater of operations to the exclusion of the rest, and a cavalier misunderstanding of the principle of civilian control of the military. Through trial after trial, Abraham Lincoln would learn a great deal about command from McClellan, almost none of it good. Yet that education would shape the president's approach to the rest of the Civil War.

McClellan's reception in Washington was a Roman triumph, with people shouting his praises and lining the streets to see him. "I find myself in a new & strange position here," he wrote his wife. "Presdt, Cabinet, Genl Scott & all deferring to me—by some strange operation of magic I seem to have become *the* power of the land. I almost think that

were I to win some small success now I could become Dictator or anything else that might please me—but nothing of that kind would please
me—*therefore* I *won't* be a Dictator. Admirable self denial!" He visited
the Senate and found that "they give me my way in everything." People
began calling the diminutive general "the Young Napoleon." He had
heard that the rebels in Richmond said "that there was only one man they
feared & and that was McClellan." A few days later he was sure "that
God has placed a great work in my hands." His transformation from general to Caesar to Messiah had taken a little over two weeks. He had no
choice, he protested; "the people call upon me to save the country—I
must save it & cannot respect anything that is in the way."[10]

Winfield Scott was in his way. Three weeks earlier, McClellan had
been at pains to thank General Scott for his kind words of welcome, hoping always "to merit your praise & never to deserve your censure." He
had flattered the general-in-chief for his fine example: "All that I know of
war I have learned from you, & in all that I have done I have endeavored
to conform to your manner of conducting a campaign." Now, after Mc-
Clellan's epiphany that he was heaven-sent to save the country, he noted
that his hero was "fast becoming very slow & very old" and could not
"long retain command," in which case "I am sure to succeed him."[11] Less
than a week later McClellan angrily wondered "how I can save this
country when stopped by Genl Scott—I do not know whether he is a
dotard or a *traitor!* I can't tell which. . . . If he cannot be taken out of my
path I will not retain my position, but will resign & let the admin take
care of itself . . . that confounded old Genl."[12] Scott was an obstacle to
McClellan's strategy for winning the war.

The loss at Bull Run had done nothing to restore Lincoln's confidence
in Scott, so the president asked McClellan to present a plan to win the
war. That request was unwise, as such advice was Scott's rightful province, and any plan McClellan presented was likely to stir conflict between him and Scott. Five days later McClellan submitted a grandiose
plan with his own army as the main effort. McClellan insisted on an
offensive against the South rather than Scott's scheme of passively surrounding it. He outlined supporting efforts into western Virginia and
eastern Tennessee, a movement down the Mississippi, driving the rebels
from Missouri, seizing key rail junctions in the South, employing the
navy to assist with reducing important ports, and a two- or three-pronged
offensive into Texas from Kansas moving south, from California west
through New Mexico territory, and possibly from the Mexican Gulf

coast (an alliance would be necessary) north across the Rio Grande. Mc-Clellan's own army would have to be reinforced to *273,000 men* in order to destroy the Confederate forces in Virginia before taking Richmond and then continuing through the lower rebel states "to occupy Charleston, Savannah, Montgomery, Pensacola, Mobile, and New Orleans." McClellan's colleagues in other theaters could surely make do with ten or twenty thousand soldiers apiece. Parts of this plan were politically impossible, others unnecessary or fanciful, and all were impractical with the resources currently at hand. Yet once McClellan had committed himself in writing, nothing else would do.[13]

If McClellan's strategic planning vexed Scott, the old general did not commit his concerns to paper, but he was livid a few days later when he received a peremptory letter in which McClellan declared the capital to be in *"imminent danger"* because the forces there were "entirely insufficient for the emergency." The Confederates in northern Virginia threatened Washington with one hundred thousand men, he insisted. (The actual number was less than half that.) He implored Scott to rush reinforcements forward to bring the capital's defenders at least to parity. For good measure, duty compelled McClellan to state that "military necessity demands" that all forces in Virginia, Maryland, the District of Columbia, and Pennsylvania be placed under his command. McClellan thus challenged Scott's competence in a primary responsibility of any military commander—maintaining the security of his capital. Adding insubordination to insult, McClellan sent a copy of the letter directly to the president.[14]

Scott wrote to Secretary of War Simon Cameron, refusing to correspond further with his subordinate. McClellan had not bothered to discuss these matters in person, Scott explained, although they had had several meetings during which the young general was usually uncommunicative. Scott scoffed at the idea that Washington was in "imminent danger. In fact, I am confident in the opposite opinion. . . . I have not the slightest apprehension for the safety of the Government here." Then, giving way to melodrama, Scott pleaded the "general infirmities of age" for making him "an incumbrance to the Army." He begged to be retired so that he might give way to a younger commander.[15]

Lincoln personally intervened to patch up the conflict, giving Scott an opportunity to complain that McClellan was continually going around him to the cabinet and the president. McClellan apologized and withdrew his letter, giving "the most profound assurances of respect for General Scott and yourself." A week later, McClellan was howling to his wife that "Genl Scott is the most dangerous antagonist I have—either he or I must leave . . . the Presdt is an idiot, the old general in his dotage—they cannot or will not see the true state of affairs."[16]

McClellan cultivated a reputation as a charismatic leader and an exceptional army organizer and trainer. His soldiers idolized him. He soon drilled the Army of the Potomac into parade-ground perfection. Whether it could fight was another matter. With the help of his intelligence contractor, Allan Pinkerton, McClellan continued to magnify the strength of Confederate forces. They estimated 100,000 rebels across the river on August 8, when in fact there were 40,000. A week later "the enemy ha[d] from 3 to 4 times my force." On August 19, the host had grown to 150,000 and by mid-September 170,000 (more than three times the actual amount). McClellan was at a loss to explain why the enemy had not attacked Washington.[17]

His enemies were multiplying not only across the river, but in the capital as well—most imagined, some real. Secretary of State Seward was a "meddling, officious, incompetent puppy." The secretary of the navy was "weaker than the most garrulous woman you were ever annoyed by." Secretary Cameron was a "rascal" and the attorney general "an old fool." Lincoln had devolved into "nothing more than a well meaning baboon."[18]

McClellan never gave Scott a moment's rest. After two months of drill, the Army of the Potomac showed no sign of advancing on the enemy, and Republican members of Congress became restless. They determined to form a committee to oversee Lincoln's prosecution of the conflict, called the Joint Committee on the Conduct of the War. McClellan met with the committee's leaders, Republican Senators Benjamin Wade, Lyman Trumbull, and Zachariah Chandler, telling them that he wanted to attack, but Scott was holding him back. One of the joint committee's first actions was to prevail upon Lincoln to accept Scott's request to retire.[19]

On October 31 Scott stepped down. McClellan had secretly maneuvered to elbow Scott's choice, Henry W. Halleck, out of the running to succeed him. The night before, McClellan swore to his wife that he had not sought the post: "it was thrust upon me. I was called to it, my previous life seems to have been unwittingly directed to this great end." Lincoln anxiously appointed him general-in-chief as well as commander of the Army of the Potomac, warning him that he was taking on immense responsibility. McClellan calmly replied, "I can do it all."[20]

During his previous years in the army he had barely reached the rank of captain. Now, six months after returning to uniform McClellan was the youngest commanding general the United States Army has ever had. With Scott no longer restraining him, the responsibility was all his.

☆ ☆ ☆

McClellan immediately and preemptively began establishing alibis against potential failure. His best judgment was that the Army of the Potomac was not ready to advance against a superior enemy at Manassas and should go into winter quarters. Yet if "political considerations" forced him to move, he estimated that he needed 150,000 soldiers for the operational army. He had just over 168,000 at hand, but after subtracting those who were sick, absent, poorly equipped, or required for defense of Washington, Baltimore, and other points, his effective maneuver force was just 76,285, half of what a prudent commander would need. Nonetheless, if allowed to scour the rest of the army for every available man and musket, and straining every nerve to hasten mobilization, he could be ready for an advance that "should not be postponed beyond the 25th Nov." He finished with an admonition that it was his "fixed purpose by no act of mine to expose this government to hazard by premature movement."[21] Thus, in McClellan's mind, he would bear no responsibility if the administration ordered him to fight, but all glory would be his if he succeeded in battle against an entrenched and superior enemy.

After submitting his strategic plan in early November, McClellan had become far less forthcoming with Lincoln, even though the president walked over to army headquarters almost daily. To give him his due, the general was terribly busy organizing the army, and over time he began to resent these meetings and social engagements with the president, which always included a heavy dose of backwoods fables. Never enamored of the president, McClellan quickly lost all respect for him, as he had done with almost every superior in his life. One November night Lincoln, Seward, and presidential secretary John Hay stopped by McClellan's home. A steward reported that the general was out, but would be home soon, and showed them to a sitting room. An hour later, McClellan returned, learned of his distinguished guests, and went straight upstairs. After another half hour, the president asked after the general, and the embarrassed servant announced that he had gone to bed.[22] Lincoln, ever patient, overlooked the slight, and called on the general on subsequent occasions. That spirit of forgiveness, even deference, was wasted on Mc-Clellan, who was coming to believe that he could bully the president.

McClellan underestimated Lincoln, questioning his leadership, his courage, his intellect, and even his humanity. He wrote his wife a few days later that he had visited the White House "where I found 'the *original gorrilla*,' about as intelligent as ever. What a specimen to be at the head of our affairs now!" Yet the president's folksy manner was deceptive, and intentionally so. It masked a keen and probing intellect, although one without the benefit of formal education. An autodidact, Lincoln felt compelled to master any subject that offended his ignorance. He taught himself both the law and Euclidean geometry. He had read deeply of the Bible and the works of Shakespeare. In 1861 he determined to teach himself military history and theory, reading voraciously and inquiring on logistics and operations. He made a habit of visiting army headquarters to read telegrams coming in from the field, especially when battles were ongoing. He daily cultivated his understanding of military art and science so that by the end of 1861 he was becoming better versed than many of his generals in their own body of professional expertise.[23]

The Army of the Potomac did not advance on the twenty-fifth of November. By that time, Lincoln had learned that the fall was the best time for campaigning because roads were generally dry and solid and troops and horses could be well supplied by recent harvests. McClellan had wasted the entire season by waiting until he felt strong enough to move against the enemy. A week after McClellan missed his own deadline, Lincoln prodded the general with a plan of his own. A force of fifty thousand troops could advance on Centreville and fix the Confederates in place, suggested Lincoln, while the rest of the army moved down the Potomac to the Occoquan River, marching up the valley to envelop the rebel flank. The plan was feasible, relatively simple, and one the Confederate commander, McClellan's friend and mentor from the old army, Joseph E. Johnston, most feared. McClellan waited more than a week to rebuff the idea, offering only that "I have now my mind actively turned towards another plan of campaign that I do not think at all anticipated by the enemy nor by many of our own people." He gave no details, and Lincoln deferred to him, asking no further questions.[24]

The Army of the Potomac was still resting in camp on Christmas Eve, and the same politicians who had lobbied Lincoln to remove Scott began to sour on his successor. The Committee on the Conduct of the War convened hearings to goad the administration to action. McClellan had fallen ill with typhoid fever and could not appear, so the committee called his generals to testify about what they knew of his plans. The panel discovered a rift: McClellan's cronies apparently knew his plans but would not divulge them; those in his favor had never been consulted or briefed. The committee met with Lincoln on New Year's Eve, and forcefully remonstrated with him to command McClellan to act. Dissatisfied with the president's support for the general, the committee demanded another meeting a week later with the entire cabinet. Five members of the committee vigorously urged offensive action and recommended that Irvin McDowell replace McClellan as commanding general of the Army of the Potomac. The president defended McClellan, but the committee was amazed to "learn that Mr. Lincoln himself did not think he had the *right* to know" what the general's plans were. He expressed confidence in McClellan and felt compelled to trust his military judgment.[25]

Nonetheless, the congressional pressure weighed heavily on the president. A few days later Lincoln conferred with Quartermaster General Montgomery C. Meigs. "General, what shall I do?" he asked in despair. "The people are impatient; [Secretary of the Treasury] Chase has no money . . . the General of the Army has typhoid fever. The bottom is out of the tub. What shall I do?" Meigs advised the president to convene a council of McClellan's division commanders. Lincoln immediately summoned McDowell and William B. Franklin to the Executive Mansion. He summarized the dire strategic situation and told the generals that he had gone to McClellan's quarters to discuss matters, but—once again—"the general did not ask to see him." Lincoln announced that "if General McClellan did not want to use the army, he would like to *borrow* it." He ordered the two generals to return the next day for a cabinet meeting with recommendations for a campaign plan.[26]

McDowell sketched an operation that closely resembled Lincoln's plan of the previous month. Franklin, one of McClellan's inner circle and privy to his thinking, suggested a massive movement down the Potomac to the York River town of Urbanna for a drive on Richmond. Most of the cabinet preferred the McDowell plan, and the group agreed to meet again to go into detail. News of these conferences worked wonders for McClellan's health, and he appeared at a January 13 cabinet meeting with Generals McDowell, Franklin, and Meigs. Franklin and McDowell were in a most uncomfortable position, being at pains to explain how they had come to offer the president such detailed advice in their commander's absence. At Lincoln's direction McDowell briefed his plan, after which McClellan stonily intoned, "You are entitled to have any opinion you please!" and offered no further comment. Meigs moved his chair closer to McClellan and urgently whispered, "The President expects something from you." McClellan seethed, "If I tell him my plans they will be in the New York *Herald* tomorrow morning. He can't keep a secret." As the tension in the room thickened, Meigs replied, "That is a pity, but he is the President,—the Commander-in-Chief; he has a right to know; it is not respectful to sit mute when he so clearly requires you to speak. He is superior to all." Presently, Secretary Chase extracted from the general his intention to push the army in Kentucky forward before his own forces attacked. Pressed for his own plans, McClellan refused to reveal them unless ordered by the president: "No General fit to command an army will ever submit his plans to the judgment of such an assembly . . . there are many here entirely incompetent to pass judgment on them; . . . no plan made known to so many persons can be kept secret an hour." Lincoln asked McClellan if he had at least determined a definite date for the Army of the Potomac to advance. He did not ask what the date or the plan was. McClellan curtly told the president that he had settled on a date. With that, Lincoln deferred to his commander once more, and adjourned the conference.[27]

The next evening, McClellan invited a *New York Herald* reporter to his home for dinner and treated him to a three-hour briefing on his plans for the entire Union army, including the army's move to Urbanna.[28]

These conferences marked a turning point in the Lincoln-McClellan relationship and in Lincoln's evolution as commander in chief. Because of congressional pressure and his own dissatisfaction with all his commanders' failures to act, Lincoln determined that the direction of the war required a firmer hand. The president sacked Secretary of War Simon Cameron in the midst of these discussions, replacing him with a McClellan ally, Edwin M. Stanton, although the general soon found that the new war minister was far less forgiving than his predecessor or the president. Within days the energetic Stanton promised, "As soon as I can get the machinery of the office going, the rats cleared out, and the rat holes stopped, we shall *move*. This army has got to fight or run away; . . . the champagne and oysters on the Potomac must be stopped." Stanton was a passionate, blunt, and driven man, but Lincoln was glad to have him nearby and drew energy from him. In late January Lincoln signed General Order No. 1, making February 22 a "day for a general movement" of all U.S. forces against the enemy. He specifically directed the Army of the Potomac to execute an offensive on Manassas Junction, essentially the Lincoln-McDowell plan, by the same date.[29] Employing his new understanding of military matters, the president began to ask probing questions and critiquing the answers he received. Inch by inch, McClellan's leash got shorter, but the egocentric general failed to perceive the change.

The same day as the cabinet session with McClellan, Lincoln sent identical messages to Major General Henry W. Halleck, commander of the Department of Missouri, and Major General Don Carlos Buell, commander of the Department of the Ohio. Neither was manifesting any initiative, and both had given the president excuses for failing to advance. Buell enjoyed a two-to-one advantage over the enemy. Halleck described himself as a carpenter trying "to build a bridge with a dull ax, a broken saw, and rotten timber," even though his forces, which could easily be reinforced, already outnumbered the Confederates by 20 percent in western Kentucky and Tennessee. Neither officer was aware of the other's plans, a failure on both their parts and McClellan's.[30]

Halleck, known as "Old Brains" for his treatises on military theory and international law, took the opportunity to lecture the president on the finer points of strategy: "To operate on exterior lines against an enemy occupying a central position will fail . . . in ninety-nine cases out of a hundred. It is condemned by every military authority I have ever read." Of course, by this time Lincoln had read the same authorities (including Halleck himself) and demonstrated his strengthening grasp of strategy as he offered a few elementary points for his generals' consideration: "We have the *greater* numbers, and the enemy has the *greater* facility of concentrating forces. . . . We must . . . find some way of making *our* advantage an over-match for *his* . . . by menacing him with superior forces at *different* points, at the *same* time." Lincoln understood the concepts of interior and exterior lines—because Federal forces operated on the periphery of the southern states, the Confederates could conceivably reinforce from one area to another faster because they enjoyed a shorter route. Yet with simple application of logic to the situation, the president leaped over the classic Jominian military theory that the professionals had studied at West Point. He refused to believe, as McClellan did, that the North was outnumbered. Therefore, Union forces could attack several points at once, putting all Confederate commanders on the horns of a dilemma. The rebels, being everywhere pressed and inferior, could not reinforce every threatened point. Lincoln's concept of concentrating military power "at the same time" surpassed Halleck's theoretical understanding and was strategically superior to McClellan's plan to weaken every other Union formation to reinforce the Army of the Potomac.[31]

In February Brigadier General U.S. Grant's assaults on Forts Henry and Donelson demonstrated the efficacy of Lincoln's thinking. By threatening Confederate general Albert S. Johnston's left, Grant forced him to weaken his right. Modest pressure from Buell then pushed the rebels out of Kentucky and much of Tennessee as well. Lincoln continued to gain confidence in his strategic abilities, and he began to pay attention to the once obscure General Grant.

McClellan protested Lincoln's decision to force him to attack at Manassas. Lincoln allowed him to present his argument for the Urbanna plan, but asked him to compare the two options in light of five incisive questions:

> 1st. Does not your plan involve a greatly larger expenditure of *time,* and *money* than mine?
>
> 2nd. Wherein is a victory *more certain* by your plan than mine?
>
> 3rd. Wherein is a victory *more valuable* by your plan than mine?
>
> 4th. In fact, would it not be *less* valuable, in this, that it would break no great line of the enemie's [sic] communications, while mine would?
>
> 5th. In case of disaster, would not a safe retreat be more difficult by your plan than by mine?[32]

McClellan responded with twenty-two pages addressing the president's questions, with the exception of cost, in some detail. He argued that his plan was bolder than Lincoln's and thereby promised greater results. McClellan might have been right. Had the Urbanna plan been executed, it might have forced the Confederates to abandon their prepared positions to address a threat on Richmond. Lincoln acquiesced to McClellan's proposal, with the reservation that he leave behind a defensive force adequate to protect Washington. Perhaps the most important outcome of this exchange was that Lincoln had forced his general-in-chief to bring him into his confidence and outline his plans fully.[33]

Lincoln's February 22 deadline passed with no movement by the Army of the Potomac. Its idleness contrasted sharply with offensive success in the West. The Committee on the Conduct of the War, unimpressed when McClellan finally testified in January, met with Lincoln twice in February and March, pressing the first time for a reorganization of the Army of the Potomac into several corps and the second for McClellan's relief. When Lincoln asked Senator Benjamin Wade who should replace him, Wade shouted, "Well, anybody!" The exasperated president replied, "Wade, anybody will do for you, but I must have somebody." Nonetheless, as before, the committee's concerns weighed on the president, and he acted soon thereafter.[34]

On March 9 the Confederates abandoned their Manassas lines and moved south of the Rappahannock, making both Lincoln's and McClellan's plans moot. An inspection of rebel defenses embarrassed McClellan, showing that they had sheltered half as many soldiers as the general had claimed and that several "Quaker guns"—logs painted black to look like cannons—had afforded dubious protection. The phrase "all quiet on the Potomac" had gone from being a comfort to a joke and, finally, an epithet. McClellan's professional credibility suffered a blow from which it never recovered.

McClellan quickly proposed another campaign plan, to deploy the Army of the Potomac down the Chesapeake to Fort Monroe on the Virginia Peninsula, thirty miles south of Urbanna. Lincoln had mixed feelings about the proposal. He retained the same reservations he had earlier voiced, but he was glad to have a commitment for some kind of forward movement. The president approved the operation, so long as McClellan left Washington well protected. Yet before the operation commenced, Lincoln took two actions that showed his patience was wearing thin. First, he ordered the Army of the Potomac reorganized into four corps as the committee had demanded but McClellan had resisted. Then, a week before the army embarked, Lincoln relieved McClellan as general-in-chief. The action made sense on a number of levels. First, it gave Lincoln a way to respond to congressional pressure without losing McClellan's services in command of the Army of the Potomac. The demotion made McClellan coequal with Halleck and Buell, so he might have become less of a lightning rod for the Committee on the Conduct of the War. Moreover, the move solved a problem created by McClellan's management style—his inability to delegate details had forced him to deal personally with a mountain of trivia. Inevitably many important matters fell through the cracks, such as coordination of Halleck's and Buell's operations. Clearly, McClellan could not "do it all." Perhaps Stanton's more forceful leadership of the War Department made the president think that he could live without a general in overall command, at least for the time being. Moreover, Lincoln's order allowed McClellan to focus all his energies on the coming Peninsula Campaign.[35]

The Army of the Potomac finally embarked on March 17, almost eight months after McClellan had taken command. The demons that had plagued him in Washington sailed with him down the Chesapeake to Fort Monroe. Confederate forces were greater than his own and always growing. McClellan's army was never quite ready to attack, needing only another few days or ten thousand more troops or a few more batteries of artillery. Of course, McClellan had not bothered to explain to Lincoln or Stanton his plans for protecting Washington, leaving no clear chain of command and apparently too few troops for the task. As a result, Lincoln held back McDowell's entire corps to guard the capital. McClellan felt that the president had betrayed him—"the most infamous thing history has ever recorded"—sending him off on a mission that was now doomed to fail for want of adequate power. McClellan insisted that Joseph E. Johnston was entrenched in large numbers across his front. The reality was that the bulk of Johnston's army was close to Richmond and that only thirteen thousand Confederates defended near Yorktown against sixty thousand Union soldiers, with more arriving every day. Southern generals played on this paranoia with deception, marching battalions in and out of wood lines to appear more numerous than they were. Moreover, McClellan counted only those Union enlisted soldiers who were healthy and carrying weapons in the front lines, while his estimates of the enemy included every man consuming rations.[36] Lincoln found a discrepancy of twenty-three thousand soldiers between the numbers McClellan professed to have and the amount that the president knew had been sent south. Refusing to share McClellan's pessimism, Lincoln insisted that time was of the essence, that the army should attack immediately before the enemy had a chance to fortify its defenses:

> And, once more let me tell you, it is indispensable to *you* that you strike a blow. *I* am powerless to help this. You will do me the justice to remember I always insisted, that going down the Bay in search of a field, instead of fighting at or near Manassas, was only shifting, and not surmounting, a difficulty—that we would find the same enemy, and the same, or equal, intrenchments, at either place. The country will not fail to note—is now noting—that the present hesitation to move upon an intrenched enemy, is but the story of

141

Manassas repeated. I beg to assure you that I have never written you, or spoken to you, in greater kindness of feeling than now, nor with a fuller purpose to sustain you, so far as in my most anxious judgment, I consistently can. *But you must act.*[37]

McClellan paid no attention to Lincoln's entreaty. He resolved to besiege the Confederates rather than assault them. When Johnston, his opposite number and old friend, inspected the defensive lines two weeks later, he marveled that they had held so long. "No one but McClellan," Johnston insisted, "would have hesitated to attack."[38]

Johnston evacuated the Yorktown defenses when McClellan began firing his siege guns, but he had bought seven weeks to improve the defenses of Richmond. McClellan slowly followed the rebels up the peninsula, continuing to insist that his army was outnumbered, never bothering to wonder why a superior and defending enemy was retreating before him. He repeatedly begged for McDowell's corps to be sent to him. Lincoln offered to have McDowell march overland to meet McClellan northeast of Richmond, so as to be able to offer continuing support to Washington, but McClellan insisted that the corps sail down the Chesapeake. Then "Stonewall" Jackson commenced his legendary campaign in the Shenandoah Valley, appearing to be everywhere at once with far more troops than he had. Without a general-in-chief to interpret the threat or coordinate a response, the president reversed himself, refusing to send more Federal forces to McClellan until Washington was safe. McClellan's subsequent protests fell on deaf ears because his professional judgment was no longer credible. Lincoln determined that he had violated express orders to protect the capital. McClellan's army had more troops than he reported, and the Confederates could not possibly field the numbers he estimated.

By the end of May McClellan was six miles from Richmond with 105,000 men facing a Confederate force of 85,000, which he estimated at 200,000. "Situated as I am I feel forced to take every possible precaution against disaster & to secure my flanks against the probably superior force in front of me." He so completely surrendered the initiative that the rebels attacked him in a desperate effort to save their capital. Union forces got the better of a bloody two-day fight in which Johnston was badly wounded and replaced in command by Robert E. Lee. McClellan was at first buoyed by success, but predictably balked again, fearing the worst when word arrived that Jackson's forces had arrived from the

Shenandoah Valley. For the next three weeks he promised daily to attack soon: he was only waiting for the rain to stop, the roads to dry, the river to fall, bridges to be built, more troops to come up, defensive works to be completed, and then he would attack "as soon as Providence will permit." Instead, on June 25 Lee commenced a relentless attack in what became known as the Seven Days Battles. McClellan was unnerved. If his "splendid Army" were destroyed by "overwhelming numbers," he preached to Stanton, he would "at least die with it & share its fate." But should that disaster occur "the responsibility cannot be thrown on my shoulders—it must rest where it belongs," with those who had so long ignored his requests for reinforcements. After three days of grim fighting and retreating, he again blamed his superiors: "the Govt has not sustained this Army." With ten thousand fresh troops he could have won, but that was no longer possible. In a final passage so inflammatory that the chief telegrapher deleted it before it reached Stanton, McClellan accused his superiors of treason: "If I save this Army now I tell you plainly that I owe no thanks to you or any other persons in Washington—you have done your best to sacrifice this Army."[39]

A general who thinks he is defeated is certainly right. The Army of the Potomac was saved only because Lee's attacks were poorly coordinated. Yet at the end of the Seven Days there was no fight left in McClellan. He made unrealistic demands for reinforcements—50,000 soldiers, 100,000 soldiers—that he knew were impossible to fulfill. Lincoln told him that "the idea of sending you 50,000, or any other considerable force, promptly is simply absurd."[40]

McClellan's army had been close enough to see the church steeples of Richmond. Now it was thoroughly defeated, and its failure spread despair across the North. Congressional reaction was swift and fierce. Senator Chandler denounced McClellan on the floor of the Senate as a traitor who "deserves to be shot," and demanded that all correspondence between McClellan and the War Department relating to the Peninsula Campaign be published. A week later he railed against McClellan's mishandling of the campaign, "Human ingenuity could not have devised any other way to defeat that army." The Radicals in Congress pressed for McClellan's relief and for a widening of war aims to include abolition. McClellan, heedless of criticism and seemingly unhinged from reality, assured Lincoln that he had indeed saved his army with a movement "unparalleled in the annals of war." The president knew better. He sailed to the front in early July to inspect the army and found them in better spirits than he had expected. McClellan chose this moment of "success" to proffer a letter to the president on the future conduct of the war. He argued for a clear statement of policy and that the war should be prosecuted "against armed forces and political organizations," but not the southern population. He urged strict compliance with civil law and protection of property, and specifically: "Military power should not be allowed to interfere with the relations of servitude." He felt that a "declaration of radical views, especially upon slavery, will rapidly disintegrate our present Armies." McClellan noted that to prosecute the war "you will require a Commander in Chief of the Army." He did not request that post, but offered to serve wherever ordered. Lincoln read the letter and put it in his pocket, thanking the general without further comment, then or later. While it was not improper of McClellan to offer confidential advice, it was clumsily impolitic, given his recent battlefield failures. He could not have known that Lincoln was even then considering an expansion of the war, including an emancipation proclamation that would radically alter Union war aims in the opposite direction of McClellan's counsel.[41]

Two days after his return to Washington, Lincoln reestablished the position of general-in-chief in the person of Major General Henry W. Halleck. With a dumpy figure and bulging eyes, Halleck had a command presence that left much to be desired, but "Old Brains" was steeped in military theory and had enjoyed a great deal of success in the West, most recently with Grant's victory at Shiloh and the subsequent occupation of Corinth, Mississippi, and its all-important rail junction. Halleck went to work first to determine what to do with the Army of the Potomac. On a visit to the Virginia Peninsula, he offered to allow McClellan to resume the offensive with reinforcements of twenty thousand. As usual, McClellan wanted more, but reluctantly agreed. Soon after Halleck returned to Washington, McClellan began asking for greater additions to his strength. Halleck ordered the army to return north to defend the capital. McClellan quickly added Halleck to the list of his incompetent superiors.[42]

McClellan received his orders on August 3, but did not begin embarking units for ten days, taking a full month before the last troops left Fort Monroe. By that time, Lee had marched north and executed a turning movement, splitting his forces and placing them front and rear of Major General John Pope's Army of Virginia. McClellan was concerned that if his army joined Pope's, he might be forced to serve under him, "which would be too great a disgrace." While Lee, Jackson, and Longstreet closed on Pope at Manassas, Halleck ordered McClellan to speed his divisions forward in support. McClellan blatantly disobeyed those orders, dissembled about his actions, and suggested moving his army to Washington and to "leave Pope to get out of his scrape." Lincoln was outraged, believing that McClellan wanted Pope to lose. Stanton suggested a court-martial for treason. Halleck broke down under the strain and frustration. Most of the cabinet signed a letter demanding McClellan's relief, but Lincoln, swinging from anger to despair, demurred. Indeed, the president's options to replace him were few. Pope was beaten, and his army had no confidence in him. Halleck had just shown that he could not stand the pressure of command. Ambrose Burnside had turned Lincoln down when offered command of McClellan's army. U.S. Grant had just succeeded to command of the armies in the West, but that theater was as critically important as its eastern counterpart. Insisting that the defense of the capital was an emergency that demanded McClellan's abilities, Lincoln explained to the cabinet, "If he can't fight himself, he excels in making others ready to fight."[43]

Yet rather than attacking Washington, Lee marched into Maryland in hopes that a successful offensive would weaken Northern morale and gain European diplomatic recognition for the Confederacy. By default McClellan, defender of the capital, became commander of the field army. Lincoln saw the invasion as an opportunity and told McClellan to "destroy the rebel army if possible." McClellan followed Lee north, hoping to force him back into Virginia rather than risk a decisive fight. Then, on September 13, McClellan received a gift of luck seldom equaled in military history. Union soldiers found a copy of Lee's order to his dispersed forces that divulged their plans—to converge on Harpers Ferry—and their locations—separated in four parts over thirty miles. "Here is a paper with which if I cannot whip Bobbie Lee," crowed McClellan, "I will be willing to go home." Taking advantage of that paper required quick decisions, fast marching, and hard fighting, none of which were in McClellan's repertoire. Eighteen hours passed before Union soldiers engaged the enemy, a delay that allowed Lee to see his peril, order a concentration of forces, and establish a hasty defense at Antietam Creek near Sharpsburg. McClellan spent another day and a half studying his outnumbered foe (eighty thousand Union troops against thirty-seven thousand Confederates, which McClellan put at one hundred thousand), hoping that he would retreat south. Then on September 17, McClellan offered a series of piecemeal attacks. Although stretched to the breaking point several times, Lee maneuvered his forces from one threatened sector to another and staved off defeat. McClellan bungled the affair from start to finish, failing to coordinate his subordinates' efforts and leaving almost a third of his force out of the battle while their comrades were fighting on the bloodiest single day in American history. After suffering a total of twenty-five thousand casualties, both armies licked their wounds the following day, neither offering to fight. Lee withdrew across the Potomac under the cover of night.[44]

Characteristically, McClellan boasted of victory, telling his wife that his supporters said "I fought the battle splendidly & that it was a master-piece of art." He decided that his position was so secure that he might demand that Stanton and Halleck be fired and that he replace Halleck as general-in-chief. Lincoln lamented the lost opportunity to "destroy the rebel army." Nonetheless, the president was politically astute enough to declare a victory and to use it to broaden the scope of the war. Days after the battle, he announced the preliminary Emancipation Proclamation, declaring that on January 1, 1863, slaves in all states still in rebellion would be "forever free." The decree was tantamount to a demand for unconditional surrender, for no one expected that any Confederate states would return to the Union under the threat and that all would fight to the last exigency to maintain the peculiar institution.[45]

McClellan was outraged. He had insisted since the outset that he was not fighting for abolition. His views on slavery were an open secret in Washington and a large part of Radical Republicans' distrust of him. "Help me dodge the nigger," he had implored a friend in 1861. "I am fighting to preserve the integrity of the Union & the power of the Govt—on no other issue." He had found Lincoln to be "really sound on the nigger question—I will answer for it that things go right with him." Now, he sought advice from other friends and subordinates on how to react to the proclamation. He told his wife that "the Presdt's late Procla-mation, the continuation of Stanton & Halleck in office render it almost impossible for me to retain my commission & self respect at the same time. I cannot make up my mind to fight for such an accursed doctrine as that of a servile insurrection." His friends advised him to accept the presi-dent's authority to make national policy and to carry out his orders as a soldier. Accordingly, on October 7 McClellan issued a general order that was, for the most part, a clear and proper statement of "the true relation between the soldiers and the Government." The Constitution gave "Civil Authorities" power over the three branches of government. "Armed forces are raised & supported simply to sustain the Civil Authorities and are to be held in strict subordination thereto in all respects." It was the province of government to determine "the principle upon which & the objects for which Armies shall be employed." Political dissent in camp was destructive of good order and discipline, the general admonished. So far, so good. Yet McClellan could not resist asserting that "the remedy for political error if any are committed is to be found only in the action of the people at the polls." That sentence was a none-too-subtle reminder that the midterm elections of 1862 were soon to be contested.[46]

It was in the first week of October that Lincoln visited the camp at Sharpsburg and discovered "McClellan's bodyguard." The day he returned to Washington the president directed Halleck to issue McClellan a clear order: "The President directs that you cross the Potomac and give battle to the enemy or drive him south." McClellan ignored his instructions. Instead, he remained in Maryland for another three weeks complaining of shortages of supplies, reinforcements, horses, and transportation. A week after his visit Lincoln reminded McClellan of their conversations, which centered on "what I called your overcautiousness. Are you not overcautious when you assume that you cannot do what the enemy is constantly doing? Should you not claim to be at least his equal in prowess, and act upon the claim?" He reminded McClellan that Lee was not nearly as well supported as his own forces. Waiting for better logistical support before attacking "ignores the question of time, which cannot and must not be ignored." Lincoln quoted Jomini, one of the theorists he had been studying: a standard maxim of war "is to 'operate upon the enemy's communications as much as possible without exposing your own.' You seem to act as if this applies against you, but cannot apply in your favor." McClellan was concerned that Lee might return north, but if he did, Lincoln instructed, the Army of the Potomac could threaten his line of communications and force him to fight. If Lee marched south into the Shenandoah Valley, so much the better. Marching east of the Blue Ridge, McClellan would be closer to Richmond than Lee: "His route is the arc of a circle, while yours is the chord." Here was the correct application of the concept of interior lines. McClellan could protect Washington on his march, gaining part of its garrison as he did so, threaten the mountain gaps, and force Lee to fight somewhere: "We should not so operate as to merely drive him away." It was a matter of aggressiveness and movement. "It is all easy if our troops march as well as the enemy, and it is unmanly to say they cannot do it." With this letter,

Lincoln demonstrated that he understood strategy and its execution far better than his timid general.[47]

While Lincoln was sending those instructions to McClellan, J. E. B. Stuart's Confederate cavalry rode completely around the stationary Army of the Potomac, repeating a feat that had embarrassed Union forces on the Peninsula. In turn, McClellan complained of a lack of cavalry mounts. Quartermaster General Meigs responded that he had sent thirteen thousand horses to the Army of the Potomac since the first of September. McClellan then complained that his horses were broken down, fatigued, and had sore tongues.[48] Lincoln lost his patience:

> Major-General McClellan: I have just read your dispatch about sore-tongued and fatigued horses. Will you pardon me for asking what the horses of your army have done since the battle of Antietam that fatigues anything?
>
> A. Lincoln[49]

The president later apologized for his sarcasm, and McClellan finally crossed the Potomac, taking six days to accomplish what Lee had done in a single night. Soon enough, Lee, Jackson, and Longstreet had outmaneuvered McClellan, blocking the army front and flank. Shortly after the national election results were in, Lincoln finally relieved McClellan, putting Ambrose Burnside in his place. McClellan spent the rest of the war in New Jersey "awaiting orders" and running unsuccessfully for president against his commander in chief.[50]

Determining a new war policy of union and emancipation seemed to settle Lincoln as commander in chief. He had upbraided Scott for mixing political and military advice. He had made no direct reply to McClellan's letter arguing for a conciliatory approach to the Confederates. Now, he would no longer tolerate political advice from generals. By declaring emancipation, the president embarked on a "hard war" that would only end with surrender by one side or the other. What he wanted now were generals who would implement policy with military strategies designed to succeed.

Lincoln explained his decision to fire McClellan, saying that he had "tried too long to bore with an auger too dull to take hold." Once he began thinking of his generals as implements, he gained a much firmer control of the army. In late October, after repeated attempts to get Buell to follow up the battle of Perryville with an offensive into east Tennessee, Lincoln relieved him in favor of Major General William S. Rosecrans, who had just won a battle at Corinth, Mississippi, and appeared to be a sharper instrument. Major General Ambrose Burnside had turned down the opportunity to succeed McClellan twice, pleading that he was not capable of independent army command. He turned out to be a better judge of his talents than was Lincoln, waging a costly frontal assault on Lee's well-entrenched troops at Fredericksburg. He followed up that debacle with the "Mud March," an ill-fated attempt to march around Lee's flank that ran into a driving rain that sank horses, wagons, and guns into an unforgiving ooze. The president accepted his resignation from command in January 1863 but reassigned him to corps command, at which level he served for the rest of the war.[51]

Lincoln replaced Burnside with Major General "Fighting Joe" Hooker, a brash, hard-drinking, egotistical general with an excellent combat record. But Hooker had been an active participant in the intramural intrigues that plagued the Army of the Potomac. Burnside and he detested one another; Burnside had finally accepted the command only when Halleck let him know that Hooker would get the job if he refused again. On January 26, 1863, the president notified Hooker of his elevation in a letter that encapsulated all that he had learned about working with generals during two years of war. Lincoln fully explained the qualities he needed in a commander, and hinted that he knew that he would not get all he sought from Hooker. Yet the president was confident enough to place Hooker in command of one hundred thousand troops within a short march of the capital in the midst of civil war, even though he knew that the general had suggested the possibility of overthrowing the government. In an unsettlingly droll passage Lincoln taunted Hooker to meet the enemy and defeat him in battle before trying to become Caesar. Lincoln solemnly promised to do his duty as commander in chief, to support the general and his army to the best of his ability. He ended by demonstrating that he understood the limitations of the army and its new commander, charging him to overcome both. Lincoln had matured as commander in chief. He had expanded the capacities of his office to exercise constitutional authority over a military establishment of immense prowess, serenely confident that it would remain obedient even as he worked to make it more effective. The most extraordinary exposition of political-military relations in American history, Lincoln's letter to Hooker also marks the moment when civilian control was firmly established over the military, not to be seriously contested for almost a century.

Hooker missed Lincoln's doubled admonition to "beware of rashness." He soon bragged that he hoped God would have mercy on General Lee, for he would have none. In early May, Lee broke all the Jominian rules of war by dividing his numerically inferior army four times to pen Hooker on three sides at the battle of Chancellorsville. The Army of the Potomac retreated across the Rappahannock, allowing Lee to march north into Maryland and Pennsylvania. Lincoln discarded Hooker as another dull implement.[52]

He soon found a sharper one.

II

THE POLITICS
OF COLLABORATION

★ From Lincoln's administration to FDR's the power of the presidency came into full maturity, with the professional military its usually reliable servant. When Lincoln sacked McClellan he showed that he had gained full confidence in his own judgment as commander in chief. With Ulysses Grant he forged one of the most effective political-military collaborations in American history. Over the following decades the military establishment returned to a relatively modest force, a small burden on the economy and the body politic in peace, but it mushroomed to gargantuan proportions in wartime. By World War I the professional military was accepted as a normal part of American government, so much so that Woodrow Wilson all but delegated the running of the war to General John J. Pershing.

Franklin Delano Roosevelt had a far broader conception of the role of the commander in chief. He maintained a dominance over policy and strategy that frustrated his military advisers, at first. Yet over time, General George Marshall and the Joint Chiefs of Staff learned to work with FDR's idiosyncratic leadership style, so that by the middle of World War II they had become an effective and eventually victorious team. By this time the Congress was little more than a bit player in national security matters.

The latter parts of the Civil War and World War II proved the high points in effective political-military relations, largely because presidents and their generals managed to work through early setbacks to attain mutual trust. Over this period the military profession came into full flower and became almost entirely nonpartisan, even if the soldiers and junior officers necessary for nationwide mobilization were still largely citizen-soldiers.

After World War II, the national security state codified FDR's ad hoc military establishment even as the presidency and the military each gained ever greater governmental power, largely at the expense of Congress.

6

War magnifies every human trait. Fortunately for the nation, the war separated the sheep from the goats, as the folksy president might have said. Talented leaders like William T. Sherman and Philip H. Sheridan, and especially U. S. Grant, naturally demonstrated their abilities, and Lincoln was wise enough to promote them. They manifested aggressiveness, courage, intelligence, and insight. Grant, more than any of the rest, showed a steadiness of character that perfectly suited him to high command. The Union thus had two such men, a soldier and a statesman, to guide its fortunes in its darkest hour. Together Lincoln and Grant forged a strategic partnership that won the war and remains the most effective political-military relationship in American history.

The first time U. S. Grant found himself commanding troops moving to engage an enemy, he felt his heart rising into his throat and a desperate desire to be at home. Yet, as he uniquely put it, "I had not the moral courage to halt and consider what to do; I kept right on." For most mortals the challenge would have been to muster the physical courage to go forward. When he reached the enemy's camp, he found it hurriedly deserted. His approach had frightened the Confederates away. "This was a view of the question I had never taken before; but it was one I never forgot afterwards. From that event to the close of the war, I never experienced trepidation upon confronting an enemy, though I always felt more or less anxiety. I never forgot that he had as much reason to fear my forces as I had his. The lesson was valuable." Indeed, it was.[1]

The combination of moral "cowardice" and battlefield experience propelled Grant to a swift victory at Fort Henry, a confident counterattack followed by a calm demand for "unconditional surrender" at Fort Donelson, and a quiet but firm resolve to "lick 'em tomorrow" after a disastrous first day at Shiloh. It allowed him to overcome a setback at

Holly Springs and to learn that his army could subsist off the land, ignoring the tether of supply lines. And it kept him moving forward through months of unsuccessful attempts to reduce the Confederate garrison at Vicksburg, before he finally hit upon an operational plan so novel that it surprised friend and foe alike. Grant marched his army down the right bank of the Mississippi, coordinated with Admiral David Porter to rush transports and gunboats past the gauntlet of Vicksburg's guns, then ferried his troops back across the river to Bruinsburg, Mississippi, below the fortress. Grant severed his line of communications and attacked Confederate forces in two directions in one of the most daring campaigns in military history. With relentless aggression he defeated rebel forces in a series of battles culminating in a siege that forced the surrender of Vicksburg and General John C. Pemberton's Confederate army on the Fourth of July, 1863. Lincoln wrote Grant to thank him "for the almost inestimable service you have done the country." The president acknowledged that he had not thought much of Grant's plan or his chances. In a magnanimous sentence that commenced a most remarkable collaboration, Lincoln admitted, "I now wish to make the personal acknowledgment that you were right, and I was wrong."[2]

Over more than a year Grant's star had been on the rise. With each victory he gained fame that came with jealous enemies. The general had been a binge drinker before the war, and some of his opponents used his reputation for alcoholism to tar him with drunkenness without substantiating facts. Halleck made such an insinuation shortly after Grant took Fort Donelson. John A. McClernand, a Democratic politician from Illinois commissioned as a volunteer general, angled tirelessly to succeed Grant and frequently spread rumors of his drinking and incompetence. Shortly after the victory at Shiloh, a delegation visited Lincoln, blaming Grant's drinking for horrific Union losses on the first day and insisting that the president relieve him. Lincoln was blunt: "I can't spare this man. He fights." Grant succeeded Halleck in the West when "Old Brains" became general-in-chief. Yet the seed of doubt was planted in Lincoln's mind. As months went by with no result in the Vicksburg Campaign, the president feared he might have a drunken McClellan on his hands. Lincoln dispatched Assistant Secretary of War Charles Dana to Grant's headquarters on a thinly veiled inspection tour. Seeing the visitor for what he was, Grant welcomed him, gave him a tent next to his own, and took him into his confidence. Dana sent seventy reports to Washington over the next one hundred days, and Grant's reputation grew with each dispatch. By that time, Grant was moving on Vicksburg with a sure step. When another delegation arrived at the White House to vilify Grant as a drunkard, the president reportedly asked to know his brand of whiskey so that he might send barrels to all his generals.[3]

Lincoln found a number of things to like about Grant, beyond his willingness to fight. Grant made a habit of using the resources he was given without complaint and executing his orders, which made him most unusual in Lincoln's experience. Furthermore, Grant had no interest in making government policy, telling his friend, Representative Elihu B. Washburne, "So long as I hold a commission in the Army I have no views of my own to carry out. Whatever may be the orders of my superiors, and law, I will execute. No man can be efficient as a commander who sets his own notions above law and those whom he is sworn to obey." Washburne, a Lincoln confidant and tireless Grant supporter, probably conveyed those sentiments to the president, as he did other Grant letters. When Lincoln declared emancipation, Grant grasped the policy's value as a war measure and began freeing slaves and arming black soldiers, even though his previous views on slavery had been ambivalent. Grant also showed a light touch with General John A. McClernand, whose conniving, incompetence, and self-promotion were reminiscent of Gideon Pillow, complete with political connections with the president. Charles Dana regularly reported on McClernand's perfidy, so that when Grant determined to relieve him two weeks before Vicksburg fell, no support remained for the politician-general in Washington. Lincoln let the relief stand.[4]

In October 1863, Lincoln combined all forces between the Appalachians and the Mississippi River and placed them under Grant's command. Grant went directly to Chattanooga to retrieve crumbling Union fortunes in the wake of a devastating defeat at Chickamauga. He replaced the army commander there, reopened supply lines to the starving forces, marched in reinforcements, punished the rebels in a series of ferocious attacks, drove them twenty miles into Georgia, and secured much of east Tennessee—all within a month of his arrival. Unlike his predecessors, he then proposed a winter campaign to start from New Orleans toward Mobile and possibly into Georgia, whereby he hoped to secure the Deep South "or force Lee to abandon Virginia and North Carolina. Without his force the enemy have not got army enough to resist the army I can take." Yet Lincoln had developed a concern about Texas and the possibility that France and Mexico might see an opportunity during the

American war to invade there. As a result, Halleck told Grant that "less for military reasons than as a matter of State policy," his plans for a raid across Mississippi and Alabama would have to wait. The subsequent campaign on the Red River came to grief and deprived Grant of much-needed forces to maintain pressure on the rebels in Georgia, east Tennessee, and along the Mississippi.[5]

This exchange of ideas was the first time Grant had the chance to offer his views at the strategic level. Unlike Zachary Taylor, he rose to the challenge. Grant demonstrated his aggressive bent, as well as an understanding of Lincoln's concept of concentration in time. Strangely, Lincoln was now chasing ghosts with an overweening concern for east Tennessee and fear of an improbable foreign invasion of Texas. Perhaps the president had been saddled with timid commanders so long that he did not yet know how work with a general who could and would keep the enemy off balance through continuous offensive action. For two and a half years Lincoln had painfully reminded his commanders that the enemy army, not some fixed point, however important, was their objective. Although he may not have known it, he was fighting against a habit of professional military thought fostered by West Point. Ostensibly extolling the virtues of Napoleonic warfare, the antebellum Military Academy had promulgated Jomini's tortured interpretations of those campaigns—reducing strategy to geometry—and further distilled them by conflating military engineering with military thought. McClellan, second in his class, became the apotheosis of such set-piece strategic thinking. Halleck, another stellar West Point student, was one of its foremost theoretical proponents. His writings further hobbled offensive warfare by demanding concentration in space.[6]

Grant and his gifted lieutenant, Sherman, had fared poorly at West Point, showing far more promise as artists than engineers. Their creative minds had developed a raiding strategy that harked back to the best Napoleonic offensives, rather than the mathematical methods of their poorly remembered lessons in fortifications and siegecraft. They understood the importance of focusing on the enemy's army, but went even further. They had seen firsthand in one bloody battle after another the destructiveness of modern war. They grasped intuitively that the "hard war" approach that Lincoln had unleashed with the Emancipation Proclamation had set them free to make war on the Southern nation. In January 1864, Grant responded to Halleck's request for a plan for the eastern theater. He suggested a raid that would bypass both Lee's army and Richmond, reaching well into North Carolina and cutting the railroads that supplied both army and capital. There is no record of Lincoln's reaction, but Halleck echoed the president's oft-repeated injunction that the Army of Northern Virginia should be the objective point. Grant was seeing beyond the president's habitual corrective to unimaginative strategy, instead intending to starve Lee's army and force him to abandon Virginia, follow the Union army, and fight on its terms to meet Grant's threat. With superior numbers, aggressive command, and hard marching, he would deprive Southern armies of their foodstuffs, Southern planters of their slaves, Southern families of their security, and the Southern people of their will to continue the war. Lincoln had yet to catch up to such novel strategic thinking.[7]

Halleck communicated Grant's designs to the president, even when he disagreed, and he explained Lincoln's decisions to Grant, but he was not up to offering his own forthright professional analysis of Lincoln's strategic notions. Lincoln had made him general-in-chief for just that purpose and to command the army, but had long since lost confidence in Halleck's capacity for either role. After Second Manassas, the president said, Halleck "had broken down—nerve and pluck all gone—and has ever since evaded all possible responsibility—little more than a first-rate clerk." If Lincoln's strategic thinking left something to be desired in early 1864, he nonetheless recognized that he needed better professional advice.[8]

Grant cleared the final obstacle in Lincoln's mind by renouncing any desire to run for president. The president had cause for concern. Fully one-third of his predecessors had been generals, and Grant's battlefield record rivaled any of theirs. McClellan was already seeking the Democratic nomination, and rumors were circulating in newspapers about a Grant candidacy. Grant began ritually disavowing political ambitions. "I would regard such a consummation unfortunate for myself if not for the country," he assured one correspondent. "Nobody could induce me to think of being a presidential candidate, particularly so long as there is a possibility of having Mr. Lincoln reelected." Elihu Washburne saw to it that Lincoln read a similar letter in which Grant told a Democratic Party official, "Nothing likely to happen would pain me so much as to see my name used in connection with a political office." Reassured that the "presidential grub" was not gnawing at Grant, the president lent his weight to a bill to create a lieutenant general, the first since George Washington, and nominated Grant for the commission and appointment as general-in-chief.[9]

Grant arrived in Washington in March 1864 to public adulation not accorded a general since McClellan's heyday. He reacted with businesslike reserve. His first decisions were to elevate Sherman to Grant's own former command in the West and to retain Meade in command of the Army of the Potomac. Grant hoped to make his headquarters in the West after his initial consultations in Washington, but quickly learned that political considerations would not allow it. Congress, the press, and the president were all too concerned with the troublesome war in Virginia for him to be so far from Washington. He compromised by placing his headquarters near Meade's for the rest of the war, while leaving Halleck in Washington as army chief of staff. Halleck's post was far less potent than the modern term now connotes, but he relieved Grant of administrative burdens, allowing him to focus on operations and strategy, which Grant began immediately to do.

Grant's plan for the 1864 campaign encompassed ideas that Lincoln had been pressing on his generals since early in the war. "It is my design," he told Sherman, "to work all parts of the army together and somewhat toward a common center"—Lincoln's concentration in time. In Louisiana Nathaniel Banks would wrap up the bootless Red River campaign and "commence operations against Mobile as soon as he can. It will be impossible for him to commence too early." (Grant would find himself frustrated with Banks's feeble execution.) Ben Butler would drive from Norfolk toward Richmond on the south bank of the James River. Franz Sigel would move up the Shenandoah Valley toward the Virginia and Tennessee Railroad. The object of the latter two operations was to force Lee to expend scarce resources protecting lines of communication and the industrial, rail, and political hub of Richmond. The main effort in the east was the Army of the Potomac. Grant's order to Meade was characteristically direct: "Lee's army will be your objective point. Wherever Lee goes, there you will go also."[10]

Grant gave Sherman broader guidance: "You I propose to move against Johnston's army, to break it up and to get into the interior of the enemy's country as far as you can, inflicting all the damage you can against their war resources. I do not propose to lay down for you a plan of campaign, but simply to lay down the work it is desirable to have done, and leave you to free to execute in your own way." He asked for Sherman to share plans with him as soon as possible.[11]

Lincoln was enthusiastic about Grant's plan. Moreover, he was delighted to have a commander who could see the war as a whole and take responsibility for directing it. When Grant wrote his memoirs two decades later he remembered that Lincoln "told me he did not want to know what I proposed to do," and that he had not shared his plans with the president or Secretary Stanton. Lincoln himself made the same claim, telling one visitor that Grant "hasn't told me what his plans are. I don't know, and I don't want to know." Yet both men overstated the case. They conferred regularly on strategy in the first few weeks of Grant's command. Grant even employed Lincolnian phrases in his orders, such as "Lee's army is your objective point." When Grant explained his campaign plan to Lincoln, the president exclaimed, "I see it! Those not skinning can hold a leg!" A few days later Grant employed the phrase in his order to Sherman, explaining that while he did not expect much from Sigel, "if Sigel can't skin himself he can hold a leg whilst some one else skins." Lincoln did not relinquish his supervision of strategy when Grant took command. He continued his visits to the telegraph office to track the progress of battles. He maintained a regular correspondence with Grant. Perhaps the best explanation of how the political-military relationship changed when Grant took command comes from a conversation with a White House visitor who asked Lincoln what sort of man Grant was.[12] Lincoln smiled and said,

> He's the quietest little fellow you ever saw. . . . The only evidence you have that he's in a place is that he makes things git! Wherever he is, things move! Grant is the first general I've had! He's a general! . . . I'll tell you what I mean. You know how it's been with all the rest. As soon as I put a man in command of the Army, he'd come to me with a plan of campaign and about as much as say, "Now, I don't believe I can do it, but if you say so I'll try it on," and so put the responsibility of success or failure on me. They all wanted me to be the general. Now it isn't so with Grant. He hasn't told me what his plans are. I don't know, and I don't want to know. I'm glad to find a man that can go ahead without me. He doesn't ask impossibilities of me, and he's the first general I've had that didn't.[13]

Grant took responsibility. Lincoln gave support. Shortly before the campaign began, Lincoln wrote a personal letter to Grant, expressing his "entire satisfaction with what you have done up to this time." Again, he professed, "the particulars of your plans I neither know, or seek to know. You are vigilant and self-reliant; and, pleased with this, I wish not to obtrude any constraints or restraints upon you." While he was naturally "anxious," he knew that Grant had the situation in hand, and that the details of campaigning "are less likely to escape your attention than they would be mine. If there is anything wanted which is within my power to give, do not fail to let me know it." Grant replied the following day. From the beginning of the war, he said, "I have never had cause for complaint, have never expressed or implied a complaint, against the Administration." Further, since his promotion to general-in-chief, "I have been astonished at the readiness with which every thing asked for has been yielded without even an explaination [sic] being asked. Should my success be less than I desire, and expect, the least I can say is, the fault is not with you."[14] It is impossible to imagine such an exchange between Lincoln and any of his previous commanders. The president and his general had established a relationship of perfect trust, mutual respect, and shared confidence.

Within a week reports of staggering losses at the battle of the Wilderness came pouring into Washington. The pattern for the Army of the Potomac was to withdraw after such a blooding. At the end of the battle Grant sent his first word to Lincoln: "There is to be no turning back." Two days later, Grant reported that his losses were heavy, about twenty thousand men, but "the loss of the enemy must be greater." Then, in a sentence that showed that the old pattern was broken, he proposed "to fight it out on this line if it takes all summer." A delighted president exclaimed, "The great thing about Grant . . . is his perfect coolness and persistency of purpose. . . . He has the grit of a bull-dog!"[15] Grant would need it, for much hard fighting lay ahead at Spotsylvania, North Anna, and Cold Harbor.

With the presidential election months away and some papers predicting Grant would win the war that summer, Lincoln needed good news from the front. He got too little of it. Banks's Red River campaign mired in the Louisiana swamps, delaying the drive on Mobile for months. Sigel's offensive in the Shenandoah never got going before a smaller Confederate force put it to flight. Ben Butler moved hesitantly toward Richmond until P. G. T. Beauregard attacked and penned the Army of the

James against its namesake river. Grant said that Butler's army was now as useless "as if it had been in a bottle strongly corked." Sherman characteristically made better progress, but in late June he suffered a defeat at Kennesaw Mountain, still twenty miles short of Atlanta. More important than all the rest was the Virginia campaign. Grant and Meade continued to move south, eventually slipping past Lee across the James River toward Petersburg, a crucial rail junction twenty miles south of Richmond. Yet the casualties from the Army of the Potomac flooded Washington's army hospitals, weighing heavily on Northern morale. Then, in late June Lee sent Jubal Early into the Shenandoah Valley. In a campaign that drew comparisons to Stonewall Jackson's in 1862, Early knocked aside a Federal force near Lynchburg, took Harpers Ferry, crossed into Maryland, and marched on Washington. By mid-July, some Northern Democratic papers were calling Grant's coordinated campaign a failure and suggesting that it was time to negotiate with the Confederate government.[16]

Crises test political-military relationships. The summer of 1864 forced Lincoln and Grant to share decisions that were not neatly military or political. After Banks's failure in Louisiana, Grant wanted to fire him, but the general was a powerful Massachusetts Republican, a former governor and speaker of the U.S. House, and a personal friend of the president. Halleck warned Grant of a political firestorm if he were relieved. Grant offered a compromise whereby Banks would retain command of the Department of the Gulf, where he would be useful in planning for Louisiana's reconstruction, but his field forces would go to Edward R. S. Canby. Much relieved, Lincoln approved the change, and Canby led the Mobile expedition in July.[17]

Benjamin Franklin Butler was another problem. Like Banks a former Massachusetts congressman, Butler was a War Democrat whom Lincoln had commissioned major general of volunteers in a bid to gain bipartisan support for the war. Butler had an uneven and controversial Civil War career, including a turbulent administration of New Orleans, but by 1863 he was among the senior generals in the army. Lincoln appointed him to command the Department of Virginia and North Carolina, and then the Army of the James. Beauregard's inferior force then "corked" him in the Bermuda Hundred. After Grant invested Petersburg, he asked permission to transfer Butler to another theater, but the political ramifications were much the same as those for Banks. Halleck offered a similar compromise, to leave him in command of his department while another general took over his army, and Lincoln reluctantly signed the order. Whether because he lost confidence in W. F. Smith, the designated successor, or because he gained a better appreciation of the political difficulty he was causing his uncomplaining president, Grant thought better of the solution and shelved it. He waited until after the November election before asking for Butler's relief, at which time Lincoln quickly agreed.[18]

In mid-July as Early marched toward Washington, Lincoln became concerned for the safety of the capital, but he also saw an opportunity to defeat and destroy a sizable rebel force. Grant's situation was comparable to McClellan's two years earlier, but his reaction was strikingly different. He immediately sent part of a corps to Washington, and offered to come in person within the hour "if the President thinks it advisable." Lincoln opined that the army should retain enough forces to hold its positions at Petersburg, but "bring the rest with you personally, and make a vigorous effort to destroy the enemy's force in this vicinity. I think there is really a fair chance to do this if the move is prompt. This is what I think, upon your suggestion, and is not an order." The two men were collaborating, thinking together over the telegraph, rather than sparring. That same day, Grant sent the entire corps and another division along with cavalry. Yet he decided, "on reflection, it would have a bad effect for me to leave here." One of the most important and difficult decisions a commander can make is to determine where he should be to influence events. Grant had earlier decided that Washington was not that place. He now reiterated that choice, and he was probably right, as he would soon have active operations on his hands around Petersburg. Moreover, if he went north he would leave Butler in charge as the senior general present. Lincoln concurred, but predicted difficulty controlling the various commands around Washington. Both men would have opportunity to regret this decision. Events soon bore Lincoln's prediction out. Union forces drove Early away from the capital, but failed to pursue him. Early headed into Maryland as Union commanders fumbled for two weeks. Stanton and Halleck did little to sort out the mess and may have actively frustrated Grant's designs. Grant suggested combining all the departments from the Susquehanna to Washington under a single commander. Meanwhile, Grant sent more reinforcements north, complaining to Halleck about slow communications: "It is absolutely necessary that someone in Washington should give orders and make dispositions of all the forces" there. The next day, Stanton put Halleck in command, but Old Brains had not gained any agility during his years in the capital. Frustrated, Lincoln decided to visit Grant to provide his general-in-chief the benefit of his hard-won wisdom on the matter of controlling generals.[19]

Before he could arrive, twin calamities struck on July 30. Early raided Pennsylvania and torched Chambersburg, raising Northern fears to a fever pitch. At Petersburg, Meade's forces exploded a huge mine beneath Confederate fortifications, blowing an enormous crater in the ground and a seam in enemy defenses. Union formations then failed to exploit the advantage while suffering losses of thirty-five hundred men. Grant called it "the saddest affair I have witnessed in the war. Such an opportunity for carrying fortifications I have never seen and do not expect again to have." The disasters cast a pall over the presidential visit, but Lincoln and Grant agreed on a plan. Grant sent Phil Sheridan to take command near Washington "with instructions to put himself south of the enemy and follow him to the death. Wherever the enemy goes let our troops go also." Yet the dashing cavalryman was junior to one of the generals in the field, so command remained muddled. Lincoln approved Grant's instructions, but hinted that Stanton and Halleck were still being obstructive: there was no sense of "following him to the death" in Washington. He gave his commander a piece of hard-won wisdom: "It will neither be done nor attempted, unless you watch it every day and hour and force it." Grant sped north two hours after receiving Lincoln's admonition. He met with his generals in the field, sent the senior one packing, and gave Sheridan full control. Sheridan's subsequent campaign in the Shenandoah Valley rivaled Jackson's in Civil War history and substantially contributed to Lee's eventual defeat.[20]

Just as important, Sheridan brought welcome news to the victory-starved North in time to affect the outcome of the election. The Democratic platform promised "immediate efforts for a cessation of hostilities." Although McClellan, Lincoln's opponent, tried to soften that pledge, his election would have brought enormous pressure for a negotiated settlement. Sherman's capture of Atlanta in September, followed by Sheridan's success in the Valley in mid-October, secured Lincoln's reelection, assuring that the war would continue under the policies of reunification and emancipation.

Lincoln and Grant spent the rest of the war in a candid and continuous negotiation, usually agreeing, sometimes debating, but always of one mind on policy and the need to keep pressing the rebel army. In the summer of 1864 Halleck had feared a repeat of the previous year's draft riots and suggested to Grant that he detach units from the Petersburg siege to enforce the law. Grant declined, telling Halleck to ask governors to mobilize the militia. Moreover, "my withdrawal now from the James River would insure the defeat of Sherman." Lincoln, eavesdropping on the cable traffic as usual, wired Grant that he had seen his response, "expressing your unwillingness to break your hold where you are. Neither am I willing. Hold on with a bull-dog grip, and chew and choke as much as possible."[21]

After Sherman captured Atlanta, he asked Grant for permission to make what would become known as the March to the Sea. For several days, Lincoln, Stanton, Halleck, and Grant all expressed reservations at his making so bold a move, especially with Hood's army still intact in Georgia. Finally, Grant decided to let him try. Lincoln, still concerned, acceded to his commanders. Sherman was out of contact for over a month after he severed his communications in Atlanta. Just before Christmas, he sent Lincoln a message by a navy ship, offering captured Savannah as a yuletide gift. Lincoln magnanimously wrote back, thanking Sherman and saying that he had been "anxious, if not fearful; but feeling that you were the better judge, and remembering that 'nothing ventured, nothing gained,' I did not interfere. Now, the undertaking being a success, the honor is all yours; for I believe none of us went further than to acquiesce."[22] The president's willingness to give all glory to his commanders went a long way toward giving them confidence to dare to achieve great results.

On the day before Lincoln's second inauguration the military situation around Petersburg was heading toward a southern surrender. Lee asked Grant if he would be willing to discuss a cease-fire. Grant properly asked for instructions, and Stanton immediately replied with a telegram Lincoln had drafted in his own hand: "The President directs me to say to you that he wishes you to have no conference with General Lee, unless it be for the capitulation of General Lee's army or on some minor and purely military matter. He instructs me to say that you are not to decide, discuss, or confer upon any political question. Such questions the president holds in his own hands, and will submit them to no military conferences or conventions. Meantime you are to press to the utmost your military advantages."[23] As much as he trusted Grant, Lincoln rightly retained authority over matters of policy, even to the last day of the war.

On March 20, as the campaign's denouement was approaching, Grant sent the president a telegraph that reads more like a missive between old friends than between soldier and statesman: "Can you not visit City Point for a day or two? I would like very much to see you, and I think the rest would do you good." Lincoln was so excited that he seemed to be packing for the trip even as he dictated his reply. The president stayed with the Army of the Potomac three weeks as the final act wound to a close. He visited Petersburg and Richmond as each fell to Federal troops, and took great satisfaction in sitting in Jefferson Davis's chair. He began to feel guilty for staying so long away from Washington, but Stanton reassured him, insisting that he was just where he should be at that moment. When Lee made one final attempt to save his army, Sheridan cut him off, telling Grant, "If the thing is pressed I think Lee will surrender." The president, reading telegrams to the end, wired back, "Let the *thing* be pressed."[24] Two days later with Lincoln's blessing, Grant and Lee sat together at Appomattox Court House to discuss terms of surrender.

To gain the confidence he and Grant shared, Lincoln had to travel farther and faster than any president in American history. A one-term congressman during the Mexican War, Lincoln never held another elective office until he assumed the presidency. He had almost no formal education, less than two months of military service, and no executive experience. By his own admission, he knew little about being president and less about being commander in chief. Yet the challenges he faced were more daunting than any president's before or since. The nation was coming apart before he took office; states were seceding from the Union *because* of his election. Had Lincoln failed to reunite the country, historians would surely have blamed his lack of experience and education. Yet Lincoln brought to the presidency a powerful intellect, a thirst for learning, natural political acumen, and strength of character that allowed him to grow quickly into his role as commander in chief.

In his chapter "On Military Genius," Clausewitz describes war as the environment of "danger, exertion, uncertainty, and chance." Danger engenders fear, and courage is required to overcome it. Exertion wears on soldiers, machines, and armies, making them tire and weaken. "War is the realm of uncertainty; three quarters of the factors on which action in war is based are wrapped in a fog of greater or lesser uncertainty." Moreover, "war is the realm of chance. No other human activity gives it greater scope: no other has such incessant and varied dealings with this intruder." In such a chaotic environment, the pressures on a military commander are enormous. The intellectual and moral qualities necessary for command are different from those of any other calling. "If the mind is to emerge unscathed from this relentless struggle with the unforeseen, two qualities are indispensable: *first, an intellect that, even in the darkest hour, retains some glimmerings of the inner light which leads to truth; and second, the courage to follow this faint light wherever it may lead.*"[25]

This mind, says Clausewitz, must be "a strong rather than a brilliant one." That is not to denigrate intellectual ability, for skills of memory, observation, terrain sense, discrimination, analysis, and critical thought are likewise indispensable in making sense of and making decisions in the bewildering array of stimuli that bombard the mind of a commander. A general needs to have the capacity "*to act rationally at all times.* Therefore, we would argue that a strong character is one *that will not be unbalanced by the most powerful emotions,*" especially the doubt that plagues an officer charged with life-and-death responsibilities for large masses of soldiers. Self-confidence, born of experience and strength of character, combined with a balanced temperament comprising "emotional strength and stability," is imperative. The commander cannot be indecisive, but neither can he be obstinate. Perseverance and insight are needed: "In all doubtful cases [one must] *stick to one's first opinion and . . . refuse to change unless forced to do so by a clear conviction.*" Moreover, "the burdens increase with the number of men in his command, and therefore the higher his position, the greater the strength of character he needs to bear the mounting load." History shows that "no case is more common than that of the officer whose energy declines as he rises in rank and fills positions that are beyond his abilities." Furthermore, at the highest level of responsibility, the differences are of kind rather than degree: "A major gulf exists between a commander-in-chief—a general who leads the army as a whole or commands in a theater of operations—and the senior generals immediately subordinate to him. . . . On that level strategy and policy coalesce: the commander-in-chief is simultaneously a statesman." In sum, supreme command calls for "the inquiring rather than the creative mind, the comprehensive rather than the specialized approach, the calm rather than the excitable head."[26] Clausewitz penned those observations more than a generation before the Civil War, yet he might easily have been drawing a sketch of Ulysses S. Grant.

For the first time in the war, Lincoln had a man who would take responsibility: "Grant is the first general I've had! He's a general!" The two men quickly established mutual trust that fostered a symbiosis of shared responsibility. Grant respected Lincoln's political skills and never questioned his absolute primacy in policy. Lincoln prized Grant's loyalty and soon appreciated that for the first time he had a general whose strategic acumen outstripped his own. The two men did not attempt to draw some artificial wall between policy and strategy where Lincoln presided in the former and Grant commanded in the latter. Almost every political decision Lincoln made had strategic consequences, just as Grant's strategic and operational methods and their outcomes had significant political ramifications. Grant offered Lincoln bold strategic advice that the president could not yet grasp and which he sometimes overruled, both men's statements to the contrary notwithstanding. When Lincoln delayed the raid on Mobile or vetoed Grant's plan to bypass Lee and Richmond for a campaign into North Carolina, Grant obeyed with alacrity. As the casualties of the Overland Campaign mounted, blood that Grant had tried to avoid spilling through more imaginative strategy, losses that had the Northern press calling Grant a "butcher," Grant never protested, never considered suggesting, à la McClellan, that "the responsibility cannot be thrown on my shoulders." Instead, he proposed "to fight it out on this line if it takes all summer." Lincoln was gratified: that summer of 1864 was crucial for the war because it was crucial for Lincoln's reelection. Failure in one sphere meant defeat in the other. Lincoln's defeat would likely have ushered in a President McClellan uncommitted to a policy of reunion under the U.S. Constitution, and who had repeatedly demonstrated his inability to withstand pressure. Lincoln trusted Grant to deliver military success, and he was not disappointed. Sherman's capture of Atlanta and Sheridan's success in the Shenandoah secured Lincoln's reelection, which meant that the war would go on until reunion was achieved.

Grant and Lincoln learned from one another. Lincoln, with long experience supervising senior generals, coached Grant as he leapt the Clausewitzian gulf to supreme command. Grant, gaining Lincoln's trust, coaxed the president to approve Sherman's bold strategy to cut his lines of communication and march across Georgia. In time, their continuous negotiation ripened into a personal relationship born of shared responsibility, mutual respect, and abiding trust.

Although Clausewitz was describing ideal qualities for military command, his prescriptions for mind and character apply equally well to a wartime head of state. The Lincoln-Grant collaboration succeeded because both men had deep reserves of emotional strength, moral courage, and intellectual stability: *"an intellect that, even in the darkest hour, retains some glimmerings of the inner light which leads to truth; and . . . the courage to follow this faint light wherever it may lead."* Despite sometimes unbearable pressure, Lincoln never wavered from his truth—that the Union must and would be restored. Grant never doubted that the Confederate army could and would be defeated. Lesser politicians sometimes counseled conciliation and negotiation without preconditions. Lesser generals lost confidence in themselves and their armies. The Lincoln-Grant partnership worked because both men possessed immense courage and determination. Character is critically important on both sides of the continuous negotiation. Lincoln and Grant forged the first true strategic collaboration between a president and supreme commander in American history, one that has yet to be surpassed.

7

After 1865 the United States enjoyed a long period of security from foreign threats. The navy retrenched and focused on patrolling the continental coastline. The small constabulary army attempted to pacify the conquered South and fought the Indian wars, but it was also involved in strikebreaking and manning coastal fortifications. Yet with the end of Reconstruction and, a little over a decade later, the final campaign of the Indian wars, the army found itself without a mission. The 1890s were a time of institutional soul-searching in both services.

The navy met the challenge with new thinking from theorist Captain Alfred T. Mahan. To become a great power, he argued, the United States needed to build a new and more powerful navy, a "fleet-in-being" capable of protecting American shipping and patrolling the seven seas, the global commons. The naval buildup began in earnest in the 1890s, centering on the new battleship. With the help of progressive internationalists, Theodore Roosevelt first among them, the United States made this blue-water fleet the main engine of its imperial designs. A five-battleship fleet successfully fought the Spanish-American War. Afterward Congress committed to funding a robust and constant naval building program. In 1907 President Roosevelt ordered the sixteen-battleship "Great White Fleet" to circumnavigate the globe, thereby demonstrating that the United States had arrived as a world naval power. By 1914 the navy comprised thirty-eight battleships, fourteen of which were the state-of-the-art, all-big-gun (twelve-to-fourteen-inch diameter), post-Dreadnoughts.[1]

The army had further to go. The Spanish-American War surprised the service, forcing it to mobilize a hundred thousand men and deploy overseas, something it had not done since the war with Mexico. Roosevelt pronounced the army's 1898 campaign in Cuba to have been "within measurable distance of a military disaster." The army's shortcomings included a cumbersome high command, poor strategic planning capability, and severe difficulties mobilizing, training, equipping, feeding, and transporting troops. The war had exposed severe institutional and organizational problems, and for a short time there was public impetus for military reform.[2]

Roosevelt and Secretary of War Elihu Root embarked on an endeavor to make the army an effective instrument of policy. Looking expansively at the foreign policy of the Roosevelt administration, Root said, "The real object of having an Army is to provide for war." He founded an army war college to educate senior officers and created a general staff to succeed the bureau system, which dated back to 1813. Root persuaded Congress to enact legislation that replaced the army's commanding general with an army chief of staff. In his 1903 annual report, Root explained why the general staff and chief of staff were so important in political-military terms. The reform provided "for civilian control over the military arm, but for civilian control to be exercised through a single military expert of high rank, who is provided with an adequate corps of professional assistants . . . , and who is bound to use all his professional skill and knowledge in giving effect to the purposes and general directions of his civilian superior." Root also expressed the hope that they had resolved "the problem of reconciling civilian control with military efficiency" that had vexed the War Department and the army for over a century.[3]

The Spanish-American War likewise heralded a long-term change in American foreign policy and military strategy. The nation's foreign policy took a decidedly expansionist, even imperialist turn. Strategic thinking changed as U.S. interests expanded. Threats to the United States and its possessions were few and predictable. Trouble from the Mexican republic was yet unlikely, but the long southern border bore watching, and guarding it was clearly an army responsibility. Germany, Great Britain, and Japan all boasted of strong naval power, and while the United States had good relations with all three, especially the British, all three nevertheless presented potential threats to the American coast and ports. Preparing for such unlikely eventualities fell on the navy and the army's coastal defense establishment. More likely were violations of the Monroe Doctrine in Panama or the Caribbean or threats to America's newly acquired possessions in the Pacific. Each of these concerns pointed up the need for a blue-water navy and ready land forces. As President Theodore Roosevelt put it, "Whether we desire it or not, we must henceforth recognize that we have international duties no less than international rights."[4]

Both the army and the navy developed general staffs to control overseas operations. Although those staffs spent years fighting bureaucratic battles to gain a full measure of legitimacy, they quickly matured sophisticated strategic planning capabilities. In 1903 the two services formed the Joint Board to coordinate planning for future wars. As these staffs explored potential contingencies, they began to crave information about U.S. foreign policy goals, so as not to plan in a political vacuum. Army and navy planners asked the State Department for direction, as well as requesting opportunities to consult on the formulation and implementation of national policy. The diplomatic corps met such requests with a narrow range of reactions, from indignation to stunned silence. They felt that the military brass was attempting to impinge on State's traditional prerogatives in foreign affairs. One level deeper, diplomats feared that consulting with the military might threaten civilian primacy in national policy making, perhaps leading to a weakening of civilian control.[5] Thus, State's reactions were more than bureaucratic turf protection, although the department was also undergoing a period of extraordinary growth.

The conflict pointed up a fundamental philosophical difference between the military and diplomatic professions of the day. These military overtures were unprecedented, having sprung from recent growth in the services' levels of overseas commitment. Soldiers and sailors saw war as a normal part of international relations. Future wars were inevitable. Therefore, it made sense to plan and prepare for them. Diplomats viewed warfare as aberrant—the outbreak of war manifested a failure of foreign policy. William Jennings Bryan, President Woodrow Wilson's eloquent if ineffectual secretary of state, summed up his department's point of view during a 1913 crisis with Japan, opining that "army and navy officers could not be trusted to say what we should or should not do, till we actually got into a war." Two years later Wilson went even further. Struggling to maintain a neutral stance toward the war in Europe, the president was appalled when the Joint Board's contingency plans for war with Germany leaked into the press. Incensed that the military was venturing into policy, Wilson suspended the Joint Board and threatened to abolish it altogether if it ever made such plans again. He pronounced that the American military officer should have "nothing to do with the formulation of [national] policy. He is to support [that] policy whatever it is."[6]

171

Even among American officers the Clausewitzian continuum, "that war is not a mere act of policy but a true political instrument, a continuation of political activity by other means," had no currency in the early twentieth century. In 1915 the army general staff drew a bright line between the statesman's formulation of policy and the soldier's execution of it: "where the first leaves off the other takes hold."[7]

In 1914 the Great War began to dominate Woodrow Wilson's presidency. Prominent Republicans led by former president Roosevelt, Senator Henry Cabot Lodge, and General Leonard Wood began agitating for military preparedness and charging that the administration was not doing enough to prepare for war. Wilson supported modest military budget increases, but insisted in his 1915 State of the Union address that the United States should not be "thrown off balance by a war with which we have nothing to do." Wilson was not opposed to any military action. During two terms he dispatched U.S. forces to Cuba, Nicaragua, Honduras, Panama, Haiti, the Dominican Republic, and Mexico. Yet he ardently desired to stay neutral in the European war because he thought it was needlessly destructive and that victory would be meaningless. Wilson hoped to broker a peace based upon a number of principles, including equality among all nations, no territorial conquest by force of arms, and his vision of "an association of nations, all bound together for the protection and integrity of each." The president had to walk a tightrope between preparedness boosters on one side and antiwar advocates, including Secretary Bryan, on the other. Even after German submarines sank RMS *Lusitania* in 1915, claiming 128 American lives, Wilson prudently sent a series of diplomatic notes to Germany warning them against attacking neutral shipping without warning and safeguards for civilians, and thereby postponed American entry into the war for more than a year. During the 1916 presidential campaign, Wilson ran and won on the slogan "He kept us out of war." Then, at the end of January 1917, the Germans announced a policy of unrestricted submarine warfare. Although he continued to advocate "peace without victory," Wilson had no choice but to break diplomatic relations with Germany and ask Congress for a declaration of war on the second of April. The first small force of American doughboys paraded through Paris on the Fourth of July. A U.S. colonel coined the phrase, "Lafayette, we are here!"[8]

Wilson concentrated on high-level policy while leaving details to trusted subordinates. He trusted no one more than Newton D. Baker, his second secretary of war, a pacifist, antimilitarist former mayor of Cleveland. When Wilson offered him the job, Baker went to see the president set to decline: I "gave him what it would seem to me were perfectly adequate reasons, and when I had finished my explanation, to which he listened with great patience, he said, 'Are you ready to be sworn in?'" Baker was an unassuming man, but an eloquent speaker, a superb administrator, and a quick study. A colleague remembered that "Baker used to sit at his desk at the War Department with one leg curled up under him on the cushion of his chair. On his desk there was always a fresh pansy, and he continually smoked a pipe. A small man physically, Baker looked boyish in the company of the tall and bulky generals who were usually around him." But he could be quietly ruthless when crossed.[9]

Among the many tasks Baker faced upon the outbreak of war was naming a commander for the American Expeditionary Forces (AEF). Of the six senior generals in the army, two were in poor health, and two more were nearing retirement. The two remaining were Leonard Wood and John J. Pershing. Wood was a former army chief of staff and the senior officer in the army. He had health problems of his own stemming from a brain injury suffered years before. Wood was exceptionally well connected, having been the first commander of the Rough Riders during the Spanish-American War, with Theodore Roosevelt as his deputy. The two men had been a thorn in Wilson's side, thumping the preparedness issue since 1914. Against direct orders, Wood made several speeches in March 1917 calling for a declaration of war. Wilson said he had "no confidence either in General Wood's discretion or in his loyalty to his superiors." Baker agreed: Wood "had no conception of loyalty. . . . [He] did not know the meaning of the word. He was the most insubordinate general officer in the entire army." Ambitious and charismatic as he was, Wood was out.[10]

That left Pershing, a fifty-seven-year-old West Pointer. He had been first captain of the corps of cadets and president of his class, graduating in 1886 as a cavalryman. During the Indian campaigns he commanded black troops, and racist subordinates later gave him the nickname "Black Jack." In the 1890s he served at West Point, in the War Department, and as a military science instructor at the University of Nebraska, where he earned a law degree. Pershing performed brilliantly in the Philippines and returned as one of the first officers assigned to the new general staff. He also studied at the Army War College in Washington, D.C., where he courted and married the daughter of influential Senator Francis E. Warren of Wyoming, chairman of the Military Affairs Committee. The next year President Roosevelt named Pershing, still a captain, over 862 senior officers for a brigadier general's commission. Warren shepherded the nomination through the Senate. Pershing held commands in the United States and the Philippines, including one at the Presidio of San Francisco. In 1915 he was away on assignment when a fire in his home there killed his wife and three daughters. His only son survived. Crushed by his losses, Pershing threw himself into his career, and was named commander of the Punitive Expedition to pursue Pancho Villa in Mexico. The campaign enjoyed mixed results, but Pershing's reputation remained intact when the expedition withdrew in February 1917.[11]

Pershing badly wanted to command the U.S. forces soon headed to the war in France. He felt he had proven himself capable and loyal, so he wrote to the army chief of staff and Secretary of War Newton Baker requesting overseas service. He sent a letter to Woodrow Wilson praising the president's war address and pronouncing himself fitted by a lifetime "as a soldier, in camp and field," to "serve my country and you." The chief of staff soon wrote Pershing to ask how well he spoke French (Pershing exaggerated). In April 1917 Baker selected Pershing to command the American Expeditionary Forces, Wilson agreed, and Pershing was summoned to Washington in early May.

When Pershing met Baker for the first time he was anxious to know what the secretary would expect of him. Baker quickly clarified their relationship. Acknowledging the impossibility of trying to control the army from Washington, he said he would give Pershing "only two orders, one to go to France and one to come home, but that in the meantime his authority in France would be supreme."[12] The day before Pershing embarked for Europe, Baker accompanied him to his only meeting with Wilson during the war. The president echoed Baker's confidence, and briefly reviewed Pershing's orders. The general was to keep in mind "that the forces of the United States are a separate and distinct component of the combined forces, the identity of which must be preserved." Pershing would decide when his forces were ready for independent action, but until then they were to "cooperate as a component of whatever army you may be assigned to by the French Government." A lot of political and military ambiguity rested between those two directives, but Pershing had full authority to make decisions "to carry on the war vigorously in harmony with the spirit of these instructions."[13]

No American general ever began his command with a more unfettered mandate. Pershing shipped for France as a general plenipotentiary. When he arrived he immediately found himself dealing with Allies on sensitive military issues, almost all of which had political ramifications. Yet seldom did Wilson or Baker insert themselves; Pershing's authority was "supreme." As more and more untrained and unready doughboys arrived in France, and as German divisions pressed ever harder along the western front, Pershing faced enormous pressure from his allies to send American units into combat under French or British command. Pershing resisted mightily, but doing so placed him in the midst of coalition politics at the highest levels. He was a general wearing many hats—trainer, organizer, combat commander, and, most difficult perhaps, his nation's highest representative in coalition councils. He soon found himself wielding more delegated political power than any general in American history. His tenure left an ambiguous legacy—harmonious political-military relations on the one hand, independent military authority on the other—which his successors would mold as they saw fit.

For the next eighteen months Pershing exercised wide discretion as he built an American army in France to join in a final victory over the Germans. Enjoying the confidence of Baker and Wilson, he was rarely in conflict with his civilian superiors. Instead, Pershing's political battles came with his allies over an issue called amalgamation: whether American units would be allowed to serve under Allied commanders or remain in a strictly American formation. Yet, near war's end, Pershing, by then long accustomed to dealing with political issues, became entangled in the question of terms of German surrender, which landed him in hot water with his superiors.

Despite his weak command of their language, Pershing charmed the French when he arrived in Paris. He soon found himself immersed in the amalgamation issue, which would complicate almost his entire tenure in command. From a purely practical standpoint, it might have made sense to place U.S. battalions under the tutelage of French or British armies, giving them seasoning with more experienced units in quiet sectors of the line. But from a national perspective America needed to make its entrée onto the world stage as a great power with its own force under its own commanders. Amalgamation was thus both a military and a political question, and a thorny one on both counts. Pershing's mandate from President Wilson and Secretary Baker made him responsible for negotiating on both levels with his coalition partners.

For the Allies who had been waiting years for the United States to enter the war, the AEF's progress was agonizingly slow. In April 1917 the regular army comprised but 133,111 soldiers, with another 185,000 in the national guard. Pershing arrived in France with a complement of 191 officers and men, and immediately asked the War Department for one million troops by the following May. Yet those men had to be drafted, inducted, organized, trained, equipped, and shipped to France, a series of herculean tasks for which the army staff would have to grow and develop to administer. Straining every fiber, the War Department estimated it could have 635,000 soldiers in France by the following June. By January 1918 the United States had but 175,000 troops in the theater, and precious few of them had seen any action.[14]

The British and French were becoming anxious, and well they might have been. Extensive Allied summer offensives in 1917 had yielded no appreciable gains and cost another million casualties. A dangerously large percentage of French forces were in mutiny or on the verge of it, refusing orders to mount any further offensives. The British were in little better shape. Moreover, a war on three European fronts had devolved essentially onto one. The Italian front had stabilized, allowing the Germans to shift divisions into France. Likewise, the Russian front collapsed after the Bolshevik Revolution, and the Germans redeployed some forty divisions to the western front, thereby enjoying numerical superiority there for the first time. Allied intelligence expected the Germans to launch an offensive soon. Seemingly idle American soldiers, the Allies thought, might have done much to stiffen their defenses and to improve morale among veterans of three years of brutal trench warfare.[15]

In December 1917 British prime minister David Lloyd George suggested sending "surplus" American companies and battalions into British lines during the emergency, after which they would be returned to the AEF. Applying diplomatic pressure on Washington, he warned that the Germans might attempt "a knockout blow to the Allies before a fully trained American army is fit." The French soon developed similar proposals. After consulting with Wilson, Baker referred the issue back to Pershing, saying he desired to keep the American army together, but that was "secondary to the meeting of any critical situation by the most helpful use possible of the troops under your command." However, Baker reiterated that Pershing had "full authority to use the forces at your command as you deem wise." It was Pershing's prerogative to determine whether the situation was critical. The French and British governments and high commands believed that the emergency was manifest. Pershing did not: "Do not think emergency now exists that would warrant our putting companies or battalions into British or French divisions," he told Baker, "and would not do so except in grave crisis." Pershing was risking that the German offensive would not deliver the fatal blow while he kept his units training under American command. He maintained his position under unrelenting Allied pressure for months to come. When the Allies continued to pressure Wilson, Baker told the president, "We ought to rely upon General Pershing to decide this kind of question, as he is on the ground and sees the needs as they arise."[16]

A snarl of transatlantic cables to and from Washington, London, Paris, and the three Allied field headquarters gave the Allies the impression that Pershing had agreed to send 150 U.S. battalions to the British in exchange for British transport of those units across the Atlantic to France. But Pershing backed out over the question of the availability of British shipping. About this same time General Tasker H. Bliss, a former army chief of staff, arrived in France as American representative to the Supreme War Council (SWC). He studied the situation and quickly came to the conclusion that the crisis was real. Pershing, in turn, suggested that six complete U.S. divisions be seconded to the British. Bliss argued that whole divisions would include only ninety combat battalions, while the rest of the troops would be headquarters, artillery, and support units. He suggested that the two of them submit their positions to Washington for a decision. Pershing rejoined that if they did that, "We would both be relieved . . . and that is exactly what we would deserve." Bliss acceded to Pershing's position. With united support from the two American generals, Lloyd George agreed to transport the six U.S. divisions for inclusion in the British sector, rather than individual battalions. Furthermore, Pershing retained the right to recall those formations any time he deemed appropriate.[17]

In early March the expected German offensive blew a hole in British lines forty miles deep. Pershing agreed to send four American divisions then in France to relieve French units, who would in turn go to the aid of the British. The disaster forced the Allies to agree to something they had theretofore avoided, naming a supreme commander. On March 26, 1918, Marshal Ferdinand Foch of France was given "the coordination of the military operation of the Allied armies on the Western Front." The next week Bliss and Pershing united to press for activation of an American army with its own sector in the line. To that end they insisted that the national armies retain "full control of the tactical employment of their forces." Foch's authority was restricted to "strategic direction of military operations," which came to mean that his power was more one of moral suasion than actual command.[18]

On March 27 the British again requested that American units be fed into Allied units during the emergency as soon as they arrived in France. Pershing responded that he still preferred that they go as complete divisions, saying that they were well enough trained to do so, even though he had insisted on thorough training programs for all divisions in France up to that time. Bliss again disagreed with Pershing, and contributed to a Supreme War Council note placing smaller American units with the Allies, and further recommending that only U.S. infantry and machine gun units be shipped for the rest of the crisis. Baker, who happened to be visiting France at the time, agreed with Bliss and overruled Pershing. To his credit, Pershing went to see the Allied commanders, where he told Foch that the Americans would be honored "to take part in the greatest battle in history." Pershing emotionally said, "Infantry, artillery, aviation, all we have are yours; use them as you wish."[19]

The Allies continued to press. Lloyd George prevailed upon President Wilson to send only infantry and machine-gun units to France, asking for 120,000 soldiers per month from April through July—a total of 480,000 men. The next amalgamation controversy arose over Wilson's failure to prescribe a certain number of battalions or time frame for their deployment, and Lloyd George's deceitful representations that Wilson had done so. To complicate matters further, the French complained that they had been left out of the Anglo-American negotiations. Wilson and the Americans lost trust in Lloyd George, and the president and Baker once again determined to leave the amalgamation question in Pershing's hands.

On 1 May the Supreme War Council, which included Lloyd George, French premier Georges Clemenceau, and Italian premier Vittorio Orlando, met at Abbeville to discuss the continuing crisis. The British thought Pershing was reneging on an agreement to send 480,000 doughboys to their lines. The French thought half those men should reinforce their army. Pershing, having seen too many confusing transatlantic cables, denied that any concrete agreements had been reached and insisted on recognition of an American army under its own commander and flag. All the allies ganged up on Pershing, arguing that the war might be over before a U.S. army was ready to take the field. Finally, Pershing slammed his fist on the table, shouted that he "would not be coerced," and stomped out of the meeting. When he returned the next day, Foch proposed that America ship 120,000 infantrymen and machine gunners in each of the months of May, June, and July. He further suggested that the council should submit this request to President Wilson, going over Pershing's head. Isolated, Pershing agreed to send those units to the French and British in May and June, then to assess the situation before making a decision about July. With minor amendments, and a commitment to recognize an independent American army, the Allies agreed, but none of them was happy. When the Allies then complained about Pershing's obstinacy, Baker prevailed upon Wilson to back his commander. On May 7 Baker cabled Bliss: "I am very glad that we have from the first insisted upon leaving these questions to the discretion of General Pershing, . . . as [he] is the American Commander-in-Chief we must continue to be guided by his judgment of the military exigencies in France." Baker told Pershing that he and Wilson fully trusted his judgment as the commander on the ground, but hoped that he would approach Allied concerns "as sympathetically as possible."[20]

Fully immersed in high-level statecraft with heads of Allied governments, Pershing found that his original ambiguous orders continued to complicate his political position. But he remained fixed on his goal of establishing an independent army.

A month later the Germans were still gaining ground at the second battle of the Marne, and Parisians were evacuating the capital. The French government was packing up to move as well. A few miles away at Versailles the SWC and heads of government met again, going over the same ground they had covered in May. Foch asked Pershing if he was willing to risk the Allies being pushed back to the Loire. Pershing said he was. "Well," said Lloyd George, "we will refer this to your president." Pershing retorted, "Refer it to the president and be damned. I know what the president will do. He will simply refer it back to me." As it happened, the Allies were even then blunting the German offensive, and American troops were arriving much faster than anticipated. The United States landed 250,000 troops in June, for a total of 900,000, far more than they had estimated a year earlier—almost the million Pershing had requested—and five months ahead of their own schedule. Pershing felt more able to accede to Foch's requests for assistance, and after the German offensive failed in the face of a Franco-American counterattack,

Foch ordered formation of the U.S. First Army in late July. The amalgamation controversy was over.[21]

Pershing was proud of his accomplishments, but so far his major victories had been over his allies, not the Germans. Furthermore, his attitude toward the Allies, especially the heads of government, showed that his civilian superiors had delegated far too much authority in the political realm to their commander in the field.[22]

Between German casualties and American arrivals, the Allies began to enjoy a numerical advantage that soon grew large enough to warrant planning a war-winning counteroffensive. The German offensives had created bulges in the front that the Allies began to eliminate in the middle of July. German forces fell back under heavy pressure, and Field Marshal Erich Ludendorff called August 8, 1918, "the black day of the German army." The main American contribution—under their own commander and flag—came on the right of the Allied line at Saint-Mihiel and the Meuse-Argonne. As the Germans retreated, the Allies began planning for victory.[23]

When the United States entered the war, Wilson had insisted that it had done so as an associated, not an Allied power. His purpose was to retain flexibility to broker a peace. Therefore, he refused to allow Pershing to attend Allied conferences, which put Pershing in a most difficult position as he tried to coordinate with the Allies. It was not until the fall of 1917 when the Allies agreed to create a Supreme War Council that Wilson changed his mind. He and Baker dispatched General Bliss to France as the American representative in January 1918.[24]

That same month Wilson gave the most important speech of his presidency when he outlined American and, he hoped, Allied war aims. He articulated what came to be known as the Fourteen Points. The first five were sweeping aspirations:

    I. Open covenants of peace, openly arrived at . . .
    II. Absolute freedom of navigation upon the seas . . .
    III. The removal, so far as possible, of all economic barriers . . . among all the nations consenting to the peace . . .
    IV. Adequate guarantees . . . that national armaments will be reduced to the lowest point consistent with domestic safety . . .

V. A free, open-minded, and absolutely impartial adjustment of
all colonial claims . . . [in which] the interests of the populations concerned must have equal weight.

Wilson followed these with several specific territorial goals, the gist of
which was to maintain historic national frontiers and self-determination
to the extent possible. The final point was his call for a worldwide league
of nations: "A general association of nations must be formed under specific covenants for the purpose of affording mutual guarantees of political independence and territorial integrity to great and small states alike."
Wilson's breathtaking purposes were equal treatment of all peoples and
nations and removal of the causes for future war. On that basis, he said,
the American people were "ready to devote their lives, their honor, and
everything that they possess." The speech was a detailed explication of
"peace without victory," and it remained fully in force as American policy later that year when the Germans began to request armistice terms on
the basis of the Fourteen Points.[25]

Wilson responded with a series of notes to the Germans, whose government was collapsing, applauding their acceptance of the Fourteen
Points, but insisting that he deal with a government that could speak for
the German people. American midterm elections were a month away,
and political reaction was swift and negative. Roosevelt and Lodge were
demanding unconditional surrender and a crushing victory. The Senate
passed a resolution calling for German disarmament and the payment of
reparations. Senate Democrat Henry Ashurst privately told Wilson that if
he did not follow the wishes of the people, "you are destroyed." Wilson
angrily said, "I am willing if I can serve the country to go into a cellar
and read poetry for the remainder of my life." Then, in a comment that
revealed a great deal of confusion, he said he was not making armistices,
which should be the purview of commanders in the field. Presumably,
Wilson meant that he was looking beyond the armistice toward the peace
treaty talks that would follow.

Later that day, in a move that complicated matters further, he dispatched his closest adviser, Edward M. House, to Europe as his personal
representative to the SWC as they discussed the armistice. "I have not
given you any instructions," he told House, "because I feel you will know
what to do."[26]

Baker loyally supported his president. In an October 21 White House
meeting, the secretary overruled his stateside military advisers, who were

also calling for harsh terms, insisting Pershing be allowed to negotiate the armistice. Yet he also wrote a memorandum on behalf of Wilson instructing that the armistice be settled along the terms of the Fourteen Points, to which the Germans seemed to be agreeing. Baker wanted a quick end to the war on Wilson's terms, but his actions also confused matters.[27]

Pershing was still heavily focused on the fighting in front of him. The Meuse-Argonne offensive was not going nearly as well in his sector as he hoped, and he wanted a few more weeks to ensure that the Germans were thoroughly beaten. For that reason, he inclined toward unconditional surrender. House had not yet arrived on October 25 when Pershing cabled Wilson with a seven-item proposal with "no tendency toward leniency." Along with surrendering their weapons, ceasing hostilities, and repatriating foreign nationals, he wanted the Germans to evacuate past the Rhine, to surrender all their U-boats and their bases. The proposal was not unconditional, but it was certainly harsh.[28]

Baker consulted with Wilson and replied saying the president was "relying upon your counsel and advice in this matter, and . . . he will be glad to have you feel entirely free to bring to his attention any consideration he may have overlooked." Baker then offered caveats that limited five of Pershing's seven terms. The president wanted terms that would end hostilities, but not so stiff as to be humiliating, "as such terms would throw the advantage to the military party in Germany." He asked Pershing to confer with House, who would soon be arriving in France.[29]

Pershing had contracted influenza and was confined to bed and unable to confer when House arrived. Pershing sent a note to the SWC, copying House, laying out arguments for unconditional surrender, contrary to what he had told the president a few days earlier and the instructions he had just received. He seems to have taken "relying upon your counsel" to mean that he was at liberty to change directions. Lloyd George and Clemenceau were incensed when they read the note, the former commenting that its contents were "political, not military." House was likewise concerned, and began to think that Pershing was positioning himself for a 1920 presidential bid. He, too, felt that Pershing had crossed the line into political matters that only heads of government, and House, as Wilson's representative, should address.[30]

News of Pershing's position exploded in Washington. Baker, Pershing's steadfast supporter, told Wilson, "He is obviously on record one way with you and another way with the Supreme War Council! It is really tragic." Pershing protested that Baker's cable had left him "entirely free" to raise other matters. Baker felt strongly that "a bad matter is made much worse by this cablegram." He drafted for Wilson a letter of reprimand to send to Pershing, but the president decided to let the matter drop, expecting House to work things out. Pershing was soon up and around, and he apologized to House for not having consulted and for sending his document to the SWC. The two men put the matter to rest.[31]

The war ended the next week when the Germans accepted the harsh surrender terms Foch presented to them.

In 1917 America once again mobilized for war, this time in fulfillment of its obligations as a great power, much as Roosevelt and Root had foreseen. The army general staff grew to over one thousand officers who developed war plans, a conscription and voluntary enlistment regime, a training base, a matériel procurement system, and a deployment schedule. They also participated in broader plans to mobilize the national industrial base. From April 1, 1917, to Armistice Day nineteen months later, the army grew from 133,111 soldiers to a strength of 3,685,458, more than a sixteen-fold increase. In November 1918 the U.S. Army in France consisted of seven corps comprising twenty-nine combat divisions, a badly needed infusion of power that was sufficient to enable the Allied forces to win the Great War. A total of 1.3 million Americans served in France. U.S. forces provided the margin of victory on the western front.[32]

Pershing had deployed to France with ambiguous instructions: to keep his army together and to help the Allies as circumstances warranted. Yet he sailed with a broad mandate from the president to use his discretion. Wilson and Baker promised to back him, and they almost always did. The paradox, given Wilson's early belief in a wall between policy and strategy, was that his hands-off wartime leadership, almost an abrogation of authority, left Pershing supreme in both realms through most of the war.

Pershing worked under tremendous pressure to build and train his army, to organize it into combat formations, to supply it across three thousand miles of ocean and several hundred miles of mud. He had tactical, operational, strategic command, as well as acting as the senior American in Allied councils that frequently put him in negotiation with the prime ministers of Great Britain, France, and Italy, as well as his fellow commanders. He acquiesced in amalgamation from time to time, but only under tremendous pressure and after a donnybrook in the SWC. He leaned heavily toward keeping the American forces together and finally succeeded. Pershing's accomplishments were monumental. Tireless, optimistic, relentless, and uncompromising, he built from scratch an army of 1.3 million, over thirteen times the size of the Army of the Potomac. At last, the success of American arms went a long distance toward giving the president what he wanted, a powerful seat at the Versailles peace conference where he could negotiate a new world order based on his vision of an end to human conflict.

The controversies with Allies were not the only conflicts Pershing faced. When Bliss came to France, Peyton C. March took his place as army chief of staff. Driven, efficient, tactless—in other words, a man very much in the Pershing mold—March "took the War Department like a dog takes a cat by the neck, and he shook it." And although he had been subordinate to Pershing in France, he had no qualms about asserting his prerogatives as chief of staff. March and Pershing clashed repeatedly over promotions, rotation policy, the number of divisions that would be needed in France, and even about officers wearing the Sam Browne belt, an accoutrement that Pershing favored and March did not. But the crux of their dispute was over who was superior to whom. Pershing thought along the lines of the Grant-Halleck model, with March as a loyal helpmeet. March asserted General Order Number 80, which reiterated the principles of Root's General Staff Act that made the chief of staff the army's senior officer. Baker never resolved the controversy, considering it a mere technical matter, and in fact the two generals cooperated more than they competed. The matter only came to resolution after the war when Pershing succeeded March, and forthwith asserted the seniority of the army chief of staff.[33]

Pershing brought the same hard-driving traits to his role as a coalition partner. With no civilian superior in France, he played to the hilt his part as the senior American in the councils of war. More than once he stood up to the combined pressure of all his Allied partners, generals and heads of government alike. With very little interference, sometimes little guidance from Washington, Pershing became accustomed to his role as both political and military leader in the theater of war. About the only times his writ was not supreme were when Baker or House happened to be visiting. His superiors should not have been surprised that Pershing flexed his policy muscles when it came time to craft an armistice.

Pershing's command in the Great War bequeathed two models of political-military relations for the next generation. His protégé George C. Marshall followed Pershing's example of harmonious relations with his civilian superiors, loyally supporting them in public, giving his best advice without reservation in private. Douglas MacArthur, an assistant division commander in the AEF, learned a different lesson, the notion that the commander in the field should not negotiate with his superiors, indeed should brook no interference from them. When MacArthur became army chief of staff in 1930s, an army manual defined policy and strategy as "radically and fundamentally things apart. . . . Strategy begins where politics end."[34] There matters stood as Hitler rearmed Germany and Japan menaced Asia.

8

It was mid-November 1938. Brigadier General George C. Marshall had found a seat "way off to the side" of the Oval Office meeting. He was relatively junior in this company, which, in addition to President Franklin Delano Roosevelt, included several high-ranking administration figures from the Treasury, Justice and War Departments. Harry Hopkins was there, seemingly more in his role as political adviser than as head of the Works Progress Administration (the others were unaware that FDR had recently sent him on a tour of U.S. aircraft factories). Six weeks earlier British prime minister Neville Chamberlain had capitulated to Adolf Hitler's demands in the Sudetenland, then announced that he had secured "peace in our time." FDR was sympathetic. He believed that Nazi air power had put the British and their French allies in a hopeless negotiating position. Therefore, Roosevelt convened his senior advisers to tell them that he had decided to ask Congress for a program to build ten thousand aircraft, an air armada to protect North and South America from Axis attacks. What he did not say aloud was that he intended to ship many of the new planes across the Atlantic to the British and French air forces.

Marshall silently noted that the president was doing almost all of the talking and that no one was questioning him. As the army's deputy chief of staff Marshall knew that the president had no plans to recruit and train additional pilots or to procure munitions for the aircraft. After his summation, FDR canvassed the room, harvesting mumbled concurrences for his proposal, finally landing on Marshall. Flashing his trademark smile, Roosevelt boomed out his request for Marshall's approval, "Don't you think so, George?" Marshall found the president's pretension of familiarity presumptuous and his demand for unanimity arrogant. Stiffly but politely he replied, "I am sorry, Mr. President, but I don't agree with that at all." FDR looked shocked and abruptly adjourned the meeting. As they stepped outside, Marshall's colleagues shook his hand and wished him well, thinking he had just ended his career.[1]

Six months later, FDR reached past thirty-four senior generals to tap Marshall as army chief of staff. If the president had been offended by Marshall's bluntness, he put such feelings aside in favor of naming a general who would tell him the truth as he saw it. Roosevelt, who was capable on the one hand of seeing the gathering war as a global political phenomenon, was also liable to concoct strategies and devise procurement plans that were little short of harebrained from a military standpoint. On the other side, Marshall could quickly see the flaw in the president's scheme to build ten thousand planes without pilots or bombs, but he was slower to appreciate the presidential tacking that FDR thought necessary to keep the electorate behind him while he quietly mobilized for war. In the years before Pearl Harbor, the president navigated between a solidly isolationist American public and increasingly potent threats overseas. He both led the electorate and followed public opinion, trusting in political instincts that were as keen as any president ever possessed, yet far from infallible. FDR painstakingly maneuvered America through an unpredictable series of strategic shocks that transformed popular attitudes and psychologically prepared the nation for a war that he had long known to be inevitable. Marshall shared that sense of impending war, but as a professional soldier he focused on the military necessity of making the small and under-equipped United States Army ready to fight. Marshall and his fellow chiefs disagreed with FDR on a number of strategic decisions—Lend-Lease aid to the British and the Soviets; the decision to invade North Africa, thereby postponing a cross-channel offensive into Europe; the relative priority to be given to European versus Pacific and South Asian operations, to name a few. But the crux of their conflict was that the professional military always sought more clarity in both policy and strategic objectives, while Roosevelt continuously adhered to a few broad principles, keeping his options open and allowing events to shape his decisions, as he believed they inevitably must.

The Roosevelt-Marshall relationship was often tense and frustrating, but it became more and more effective over time, largely through the agency of Harry Hopkins, a liberal New Dealer with no military background. A tireless domestic policy adviser, Hopkins taught himself to be a strategic assistant to a wartime president. Fiercely loyal to both men, he taught Marshall and Roosevelt to understand and trust one another, but not before their disparate natures collided in a political-military conflict over the most fundamental Allied war aims in the Second World War.

Ultimately, FDR, Marshall, and Hopkins renegotiated the political-military dynamic in America. In the late 1930s the army and navy were unprepared for the war to come. The services fought with each other for scarce resources and often had diametrically opposed strategic views and plans. They had little influence on foreign policy. By the end of the war, all that had changed. By 1945 the Joint Chiefs of Staff eclipsed the State Department and their own civilian superiors in terms of their influence with the president, their mastery of global strategy, and their disposition of national resources. FDR personally granted this influence to the Joint Chiefs of Staff but, much to their consternation, never clearly or officially. Yet after the war the idiosyncratic arrangements that the president, Marshall, and Hopkins had worked out were largely codified in law and practice as America built a "national security state."

During his first term as president, Franklin Delano Roosevelt focused on domestic matters, feverishly building the New Deal to save the nation from the Great Depression. Roosevelt's priorities reflected the concerns of the American people, whose confidence had been badly shaken by the economic crisis. Turning inward, a majority of Americans embraced a relatively new form of public sentiment, isolationism. Isolationists came from all parts of the political spectrum, and while they differed on other issues, they shared several assumptions about foreign affairs. They made no moral distinctions among other nations. Americans had long seen Europe as a cockpit of never-ending war, and most felt U.S. intervention in the Great War had been a mistake. Unable to solve its economic problems at home, the United States could do little good overseas. Moreover, foreign problems did not threaten American security. Isolationists were not passive; they pressured the government to forswear overseas involvement. In 1935 Roosevelt felt compelled to sign a Neutrality Act, which placed a mandatory embargo on arms sales to all foreign belligerents. As the 1936 election neared, FDR signed an extension of the original law. That year alone an estimated half million antiwar students protested on college campuses around the country. In February 1937 a poll concluded that 95 percent of Americans agreed that the nation should never participate in any future war. Wilsonian internationalism was dormant.[2]

After his reelection, FDR's political agenda changed little at first, but as German rearmament and Japanese incursions into China raised alarms, he began to devote increasing attention to the army and navy. In 1936 he had enhanced the service chiefs' authority, giving them control of their general staffs and full command over their fleet and field forces. He began reviewing military readiness and scrutinizing war plans. FDR shared the public's aversion to war, but he had to walk a tightrope, trying to deter aggression without exciting isolationist fears. He developed a principle that would guide much of his strategic thought in the years to come—the best way to keep the United States out of war was to assist America's friends without appearing to intervene in international disputes.[3]

In September 1938 Hitler shocked the international system. At a conference in Munich with British and French leaders, the Nazi dictator demanded and received the cession of the Sudetenland from Czechoslovakia. The agreement satisfied no one, not even Hitler (who had hoped to provoke war), but from the Allied perspective it seemed a small price to pay for peace. FDR concluded that Hitler was a "wild man" who could not be trusted and was likely bent on expansionist war. Roosevelt changed course, deciding to seek both repeal of the Neutrality Act and a vast increase in aircraft production, hoping to sell planes to Britain and France for their looming war with Germany. Yet while Munich jolted FDR and his administration, it failed to register with the isolationist American electorate. Politically weakened by his Supreme Court–packing scheme, Roosevelt lost many Democratic allies in the November elections. Congress refused to act on his proposals.[4]

In 1938 FDR's most trusted adviser and political fixer, WPA administrator and soon-to-be secretary of commerce Harry Hopkins, began to shift his focus from domestic to foreign policy issues in keeping with his chief's concerns. The president sent him on a secret tour of West Coast aircraft factories. When he returned, Hopkins sent word to the army that its budget was likely to increase and he would like a meeting with the chief of staff or his deputy. Shortly thereafter Hopkins encountered Brigadier General Marshall during the latter's Oval Office "disagreement" with FDR. A shrewd staffer advised Marshall that "the entry to the President is through Mr. Hopkins." So, in December Marshall paid Hopkins a call, a meeting that marked the beginning of their long and fruitful friendship.[5]

In late 1938 FDR and his military advisers shared a view that war was on the horizon. They differed over how to prepare for it. The president saw the European democracies as "the first line of defense." If they could defeat fascism, America need not get involved in the war. Thus, it made sense, especially in light of popular isolationism, to provide material support to Great Britain and France. The army and navy chiefs, responsible for equipping their own services, did not share Roosevelt's opinion. They were not at all sure that Western Europeans could stand against Hitler and Mussolini. If they could not, every truck and plane sent to them was a wasted asset. Moreover, if and when the allies failed, the American army and navy would have to be ready to fight the Axis, and that was something for which they were then unprepared. Mobilizing for the coming war would tax the nation's human and material capacities to their limits. America, the chiefs believed, had nothing to spare.

The chiefs were not simply being pessimistic; they had done the analysis. Since the Great War the services' war plans divisions and the Joint Board had developed a series of contingency plans for wars against potential enemies east or west. One prescient plan posited a two-front, two-ocean war. In such a scenario, planners agreed, the United States would initially defend in the Eastern Hemisphere until it had won the Atlantic war, then shift back to the Pacific. Years in preparation and revision, these plans were comprehensive in scope and detailed down several echelons of command, including the demands of manpower, matériel, logistics, and fleets and armies necessary to vanquish the putative foe.[6] Within the army and the navy the continuous thinking and rethinking that such work demanded honed strategic planning capabilities that mark the zenith of professional military expertise.

The Munich crisis spurred planners to revise their scenarios because their assumptions of nearly two decades were no longer realistic. Britain was surely no threat, but Germany and Italy were, and a coalition comprising Germany, Italy, and Japan would be formidable indeed. Moreover, the United States might have to face those hosts in radically variant situations: either alone, or in alliance with Britain, France, and others.[7]

On September 1, 1939, Germany invaded Poland. Six months earlier, after Hitler abrogated the Munich agreement and marched into Czechoslovakia, Great Britain and France had vowed to defend Poland. They had been dumbstruck when Germany and the Soviet Union announced a nonaggression pact in August. Now they would be pushed no further. Both countries declared war on Nazi Germany, and the Second World War began in Europe. Bound by the Neutrality Act, FDR shut off American aid to all belligerents, but he told the people that the war would surely affect them: "When peace has been broken anywhere, peace of all countries everywhere is in danger." While declaring neutrality and a limited national emergency, he, unlike Woodrow Wilson, could not ask Americans to "remain neutral in thought." Poland fell on October 6, 1939.[8]

Coming a year after Munich, this second international shock began to awaken the American people. While they yet hoped to remain neutral, the invasions of Czechoslovakia and Poland and the Soviet-German pact aroused popular fears for U.S. security and sympathy for the invaded peoples and their French and British champions.[9]

On the day Germany invaded Poland, FDR named Admiral Harold K. "Betty" Stark as chief of naval operations and General George C. Marshall as army chief of staff. Marshall's elevation was something of a surprise: he was relatively junior and had famously disagreed with FDR in the Oval Office a year earlier. Marshall had wanted the job, but was careful to do nothing that would appear to be campaigning for it, unlike others, such as General Hugh Drum. "Drum, Drum, Drum," lamented FDR at one point, "I wish he would stop playing his own drum!" Instead, Hopkins privately sang Marshall's praises to the president, an advocacy that Marshall believed was largely responsible for his nomination. In April 1939 the president secretly summoned the general to the White House to tell him of his selection. Characteristically, Marshall told FDR that he "wanted the right to say what I think and it would often be unpleasing." The president agreed. Marshall refused to let his commander in chief off so easily: "You said *yes* pleasantly, but it may be unpleasant."[10] In a sentence Marshall encapsulated the future of their relationship.

A few months earlier Roosevelt had brought the Joint Board and the army-navy munitions board into the newly created Executive Office of the President. With that act he greatly increased the powers of the service chiefs and centralized military command under himself. The army chief of staff and the chief of naval operations now reported directly to the president, making them his personal military advisers. Moreover, FDR became the "sole coordinating link" between foreign policy and military strategy. He was now, in effect, his own secretary of state, secretary of war, and secretary of the navy. The incumbents in those positions were marginalized. Soon, they would be deleted from the distribution lists for important strategic papers. On the other hand, Harry Hopkins quietly became, as one historian put it, "an invisible member of the Joint Chiefs, indeed of the Combined Chiefs of Staff."[11]

That untidy blurring of bureaucratic lines perfectly suited Roosevelt. His methods appeared chaotic, but were merely idiosyncratic. He thought of himself as a "juggler," an improviser capable of keeping any number of balls in the air: "I never let my right hand know what my left hand does." He could be secretive and duplicitous. "I may have one policy for Europe and one diametrically opposite for North and South America. I may be entirely inconsistent, and furthermore I am perfectly willing to mislead and tell untruths if it will help to win the war." He liked his official relationships to be personal, not institutional. He resisted regular meetings with his chiefs, but saw them as often as he liked, together or individually, as the need struck him. The chiefs continually asked him for a formal charter, which he continually refused to grant. He asked for and received their candid advice on both political and military matters, and he felt free to overrule them on both political and military grounds. He detested organizational charts and strictly hierarchical chains of command. He reveled in creating offices with overlapping responsibilities, thus setting his subordinates at odds with each other. Moreover, FDR would allow no written record of his discussions. Marshall once brought a staff officer "with a big notebook" to the Oval Office, and "the president blew up." They tried again at the next meeting, but that time the notebook was "so little he couldn't use it." Marshall had to give up on note taking.

Bringing the service chiefs into his inner circle was in keeping with FDR's modus operandi: the brass reported to him *and* their service secretaries, and confusion was inevitable. Yet the president was not lacking in skills: after six years as architect of the New Deal with its alphabet soup of agencies, he thoroughly grasped the capabilities and limitations of bureaucracy. He recoiled at being confronted with binary, "either/or" decisions. His long political career had taught him to keep his options open as long as possible. He preferred to bide his time, to commit to decisions only when absolutely necessary. Indeed, he knew that one way to decide is not to decide. Moreover, if his subordinates were in conflict with one another, they would always have to appeal to him for decisions, bringing a range of alternatives from which he would be free to choose, or not. FDR had more respect for the logic of events, which might open his options as well as close them, than for the prescriptions of planning.[12]

Thus, the president viewed the services' contingency planning not as a prudent hedge against the future, but as an institutional gambit to box him in. He refused to issue the kind of clear policy guidance that military planners craved. He balked at approving strategic plans, or to be bound by their assumptions or prescriptions, but happily latched onto the parts he liked while ignoring the rest. He also had a worrisome habit of thinking aloud about possible strategic initiatives: "Roosevelt had a habit of tossing out new operations," Marshall later recollected; "I called it his cigarette lighter gesture." Needless to say, the service chiefs often thought the president feckless. His seeming indecision frustrated them and made their war preparations more complex. Yet FDR affected not to care about their difficulties. Keeping his options open made the president's world leadership challenges a bit easier, and that was the point.[13]

The president, a former assistant secretary of the navy, had more affinity for and paid more attention to the maritime services than the army. He meddled in naval affairs, selecting officers for promotion and command and moving ships from one theater to another at his whim. He was far less interested in and attentive to the army. As a result, Marshall had a freer hand than his naval counterpart, but he continually had to fight for resources that the navy received as a matter of course. In one of his few recorded attempts at levity with FDR, Marshall once asked the president if he would stop referring to the navy as "us" and the army as "them."[14]

FDR was among the most gifted American politicians of his or any generation. Moreover, years of presidential experience during a wrenching worldwide depression had taught him to think globally and to be comfortable in his role as a world political leader. As he prepared for war, he faced conflicting responsibilities—he needed to deter war, to assist his allies in prosecuting a likely war, to prepare the nation's armed forces for war, and to get the American people ready for the possibility of war. Moreover, Roosevelt had to juggle these aims knowing that his second term would end in January 1941. Thus, in addition to his other burdens, FDR had to decide whether to run for a third term, breaking a hallowed precedent established by George Washington. The challenges that Marshall and his naval counterparts faced were as complex as any military problems in American history, but they were relatively straightforward in comparison with Roosevelt's range of responsibilities.

With Hopkins's support, Marshall slowly learned how to deal with Roosevelt. His first and possibly mistaken principle was to maintain social distance from the president. The general never "dropped by" the White House at cocktail hour as so many of Roosevelt's intimates did. He declined invitations to Hyde Park and Warm Springs. Bluntly parrying the most notable weapon in the Rooseveltian arsenal, Marshall pointedly refused to laugh at the president's jokes. By remaining aloof, Marshall felt that he was protecting himself from the charms of Roosevelt the raconteur, and he probably succeeded in keeping the president on topic, a task at which so many others failed. He kept the relationship on a strictly professional level. He never faced a morning in which he had to retract a commitment made over a convivial dinner the night before. Despite such stiffness, Marshall tried to win the president's confidence through demonstrated loyalty and absolute candor in private. He spoke to FDR forthrightly but dispassionately. "I never haggled with the president," he later recalled. "I swallowed the little things so I could go to bat on the big ones." Still, it took FDR some time to warm up to Marshall, and the general labored long to gain the president's full support in building the army for war.[15]

Marshall studied how the president's mind worked. When FDR was planning a trip to the infantry school at Fort Benning, Georgia, in late 1939, Marshall sent the school commandant instructions that encapsulated much of what he was learning about FDR's mental habits. Give him "one sheet of paper," Marshall advised, "with all high-sounding language eliminated, and with very pertinent paragraphed underlined headings. . . . A little sketch of ordinary page size is probably the most effective method, as he is quickly bored by papers, by lengthy discussions, and by anything short of a few pungent sentences of description. You have to engage his interest, and then it knows no limit."[16] George Marshall thought in prose, one well-supported sentence flowing into another, trip-hammers driving to a logical conclusion. Franklin Roosevelt thought intuitively, giving his imagination free rein to gather insights from a range of sources—from childhood memories to cocktail conversations to opposition newspapers—combining all to reach a creative, even artistic, solution. Each man's process worked—for him. Marshall was among the most effective military planners and organizers in history. Likewise, FDR had no peer as a political strategist. Yet Marshall was subordinate and self-effacing and canny enough to understand that he would have to adjust his way of seeing the world to Roosevelt's, not the other way around. He violated that principle on only one occasion, bringing on the political-military crisis of the war.

For all his correctness in dealing with Roosevelt, Marshall was no political naïf. He carefully cultivated allies, including Treasury Secretary Henry Morgenthau, presidential confidant and industrialist Bernard Baruch, and in 1940, Secretary of War Henry Stimson. At Morgenthau's request, Marshall briefed him on the army's extensive needs for mobilization. Morgenthau listened and confessed that the enormity of the problem made him "dizzy," but he arranged a meeting with the president for the general to make his case. Likewise, Marshall frequently sent aides to New York to listen to Baruch's views on the military, and flew Baruch to various army posts to review training. All these men became Marshall votaries who happily and deftly assisted the chief of staff in carrying his arguments to the president. None, however, was more important than Hopkins, the driven, chronically ill jack-of-all trades and, many critics said, evil genius of the Roosevelt administration. Hopkins knew the workings of the presidential mind intimately. He knew precisely when to press and what kind of argument to make in order to sway the commander in chief. Whenever Marshall "hit a tough knot," he later remembered, he would call upon Hopkins to arrange a meeting with FDR. In a number of private sessions with just the chief of staff and the president, Hopkins was an inveterate and reliable sponsor for Marshall's point of view: "He was always the strong advocate, it seemed to me, of almost everything I proposed, and it required quite a bit of explanation [to make] the President see that the set-up could not be handled [as] he sometimes suggested." Marshall felt that Hopkins was "courageous" in his advocacy and "quite invaluable to me." Marshall recalled that "I couldn't get at the President with the frequency he could, nothing like it, nor could I be as frank nor could I be as understanding." Hopkins made "the military position . . . plainer to the President than I could possibly have done myself." The Hopkins-Marshall partnership was one of the least heralded but most influential relationships of the war.[17]

An unexpected Marshall strength was the influence he gained on Capitol Hill. Members of Congress quickly came to trust him, partly because of his air of command and well-earned reputation for integrity, but largely because he had no personal agenda or political aspirations. When asked about his politics he would reply, "My father was a Democrat, my mother a Republican, and I am an Episcopalian." He sometimes deprecated his ability to communicate with Congress, but influential members would have none of it. Senate Appropriations Committee chairman Alva Adams once teased him that "you came before the committee without even a piece of paper and got every damned thing you asked for." Speaker of the House Sam Rayburn said Marshall was the most effective committee witness he had ever seen: "When he takes the witness stand, we forget whether we are Republicans or Democrats. We just remember that we are in the presence of a man who is telling the truth, as he sees it, about the problems he is discussing." Marshall's expertise, judgment, and patriotism were beyond question. Both Congress and the president trusted his integrity and loyalty.[18] Still, Marshall was a canny operator, as he showed when analyzing his own influence on the Hill: "If Republicans could assure their constituency that they were doing it on my suggestion and not on Mr. Roosevelt's suggestion, they could go ahead and back the thing. He had such enemies that otherwise the member of Congress didn't dare seem to line up with him. And that was true of certain Democrats who were getting pretty bitter."[19] Marshall never used his influence to go around FDR, even when they disagreed, as they often did over army appropriations. Instead, Marshall employed his credibility in pursuit of administration policies regardless of his personal views. His clout on the Hill aroused the president's jealousy, but Marshall began to gain Roosevelt's trust because he was a team player for the executive branch and the war effort. As a result, for all his political savvy, Marshall rose above politics.[20]

During his first several months as army chief of staff Marshall tried without much success to persuade the president to increase army manpower and to provide more funds for equipment and training. The fall of Poland was enough to prod Congress into passing a "cash-and-carry" bill allowing the Western allies to buy armaments in the United States and transport them in their own ships. Yet as months went by without further Nazi aggression, the nation lost its sense of insecurity. If war came, traditional thinking held, citizen-soldiers would rally to the colors as they had always done, and American "know-how" would rapidly put weapons in their hands. Marshall failed to persuade the president merely to increase the actual strength of the army to levels authorized back in 1920—280,000 soldiers in the regular army and a similar number in the national guard. Instead, he had to make do with 227,000 regulars and 235,000 national guardsmen and small budgets for their training and armament. In April the House Appropriations Committee voted to *cut* the armed forces budget almost 10 percent.[21]

The "phony war" ended in the spring of 1940 as German forces invaded Norway, the Low Countries, and France. Hitler had accomplished in three months what his Great War predecessors had failed to achieve in four years. Americans were shocked. This time, Nazi aggression shook the American public and made them feel truly vulnerable. It was a popular watershed. For the first time since the Great War private citizens organized to pressure the government to rearm.[22]

Having dithered during the long months since the fall of Poland, FDR sprang into action. Two years earlier he had called for ten thousand military aircraft; he now demanded a seemingly impossible fifty thousand. He sacked his inconsequential service secretaries and replaced them with two Republican elder statesmen. Henry Stimson, former secretary of war and secretary of state, resumed his old post at the War Department, and Frank Knox, a former Rough Rider, Chicago publisher, and 1936 vice presidential candidate, became secretary of the navy. These selections made the cabinet all but a national unity government and the most bipartisan presidential team since the Washington administration, before the advent of formal parties. Despite the unprecedented arrangements that cut them out of the chain of command, the secretaries were useful administrators and Stimson an especially effective ally for Marshall and adviser to FDR. Having secured his political flank, the president had Hopkins manage the Democratic National Convention, where he engineered a "We Want Roosevelt" demonstration that "forced" FDR to answer the call to duty and stand for a third term.[23]

Marshall, too, recognized the opportunity that the fall of France presented. Aiming to reinstate the budget that Congress had cut in April, Marshall enlisted the help of Treasury Secretary Morgenthau in May. As the Nazis overran Belgium and the Netherlands, Marshall briefed a plan to the president to restore the army to its authorized strength of 280,000 by September, and to expand it to 750,000 complete with equipment by September 1941. The price tag was $657 million. The ineffectual Harry Woodring, in his last days in office as war secretary, sat mute. Morgenthau supported Marshall in the face of FDR's attempts to dominate the conversation, a standard ploy when the president didn't want to have a discussion about a controversial topic. When Morgenthau pressed the case, the president sniffed, "Well, you filed your protest," and began waving his advisers out of the office. However, Morgenthau had encouraged Marshall to "stand right up and tell him what you think and stand right there. There are too few people who do it and he likes it." Morgenthau asked the president to hear Marshall out. FDR smiled, "I know exactly what he would say. There is no necessity for me to hear him at all." In a controlled fury Marshall strode across the room, stared down at the wheelchair-bound Roosevelt, and asked, "Mr. President, may I have three minutes?" FDR's mood changed in an instant, and he graciously said, "Of course, General Marshall." The chief of staff rapidly and precisely detailed the army's urgent needs. "If you don't do something . . . and do it right away," he finished, "I don't know what is going to happen to this country." Astonished and impressed, the president gave Marshall part of what he wanted in the administration's request to Congress, and promised to deliver more in an executive order. Then he asked Marshall to return with a complete list of the army's requirements. Marshall believed this meeting broke the logjam in preparation for war. In April, he had labored in vain to restore $18 million to his budget. After this tense Oval Office interview, FDR asked Congress for a defense increase of $1 billion.[24]

Of course, not everything went Marshall's way. Winston Churchill became British prime minister as France was falling. Before long Churchill and FDR began forming the most crucial personal relationship of the war. Soon, over the protests of his military advisers, the president was insisting on all-out assistance to Great Britain. In the autumn as Nazi warplanes were attacking England, Roosevelt and Churchill concluded a "destroyers for bases" deal in which the United States gained use of several British naval bases in exchange for fifty destroyers. A few months earlier Congress had explicitly banned arms transfers unless the chief of naval operations and the army chief of staff certified that the matériel was obsolete and not "essential" for American defense. That provision put Marshall and Admiral Stark in an untenable position—Marshall later opined that requiring such a certification from a service chief was unconstitutional: "for a subordinate of the commander-in-chief to be able to tell him what he can or can't do is kind of ridiculous." How could the service chiefs prove that sending weapons abroad to shore up Allied defenses was less essential than keeping them for use in an American war that had yet to be declared? One army planner, Major Walter Bedell Smith, put the case pungently: "If we were required to mobilize after having released guns necessary for this [British] mobilization and were found to be short . . . everyone who was a party to the deal might hope to be hanging from a lamp post."[25] Yet Marshall found ways to support the president's policy while maintaining his own integrity. Indeed, he went out of his way to aid the Allies so long as he could do so without shortchanging the equipping of the United States Army.

FDR did not hesitate to overrule his military advisers on strategic matters. Against their misgivings he increased economic and diplomatic pressure on Japan, ratcheting up the possibility of a Pacific war. He rejected the chiefs' advice to move part of the Pacific Fleet to the Atlantic for defense against the German threat. Instead, he ordered the fleet from the California coast to Pearl Harbor. The fleet commander objected so vehemently that Roosevelt sacked him. The Pacific Fleet was necessary for deterrence, FDR said, for sending a signal to the Japanese that the United States was serious in its diplomatic negotiations. Stark privately considered such presidential orders "childish," and one naval planner said that the CNO spent much of 1940 "knocking down harebrained schemes of the president."[26]

Fed up, Stark drafted a memorandum for FDR in late October 1940, hoping to elicit clear policy guidance for strategic planning. After carefully outlining and then logically dispensing with three alternatives—Plan A, hemispheric defense and war avoidance; Plan B, preparing equally for war in the Atlantic and the Pacific while sending maximum military assistance to the Allies; and Plan C, preparing for a strategic offensive in the Pacific—Stark chose a fourth, Plan D or Dog, which insisted on the imperative of Great Britain's survival as a crucial member of the alliance, the necessity of defeating Germany first and probably with a land campaign in Europe, and defending in the Pacific until the German surrender, then defeating Japan. After some negotiation, Marshall offered his "general agreement" with the plan, while taking exception to any mention of war in the Pacific. Nonetheless, Stark's memo deftly fused policy and strategy, secured army-navy agreement, and linked American war aims to Great Britain's survival without making them hostage to Britain's strategic intentions. Stark and Marshall worked together to gain approval of Plan Dog. Stimson and Knox quickly signed on, but Secretary of State Cordell Hull refused, insisting that it would be inappropriate for him to endorse a "technical military statement." True to form, FDR refused to commit to any decisions that might limit his future political options. He neither approved nor disapproved the plan, merely voicing his agreement with some parts—the defensive in the Pacific and a call for combined staff talks with the British chiefs—and disagreement with others, namely U.S. entry into the war and the Germany-first strategy. Still, he allowed Stark and Marshall to proceed with military planning, without assurance that their efforts would have full presidential backing.[27]

FDR held and maintained the upper hand in the relationship. His relations with his military advisers were not always close and harmonious, and he certainly did not simply accede to their professional judgment in strategic matters. Indeed, he overruled the chiefs on major strategic matters some twenty-two times between 1938 and the end of the war. On thirteen other occasions the initiative for strategic decisions came from the president rather than the chiefs. FDR relished the title "commander in chief" and was quite comfortable challenging the military brass in the arena of their own professional expertise.[28]

During the 1940 election campaign FDR continued to frustrate his military advisers while carefully tacking between the isolationists and the interventionists. For months he promised American mothers that "your boys are not going to be sent into any foreign wars except in case of foreign attack." Then, toward the end of the campaign, as Nazi planes were bombing Britain, he omitted the final qualifying phrase, seeming to deny the possibility of American entrance into the war. His Republican opponent, Wendell Willkie, who had largely supported FDR's foreign policy rather than playing to his party's isolationists, thought Roosevelt's rhetorical omission callous and deceitful, and that it probably secured the president's reelection. On the other hand, after Congress had authorized resumption of the draft by one vote in the House, FDR agreed to start the lottery just days before the election, a startlingly courageous and seemingly apolitical move. Roosevelt won an unprecedented third term in the first week of November 1940.[29]

After his election victory Roosevelt and Hopkins took a ten-day Caribbean voyage on a navy cruiser to reflect on the world situation and to refocus for the term ahead. Hopkins let the president relax and "refuel," as FDR often did on such vacations. They fished and played cards, and Hopkins had no idea what FDR was thinking. "Then, one evening, he suddenly came out with it—the whole program," which became known as Lend-Lease, a way to furnish arms to the Allies without requiring immediate payments that the war-torn countries could not afford.[30] Over the next four months FDR threaded a narrow course between helping the Allies, building the U.S. armed forces, and preparing the nation for possible war, all the while trying not to alarm the country. He employed the "bully pulpit" of the presidency to sustain an argument against Hitler and Nazism and for democracy and freedom.

The day after he returned from the Caribbean, FDR met informally with the press corps, and casually likened America's relationship to the war in Europe with that of a person whose neighbor's house is on fire. "If I have a length of garden hose" to lend him, Roosevelt supposed, "I may help him to put out his fire." But the hose cost fifteen dollars. Should one ask the neighbor to pay for the hose while the fire is blazing? Certainly not, "I don't want $15—I want my garden hose back after the fire is over." If the hose were damaged in the fire, the neighbor could later replace it. "Now what I'm trying to do is to eliminate the dollar sign," said the president, to "get rid of the silly, foolish old dollar sign" and help our neighbors put out the fire.[31]

A few days after Christmas 1940 Roosevelt delivered a radio address on the theme of "national security," one of the first usages of a phrase that fused the spheres of diplomacy and military power. Never in its history had "American civilization been in such danger as now," he warned, directly acknowledging the enormity of the Nazi threat. There could be no appeasing or negotiating with Hitler, who had proclaimed his intention "to enslave . . . Europe and dominate the rest of the world." That did not mean that the United States was going to war. Instead, America should "do all we can now to support the nations defending themselves against attack by the Axis." The nation should put its efforts behind producing weapons and munitions to aid the Allies. "Our national policy is not directed toward war. Its sole purpose is to keep war away from our country and our people." With that aim in mind, FDR intoned, "We must be the great arsenal of democracy." The effect of his address was apparent when White House mail and telegram counters tallied a ratio of one hundred to one in favor of the president's plan.[32]

Having given the people something to oppose—Nazism and fascism—the president used his January State of the Union message to set forth a vision of "a world founded upon four essential human freedoms"—freedom of speech, freedom of worship, freedom from want, and freedom from fear. This was "no vision of a distant millennium. It is a definite basis for a kind of world attainable in our own time and generation."[33] Between his reelection and his inauguration, Roosevelt established the framework for his third term, gaining popular approval for his support of the Allies and his opposition to the Axis. As a champion of freedom and democracy and an implacable foe of Nazi tyranny, he proposed Lend-Lease, a plan that would force Congress to reverse its adherence to isolation and neutrality in order to face the gathering crisis. FDR sought to enlist all Americans and all of mankind in the struggle to build a better world resting upon fundamental human rights. In four months of carefully orchestrated appearances, FDR transformed himself from "Dr. New Deal" to "Dr. Win the War," guiding the public conversation from one that was primarily focused inward on the national economy to one that looked outward to a threat to civilization itself.

Within the quiet councils of government, FDR began to enunciate three fundamentals of the policy that would guide his decisions. He aimed to keep America out of war if possible, and the best way to do so was to aid the British in their fight against Hitler. However, the United States needed to prepare for the eventuality in case war became unavoidable. FDR's masterly political schemes present a prima facie argument for civilian control of the military, as the governing presumption of the Constitution is that political leaders alone possess the requisite skill and accountability to the people to make such critical judgments.

From late January to late March 1941, American and British military planners met secretly in Washington to discuss strategy in the event of U.S. entry into the war. After his reelection campaign, FDR could not afford to be seen planning to send American sons into foreign wars. Except for a plenary meeting, even Marshall and Stark stayed away from these sessions to avoid drawing attention to them. The conferees agreed on the primacy of the European theater for military operations and an initial defensive in the Pacific. The Americans acquiesced to an "indirect approach" to defeating the Germans, that is, fighting on the Mediterranean periphery, a stance they would later regret. After the American-British Conversations (ABC-1) concluded, FDR characteristically approved those parts of the agreement that he liked and ignored those he did not. Nonetheless, the conference left the United States better prepared in terms of strategic planning—knowing in broad terms the plan the administration would follow when the war began—than it had ever been on the eve of a war, an accomplishment all the more astonishing because of the complexities of the coalition war that would begin before 1941 was out. That preparedness was also a tribute to the professionalization of the military over the past several decades.[34]

During the talks Congress took up the Lend-Lease bill. Some members of Marshall's staff were surprised when he employed his considerable influence to support the plan. Yet Marshall always tried to support the president, regardless of his own feelings; and in this case he had analyzed Lend-Lease in terms of its favorable effect on the American defense industry. British demand for war matériel would accelerate American mobilization by making defense production profitable faster. Even though some armaments and munitions would be going to Great Britain, the defense industry would be equipping the U.S. Army more rapidly than it would have done without the demands of Lend-Lease.[35]

Marshall's support was important because he had gained a reputation as the best administration spokesman on Capitol Hill. The president's opponents attempted to place amendments on the Lend-Lease bill that would have restricted the president's freedom of action. Secretaries Hull, Morgenthau, and Stimson made little headway with Senate leaders, until Stimson arranged for Marshall to "drop by" a negotiating session. The general "gave a ripping good speech" on Lend-Lease and "made a great impression on the Senators." Within a week both houses passed it, and FDR signed an effective Lend-Lease Act. Marshall was back on the Hill the next week, lobbying successfully for $7 billion to fund the program— ten times what he had requested for the entire army less than a year earlier.[36]

The spring of 1941 was a dark time for the Allies. German U-boats were inflicting significant losses in the Atlantic, and shipping Lend-Lease matériel to Great Britain soon gave the Nazi fleet even more targets. Yet FDR could not risk inflaming isolationist suspicions by authorizing U.S. Navy convoys to escort the ships. The U-boats enjoyed a field day. Although the Germans abandoned the Battle of Britain, they abrogated their nonaggression pact with the Soviet Union and attacked on June 22, 1941. Marshall and Stark, having carefully observed as the Wehrmacht made quick work of Poland and France, expected the Red Army to collapse in the face of the Nazi onslaught. They advised FDR to leave the Russians to their fate. The president, however, disagreed with their judgment and insisted on extending Lend-Lease aid to the Soviets. Once again, he challenged the military experts in their own field, and he was right.[37] The Soviets won their defensive campaign against the Germans, and over the next four years, contributed more to the defeat of Nazi Germany than the United States, Great Britain, and all other allies combined. Yet that spring Allied prospects had never looked bleaker.

With war raging in the Atlantic, Eastern Europe, and Asia, Marshall had confronted the possible erosion of military manpower. The previous

October Congress had passed a conscription bill under which draftees were required to serve one year. In the summer of 1941, the army that Marshall had so painstakingly built was set to dissolve in a few short months as those enlistments expired. Still smarting from the Lend-Lease defeat, conservative isolationists in Congress were ready to pounce if FDR tried to renege on the one-year deal. The president was unable to take the lead on extending enlistment terms, but knowing his intent, Marshall did. In early July he drafted an official report on his first two years as chief of staff, touting all the gains the army had made in personnel, equipment, and training. He warned that all could be lost if the army lost the bulk of its manpower. He asked Congress to grant the War Department authority to extend the service obligations of draftees, reservists, and the national guard. Again, largely owing to Marshall's influence, the Senate passed the extension handily. However, in the House a coalition of isolationists, Republicans, and Roosevelt-haters joined in opposition. A GOP sponsor of the original conscription bill invited Marshall and forty Republican opponents to the Army-Navy Club to debate Marshall's request. The session went long into the night. Marshall felt he was making progress until one representative said, "You put the case very well, but I'll be damned if I'm going along with Mr. Roosevelt." His blue eyes flashing with anger, Marshall rebuked the congressman, "You're going to let plain hatred of the personality dictate to you to do something that you realize is very harmful to the interests of the country." He then went much further than any general should have gone, offering to campaign in 1942 for anyone present who agreed to vote for the bill. A few weeks later, the House passed the bill 203–202. One representative who had been present at the Army-Navy Club credited Marshall with changing his vote. One vote was enough to sustain the army.[38]

As the House was voting, Roosevelt and his military advisers were afloat in Placentia Bay off the coast of Newfoundland. Harry Hopkins had been prodding FDR to meet with Churchill for months, and the president finally agreed. In his new role as Lend-Lease coordinator, Hopkins had just flown to England, then Moscow, and back to England in time to accompany Churchill to the first strategic summit meeting of the war. After an elaborate ruse to cover his absence, FDR boarded an American warship and steamed north for the rendezvous. To preserve secrecy, Marshall and Stark had been asked to attend the conference at the last possible moment. As a result, the chiefs and their planners were unprepared to negotiate with their British counterparts. They had only one shipboard meeting with FDR before Churchill arrived. Ironically, the lack of coordination might have been an advantage for the Americans. The British military leaders hoped to gain specific commitments on Lend-Lease, U.S. Navy convoys across the Atlantic, and a strategy of harassing Hitler in the Mediterranean, but their American counterparts were not empowered to make any agreements on material aid or strategic designs. Churchill pressed Roosevelt on those matters as well as on issuing a joint ultimatum to Japan to desist from further moves into the southwest Pacific. FDR, as always, was unwilling to be pinned down. In the end the Argentia Conference, named for the sleepy fishing village near which they anchored, was significant for two outcomes. It allowed Churchill and FDR to get acquainted and take each other's measure, and it produced the Atlantic Charter, a statement of joint principles for the postwar world based upon self-determination and economic freedom.[39]

Argentia provided important clues about the style of FDR's war leadership. He had left his secretaries of state, war, and navy back in Washington, as he would for almost every major conference of the war. FDR had brought the service chiefs into his own executive office, and their presence at Argentia confirmed that they had eclipsed their civilian superiors as strategic advisers to the commander in chief. FDR had effectively neutered the secretaries of war and navy, and those offices would never truly recover, with civilian control of the military the poorer for their weakness. Furthermore, the chiefs' newly confirmed status only counted for so much. Marshall and Stark were in the dark about the summit until almost time to pack for the trip. They had no time to prepare and little opportunity to check signals with the president. This time, because the president had kept the agenda symbolic and the allied relationship personal, the lack of concourse with his chiefs hardly mattered. They would not be so lucky again.

At Argentia Churchill argued for a hard line against the Japanese, although it was in neither the American nor the Japanese interest to provoke a war. Yet both sides practiced ham-fisted diplomacy that caused them to lurch in that direction. The service chiefs argued vigorously against provoking Japan, both because Germany was the more dangerous enemy and because neither the army nor the navy was ready for war.[40]

As war pressures mounted that summer, General Marshall saw a need for more definitive plans than FDR had thus far been willing to countenance. When FDR requested production estimates necessary to defeat "potential enemies," Marshall and Stark seized on the opportunity to think globally about the services' recommendations. The resulting report, known as the "Victory Program," was a comprehensive review of American policy, strategy, and mobilization plans for the coming war, all from the standpoint of the service chiefs. It outlined five broad policy objectives, among them maintaining the security of the Americas, and preventing both Japanese expansion and the "disruption of the British empire." Achieving these goals could only be accomplished through military victories against the Axis powers. For the immediate future, the United States would offer support to Great Britain and the Soviet Union in their quest to defeat Germany; eventually, the plan estimated, large American ground forces, as many as nine million men in 215 divisions by the middle of 1943, would be required to defeat the Nazis. War with Japan would necessarily follow. The military had made a psychological and intellectual shift to a global strategy.[41]

Marshall found that he still could not get the president's full attention on important matters. "I didn't understand that I must find a way to do the talking," he recalled, rather than allow the president to filibuster meetings with old anecdotes to avoid unpleasant topics. In the fall of 1941 both men were dealing with myriad pressures—Lend-Lease aid to the British and the Russians, an expanding security zone in the Atlantic where a tense standoff with German submarines had become a shooting war, concerns about American interests in the Philippines, and a hundred others. The global situation was complex and confusing. FDR still hoped that by aiding the British and the Soviets he might avoid American entry into the war. Meanwhile, the armed services had to prepare, but without a declaration of war they were competing for the same scant resources. "The opposition to a large army was very widespread and there was a feeling that such an army was possibly no longer needed," Marshall later recalled. "Everybody was fighting for something. Each service wanted to get an increase—each service wanted more money—and we had the regrettable state of one service working against another." Thus, in September 1941, despite the recommendations for 215 divisions in the Victory Program, FDR called Marshall to the White House to discuss *cutting* the army in favor of Lend-Lease, the navy, air power, and industrial mobilization. "This was a very serious affair," Marshall concluded, and even though Roosevelt backed off his proposal, "it remained serious until the real fighting began and the people's understanding" of what was needed in a war changed.[42]

In late November 1941 Secretary Hull's negotiations with the Japanese were irretrievably breaking down. On November 26, 1941, he issued Japan a ten-point ultimatum that was arrogant, provocative, and moralistic. Afterward, he told Stimson, "I have washed my hands of it, and it is now in the hands of you and Knox—the Army and the Navy."[43] Hull was correct in assessing the eclipse of the State Department's influence over foreign policy in wartime, but he was wrong in predicting where that influence would land. Stimson and Knox would be important administrators, but the conduct of strategy was now in the hands of the army chief of staff and the chief of naval operations, subject always to the dominant and idiosyncratic control of the commander in chief, Franklin Delano Roosevelt.

Ten days after Hull's démarche, Japan attacked Pearl Harbor and the Philippines.

On the evening of December 7, 1941, Churchill was at his country retreat, Chequers, when the news of Pearl Harbor came over the wireless. He called President Roosevelt, who confirmed the report: "We are all in the same boat now." Grieving for his American friends, Churchill was nonetheless joyous to gain them as new allies. He summoned Parliament into session the next day to declare war on Japan and "went to bed and slept the sleep of the saved and thankful." He wrote FDR, inviting himself to Washington to "review the whole war plan in the light of reality and new facts." He sailed with his military advisers and arrived before Christmas, ensconcing himself in a second-floor bedroom in the White House.[44]

Over the next nine months the Allies worked out the parameters of their strategic partnership in a series of conferences in Washington and London. FDR and Churchill grew politically and personally close. Their military leaders offered strategic advice for a coalition with global responsibilities and means that were growing to match them. Having become the foremost uniformed leader in Washington both militarily and politically in 1941, Marshall pursued political-military relations on a broader, international stage during 1942, employing the skills that he had shown to such advantage in the previous year. Yet the next several months were frustrating for Marshall as he negotiated with the British, labored to reorganize the army, and tried to establish an effective relationship with the president. By the summer, Marshall and his colleagues broke with FDR over the fundamental strategic principle of Germany first, bringing on the gravest political-military crisis of the war. During this period Hopkins was an indispensable ally to Marshall. Although intensely loyal to both FDR and Marshall, he could forthrightly disagree with either of them in the interest of winning the war. Although Marshall eventually lost this struggle with FDR, he steadily grew in stature and in the estimation of his military colleagues and political superiors, becoming first among equals in combined military councils. As Churchill would later write, he was "the true organizer of victory."[45]

Churchill's trip to Washington was a celebration of the transatlantic alliance (president and prime minister lighting the White House Christmas tree, Churchill addressing a joint session of Congress). It was also a three-week marathon. Most nights the hard-drinking Churchill kept the president up until the wee hours smoking cigars and drinking whiskey, negotiating the strategies of the United Nations, as they declared themselves on New Year's Day, 1942.[46]

Churchill's greatest concern was that Japan's surprise attack might have weakened American resolve to defeat Germany first. Fundamental assumptions of the American-British conversations of the previous winter were now invalid. The American Pacific Fleet had taken a beating, as had the British fleet at Singapore. With a string of victories in the western Pacific, Japan had become a regional hegemon and a potent threat from New Zealand to India. Stark, author of Plan Dog, was on his way out because of the U.S. failure at Pearl Harbor. His heir apparent, U.S. Fleet commander Admiral Ernest J. King, was not wedded to Stark's plan and wanted to avenge the Japanese attack. The right-wing isolationists who had accused FDR of maneuvering the country into war were now hawkish, insisting on attacking the Japanese rather than the Germans. General Douglas MacArthur, U.S. commander in the Philippines, a conservative darling and potential Republican presidential candidate, was a significant dissident. Minding his right political flank, Roosevelt ordered MacArthur to escape from Corregidor and flee to Australia to build a force to defend the southwest Pacific. Not surprisingly, MacArthur became another vocal proponent for a "Pacific first" strategy.[47]

Yet the men who mattered most were steadfast. Roosevelt and Marshall quickly assuaged Churchill's concerns—Plan Dog was still in effect, and the United States would focus on Germany first. Hitler's foolish decision to declare war on the United States made it politically easier for Roosevelt to keep that commitment. Indeed, even at this early date FDR had built upon the principles that guided his prewar decisions to establish policy fundamentals that would guide him through the war. First, this war would be fought and won by the United Nations, not the United States alone. Maintaining the integrity of that alliance was paramount, which meant maintaining effective strategic coordination among, and providing material aid to, the Allies. Second, Germany was the primary enemy and would have to be defeated first. Indeed, the defeat of Japan would likely come as a matter of course after a victory in Europe. Third, because the Soviets were doing the lion's share of the military work in defeating Germany, they must be given unstinting assistance to sustain them through the war. Fourth, the Allied war aim should be the unconditional surrender of the Axis powers. Finally, the cooperative efforts of the United Nations should continue into the postwar world. Although aversion to public commitments kept FDR from enunciating them fully and forthrightly, these principles constantly and consistently governed his thinking and actions, and his advisers and allies understood them.[48]

With strategic priorities established, the conference dubbed Arcadia moved onto the details of strategy in Europe. Once again the British were better prepared for the meetings than their American cousins. Churchill and his advisers had been at war with Germany for two years. They worked together within a well-defined institutional framework, and had rehearsed their briefs well. By telling contrast, the Americans scheduled the first day's session in a room that was too small for the conferees. They had a diminished sense of their own competence simply because the British had been fighting for so long. Britons exacerbated that feeling with characteristic condescension, despite the common understanding that Americans would soon be providing not only the lion's share of matériel but the bulk of the manpower as well. The Americans worried that the British would dominate early planning, establishing priorities that would later be difficult to renegotiate when the United States became the senior partner. U.S. conferees, Marshall included, were especially worried about the influence that Churchill seemed to wield over Roosevelt in their nightly negotiations over cocktails. Eleanor Roosevelt, seeing her husband and Churchill together in the new White House map room that FDR had built to mirror the prime minister's own, said "they looked like two boys playing soldier. They seemed to be having a wonderful time, too wonderful in fact."[49]

The chief of staff tried to rein in these tendencies by sticking to the principle of "Germany first." Yet following the agenda Churchill had drafted, the Americans found themselves agreeing to a stabilization of the Pacific front, Lend-Lease aid to Russia, regaining command of the Atlantic, defeating the Germans in North Africa, and preparing for a 1943 offensive in Europe. The wherewithal to accomplish all those tasks in such a short time simply did not exist. The war-weary, resource-starved British looked at the United States as a newly opened warehouse. The inexperienced Americans were unable to make them see that the storage space was still mostly empty, however grand their plans to fill it.[50]

Marshall promulgated another principle aimed at avoiding such mistakes in the future—unity of command. When the British conferees turned the agenda toward allocating forces to the Pacific, Marshall insisted that the discussion was premature. He argued that the Allies had spent the first three bloody years of the Great War learning the lessons of divided command. If the Allies now failed to appoint theater commanders, small questions of local defense arrangements and theater logistics would consume time and frustrate global efforts. He proposed naming a single commander in the southwest Pacific to control the combined air, ground, and sea forces of the United States, Great Britain, the Netherlands, and Australia. The British and Admiral Stark were skeptical at first, as was Roosevelt, who joked that Marshall knew nothing about ships, and the navy knew nothing about soldiers. Yet over the next several days, Marshall won over the president and the navy leadership. After he proposed a British general, Archibald Wavell, for the command, the British chiefs of staff came around, even arguing that the theater commander should be given additional authority. Still, Churchill remained opposed. Lord Beaverbrook passed Hopkins a note telling him to "work on Churchill." The next morning Hopkins, whom Churchill had dubbed "Lord Root of the Matter" for his ability to focus Allied negotiations, steered Marshall into the prime minister's White House bedroom. As usual Churchill had slept late and was still abed with His Majesty's state papers scattered about him. Towering over his quarry, Marshall walked back and forth across the room making his unity of command argument and parrying Churchill's interruptions with vehement rejoinders. Marshall, at his best in small groups and under pressure, told the prime minister that if the

Allies didn't act, they were "finished in the war." Refusing to concede, the prime minister excused himself to take a bath, returned a few minutes later naked save a towel, and told Marshall that he would have to take the worst with the best. Marshall decamped, unsure what that meant. Later that day, Churchill told FDR that he would agree to the plan "most strongly endorsed by General Marshall."[51] Having established unity of command in the southwest Pacific, the Allies would find it logical to do so in every theater, which greatly simplified and strengthened their efforts.

Marshall next raised the question of Wavell's boss—to whom would he report? As a coalition commander rather than just a British general, he ought not answer only to London. The Arcadia conferees agreed to create a new military council called the Combined Chiefs of Staff (CCS), with its headquarters in Washington. Wavell would report to the CCS, who would be responsible to Roosevelt and Churchill. The British chiefs of staff found that the CCS worked seamlessly with their own institutions, but the Americans had no counterpart. As the scribes were drawing up the agreement, Marshall cajoled one of Roosevelt's secretaries to list Lieutenant General Henry H. "Hap" Arnold, commander of U.S. Army Air Forces, as one of the American members, along with himself and Admiral Stark. Shortly thereafter, when the United States informally created a counterpart to the British chiefs—the Joint Chiefs of Staff—it naturally consisted of the American members of the CCS: the army chief of staff, the chief of naval operations, and the chief of the army air forces. The CCS governed coalition decision making for the rest of the war, and rarely in history has a coalition operated as smoothly. Likewise, the Joint Chiefs of Staff, an "accidental" organization never granted a formal charter by FDR, continues in a different form as the supreme American military council to this day.[52]

During the conference Hopkins and Lord Beaverbrook studied the allocation of war matériel. Beaverbrook suggested a two-member civilian board, one British and one American, to advise the political leaders. By the end of Arcadia, this idea had evolved into two committees, one to advise FDR and Churchill and another to report to the CCS. On the final morning of the conference, FDR showed Marshall and Hopkins the proposal for two war resources boards, one of which would bypass the CCS. Marshall calmly told the president that under those circumstances, he could no longer remain as chief of staff. In effect, Marshall threatened to resign. To Marshall's surprise, Hopkins agreed with him. Roosevelt got the message. In the meeting that followed, FDR asked the two men to present their plan to Churchill. Hopkins suggested that a single civilian board could report to the CCS, with the right to take disputes to FDR and Churchill. Reluctantly, Churchill agreed to try it for a month. FDR seized on the compromise, and the "temporary" solution lasted through the war.[53]

Marshall had won the day on fundamental questions of command, issues that were of paramount importance for the rest of the war. But on more immediate but still profound matters, such as the focus of strategy for the coming year, the better-prepared British had bested him by relying on divisions within the American camp. The British demanded a primary focus on defeating the Axis in North Africa in 1942. An invasion of Europe, they said, would follow, preferably in 1943. Roosevelt agreed, insisting that American soldiers go into action against the Germans as soon as possible, but certainly in 1942, and (he hoped) before Election Day. Greater disputes festered among FDR's military advisers. The navy and MacArthur demanded a concentration in the Pacific; they had little interest in Plan Dog. Marshall's army planners supported their boss, insofar as they trusted the British to commit to a 1943 offensive in Europe, which was not far. Marshall was amenable to putting Americans in action in North Africa, but he knew that the army was not yet fully ready. Moreover, he knew that resources committed in Africa would be unavailable for the more important European invasion. The Arcadia meetings papered over these disagreements in a cloud of goodwill and a Declaration of the United Nations organization and aims. Yet trials for American and British soldiers and statesman lay ahead.[54]

After the British left Washington, Marshall moved quickly to solve long-standing organizational problems within the army. Since the Root reforms—four decades that had seen a world war, rapid technological change, and unprecedented economic upheaval—the army had grown and contracted, taken on new missions and cast others off, all the while sprouting new agencies, many resembling their antiquated predecessors of the nineteenth century. At the end of 1941, sixty-one subordinates reported directly to the chief of staff. Now, Japan's surprise offensive provided a strategic impetus and a political opportunity for Marshall to clean house and to get his headquarters into fighting form.

In late January 1942 Marshall quickly, quietly, and ruthlessly reorganized what he called the poorest command post in the army, his own. In early March the president signed an executive order to implement Marshall's reforms. With the help of a now-streamlined general staff, Marshall commanded just three subordinate but exceptionally powerful organizations: Army Ground Forces, Army Air Forces, and Services of Supply (later Army Service Forces). Marshall had taken just six weeks to effect this sweeping realignment. The shock of a world war both allowed and demanded that Marshall act with dispatch, and new wartime executive powers allowed FDR to enact the changes without appealing to numerous congressional committees for permission. No longer choking on minutiae, Marshall felt far more able to command the army and concentrate on global strategy.[55]

Admiral King became chief of naval operations in March 1942, combining that office with his old one, commander in chief of the U.S. Fleet. He was the president's primary naval adviser and the admiral authorized to execute strategic decisions, a theretofore unimaginable accretion of power that both he and Marshall now enjoyed. King was one of the most broadly experienced sailors of his generation—brilliant, aggressive, well read, and politically astute. He was also a binge-drinking, bigoted philanderer who was abusive to his officers, suspicious of the British and the army, and abrasive in his dealings with almost everyone. One of his six daughters laughed that her father was "the most even-tempered man in the Navy. He is always in a rage." Marshall, usually circumspect to a fault in his assessments of others, later said that King "was always sore at everybody. He was perpetually mean." He made negotiations with the British difficult by being "perpetually quarrelsome, ready to fuss with them or us." Recognizing those traits early, Marshall went out of his way to cultivate his counterpart. The two men were never close, but they learned through hard knocks the value of working together.[56]

King and Marshall, together with Arnold as a junior partner, constituted the JCS. As the senior officer, Marshall presided at their meetings, but he was uncomfortable having two votes to the navy's one, especially since King could effectively veto any proposal by withholding consent. Marshall wanted to establish a fairer process with a neutral chairman of the JCS, and he enlisted Hopkins's aid to lobby FDR. They proposed Admiral William Leahy, former chief of naval operations and an old friend of FDR's, for the post. The president refused at first, insisting that Marshall was the chief of staff. Marshall explained that they needed a chief of staff of all the military services. "Well," said Roosevelt, "I'm the chief of staff. I'm the commander in chief." Marshall persisted for months while FDR continued to balk, but finally FDR relented and appointed

Leahy to be his "legman" on the Joint Chiefs of Staff. Leahy became more of a military chief of staff to FDR than a real chairman of the Joint Chiefs. Nonetheless, interservice coordination began to improve with his arrival, both because the chiefs worked together better and because Leahy had more ready access to the president.[57]

In the spring of 1942 the daily demands of fighting a global war were starting to tax America's resources and diffuse its strategic focus. Fearing a reprise of the carnage of the trenches, Churchill persisted in advocating peripheral operations as long as possible. This dispersion of strategic effort irritated Marshall, and the expansive Roosevelt tossing off potential Mediterranean operations with a flick of his cigarette lighter exacerbated his vexation. With some difficulty, Marshall steered FDR back to Europe and gained his approval for an amphibious offensive across the English Channel. The president ordered Hopkins and Marshall to take the plan to London.[58]

In early April Marshall and Hopkins flew to England. Marshall was now engaged in coalition relations, advising Churchill as well as FDR. Stoically enduring Churchill's fondness for late hours and histrionics, Marshall engaged the prime minister with straightforward doggedness. Hopkins, by this time a Churchill confidant, reinforced Marshall's efforts. After ten days of give and take, the Americans thought they had a deal: Churchill would support a cross-channel attack in 1942 if possible and 1943 for certain. But the prime minister was mainly interested in getting his allies into the war. He was less than forthcoming with his reservations about the early feasibility of cross-channel operations, but he agreed because doing so would force the Americans to mobilize divisions quickly to fight the Germans. Marshall and Hopkins went home happy, but deceived.[59]

In May Soviet foreign minister Vyacheslav Molotov arrived in Washington to demand the opening of a second front in Europe. Just back from London, Marshall and Hopkins counseled FDR to agree to a European invasion, but not to a specific date. Roosevelt plowed ahead, publicly committing the United States to putting troops in Europe in 1942.[60] Like Churchill before him, FDR had committed to a strategy for which he had no capability and perhaps no intention to carry out.

In early June a victory in the Pacific ironically complicated strategic deliberations further. At the end of a three-day battle at Midway the United States gained the strategic initiative in the Pacific, never to lose it again. Marshall and Stimson maintained that Midway had secured the prerequisite for Plan Dog, the safety to defend in the Pacific while pursuing a strategic offensive in Europe. King and MacArthur, however, seized on the victory to argue for reinforcing success with an offensive against the Japanese and effectively abandoning "Germany first." The American military could not agree on this most fundamental strategic priority.[61]

Churchill returned to the United States a few days later for more consultations. The British War Cabinet had already decided to renege on their commitment to invade Europe in the coming year. Churchill flew directly to Hyde Park for a private weekend with Roosevelt, who had already shown signs of wavering on the issue, notwithstanding his blithe promise to Molotov.[62] Marshall rightly feared that the prime minister would employ his considerable persuasive talents in favor of a North African landing: "We were largely trying to get the president to stand pat on what he had previously agreed to. The president shifted, particularly when Churchill got hold of him. . . . The president was always ready to do any sideshow and Churchill was always prodding him. My job was to hold the president down to what we were doing." Alone with FDR, Churchill prosecuted a vigorous case against a cross-channel attack into France, and Churchill convinced him to shift to an invasion of North Africa.[63]

The day after FDR and Churchill returned to Washington, Great Britain suffered a most devastating defeat in North Africa, making the case for an invasion there all the more poignant. The two leaders were together in the White House when they learned that the thirty-three-thousand-man British garrison at Tobruk had surrendered after a one-day battle with German forces half as numerous. Later, in a meeting with their chiefs of staff, Roosevelt expressed his sympathy practically: "What can we do to help?" Marshall immediately dispatched three hundred new Sherman tanks and one hundred self-propelled artillery pieces to the Middle East. Nothing, Churchill said of FDR and Marshall, "could exceed [their] sympathy and chivalry."[64] American generosity in the Britons' hour of need helped cement bonds of trust between the two allies. Yet the conference left important strategic decisions in the air, except that Churchill and Roosevelt agreed on the necessity of putting American troops into action in 1942 in the European theater. The geographical definition of that theater was now broad enough to include both France and North Africa.

Marshall's planners were poorly prepared to respond to the rapidly changing strategic picture. The navy and MacArthur held no brief for

Germany first, so American counsel was divided. Churchill, whose government was teetering over the Tobruk debacle, desperately needed a demonstration of U.S. commitment. The president wanted to put American soldiers into action against the Germans soon, and he wasn't getting sound or consistent advice from his own military. Shortly after he returned to London, Churchill informed FDR that the British would not support an invasion of France and insisted on a North African offensive instead. That announcement triggered the war's gravest upheaval in both Allied strategy and American political-military relations.[65]

Marshall told Stimson that the British veto presented "a new and rather staggering crisis . . . in our war strategy." Together with King he determined to force a confrontation with both the president and the British. The two chiefs wanted clear strategic direction from the commander in chief. Marshall wanted a firm commitment from the British for an invasion of Europe that would relieve pressure on the Soviets and present Hitler with a two-front war.[66]

On July 10 Marshall, King, and Arnold wired FDR at Hyde Park that if the British insisted on a North African offensive, then the JCS were "definitely of the opinion that we should turn to the Pacific and strike decisively against Japan." In other words, the strategic priority should become "Pacific first." Later in the day, Marshall sent FDR another message stating that he intended "to force the British into acceptance of a concentrated effort against Germany." Seething, the president sensed a bluff and called it, demanding that the JCS immediately dispatch their detailed plans for a Pacific offensive along with estimates of what such a strategy would mean for the Middle East and Russia.[67]

Of course, the Joint Chiefs had to admit that they had no comprehensive plans and that their proposal would not help the strategic situation with respect to the Soviet Union or the Middle East. Reading their response, Roosevelt grew livid. He might have expected such petulance from King, who had never supported "Germany first." Marshall was another matter. FDR had come to trust Marshall's judgment, his maturity, his forthrightness. Now the president had caught him playing games over the most important strategic decision of the war—where to concentrate American military power. FDR angrily dashed off a handwritten reply: "My first impression is that it is exactly what Germany hoped the United States would do following Pearl Harbor. Secondly it does not in fact provide use of American troops in fighting except in a lot of islands whose occupation will not affect the world situation this year or next. Third: it does not help Russia or The Near East. Therefore it is disapproved as of the present."[68] Emphasizing his constitutional role and his pique, he signed himself "Roosevelt C in C." Deciding to return to Washington quickly to resolve the conflict, the president wired ahead for Marshall, King, and Hopkins to pack for an immediate trip to London. During a tense White House session Marshall argued vigorously for the "Pacific first" gambit and against a "cigarette lighter" operation in the Levant. FDR scolded his advisers for their petulance— you can't have everything you want so you are "taking up your dishes and going away"—and reaffirmed his support for a cross-channel invasion. The next day he sent them across the Atlantic to plead for an agreement to put American troops in action against the Germans by the end of 1942. Marshall backed off of "Pacific first," but he knew that he was in an untenable position: entering negotiations with the Allies without the firm backing of his president.[69]

The outcome of the London meetings was a foregone conclusion. The British chief of the Imperial General Staff, Field Marshal Sir Alan Brooke, knew that the Americans were divided: "Hopkins is for operating in Africa, Marshall wants to operate in Europe, and King is determined to stick to the Pacific." Marshall and King attempted to forge a compromise, but Harry Hopkins scuttled that plan by prompting FDR to set a firm date for Torch, the invasion of North Africa—October 30, 1942.[70] When push came to shove, Hopkins sided decisively with the president and his policy, not Marshall. In doing so, he may also have saved the alliance.

Recording the decision, the official JCS minutes ruefully noted that "our political system would require major operations this year in Africa." Many years later, Marshall admitted that in 1942 he still had something to learn about the continuous negotiation. "We failed to see that the leader in a democracy has to keep the people entertained. That may sound like the wrong word, but it conveys the thought. The people demand action." Roosevelt was the political leader of a nation that wanted to avenge a dastardly Japanese attack. He was also a commander in chief whose policy was to defeat "Germany first." He had to reconcile those disparate realities with political and strategic leadership. He could not allow the first anniversary of Pearl Harbor to arrive without demonstrating his resolute commitment to the strategy under which he had led his citizens to war. In practical partisan terms, FDR the Democrat needed to show progress to the electorate. Marshall later noted that in their next conversation about Torch, FDR held up his hands in mock prayer and said, "Please, make it before election day." Yet when Marshall had to postpone the operation by a week, so that it commenced just after the 1942 midterms, FDR "never said a word; he was very courageous."[71] The Democrats suffered at the polls, but Roosevelt had put U.S. troops into action against the Germans in North Africa in 1942.

On another level, however, Marshall's fears were borne out. The Soviets never accepted Torch as a true second front against Germany—it was a pinprick compared to their own efforts on the eastern front. Churchill continued to pursue Mediterranean sideshows along the "soft underbelly of Europe," which tied down forces that might have begun building toward a cross-channel invasion of France. A second front in northwestern France would have satisfied the Russians, but it had to be postponed beyond 1943 into 1944, a delay that remained the sharpest point of contention among the Allies until D-Day.

Worse, the Joint Chiefs subverted FDR's clear decision to stick with Germany first. Despite their apparent acquiescence to the Torch decision, for several weeks the chiefs acted as though the matter were not settled. They engaged the British chiefs of staff in a "transatlantic essay contest" over the size of Torch forces until early September. Meanwhile, U.S. campaigns in the South Pacific began to consume men, matériel, and transportation assets in ever increasing quantities. The chiefs might have slowed that expansion, but they did not. When Leahy joined the JCS, he made clear that he saw Japan as the main enemy and insisted on opening the Burma Road to aid the Chinese. As late as an August 11 JCS meeting, Marshall declared that "the big issues to be decided were whether the major U.S. effort was to be made in the Pacific as against Europe and the Middle East." These actions petulantly contravened the commander in chief's clearly and repeatedly expressed strategic priorities. By the end of 1942 more American combat forces were in the Pacific than in the European theater.[72]

By New Year's Day 1943 the Allies faced an entirely different and considerably brighter global situation. The Americans had secured Guadalcanal. In North Africa British forces on the east and Americans on the west were pushing the Germans back into Tunisia. The Red Army had counterattacked the Germans at Stalingrad and would soon destroy the German Sixth Army, so all concerns of Soviet collapse were moot. However, large commitments of American forces in the South Pacific and North Africa rendered a buildup for a cross-channel offensive strategically and logistically problematic. Each military adviser analyzed the situation through the prism of his own view of military power. Sailors Leahy and King focused on defeating Japan by aiding China and retaining the initiative in the Pacific. Airman Arnold insisted upon a bomber offensive against Germany from both the Mediterranean and Britain. Marshall the soldier reverted to a cross-channel offensive to defeat Germany first. The Joint Chiefs were hopelessly divided.[73]

Torch was so successful that Churchill and Roosevelt chose to convene their next strategic conference in the North African city of Casablanca in January 1943. FDR held only one preparatory session with his chiefs before the trip, and they arrived at no consensus. He warned them that the British would "have a plan and stick to it." He was right, and the cacophony of strategic counsel coming from the JCS drove FDR into Churchill's arms. One British planner said that if he had drafted his preferred outcome before the summit convened, "I could never have written anything so sweeping, so comprehensive, so favourable to our ideas." Roosevelt and Churchill agreed to an invasion of Sicily, a buildup in England with an unspecified date for a cross-channel offensive into France, and subordination of the Pacific war to the European theater. Marshall's chief planner, Brigadier General Albert Wedemeyer, ruefully paraphrased Caesar, "we lost our shirts. . . . One might say we came, we listened, and we were conquered."[74]

Casablanca represented the nadir of American political-military relations in World War II, but the solutions to the problem were already in the making. Six months earlier, the Joint Chiefs had recognized the importance of presenting a unified front to the president and to the Allies. They knew that the British had better planning processes, so the JCS established subordinate committees to iron out differences in strategy to guide planning, logistics, wartime manufacturing, and postwar objectives. One of those, the Joint Strategic Survey Committee, drafted its own charter, demanding a global portfolio based on the imperatives of grand strategy: "The Military authorities of the nation should share with the diplomatic and economic authorities the responsibility for shaping the national policy in peace as well as war. Since grand strategy

looks beyond the war to the subsequent peace, its scope includes all factors that will affect the peace, and extends to the relations of a nation to
its allies and to neutrals as well as to its opponents." That ambition was
a far cry from the prewar notion that strategy should begin only when
policy had failed. Although American joint planning procedures had
not matured in time for Casablanca, they did soon thereafter and, more
broadly, established the framework for military dominance of national
security planning after the war as well.[75]

Most importantly, the Allies began to win the war. They seized the
initiative in the Mediterranean, which they ratified with an amphibious
assault on Sicily followed by a series of offensives in Italy itself. Millions
of Soviet soldiers began pushing the Wehrmacht back all along the bloody
eastern front. And in the supposedly secondary Pacific and Southwest
Pacific theaters, the Americans steadily forced the Japanese to retreat, or
hopped around their island strongholds that no longer enjoyed naval or
air support. Strategic agreement was far easier to achieve when the coalition was advancing on all fronts.

To support all these offensives, American manufacturing had caught
up to Allied demand, producing guns, tanks, planes, ships, and landing
craft at astonishing rates, even dwarfing the fantastic figures FDR had
demanded before the United States entered the war. Furthermore, U.S.
armed forces mobilization and training had progressed to the point that
American manpower contributions to the fighting fronts began to out-
strip those of the British. The issue of Germany or Japan first became
moot as the Allies, especially the United States, accumulated the forces to
do both simultaneously. As 1943 wore on, Great Britain became a junior
partner to both the United States and the Soviet Union, and its material
inferiority undercut its negotiating position with its Allies.

On a more personal level, FDR was now an aging, ailing man who
had been through thick and thin with his military advisers. Unlike Lincoln, he retained the same military chiefs throughout the war (remembering that King took over from Stark shortly after Pearl Harbor and Leahy
arrived a few months later). Despite a number of conflicts and defeats, he
had grown to trust them, especially George Marshall. When he went to
strategic conferences, he continued his practice of leaving the secretaries
of state, war, and navy at home. After Casablanca, however, he traveled
to every conference with the Joint Chiefs, giving them plenty of time to
understand his thinking. As the president's health continued to fail, he

relied on Marshall and Leahy and King far more than he had done in the past. Acknowledging their critical participation, he agreed to continue their ad hoc committee, the Joint Chiefs of Staff, after the war.[76]

When it came time to select a supreme allied commander for the invasion of Europe, Churchill graciously nominated Marshall. FDR agreed that the general had earned the assignment. At one point Roosevelt worried that "fifty years from now practically nobody will know who George Marshall was. That is one of the reasons why I want George to have the big command—he is entitled to establish his place in history as a great general." Yet it was hard for anyone, especially FDR, to imagine who could fill Marshall's shoes as chief of staff, on Capitol Hill, on the JCS, and in Allied councils. Administration critics charged that FDR was plotting to move Marshall out of the way, and that the "slimy hand" of the White House Rasputin, Harry Hopkins, was wielding the knife. German radio announced that Marshall had been dismissed and that Roosevelt had taken his post, prompting Marshall to send a facetious message to Hopkins: "Dear Harry: Are you responsible for pulling this fast one on me?" Hopkins shared the note with FDR, who wrote back, "Dear George—Only true in part—I am now Chief of Staff but you are President. FDR."[77] Their years together had broken Marshall's embargo against presidential use of his first name.

In fact, the opposite of what the critics were charging was true: both Hopkins and Stimson were passionately lobbying to assign Marshall to the supreme command. At the Tehran conference in late 1943, Stalin, anxious to get a commander named for the second front, also expressed his preference for Marshall. By then, FDR could postpone a decision on the command no longer. He sent Hopkins to convey his misgivings to Marshall, perhaps to soften the blow. The two men danced around the issue until Marshall said he would "go along wholeheartedly with whatever decision the president made. He need have no fears regarding my personal reaction." The next day FDR finally sat down with his army chief to discuss the matter. True to form, Marshall refused to let the president off the hook, insisting that he "wanted him to feel free to act in whatever way he felt was to the best interests of the country, and to his satisfaction, and not in any way to consider my feelings." The president replied that he couldn't "sleep at ease if you were out of Washington."[78] General Dwight D. Eisenhower got the D-Day command and led the defeat of Nazi Germany.

Roosevelt and Marshall had traveled a long and difficult road together to reach that pass, where each could trust the other entirely, even in a decision that was painful to them both. It was entirely fitting that Hopkins acted as intermediary. Marshall later recalled that FDR did not develop complete confidence in him until after the United States entered the war and that Hopkins was largely responsible for fostering the relationship.[79]

FDR dominated the continuous negotiation until the last months of the war. Before Pearl Harbor the president brought his military advisers into his official household, granting them extraordinary access and keeping them under his inquisitive eye. He allowed them to prepare for war only on his terms, insisting on his prerogatives as political leader and commander in chief to assist the Allies, to accept or reject strategic plans in whole or in part, and not to be bound by the strictures of military necessities. After the United States entered the war, FDR made strategy at a high level, tying it to long- or short-term political objectives. He allowed his military chieftains to fight with one another, leaving them to learn the lessons of cooperation on their own, while he chose among their proposals or vetoed them all in favor of British plans. After the Torch controversy and the Casablanca conference he became less domineering, but only because the JCS had learned to support his policy and became more adept at negotiating strategy to execute it. In a sense, he had tamed the Joint Chiefs, much as an experienced horseman "breaks" a young colt. Thereafter, horse and rider worked together most effectively. Even when his health began to fail in 1945, the JCS continued to pursue his policies without his firm guidance. In the final two years of the war, the continuous negotiation became an intimate and productive partnership in which a capable president maintained control of an extraordinarily effective and powerful military instrument. Only the Lincoln-Grant partnership rivals it for effectiveness and the maintenance of American traditions of civilian control.

The relationship between Roosevelt and Marshall coupled two distinctive and forceful personalities. FDR was the consummate politician of his day, who became a master grand strategist. He focused on global policy objectives, but was quite capable of delving into strategy when the chiefs did not seem to adhere to his broad principles. His "cigarette lighter" methods could appear maddeningly chaotic to his advisers, but in historic terms he was unusually consistent in pursuit of war aims that changed little from December 1941 to the end of the war. On the other side stood Marshall, the quintessential professional soldier, who became a master politician at the national and international levels. He succeeded politically because he developed a relationship of candor, truthfulness, expertise, and disinterestedness, and because he had no personal ambitions beyond serving the war effort as best he could. Marshall did not hold himself aloof from politics. In fact, he recalled that the Joint Chiefs spent more time discussing the political aspects of strategy than anything else. For Marshall the matter was axiomatic: "Any move in a global war has political implications." There was no wall between policy and strategy.[80]

Roosevelt came to give wide latitude and great responsibility to his chiefs, but he extended it personally and as an outgrowth of his peculiar leadership style. That authority naturally grew as the armed forces expanded to unprecedented size and power to fight a global war. One man could not do it all. Yet FDR opposed a formal military advisory organization. Marshall managed to establish the Joint Chiefs only by subterfuge. FDR refused to grant the JCS a formal charter, even though the JCS established subordinate committees and structures that tended to institutionalize its authority and broaden its ambit.

After Roosevelt's death and the end of the war, the National Security Acts of 1947 and 1949 legislated what he had refused to commit to paper: a charter for the Joint Chiefs of Staff. The legislation also created the National Security Council, the Central Intelligence Agency, and the Department of Defense, subordinating within the latter the Departments of the Army, Navy, and the newly independent Air Force. What FDR had fiercely resisted—a formal national security apparatus with organizational charts and institutional fiefdoms—was now enshrined in law. Those structures and their successors are so familiar to us now that it is hard to bring to mind a world in which they did not exist. Yet there were unforeseen consequences of the new establishment. No one could guarantee that FDR's successors would have the political skills and iron will to control such a beast. Even FDR feared the consequences of making his ad hoc arrangements formal. Neither could one legislate that future members of the Joint Chiefs would be as able as their wartime predecessors or that they would have a leader as self-effacing as George C. Marshall. As the Torch controversy showed, even Marshall could have his

223

insubordinate moments. No national security act could conjure another Harry Hopkins, whom one historian described as "an invisible member of Joint Chiefs, indeed of the Combined Chiefs of Staff." It might be more apt to describe Hopkins as FDR's national security adviser *and* an informal secretary of defense. Yet Hopkins, like the Joint Chiefs, wielded such authority only to the extent that FDR personally allowed him to do so. Giving these arrangements legal standing was a well-meaning attempt to preserve the most effective political-military arrangement American governance ever enjoyed, forgetting that the success was due largely to the unusually able men who worked so long and diligently to achieve it.[81]

After the war the military came to dominate national security policy. The mere fact that "national security" displaced the old "foreign policy" speaks to this shift in the collective worldview of American governance. The National Security Acts effected much of the change, but they were also reactions to the reality that the end of war did not portend peace. The United States and the Soviet Union went from World War allies one day to Cold War adversaries the next. Creating a national security state presumed a perpetual threat, and every foreign policy problem necessitated a military component and perhaps a military solution. Under such circumstances, military leaders retained enormous authority and responsibility. That the generals and admirals of the Cold War were also the legendary victors of World War II only enhanced that power. This new "military definition of reality" was a far cry from the time when strategy began where politics ended.[82]

III

THE PERILS
OF PARTISANSHIP

★ World War II ended not with peace but with a Cold War, a bipolar conflict soon compounded by rational fears of nuclear Armageddon. In a time when war might be measured in hours rather than years, presidents accrued unprecedented sway over national security matters that Congress could scarcely contest. Concurrently, the hero-generals and -admirals of World War II gained suzerainty over burgeoning armies and fleets of ships, planes, and missiles, and their attendant budgets, placing them and their successors near the apex of the Washington power structure. Newly powerful military bureaucracies carefully groomed officers to take on institutional values. Yet Douglas MacArthur's insubordination to Harry Truman put future presidents on notice that generals warrant close scrutiny. Eisenhower, a former general himself, tried to corral the top brass, but he and his successors chafed at a succession of company men, each of whom seemed focused on the protection and growth of his own branch of service. Presidents came to mistrust the professional assembly line because they could not control it.

The major conflicts of the late twentieth and early twenty-first centuries were wars of choice. Thus, commanders in chief came to desire publicly voiced support from their military counselors, and they began to buck the profession by attempting select generals who would provide it. In Vietnam, Desert Storm, and the wars in Iraq and Afghanistan, the principal military leaders—Taylor, Powell, Franks, and Petraeus—responded by allying themselves politically with the presidents who handpicked them, rather than offering professionally nonpartisan counsel. The results in each case were amicable, even trustful, relations between those presidents and their generals, but poorly developed policy and badly executed strategy with predictably unsatisfactory effects for the nation. Moreover, succeeding administrations had reason to question whether the president could depend upon the same generals to provide the impartial expertise necessary to analyze new policy aims and formulate strategies in the best interests of national security. Over time, presidents, doubting the disinterestedness of the military profession, would be left with the necessity of finding like-minded generals of their own.

9

EXIT MacARTHUR

A consummate performer, Douglas MacArthur held his listeners spell-bound for over half an hour, no mean accomplishment with an audience as jaded as the United States Congress. Twenty million Americans were watching on television, and ten million more were listening on radio—breaking records for both media. Neither his jet-black hair, his flagpole posture, nor his perfectly modulated baritone betrayed the general's seventy-one years. The joint congressional audience had interrupted him with applause some thirty times already. Now he paused and eased into his peroration, aware that he was culminating a half-century of military service, if not his career on the international stage. "When I joined the Army," he reminisced,

> even before the turn of the century, it was the fulfillment of all of my boyish hopes and dreams. The world has turned over many times since I took the oath on the plain at West Point, and the hopes and dreams have long since vanished, but I still remember the refrain of one of the most popular barrack ballads of that day which proclaimed most proudly that "old soldiers never die; they just fade away."
>
> And like the old soldier of that ballad, I now close my military career and just fade away, an old soldier who tried to do his duty as God gave him the light to see that duty.

The House chamber erupted with a deafening roar. Congressmen and senators stood applauding and weeping. Dewey Short, a Republican representative and clergyman from Missouri, exclaimed, "We saw a great hunk of God in the flesh, and we heard the voice of God." Former president Herbert Hoover insisted that MacArthur was "the reincarnation of Saint Paul into a great General of the Army who came out of the East."

President Harry S Truman, who watched on television, offered a pithier critique: "It was nothing but a bunch of damn bullshit."[1]

A week earlier, Truman had unceremoniously relieved MacArthur of his commands in Japan and Korea. For the past year tensions had been escalating between the two men and between MacArthur's headquarters and the White House, the State Department, and the Pentagon. Differences over strategy in Korea exposed insuperable conflicts about foreign policy. While both sides agreed on the need to contain world communism, they disagreed on the geographic focus of that effort and the methods by which to effect it. Truman found the strategic crux in Europe; MacArthur located it in Asia. The president aimed to avoid a wider war, especially one with China or the Soviet Union, a conflict that might bring on a third world war. MacArthur maintained that he was already at war with China, that the enemy should be afforded no sanctuary, and that there was "no substitute for victory." Yet the more profound conflict between the two men was over the scope of the general's authority and the issue of his subordination to the president. The president's political opponents and the general's admirers were all too happy to exploit the rift for their own partisan purposes.

One legacy of World War II and the rise of the national security state was that military heroes of the war, adorned with stars and medals won in action and ensconced in positions of administrative power, had gained increasing influence in the councils of government. Out of a sense of reverence, gratitude, or fear of their constituents, civilian leaders accorded unprecedented deference to military rank and expertise. Unfortunately, with FDR's death, the nation no longer had a charismatic leader with the ability to hold such tensions at bay. Governing in his predecessor's shadow, the new president had fought a series of battles against his uniformed subordinates. The navy and marines had almost scuttled a reorganization of the military departments as a threat to their bases of power. They lost that fight, and FDR's ad hoc wartime creation, the Joint Chiefs of Staff, gained official standing in the National Security Acts of 1947 and 1949, along with a powerful new Department of Defense and a Central Intelligence Agency. Then, in what became known as the "Revolt of the Admirals," naval leaders waged a legislative end-run against postwar administration budget cuts that threatened their cherished new generation of carriers. As Soviet power grew, every national security problem took on the trappings of an existential threat. In this milieu, one of the greatest heroes of the war, General of the Army Douglas

MacArthur, had accrued all but independent sovereignty as American viceroy of occupied Japan. When war broke out in Korea, he assumed the role of supreme commander in the Far East. Yet the Joint Chiefs, the only body with prestige enough to assist the president in bringing him to heel, could not. They were too deferential to a general who was a full generation their superior and whose laurels far eclipsed their own. The MacArthur controversy thus became a critical test of civilian control of the military in American history, ranking in severity alongside the Newburgh Conspiracy.

Larger than life, Douglas MacArthur was a figure of extreme contrasts. He was charming, generous, brilliant, magnanimous, and visionary. He was arrogant, self-centered, prejudiced, thin-skinned, and myopic. MacArthur was always onstage, performing the parts of patrician intellectual, swashbuckling soldier, and worldly strategist, sometimes all three and more at the same time. It seemed impossible to be neutral about him—observers either loved or hated him. An Australian general who served under MacArthur throughout the Second World War claimed that "the best and worst things you hear about him are both true."[2]

His father was a Civil War hero who gained fame at the battle of Chattanooga. Eighteen-year-old Arthur MacArthur led an assault up Missionary Ridge, far exceeding orders to halt after carrying the first line of Confederate defenses, and causing General Grant to demand to know who had authorized such recklessness. Yet the Union charge surprised the rebels, gained the ridge, and won the battle. MacArthur later received a Medal of Honor for his gallantry. His son distilled the lesson: "It's the orders you disobey that make you famous." The father was a courageous and gifted battlefield leader who rose to become a lieutenant general and U.S. commander in the Philippines, but as an aide put it, "the most flamboyantly egotistical man I had ever seen, until I met his son." Douglas kept his father's picture at his bedside until his own death.[3]

MacArthur rose quickly. He earned his first star in World War I and became West Point superintendent just sixteen years after his own graduation. President Hoover appointed him army chief of staff—a position that had eluded his revered father—but that was a thankless position in a time of Depression-era military budgets. In the summer of 1932 MacArthur gained a measure of infamy by ruthlessly driving the Bonus

Marchers from Washington. Attired in his dress uniform complete with decorations, the chief of staff took active command of the tanks, infantry, and artillery that routed the starving World War I veterans and torched their shantytown. His aide, Major Dwight D. Eisenhower, had urged against such a conspicuous role, but learned that his chief "had an obsession that a high commander must protect his image at all costs and must never admit his wrongs." MacArthur's suppression of the Bonus March caused New York governor Franklin D. Roosevelt to conclude that the general, along with Louisiana governor Huey Long, was one of the two most dangerous men in the country. Strangely enough, President Roosevelt kept him on as chief of staff, but the two enormous egos often clashed. One day while arguing with the president in the Oval Office over proposed army budget cuts, MacArthur lost his temper and said, "When we lose the next war, and an American boy with an enemy bayonet through his belly and an enemy foot on his dying throat spits out his last curse, I want the name not to be MacArthur, but Roosevelt." FDR thundered, "You must not talk that way to the president!" Abashed for once in his life, MacArthur apologized and offered his resignation. Outside, he vomited on the White House steps.[4]

Roosevelt turned down MacArthur's offer to resign. Yet when MacArthur's tour as chief was up, FDR was happy when the general accepted a position abroad as military adviser to Filipino leader Manuel Quezon. Roosevelt passed over MacArthur's handpicked successor to choose his own chief of staff, an act for which MacArthur never forgave him.[5]

MacArthur's career in the U.S. Army appeared to be over, but he was soon named field marshal of the Filipino forces and quickly became mentor to Quezon. FDR recalled him to active duty as war threatened in 1941. Yet Philippine defenses were shockingly unprepared when the December 7 attack came. Japanese warplanes destroyed MacArthur's air force on the ground nine hours *after* the Pearl Harbor raid. Invasion of the Philippines was a relatively simple matter after that debacle, and the Imperial Japanese Army soon besieged Filipino and American forces in Bataan. Despite this failure, MacArthur remained a darling of the political right wing, and FDR ordered him to leave the Philippines to take command of Allied forces in Australia. Over the next three years, MacArthur's forces retook New Guinea, "leap-frogged" southwest Pacific islands en route to the reconquest of the Philippines, and eventually threatened an invasion of Japan. MacArthur presided over the Japanese surrender on the USS *Missouri* in the summer of 1945. He remained in

Tokyo for the next five years as supreme commander of the Allied powers, administering the occupation of Japan and rebuilding its economy and political system.

By the time the Korean War erupted, MacArthur had been out of the United States for fifteen years, having returned only once for a brief visit. Yet Republican political operatives had enticed him to float his name as a candidate for president in both 1944 and 1948. Neither gambit bore fruit, but his longing for the presidency became the stuff of political lore. Long surrounded by handpicked sycophants who thought of him as "the greatest man since Christ" or even "the greatest man who ever lived," he was accustomed to more than deference. He assumed the role of an Asian potentate, treating both Manuel Quezon and Hirohito as supplicants. He had no close ties to his military colleagues in the Pentagon and tended to make them feel like the junior officers they had been when he was army chief of staff. An admiral who served under him in World War II said that he "was never able to develop a feeling of warmth and comradeship with those about him. He had their respect but not their sympathetic understanding or their affection. . . . He was too aloof and too correct in manner, speech, and dress. He had no small talk." MacArthur staff officer and later Wisconsin governor Philip La Follette praised the general's "first-class mind" and his "will of iron."[6]

> But there was a serious flaw in this otherwise almost perfect combination of human qualities. He had no humility and hence no saving grace of a sense of humor. He could never laugh at himself—never admit mistakes or defeats. When these occurred . . . he resorted to tricks—sometimes sly, childlike attempts—to cover up. . . . His obvious warts—warts that were insignificant against his towering intellect, superb courage, and inflexible will—became important only because they were denied.[7]

Harry Truman viewed himself as a man who differentiated clearly between black and white, with little interest in shades of gray. Yet, like all people, he overlooked his own compromises. Truman professed to hate West Pointers. Denied a Military Academy appointment as a youth, he affected a lifelong disdain for the college and its graduates, a sentiment that he expanded to include all regular officers. Yet Truman admired citizen-soldiers like the Missouri national guardsmen he led as a battery commander in the First World War. He told himself that there was a world of difference between these two martial archetypes, but in fact Truman developed great respect for a number of Military Academy men, such as fellow Missourian Omar N. Bradley, and regular officers, most notably his secretary of state and secretary of defense, George C. Marshall. Indeed, he came almost to revere those men, uncritically overlooking their flaws. Truman fancied himself a man of plain thinking and no contradictions, but events proved otherwise.[8]

Truman observed the supposedly inviolable rule that "politicians have no business interfering in military operations." A student of history, especially the Civil War, Truman had drawn cautionary lessons from the Joint Committee on the Conduct of the War. When, during World War II, then senator from Missouri Truman came to chair a military oversight committee, he vowed that his board would not repeat the meddling mistakes of its predecessor. Likewise, he had studied the relations between Confederate president Jefferson Davis and his chief lieutenant, Robert E. Lee. Truman concluded that theirs was the ideal political-military partnership, wherein Davis made policy and Lee carried it out through strategy. A theoretical "bright line" delineated the gap between those responsibilities. His assessment overlooked Davis's niggling supervision of other military commanders as well as Lee's deft forays into policy. Nonetheless, in Truman's mind, the separation of policy and politicians from strategy and generals was absolute: "The commanders in the field have absolute control of the tactics and the strategy, and they always have." FDR would certainly have begged to differ.[9]

Truman was a haberdasher by trade, a small businessman, and local politician. He might have remained a county judge in Independence, Missouri, but for the support of Thomas Pendergast, Democratic boss of Kansas City. Pendergast needed a U.S. Senate candidate in 1934, and Harry Truman fit the bill. Truman won easily, but his association with the Kansas City machine cast a shadow over his career. The new senator responded with honesty, patience, and hard work, making few headlines until he became chairman of the military oversight committee during the war. Rather than grilling generals and questioning strategy as the Joint Committee on the Conduct of the War had done, Truman traveled the country investigating military contracts at army posts and naval bases. He ferreted out corruption and saved taxpayers $15 billion with diligent oversight. In the public consciousness, Truman transformed himself from protégé of a ward boss to paragon of clean government. In 1944 when FDR began casting about for a replacement for his vice president, Henry A. Wallace, several Democrats suggested that he could do worse than Harry Truman. FDR and HST won the election in November, were inaugurated in January, and Roosevelt died in April 1945. When he ascended to the presidency Truman felt as if the "world and all the stars had fallen on me."

Few presidents have inherited more daunting challenges or followed a more illustrious predecessor. Truman, an obscure legislator a few months earlier, shared the stage with Churchill and Stalin, FDR's wartime partners, at a war-ending conference at Potsdam. The new president learned of the invention of the atomic bomb, a miracle weapon that might, if effective, end the war with Japan with one blow. The first person in history faced with such a decision, Truman chose to drop the bomb, and did so again four days later. Japan capitulated. After the surrender, Truman had to decide who would command the occupation of Japan. Among the major commanders of World War II, only MacArthur lobbied for a postwar overseas role. All the rest returned home in triumph to the adulation of their countrymen, except MacArthur. Every independent American commander received stateside duty or retired from service, except MacArthur. Yet Truman felt he had little choice but to designate him supreme commander, Allied Powers (SCAP) in Japan. That decision seemed to pay off handsomely as the general, showing a broad understanding of history and politics as well as a surprisingly liberal view of human governance, transformed Japan from a destitute, militaristic oligarchy into a growing, democratic constitutional monarchy.[10]

MacArthur's success in Japan did little to endear him to Truman, who referred to him variously as the "Big General," "Mr. Prima Donna, Brass Hat," a "play-actor and bunco man," and "The Right-Hand Man of God." He admitted that FDR's hatred of "MacArthur may have influenced me some." Yet Truman chose not to antagonize the five-star war hero who had a loyal and enthusiastic following in the United States.[11]

MacArthur had returned Roosevelt's hostility. Shortly after hearing of his death, MacArthur opined, "He never resorted to the truth when a lie would suffice." Still, he respected the president's canniness and his patrician descent and demeanor. MacArthur had only contempt for Roosevelt's successor: "We're even worse off with the Jew in the White House.

(You can tell by his name. Look at his face.)" The general disdained Truman as a second-rate pol and an unwelcome outsider. But he vastly underestimated the new president's intelligence, character, determination, and his dislike of pretension and arrogance.[12]

The North Korean People's Army launched a surprise invasion of South Korea on June 25, 1950. Unclear American policy about such a contingency was partially responsible for the attack. At the end of World War II, U.S. diplomat Dean Rusk had drawn a line between American- and Soviet-controlled Korea at the thirty-eighth parallel, indicating that the United States had strategic interests on the peninsula. Yet the United States did little else to protect those interests. In two March 1949 press conferences MacArthur called the Pacific Ocean "an Anglo-Saxon lake and our line of defense runs through the chain of islands fringing the coast of Asia" from the Philippines through the Ryukyus to Japan and then through the Aleutians to Alaska. The entire Korean peninsula and Formosa lay outside the boundary. Ten months later Secretary of State Dean Acheson gave a policy address drawing an identical "line of defense." With a peace treaty in Japan still in the drafting stage, the Soviets suspected that these pronouncements, which accurately reflected administration policy, gave them a green light to consolidate the communist hold on Korea. Indeed, Stalin approved the North Korean decision to invade.[13]

The North Korean offensive surprised MacArthur as much as anyone. He had considered Korea outside his ambit and had given little thought to the possibility of a communist attack there. A year later, he accurately told a Senate committee: "I had nothing whatever to do with the policies, the administration, or the command responsibilities in Korea until the war broke out." Indeed, MacArthur was astonished when he received orders to resist North Korean aggression. He told John Foster Dulles that anyone who deployed American forces onto that peninsula "ought to have his head examined." Notwithstanding his reservations, he accepted the mission to assist South Korea and soon gained formal authority as commander in chief, United Nations Command (CINCUNC). MacArthur's impressive wartime record, his success during the occupation of Japan, and his support within the right wing of the Republican Party left Truman with little choice but to appoint a man he did not trust to the Korean command.[14]

The day after MacArthur's appointment, *New York Times* correspondent James Reston foreshadowed trouble: "Diplomacy and a vast concern for the opinions and sensitivities of others are the political qualities essential to his new assignment, and these are precisely the qualities General MacArthur has been accused of lacking in the past." MacArthur, he said, was "a sovereign power in his own right, with stubborn confidence in his own judgment."[15] Indeed, the seventy-year-old general was already showing signs of bucking administration policy.

Just weeks before the North Korean offensive, MacArthur began to voice concerns about Formosa (Taiwan).[16] Although he had never evinced much interest in the island and the Nationalist Chinese government, in May 1950 he urged the Joint Chiefs of Staff to reconsider their strategic value. Formosa, he argued, "is the equivalent of an unsinkable aircraft carrier and submarine tender." Less than three weeks later he penned an eleven-point "Memorandum on Formosa," the thrust of which was to make the island the linchpin of American defense of its "Anglo-Saxon lake." The Truman administration, feeling the pangs of criticism for having "lost China" and desiring to maintain its strategic focus in Europe, did not agree.[17]

MacArthur was flexing his independence in strategy as well. Not yet named United Nations commander, he ordered his planes to attack Pyongyang before the president authorized such an action. During his years in the Southwest Pacific command and during the occupation of Japan MacArthur had developed an "old habit of doing things in his own way, without too much concern about waiting for orders from Washington." Often commanding at several levels at once, he would claim authority to act wearing one hat, even if he had contradictory instructions wearing another. By July 1950, MacArthur was simultaneously supreme commander, Allied Powers in Japan; commander in chief, United Nations Command (all coalition forces); commander in chief, Far East (all U.S. forces); and commanding general, U.S. Army Forces, Far East. He took advantage of his proximity to the action halfway around the world from Washington and his ability to make decisions personally and quickly while his superiors—the Joint Chiefs, the secretary of defense, the National Security Council, the president, and occasionally the UN Security Council—sometimes fumbled for days to arrive at consensus. Often the general authorized actions that amounted to faits accomplis, and his superiors became accustomed to accepting those situations because they felt there was little else they could do. General Eisenhower,

MacArthur's longtime aide, warned his Pentagon colleagues against appointing "'an untouchable' whose action you cannot predict and who will himself decide what information he wants Washington to have and what he will withhold."[18]

As surprised as he was at the North Korean invasion and the U.S. decision to resist it, MacArthur soon began to view the war as a capstone to a brilliant career. Here was a contest between communism and democracy, between freedom and tyranny, and it was taking place where MacArthur had always predicted—in the Far East. Victory in such a cockpit would solidify his place among history's great captains. Now that war had begun and he had been placed in command, he would brook little interference from politicians or deskbound generals in Washington who understood "little about the Pacific and practically nothing about Korea." Indeed, he assured Dulles that he was quite "prepared to deal with policy questions." MacArthur intended to wield authority matching Pershing's in the First World War.[19]

In the summer of 1950 the UN Command attempted to arrest the North Korean invasion. American forces sent to reinforce them in the first days were likewise routed, and the Allies fell back into a defensive perimeter protecting the port of Pusan on the southeastern shore of Korea. Pusan was both an entry point for arriving forces and supplies and a potential evacuation port if the North pushed the defenders off the peninsula.

In the midst of the Pusan crisis MacArthur decided to visit Formosa. Nationalist Chinese leader Chiang Kai-shek had offered thirty-three thousand troops to the UN Command for use in Korea, but Truman declined, not wanting to broaden the war by giving affront to Communist China. On July 27, the Joint Chiefs warned MacArthur that Mao Tsetung's forces appeared to be massing on the mainland coast for a possible invasion of Formosa. That "war warning" induced MacArthur to make "a brief reconnaissance" of the island on July 31. The State and Defense Departments were still formulating Formosa policy, so the JCS suggested to MacArthur that he might "desire" to send a subordinate, someone with a lower political profile. Yet they deferred to his judgment: "If you feel it necessary to proceed personally on the 31st, please feel free to go since the responsibility is yours."[20] The Joint Chiefs were developing a habit of deference to the Far East commander that would make controlling him all the more difficult in the months to come. MacArthur made the trip as planned.

The substance of the two-day conference with Chiang was, as Mac-Arthur later said, "purely military in nature," but its political ramifications were profound. The general was photographed embracing the generalissimo and kissing Madame Chiang's hand, thereby enraging Secretary of State Dean Acheson, who had tried to keep the United States neutral in China's civil war. MacArthur's public trip report lauded Chiang, "my old comrade-in-arms," for his "indomitable determination to resist Communist domination," and noted their agreement not to deploy Chinese troops to Korea. Chiang used his press release to gain maximum political advantage. He extolled MacArthur for his commitment to fighting totalitarianism, thereby damning others in the American government, such as Acheson, by omission. He hailed a new "Sino-American military cooperation" and declared that "victory" over Mao's forces was now assured. Such rhetoric sent shivers through America's European allies and infuriated the State Department, which had the delicate task of holding coalitions together on both sides of the globe. Although fifteen senior officers accompanied him to Taipei, MacArthur found no room on his plane for his State Department political adviser. When Acheson asked for a report, MacArthur refused, saying his talks were "purely military." Acheson told his representative in Tokyo that he was "increasingly disturbed" that MacArthur was "taking foreign policy in[to] his own hands." The president, who was reading the cable traffic, became incensed and told Secretary of Defense Louis Johnson to order MacArthur to make "full and complete reports on the [war] situation" daily. The JCS watered down the order with military politesse.[21]

Shortly thereafter, the JCS received an erroneous report that MacArthur had deployed three fighter jet squadrons to Formosa on his own authority. The JCS told MacArthur that such an action was "political" and required approval at the "highest levels" of government. MacArthur replied that he had not sent the jets and only intended to do so in case of a Communist Chinese attack on Formosa. On August 4, Johnson, acting on Truman's orders, sent the Far East commander a stern message. He reminded the general that when the war in Korea broke out the president had sent the Seventh Fleet to the Formosa Strait to neutralize Formosa, in other words to deter an attack by either Chinese side on the other. "No one other than the President as Commander-in-Chief," Johnson warned, "has the authority to order or authorize preventive action against concentrations on the 'Chinese' mainland. . . . The most vital national interest requires that no action of ours precipitate general war or give excuse to others to do so." MacArthur assured Johnson that he understood and supported the president's policy.[22]

Just to be sure, Truman dispatched White House aide W. Averell Harriman to Tokyo. Harriman became a de facto ambassador to MacArthur's headquarters, which had the trappings of "a hostile and suspicious foreign government." Truman's charge to his envoy was to tell MacArthur to "leave Chiang Kai-shek alone. I do not want to have him get me into a war with Mainland China." Yet Truman also instructed Harriman to "find out what [MacArthur] wants, and if it's at all possible, I will give it to him," as if the general truly were a Pacific potentate. Harriman's trip seemed to go well. The two men had been friends since the general's assignment as superintendent at West Point, just a few miles from Harriman's Hudson River estate. MacArthur assured Harriman that he understood the administration's positions and would support them as a good soldier. Yet Harriman was troubled. "For reasons which are rather difficult to explain," he wrote the president, "I did not feel that we came to a full agreement on the way we believed things should be handled on Formosa and with Generalissimo. He accepted the President's position and will act accordingly, but without full conviction. He has a strange idea that we should back anyone who will fight communism." Nonetheless, a few days later Truman publicly declared that "General MacArthur and I are in perfect agreement. . . . I am satisfied with what he is doing."[23] It was a measure of the president's political vulnerability that he felt the need to make such a conciliatory statement three months before an off-year election. Nonetheless Truman thought he had put these troubles to rest.

He had not. That same day, August 10, 1950, MacArthur issued a press release defending his trip to Formosa, which had been "maliciously misrepresented to the public by those who invariably in the past have propagandized a policy of defeatism and appeasement in the Pacific." MacArthur did not say who the "anonymous sources" and "persons 10,000 miles away" were, but "appeasement" was a reference to Munich and "defeatism" the language of the anticommunist "China Lobby," who accused the Truman administration of having "lost China." To Truman, Acheson, and others in Washington, MacArthur seemed to be aligning himself with right-wing Republican opposition to the president.[24]

Four days later Johnson sent the general a cable reminding him of the administration's policy forbidding deployment of American forces to Formosa without the president's approval. MacArthur petulantly replied that he fully understood the president's intention "to protect the Communist mainland." Such impudence fairly begged rebuke, but none was forthcoming. Instead, Truman seemed to reward MacArthur's arrogance by granting him permission to coordinate defense plans with Chiang, which the general had already begun to do.[25]

A few days later the Veterans of Foreign Wars asked MacArthur to send a statement to be read at their annual "encampment." A boilerplate encomium to the heroism of the VFW's members would have sufficed, but MacArthur chose to address the issue of Formosa, in order "to clarify any fogginess in current American thinking generated by such misinformation being circulated in public discussions both at home and abroad." Formosa, he argued, was an "unsinkable carrier tender" located so "that in the hands of a power unfriendly to the United States it constitutes an enemy salient" into American strategic defense lines in the Pacific. "Nothing could be more fallacious than the threadbare argument by those who advocate appeasement and defeatism in the Pacific that if we defend Formosa we alienate continental Asia." Those who made such assertions did "not understand the Orient." He ended by applauding the president's decision to defend Korea as a "turning point in this area's struggle for freedom." Senator Joseph McCarthy, who had well begun his noxious anticommunist crusade, called the letter a "most intelligent, clearcut, irrefutable, and valuable document."[26]

Although MacArthur had sent an almost identical message to the Joint Chiefs a few days earlier, the VFW letter appeared to be a public disavowal of Truman's policy. Indeed, the British ambassador pointedly wondered whether U.S. policy on "Formosa was firmly based on the President's statements," a considerable departure from usual diplomatic discourse. At a Saturday morning meeting Truman, "his lips white and compressed," read the entire VFW message aloud to Acheson, Johnson, Harriman, and the Joint Chiefs. Acheson called the letter "rank insubordination." Omar Bradley found it "the height of arrogance." The president told Johnson to order MacArthur to retract the statement, but the secretary balked. Johnson revered MacArthur, the letter was already in the press, and forcing the general to recant might cause more embarrassment. When Truman discovered that Johnson (soon to be dismissed) had not complied, he dictated an order for immediate delivery: "The President of the United States directs that you withdraw your message . . . because various features with respect to Formosa are in conflict with the policy of the United States and its position in the

United Nations." Truman considered sacking MacArthur as CINCUNC and appointing Bradley in his stead, but he decided against relief, having "no desire to hurt General MacArthur personally."[27]

When MacArthur received the retraction order, he was "utterly astonished" and protested that his statement clearly supported Truman's policy. Moreover, the opinions expressed were merely his "personal" views. Still, he complied and retracted the letter, but the damage was done, as newspapers across the United States and abroad published it. MacArthur became convinced that conspirators in Washington were bent on his destruction. Bradley would later testify that the episode was the first in "an accumulation" of offenses that led to MacArthur's recall. Again, having reined in the general, Truman undermined his own action by sending a conciliatory note and lending his support to MacArthur for a most risky amphibious operation at Inchon.[28]

If Truman was having difficulty maintaining civilian control, the Joint Chiefs were finding it increasingly difficult to exercise military oversight of MacArthur. Bradley believed that the Far East commander "always considered us a bunch of kids." MacArthur had served with none of the Joint Chiefs during the war and had no personal relationships with them. Senior as they were, the chiefs were all a generation younger than their Far East subordinate, and none of them, except perhaps Bradley, had achieved anything like his wartime laurels. MacArthur referred to Bradley, his fellow five-star general, commander of American ground forces during the war in Europe, and current chairman of the Joint Chiefs, as "a farmer." As Eisenhower had warned, MacArthur was stingy with information except when providing it suited his purposes. During his years as SCAP, MacArthur trusted no one outside his intimate circle of advisers, and over time that circle had become a coterie of sycophants. MacArthur included the JCS in those he characterized as sitting ten thousand miles away perfectly ignorant of the Orient. The strains in this relationship grew worse.[29]

Over the summer of 1950 the Pusan perimeter stabilized as Allied ground forces gained strength and Allied air forces punished the North Korean army and effectively cut its lines of communication. The Eighth Army was probably strong enough to take the offensive, but MacArthur had other ideas. He conceived an amphibious turning movement reminiscent of his famous "island hopping" strategy of World War II. He would land a force at Inchon, just south of Seoul on the peninsula's western coast, trapping the North Korean army between two UN forces. The plan was daring, not least because the harbor at Inchon suffered from one of the severest tidal disparities on Earth, some thirty feet between high and ebb tide. At first, except for MacArthur, no one—even his own staff—supported the plan. But when Harriman had asked what MacArthur wanted in return for his support of the administration, the general had asked approval of this plan. Truman ordered the Pentagon to support it. MacArthur refused to provide essential details to the JCS for fear that they might find the operation wanting. When the Joint Chiefs finally understood what MacArthur had in mind, Bradley spoke for them all and called Inchon "the worst possible place ever selected for an amphibious landing." As the American land commander at Normandy, Bradley knew something about amphibious operations. Appalled, the Joint Chiefs deputized U.S. Army chief of staff General J. Lawton Collins and chief of naval operations Admiral Forrest Sherman to fly to Japan to talk MacArthur out of his scheme. MacArthur gave a masterly performance. One of the admirals present later said, "If MacArthur had gone on the stage, you never would have heard of John Barrymore." He dissected the counterarguments one by one, and finally admitted the risks, saying, "I am used to taking such odds. . . . We shall land at Inchon and I shall crush them!" His rhetoric carried the day. Sherman and Collins returned to Washington endorsing the plan. After meeting with the president and Secretary Johnson, the JCS sent MacArthur a tepid approval. Then just days before the landing, they sent him more questions, which MacArthur saw as "an anticipatory alibi in case the expedition should run into trouble." In reply, MacArthur evasively told the chiefs that "the plan remains as described to you." Then he dispatched to Washington a junior officer carrying the details of the operation, knowing that the courier would arrive too late for the JCS to act. Bradley called these antics "an act of arrogance unparalleled in my military experience.[30]

On one level the Inchon landing was one of the most successful amphibious operations in history, accomplishing its immediate objective with light losses and leading to the recapture of Seoul several days later. The Eighth Army broke out of the Pusan perimeter, drove the enemy northward, and linked up with the Inchon forces. Yet operational success yielded no strategic victory: large remnants of the North Korean People's Army withdrew past the thirty-eighth parallel because the two allied forces were unable to close the trap. Inchon failed to fulfill MacArthur's theatrical promise to crush the NKPA and, thereby, to win the war. Still, the original war aim, restoring the status quo antebellum, had been accomplished.[31]

Yet the myth of Inchon—that MacArthur, against all odds and over the protests of his timid superiors, had pulled off the impossible—was potent. His already submissive staff in Tokyo now viewed him as an infallible deity. Back in Washington, MacArthur's ostensible superiors on the Joint Chiefs became wary and timid. After worrying, dallying, and weakly concurring with the Inchon plan, the JCS "were naturally reluctant to oppose their theater commander and be embarrassed again." Bradley said they looked "like a bunch of nervous Nellies to have doubted." General Collins later admitted that MacArthur's prestige was so "overpowering, that the Chiefs hesitated thereafter to question later plans and decisions . . . which should have been challenged." Averell Harriman said that "General Bradley and the Chiefs of Staff were afraid of General MacArthur." Acheson warned that "there's no stopping MacArthur now." When the general announced his intention to preside at a ceremony to reinstate the Syngman Rhee government in recaptured Seoul, State protested and the JCS told him that "such plans must have the approval of higher authority." MacArthur wired back, "Your message is not understood. I have no plans whatsoever except scrupulously to implement the directives which I have received." The ceremony went ahead just as MacArthur planned.[32]

With the North Koreans in flight north of the thirty-eighth parallel, the United Nations could have considered their mission completed, but all in Washington agreed that new circumstances presented an opportunity to unify Korea under a democratic government. Truman had approved a National Security Council policy statement before Inchon that prospectively authorized military operations north of the parallel, but ordered MacArthur to take precautions not to draw the Chinese or Soviets into the conflict. For example, only Republic of Korea (ROK) forces should advance near the Yalu River border with Manchuria. On September 27, 1950, the JCS directed MacArthur to advance north of the thirty-eighth parallel to destroy the North Korean armed forces in accord with NSC policy. Then newly installed secretary of defense, George Marshall, muddled the JCS order by telling MacArthur, "We want you to feel unhampered tactically and strategically to proceed north of the 38th Parallel."

MacArthur replied, "I regard all of Korea open for our military operations, unless and until the enemy capitulates." The United Nations General Assembly ratified the new mission a week later. As the Allies attacked north, there was a shared feeling in Korea, Tokyo, and Washington that the war was almost over.[33]

In mid-October Truman decided to fly to the Pacific for a meeting with his field commander. Midterm congressional elections were a few weeks away, and the Democrats needed a boost. Having the president rub elbows with a winning general couldn't hurt. Marshall and Acheson counseled against the trip, and neither accompanied the president. Acheson recalled telling Truman that "while General MacArthur had many of the attributes of a foreign sovereign . . . and was quite as difficult as any, it did not seem wise to recognize him as one." Truman was aware of the stakes, confiding to a friend that he was going "to talk to God's right-hand man tomorrow." When the president and the CINCFE met at Wake Island they seemed, said *Time* magazine, "like the sovereign rulers of separate states, approaching a neutral field with panoplied retainers to make talk and watch each other's eyes." MacArthur, in open-collared khakis and his trademark crushed-brim cap, greeted the president on the tarmac at sixty-thirty in the morning. The two men had never met, but they beamed at one another like old friends. Reporters noted that MacArthur failed to salute his commander in chief. They met in two sessions, the first a private half-hour interview in a Quonset hut. A short while later they joined Harriman, General Bradley, diplomat Dean Rusk, and several other political and military aides. MacArthur pulled out a briar pipe and asked if the president minded his smoking. "No," said Truman to general laughter, "I suppose I've had more smoke blown in my face than any other man alive." Unknown to MacArthur, a stenographer sat near an open door taking notes. MacArthur reported on the military situation in Korea and the plans for political and economic reconstruction after the war. He fielded numerous questions with ease, and several participants commented on the brilliance of his performance and his command of the subject. Truman emphasized the need to limit the war to Korea and the current combatants. MacArthur said he expected "formal resistance" to end by Thanksgiving and hoped to begin returning troops to Japan by Christmas. Truman asked about the likelihood of Chinese or Soviet intervention. "Very little," the general said, offering a comprehensive estimate of the strength of Chinese ground forces (he said they had no effective air force) in Manchuria and the Russian air force in

Siberia. He assured the conference that the combination of Chinese troops and Russian air forces "just wouldn't work."[34]

After ninety minutes Truman brought the meeting to a close, marveling at how much ground they had covered. He invited MacArthur to lunch, but the general declined, pleading the need to return to his command as soon as possible. Bradley thought his refusal offensive to the president, but Truman did not let on. The conferees waited while a communiqué was prepared, then stepped outside for another photo opportunity where Truman presented the general with a Distinguished Service Medal. Despite dire predictions, at the time the conference appeared to be an unqualified success. On his way home, Truman was at pains to relate how much he and MacArthur agreed on policy. Yet the meetings were too brief to be substantive, and no new directions resulted from them. Acheson, later explaining his misgivings, said that "talk should precede, not follow, the issuance of orders." MacArthur's private meeting with the president did in fact sow the seeds of later misunderstandings. Five hours after his arrival, Truman boarded his plane for Hawaii. The two men would never see each other again.[35]

Two days later UN forces were forty miles from the Yalu; North Korean resistance seemed to have collapsed. MacArthur pressed his American troops to "drive forward with all speed and with full utilization of all their force." When the JCS reminded him that only South Koreans were to go near the Yalu, MacArthur dismissed their warnings: their directive had been temporary, Secretary Marshall's subsequent message lifted any restrictions, and further, this was a policy matter that he and Truman had privately discussed at Wake. The Joint Chiefs were in the dark, but neither they nor Secretary Marshall moved to force MacArthur to comply with their orders. Bradley later testified to a Senate panel: "I don't know what was discussed between the President and General MacArthur." Yet Truman told a press conference that he understood only ROK troops were to approach the Chinese border. MacArthur then issued his own statement, saying "the mission of the United Nations forces is to clear Korea." The JCS, on eggshells after their Inchon embarrassment, advised Truman to adhere to American military tradition of allowing the commander in the field to carry out his assigned mission without interference. That advice accorded with Truman's own belief that it was the president's role to assist generals in wartime, rather than second-guessing them. The president backed down and endorsed MacArthur's deployments of American troops, saying there would be no "privileged sanctuary" for the NKPA. On October 24 the UN forces were racing toward the Yalu.[36]

The next day the Chinese army attacked. Even before the Inchon landing, Chinese foreign minister Chou En-lai had expressed concerns about China's security. At the end of September he publicly warned the United States not to cross the thirty-eighth parallel. When the UN authorized reunification of Korea in early October, Chou broadcast another message declaring the resolution illegal and warned that the Chinese would "not stand idly by" while American forces menaced their borders. Chinese Communist forces (CCF) began crossing the Yalu that same day, a week before MacArthur assured Truman that they would not attack.[37]

The CCF inflicted significant casualties on UN troops for two weeks, then broke contact as quickly as they had attacked. MacArthur's report to the JCS indicates that he was not unduly alarmed and wanted "a more complete accumulation of military facts" before giving his appraisal of the situation. Yet on the same day and without notifying the JCS, he ordered his air commander, General George Stratemeyer, to launch a bombing campaign in northernmost Korea, targeting the Korean ends of the Yalu bridges. Stratemeyer prudently called General Vandenberg, air force chief of staff, to warn him. The possibility of bombers straying into Chinese territory and thereby widening the war escaped MacArthur, but was hardly lost on his superiors in Washington. Under Truman's instructions the JCS ordered MacArthur to suspend all bombing within five miles of the Yalu.[38]

Bradley later wrote that November and December of 1950 were when "MacArthur lost control of the battle and his emotions, leading Washington to lose all confidence in him." In response to the JCS order, MacArthur protested that the Chinese attack "threatens the ultimate destruction of the forces under my command." The bombing suspension would "be paid for dearly in American and other United Nations blood." MacArthur insisted that the JCS reconsider their order or immediately bring the matter before the president. He could "not overemphasize the disastrous effect . . . for which [he] could not accept responsibility without [the president's] personal and direct understanding of the situation." In just two days MacArthur's attitude had changed from wait-and-see to fear of "a calamity of major proportion."[39]

The Joint Chiefs did consult Truman, who, in deference to the commander "on the scene," ordered them to "give him the go-ahead" to bomb the Korean ends of the bridges as he had proposed, but to be careful of other sensitive targets such as dams and power plants. Bradley later recalled MacArthur's emotional challenge to the Joint Chiefs' authority: That night

> we committed the worst possible error . . . we sensed something was badly wrong. MacArthur had exceeded his authority in ordering the bombing of the [Yalu] bridges and had first tried to do it without Washington clearance. It was an indication that he was going off willy-nilly on his own in defiance of established policy. . . . Right then—that night—the JCS should have taken firmest control of the Korean War and dealt with MacArthur bluntly.[40]

Yet despite their fear "that a global war with the Russians could erupt at any hour," the Joint Chiefs failed to jerk MacArthur's reins. Their timidity after Inchon, their lack of clarity about the operational situation, and traditional deference to the commander in theater combined to forestall an intrusion. Secretary Marshall sent a mollifying message to MacArthur, full of understanding for his difficulty and promising fullest support, but reminding him of the worldwide implications of the war. MacArthur responded in kind, thanking Marshall and expressing "complete agreement with the basic concept of localizing, if possible, the Korean struggle."[41]

Then again, almost simultaneously, MacArthur demanded for his fighter planes the right of "hot pursuit" of enemy aircraft—both Chinese and Soviet MiG-15s had been spotted—across the Manchurian border.[42]

In light of the CCF offensive, the JCS advised MacArthur that "'the destruction of the North Korean Armed Forces' may have to be reexamined" by the National Security Council. In yet another volte-face MacArthur insisted that "it would be fatal to weaken the fundamental and basic policy of the United Nations to destroy" the NKPA. Instead, given that the Chinese had broken off their attack, he wanted to mount "an all-out offensive designed to drive the Communist Forces across the Yalu River." If the NSC restricted his objectives, it would "destroy the morale of my forces" and the ROK army might "collapse or even turn against us." In response to a JCS message alluding to the need to consult UN allies, he also disparaged the "Munich attitude" of the British and their "desire to appease the Chinese Communists by giving them a strip of Northern Korea." Obviously, MacArthur's understanding of the international implications of operations in his theater, which he had been at such pains to express to Marshall, only went so far. True to form, the JCS dithered, requested clarification, and then meekly approved CINCFE's offensive.[43]

MacArthur was planning to attack an enemy force that had driven him back with alacrity two weeks earlier. That force was resting and reinforcing, a fact that MacArthur's intelligence staff failed to discover. Supremely confident once again, MacArthur assured Washington that his offensive would end the war. During a Thanksgiving visit to the front with a press contingent in tow, he loudly promised to "get the boys home by Christmas." Reporters seized on the comment and began to write about the "Home-for-Christmas Drive," as MacArthur surely intended. The attack began November 24.[44]

The Eighth Army pushed north from positions in the Chongchon Valley on the western side of the peninsula. The X Corps was in the east and separated from the Eighth Army by some fifty miles of rugged terrain weakly held by an inexperienced ROK corps. The night after the UN offensive commenced, the Chinese counterattacked with 180,000 troops in the east, 120,000 in the west. The main Chinese effort sought to exploit the UN's weak center, driving the ROK forces back while attempting to turn the Eighth Army's right flank. The center cracked, and within days all UN forces were retreating under the pressure.[45]

MacArthur, buoyantly optimistic a few days earlier, warned the JCS that "we face an entirely new war." He began to demand reinforcements, warning that his command might be pushed into the sea. The JCS suggested withdrawal south and defending along the narrow waist of the peninsula. MacArthur refused, insisting that Eighth Army and X Corps could not regain contact, but had to establish separate beachheads on opposite sides of the peninsula for defense and possible evacuation. The Eighth Army might have to fall back as far as Pusan. Again, the JCS agreed, as "the preservation of your forces is now the primary consideration."[46]

President Truman was angry with MacArthur for having underestimated the Chinese threat. MacArthur had told him point-blank that there was little likelihood of Chinese intervention. Now the "Big General" was talking about evacuating Korea. "Home for Christmas" was a bad joke. Moreover, newspaper reports began to criticize MacArthur for his handling of the war. The thin-skinned general answered his critics in letters and interviews. The *New York Post* noted with some sarcasm that MacArthur had granted exclusive and lengthy access to four media outlets in as many days. His offensive, which he now said had really been only a "reconnaissance-in-force," had saved the UN Command from a Chinese trap. His superiors in Washington had imposed restrictions on his freedom of action that were "an enormous handicap, without precedent in military history." Truman felt that MacArthur was trying to ensure "that no blame whatsoever attached to him or his staff." Once again, the president considered relieving MacArthur, but decided against it because he didn't want it to appear that he had fired the general because the offensive failed—no general could "be a winner every day of the week." Truman hesitated to reprimand MacArthur, but the general "had to be told" that his public statements were "out of order." Accordingly, Truman told Acheson and Marshall to issue two directives admonishing their subordinates to "exercise extreme caution" in public statements and to clear all but routine releases with either State or Defense. On December 6, 1950, the so-called "gag order" went to U.S. officials around the world, but it was intended for MacArthur.[47]

Still, every national security leader in Washington shrank from confrontation with MacArthur. Yet the Chinese offensive and the UN collapse made it clear that the train was running off the rails in Korea. The strategy was questionable, battlefield leadership seemed weak, and the theater commander was growing increasingly erratic. The *New York Herald Tribune* ran an editorial entitled "MacArthur's Disaster," charging that the Far East headquarters had "compounded blunder by confusion." MacArthur could "no longer be accepted as the final authority on military matters." He began insisting on a blockade of mainland China and renewed his call for Nationalist Chinese troops to reinforce the UN Command in Korea. Acheson and his team joined Marshall and the Joint Chiefs in the Pentagon War Room on Sunday, December 3, for hours of talks on the situation. Lieutenant General Matthew B. Ridgway, the army's deputy chief of staff, remembered that no one was "willing to issue a flat order" to MacArthur. Ridgway finally spoke up, telling his superiors that they "had already spent too damn much time in debate"—they owed it to the men in the field to stop talking and do something. Acheson felt that "someone had expressed what everyone thought—that the Emperor had no clothes on." Yet no one else spoke. No decisions were made; no orders given.[48]

Walking out of the meeting, Ridgway accosted his old friend, Hoyt Vandenberg, the air force chief of staff. Why didn't the Joint Chiefs "send orders to MacArthur and tell him what to do?" Vandenberg said, "What good would that do? He wouldn't obey the orders. What can we do?" Ridgway stated the obvious: "You can relieve any commander who won't obey orders, can't you?" Vandenberg, "puzzled and amazed," just walked away.[49]

The strains were showing on everyone. At a press conference that week, Truman fumbled a question by indicating that atomic bombs might be used in Korea. Then he made matters worse. Was that option under active consideration? "Always has been," Truman replied; "it is one of our weapons." Under what circumstances would they use the bomb? Becoming more exasperated, Truman said, "It's a matter that the military people will have to decide. I'm not a military authority that passes on those things." How would such a decision be made? Truman snapped, "The military commander in the field will have charge of the use of the weapon, as he always has." Although the White House press office later clarified Truman's remarks, saying that the president was well aware that only he could authorize use of atomic weapons, the damage had been done. The British House of Commons erupted at the news that MacArthur might have control of the bomb. Prime Minister Clement Attlee flew to Washington immediately for consultations with Truman.[50]

Over the next several weeks MacArthur became more and more pessimistic, demanding a change in policy based on a false dilemma. He insisted that the administration acknowledge that war already existed with China. However, the forces at his command were too small to counter the Chinese offensive. He needed reinforcement from stateside U.S. divisions. With that help he proposed a four-part plan to: (1) bomb mainland China to "destroy its industrial capacity to wage war," (2) blockade the Chinese coast, (3) employ the Nationalist Chinese to reinforce the UN in Korea, and (4) release the Nationalists to attack the mainland. If the administration did not agree with this policy shift, the only alternative was evacuation and defeat, for which he could not be held responsible.[51]

The president and the National Security Council rejected MacArthur's plan. The JCS sent the general a polite response, saying there was "little possibility of a policy change." The mission was now to defend in Korea, protect his force, and to inflict as much damage on the enemy as possible. The Joint Chiefs requested his thoughts on the conditions that might trigger the need to evacuate the peninsula. MacArthur "shot a query right back." His forces were insufficient to hold on in Korea and protect Japan. A decision to evacuate Korea would be of "highest and international importance, far above the competence of a theater commander." What, he asked, was his mission? The morale of his troops would "become a serious threat to their battle efficiency unless the political basis upon which they are asked to trade life for time is clearly delineated." MacArthur ended with mawkish sarcasm: "Under the extraordinary limitations and conditions imposed upon the command in Korea . . . its military position is untenable, but it can hold, if overriding political considerations so dictate, for any length of time up to its complete destruction. Your clarification requested." McClellan could not have put it better.

Dean Acheson said MacArthur's reply "was a posterity paper if ever there was one." Marshall was especially peeved, telling Dean Rusk that when a general complains about his soldiers' morale, the problem is with the general, not the soldiers. Bradley concluded that MacArthur was badly out of touch with conditions on the ground. Worse, he was "incurably recalcitrant and basically disloyal." Bradley felt that "Washington was thus being placed in the position of *convincing* a subordinate commander that our orders should be carried out." Yet Truman sent a long and adulatory letter to MacArthur painstakingly explaining the importance of the effort in Korea to broader strategic objectives. Generals Joseph Collins and Hoyt Vandenberg flew to Japan to define the mission and to explain a menu of sixteen possible contingencies in the event of an evacuation. MacArthur seems to have misconstrued every message. In particular, he seized on those contingency steps—a blockade of the Chinese coast, reconnaissance flights along the Chinese border, removing restrictions on Chiang's forces—as JCS concurrence with his four-part policy proposal. All the while, he continued to complain about his restrictions and a lack of clarity in his mission. The truth was that MacArthur simply disagreed with the administration's policy and believed that he should be allowed to expand the war into mainland China.[52]

Two days before Christmas, Eighth Army commanding general Walton H. Walker was killed in a jeep accident near the front. Some in Washington had been concerned about his leadership for some time, but no one had wanted to confront MacArthur about the matter. Now MacArthur requested that General Ridgway replace Walker, and the JCS quickly agreed. Criticisms about morale and discipline in Korea may have been exaggerated. The Eighth Army had just executed a textbook fighting withdrawal, inflicting far more casualties than it took and finally establishing a solid defensive line. Still, with energy, charisma, and iron will, Ridgway turned the army into a formidable and aggressive fighting force. While in the Far East to confer with MacArthur, Collins and Vandenberg visited Ridgway at the front and found a force with renewed morale and offensive spirit, contrary to the gloomy picture that MacArthur was painting in Tokyo. The two service chiefs took that assessment back to Washington, delivering the final blow to MacArthur's credibility within the administration and the Joint Chiefs. From that point forward the JCS began to bypass MacArthur and deal directly with Ridgway. Bradley felt that "MacArthur had been 'kicked upstairs' to chairman of the board and was, insofar as military operations were concerned, mainly a prima donna figurehead who had to be tolerated."[53]

Over the next three months the situation on the ground in Korea changed significantly. Ridgway's leadership transformed the Eighth Army, which executed several offensives in early 1951. By the end of March UN forces had pushed the CCF north and were threatening once again to cross the thirty-eighth parallel. MacArthur developed a habit of flying in from Tokyo, holding a press conference announcing that he had ordered an attack, and then flying back to Japan before nightfall. Ridgway's staff was apoplectic at the breaches of operational security, to say nothing of the old man's grandstanding. MacArthur had had nothing to do with these offensives. Yet the Eighth Army moved inexorably forward. However, the administration and the United Nations had quietly recognized that there would be no unification of Korea. The UN General Assembly passed resolutions calling for a cease-fire and negotiations, but Chou had denounced those as illegal, and the war went on. Truman and his advisers repeatedly rejected MacArthur's demands for a wider war, a position that was easier taken with Ridgway in command in Korea. Sometime in March, perhaps sensing his own growing irrelevance or fearing that the last chapter of his biography might end in stalemate, MacArthur mounted the stage for the final act of his career.[54]

As UN forces approached the thirty-eighth parallel, Truman's advisers conferred over what another crossing of that symbolic line might mean for policy. Acheson canvassed the allies and found little appetite for another invasion of North Korea. The NSC therefore advised Truman to work toward an armistice with the Chinese. Accordingly, they drafted a potential armistice statement and began circulating it among the allies. The JCS concurred with the initiative and told MacArthur of it on March 20.[55]

Four times in the previous month MacArthur had made public statements that he failed to clear with the Pentagon. In them he rehearsed the usual grievances, disparaging the "unprecedented" restrictions that Washington had placed on his operations and predicting "savage slaughter" if American policies were not reversed. Despite these repeated violations of the December 6, 1950, "gag order," the JCS never questioned or confronted the CINCFE. MacArthur concluded that the gag order was a dead letter inasmuch as the Joint Chiefs were neglecting to enforce it.[56]

On March 24 MacArthur preempted the president's peace feeler with his own communiqué to the Chinese. MacArthur taunted his enemy, asserting that China lacked the capability to wage modern war. Despite the restrictions under which he labored as UN commander, China had demonstrated "its complete inability to accomplish by force of arms its conquest of Korea." He warned that if the UN decided to widen the war, China risked "imminent military collapse." Therefore, MacArthur announced, he stood ready to confer with his Chinese opposite number to effect the accomplishment of UN political objectives in Korea. This insulting, arrogant invitation to surrender scuttled any chance for armistice talks. Discussions with the allies about armistice negotiations were now moot. Truman never sent his proposal to the Chinese because "it would only have confused the world."[57]

Reaction to MacArthur's pronouncement was swift. Allied leaders deluged the State Department and the White House with queries—did MacArthur's statement indicate a change in U.S. policy? Who was making American policy? Deputy defense secretary Robert A. Lovett said MacArthur's act constituted "defiance of the Chiefs of Staff, sabotage of an operation of which he had been informed, and insubordination of the grossest sort to his Commander in Chief." Likewise, Acheson called it "a major act of sabotage." For Bradley it was an "unforgivable and irretrievable act." Some wondered if MacArthur had taken leave of his senses. Acheson quoted Euripides: "Whom the gods destroy they first make mad." The official history of the Joint Chiefs concluded, "Had he deliberately sought to do so, the UN Commander could hardly have found a more effective way to arouse the President's wrath." Arouse it he did. Truman's reaction "combined disbelief with controlled fury."

MacArthur's action "was in open defiance of my orders as President and Commander in Chief. This was a challenge to the President under the Constitution. It also flouted the policy of the United Nations. . . . By this act MacArthur left me no choice—I could no longer tolerate his insubordination." The president made up his mind: he would relieve MacArthur. The questions were how and when. Looking, as he often did, to history for guidance, Truman began to study the details of the Lincoln-McClellan relationship.[58]

Truman acted deliberately. He determined, for the time being, to keep his own counsel about his decision. He instructed the JCS to send MacArthur a terse message: the president directs that you review the 6 December 1950 "gag order." If Chinese generals requested a parley, he was to report to the JCS for instructions. As reprimands go, this was rather mild stuff. MacArthur might have thought that Washington's pattern of timidity and lenience was continuing. Indeed, he told one adviser at the time that because he was a UN commander, "There's nothing [the administration] can do to me. There has to be an international agreement."[59] That statement of hubris both underestimated Harry Truman and overstated MacArthur's standing with the UN allies.

Then, on March 20, MacArthur responded to a letter from Republican congressman Joseph Martin, House minority leader. Martin had sent MacArthur a copy of a speech in which the congressman had called for opening a second front with the help of Nationalist Chinese forces. "If we are not in Korea to win, then this administration should be indicted for the murder of American boys." He asked MacArthur for his reaction "on a confidential basis or otherwise." The general praised the speech and agreed with the need to unleash Chiang and his army. He derided those who could not see the primacy of the Far Eastern theater: "Here we fight Europe's war with arms while the diplomats there still fight it with words; . . . if we lose the war to Communism in Asia the fall of Europe is inevitable; win it and Europe most probably would avoid war and yet preserve freedom. As you point out, we must win. There is no substitute for victory." MacArthur placed no restrictions on Martin's use of the letter.[60]

On April 5, 1951, Martin went to the well of the House and read the letter aloud. MacArthur's comments made front-page news around the world. For the second time in as many weeks editors were asking who was making American policy. Foreign diplomats lined up at the State Department to register their complaints. Members of Congress broke along partisan lines, with many Republicans echoing MacArthur's concerns.[61]

Truman was calm in a storm. Over the weekend he consulted privately with the vice president, the chief justice, the Speaker of the House, and the secretary of the treasury. Truman convened his top national security advisers again on Saturday. Marshall suggested ordering MacArthur to Washington for consultations, but Acheson opposed bringing him home "in the full panoply of his commands and with his future the issue of the day." The president would be hamstrung. Their accounts differ on where each stood that morning on the question of relief. Truman announced no decision.[62]

Marshall and Bradley pleaded for more time to think and consult. The question was personally and professionally wrenching for both of them. The secretary had not been well for some time. Moreover, he still bore the scars of the political mauling he had taken for his role in the "loss" of China. During his confirmation hearing, a member of the McCarthy clique, Senator William Jenner, had called Marshall "a front man for traitors" and a "living lie." Bradley had observed the savaging of Marshall at close hand for years, but had personally "been spared attack by the right-wing primitives on the Hill." Just months from his own planned retirement, Bradley had "no stomach for going out on [such a] sour note." More broadly, he worried that a JCS endorsement of MacArthur's relief, "if the firing was construed as mainly political, . . . would have the effect of 'politicizing' the JCS." The two men considered sending a stern warning to MacArthur, but that gambit had failed several times before. At all events they wanted to avoid getting into a legal wrangle that might lead to a court-martial and a media circus.[63]

On Sunday afternoon Bradley met with the Joint Chiefs and discussed an array of options to solve the "MacArthur problem." Eventually, they unanimously agreed that he should be relieved of all his commands. They made their recommendation from "a military point of view only," recognizing that those considerations were but a small part of a broader issue. They offered Marshall and the president four reasons that MacArthur should be relieved: that he was not in sympathy with the policy to limit the war to Korea; that he had disobeyed the "gag order" and had undercut the president's peace initiative; that it was difficult to coordinate plans with him as they never knew if he would obey orders; and that failure to relieve him would damage civilian control. The president's political standing was so precarious that having the unanimous support of the JCS on this matter would be invaluable in the months to come.[64]

Bradley delivered the Joint Chiefs' recommendation to Truman on Monday. Marshall voiced his concurrence with their recommendation. The four advisers were agreed. For the first time Truman revealed that he had already reached his decision. The group agreed that Ridgway should succeed MacArthur, and Truman directed Bradley to prepare the necessary orders. Truman signed them the next day.[65]

A comedy of errors followed. Delivering the message to MacArthur was a delicate task. As Secretary of the Army Frank Pace was then touring the front in Korea, Truman decided that he should personally deliver the relief order. The night before he was to have done so, a *Chicago Tribune* reporter began asking about a "major resignation" that was rumored in Tokyo. Bradley warned Truman that MacArthur might resign if he knew he was about to be relieved. "That son of a bitch isn't going to resign on me!" Truman exploded, "I want him fired!" The White House staff prepared a statement that it released at 1:00 A.M. in Washington. Through a communications snafu, Pace never got his instructions. Bradley tried to send a radio message to MacArthur, but it arrived too late. Instead, MacArthur learned of his relief from his wife, who had heard it from a tearful staff officer, who in turn had heard the news flash over the radio. Accidental as it was, this gaffe was an unfortunate way to end a distinguished military career of some five decades.[66]

For the next several weeks the United States was awash in a tide of Truman hatred. Truman addressed the nation the day after the firing, but the speech was "a complete flop." Truman was a master at making hard decisions, but he failed at communicating his rationale to the country. The president was hanged in effigy in California. State legislatures and city councils passed resolutions condemning him. A Gallup poll showed that two-thirds of Americans opposed MacArthur's dismissal, while only one-quarter approved. The White House admitted that its mail was running twenty-to-one against the decision. Constituents sent tens of thousands of telegrams to Capitol Hill, calling for Truman's impeachment and describing him as an "imbecile," a "Judas," a "red herring," and "the pig in the White House." On April 20 the crowd at Griffith Stadium booed the president throwing out the ceremonial first pitch.[67]

The "primitives on the Hill" led the chorus. Senator Jenner charged that "this country today is in the hands of a secret coterie which is directed by agents of the Soviet Union." Freshman senator Richard Nixon of California thought "the happiest group in the country will be the Communists and their stooges." Senator McCarthy railed against "treason in the White House" and called Truman a "son of a bitch" who was drunk on "bourbon and benedictine." The president had few supporters in Congress willing to declare themselves in public.[68]

On the other hand the national press mostly stood with the president. A poll of military and political correspondents showed that 85 percent backed Truman's decision. The Scripps-Howard, Hearst, and McCormick papers—conservative bastions all—opposed the president, but a majority of editorial opinion was supportive, even among some papers usually in opposition. Influential columnist Walter Lippmann concluded that "General MacArthur chose to force the president to relieve him—or he thought from what he had seen during the past year that the president would give in and would take his orders from Tokyo." The *New York Herald Tribune* concurred:

> The most obvious fact about the dismissal of General MacArthur is that he virtually forced his own removal. In high policy as in war there is no room for divided command. . . . General MacArthur is a soldier of the highest abilities . . . yet he is the architect of a situation which really left the President with no other course. With one of those strokes of boldness and decision which are characteristic of Mr. Truman in emergencies, a very difficult and dangerous problem has been met in the only way it could have been met.[69]

Yet as one observer noted, "Truman succeeded in making a popular hero out of MacArthur—something the general was never able to do for himself." MacArthur enjoyed a triumphant return to the United States. A crowd of one hundred thousand lined a twenty-mile parade route on Oahu. In San Francisco a half million people welcomed the general, his wife, and his son. When they arrived in Washington another throng broke down restraining ropes to greet their plane. The MacArthurs waded through the scrum for a half hour to reach their awaiting limousine.[70]

Just after noon the next day, April 19, 1951, MacArthur ascended the House rostrum to address a joint meeting of Congress. The congressional leadership had extended an invitation normally reserved for the president and visiting heads of state. The events of the past week had given the address such a buildup that thirty million Americans tuned in on radio and television. Schoolchildren and federal workers had a half day off to listen to the speech. The hero of the hour exceeded expectations with one of the most moving and eloquent speeches in American history. He was forceful, but unhurried. He was dignified, but passionate. His message was clear, detailed, authoritative, and persuasive. He appeared earnest and forthright, although he was not always truthful. He began with humility and gratitude for the opportunity to address the august body in that historic chamber. He held "neither rancor nor bitterness," and had "but one purpose in mind: to serve my country." The audience, enthusiastic before he began, was now alternately holding its breath to listen and yelling itself hoarse to applaud.

He gave a lengthy appreciation of Asian history and geography, recounting his decades of experience in the region to establish his bona fides to speak as an expert on the Philippines and Japan, and more to the point, on Formosa, Korea, and China. He demonstrated mastery of his subject as he argued that the Far East was the most strategically important region on earth. The Asian peoples, he lamented, were achingly poor and long oppressed, and wanted only freedom and equality. "World ideologies play little part in Asian thinking and are little understood. What the peoples strive for is the opportunity for a little more food in their stomachs, a little better clothing on their backs, a little firmer roof over their heads, and the realization of the normal nationalist urge for political freedom."

MacArthur agreed with the president's decision to intervene in Korea and applauded his own efforts in routing the NKPA. Yet the Chinese entry "created a new war and an entirely new situation, a situation not contemplated when our forces were committed against the North Korean invaders; a situation which called for new decisions in the diplomatic sphere to permit the realistic adjustment of military strategy.

"Such decisions have not been forthcoming."

Of course, it would have been more accurate to say that the national leadership had debated those questions at length, with MacArthur's recommendations and the whole of American national security policy and grand strategy in mind, that decisions based upon those deliberations had been clearly determined, and that the JCS and the president had explained those policies in writing and in person to MacArthur repeatedly.

MacArthur rehearsed a watered-down version of the policy shift he had advocated, leaving out the imperative to destroy Chinese industrial capacity and to use Nationalist Chinese forces in Korea. He scoffed that "no man in his right mind would advocate sending our ground forces into continental China, and such was never given a thought," ignoring the probability that his prescription would broaden the war and bring on such a deployment. Furthermore, every military leader involved in the war "fully shared" these views, including the Joint Chiefs of Staff. The JCS would spend many coming weeks exposing that falsehood.

In the next sentence he passively damned those military superiors who ostensibly shared his views. "I called for reinforcements, but was informed that reinforcements were not available." He conveniently forgot the doubling of his prewar force with four stateside divisions, an infusion of strength that the JCS felt was dangerously close to imperiling the global containment strategy. MacArthur condemned anonymous critics as those who "would appease Red China." He leveled the charges of defeatism and appeasement repeatedly in his address, never naming the guilty, but leaving it to his audience to guess at their identities. He lauded the gallant men fighting in Korea who were "splendid in every way." Yet appeasement dishonored their efforts and hampered their martial efforts: "'Why,' my soldiers asked of me, 'surrender military advantages to an enemy in the field?' I could not answer."

At the end he famously begged leave to "fade away," although it soon became clear that he had no such intention.[71]

That afternoon half a million well-wishers turned out to cheer him in Washington. The next day 150,000 letters and 20,000 telegrams welcomed him at the Waldorf Astoria, his new permanent residence in New York. A day later some 7.5 million New Yorkers lined the Manhattan ticker-tape parade route. Seven hours and nineteen miles later, the Department of Sanitation swept up 2,859 tons of litter, a new record that eclipsed the old one fourfold. Although no one knew it then, MacArthur had just reached the apex of his popularity.[72]

Conservative Republicans demanded hearings into MacArthur's dismissal. The Senate agreed and gave the task to the combined Armed Services and Foreign Relations Committees with Senator Richard B. Russell, Democrat of Georgia, as chairman. Russell was an able and respected legislator and a party loyalist whose first act was to deny Republican demands for television and radio coverage of the hearings. He made the decision on national security grounds, but Democrats also intended to deny their opponents a platform for MacArthur's eloquence. The committee released "cleared" transcripts at the end of each day's session.

Forty-two days of testimony yielded a thorough public record, almost two and a half million words, which inadvertently provided an intelligence bonanza to the Chinese and Soviets.[73]

Washington's political temperature rose as the hearings drew nearer, and military leaders found themselves at the center of the controversy. James Reston noted that "prominent soldiers are supplying much of the balance, statesmanship, and confidence so sorely needed by the Administration." Columnist Drew Pearson disagreed: "It looks as if Harry Truman is going to have to fight his battle almost alone. None of the military men on whom he has leaned so heavily in the past appears ready to face MacArthur." Pearson did not know that the JCS and civilian leaders of the administration met before the hearings and began to plot strategy for the coming testimony. The secretary of the air force concluded that the administration's political fate was "in the hands of the military."[74]

MacArthur led off with three days of testimony. He appeared in character as éminence grise, master military strategist, and Far East expert. He admitted no mistakes, repeated his four-part policy prescription for ending the stalemate in Korea, expressed incredulity that the administration had chosen to tie his hands, and insisted that the Joint Chiefs agreed with his assessments and prescriptions. The senators were roundly charmed by his charisma, and impressed by his erudition. By prior agreement the committee began his daily questioning in the morning and worked through lunch until mid-afternoon. Unlike the senators, MacArthur never left his seat, causing one Democrat to marvel at the seventy-one-year-old's stamina: "Why, he must have the bladder of a college boy."[75]

Probing MacArthur's views on civilian control lay at the heart of the committee's charter. He surprised them when he said the president had every right to fire him, without giving any reason: "The authority of the president to assign officers and reassign them is complete and absolute." Yet the president had given a reason—his insubordination. MacArthur claimed to have carried out every order faithfully, "No more subordinate soldier has ever worn the American uniform."[76]

MacArthur repeated the old dichotomy between war and peace: "when you go to war, you have exhausted all other potentialities of bringing the disagreement to an end." Therefore, war becomes a matter quite separate from peace, and the "politicians" must give way to soldiers. "When politics fails, and the military takes over, you must trust the military." Later, he amplified on this principle: "There should be no non-professional interference in the handling of troops in a campaign. You have professionals to do that job and they should be permitted to do it." Of course, the worst kind of meddling was to place constraints on the use of force: there is no substitute for victory. "War never before in the history of the world has been applied in a piecemeal way," he asserted with typical MacArthur absoluteness, "that you make half-war, and not whole war. . . . That is a new concept in war. That is not war—that is appeasement."[77]

However, at one point late in MacArthur's testimony, Senator Brien McMahon, a Connecticut Democrat, asked what America should do if his oft-repeated fourfold strategy landed the nation in an all-out global war. MacArthur fell into the poorly disguised trap: "That doesn't happen to be my responsibility, Senator. My responsibilities were in the Pacific." The Joint Chiefs had responsibility for the global situation. "Now I am not familiar with their studies. I haven't gone into it." Senator McMahon then snared his prey: "General, I think you make the point very well . . . that the Joint Chiefs of Staff and the President . . . [have] to look at this thing on a global basis and a global defense. You, as a theater commander by your own statement, have not made that kind of study, and yet you advise us to push forward with a course of action that may involve us in that global conflict." MacArthur could not have it both ways.[78]

Underpinning MacArthur's entire case was his assertion that he and the JCS were in full agreement. Therefore, this was a dispute between the professional military and meddling politicians. This was a tricky argument to make, because the Joint Chiefs had already contradicted his claim that they agreed with him on policy and strategy. They had concurred with his relief. Nonetheless he plowed ahead. His proposals "were in complete accord with the military recommendations of the Joint Chiefs of Staff." Their positions and his were "practically identical." If there was "any friction between us, I am not aware of it." His military colleagues would soon take exception.[79]

After MacArthur concluded, Secretary Marshall followed him for seven days of testimony. Marshall was no longer as popular as MacArthur, but in terms of military prestige and reputation for integrity, he was more than a match. In his opening statement he began destroying the foundation of MacArthur's edifice: "From the beginning of the Korean conflict down to the present moment there has been no disagreement between the President, the Secretary of Defense, and the Joint Chiefs of Staff." Marshall, with the highest standing on both sides of the civilian-military divide, would not allow MacArthur to frame the controversy as a conflict between soldiers and politicians. Day after day, he took issue with MacArthur's strategic judgments, noting that following the general's recommendations risked "not only . . . an extension of the war with Red China, but an all-out war with the Soviet Union. He would have us do this even at the expense of losing our allies . . . [and] even though the effect of such action might expose Western Europe to attack." Marshall admitted that there was nothing new about a theater commander complaining about his orders. "What is new," he continued, "and what has brought about the necessity for General MacArthur's removal, is the wholly unprecedented situation of a local theater commander publicly expressing his displeasure at and his disagreement with the foreign and military policies of the United States."[80]

Bradley, nationally popular as the "GI general," then took questions for six days. He unequivocally endorsed the administration's policy in Korea—there was no daylight between the JCS and the administration. Using first-person pronouns Bradley lent his five-star prestige to Truman's decision to fire MacArthur. In his opening statement he said that MacArthur's proposed strategy would be a mistake because it would inevitably widen the war with Red China. In answer to a senator's hostile question about U.S. strategy, he said, "If we are following the wrong tactics [in Korea] . . . then all of our top military people that are here and who are responsible for world-wide strategy and who have knowledge of our capability are all wrong, and you are right." Most important, MacArthur's sacking was necessary because his "actions were continuing to jeopardize the civilian control over military authorities." In the most famous single line of the hearings, Bradley broadsided MacArthur's military judgment: "Frankly, in the opinion of the Joint Chiefs of Staff, this strategy would involve us in the wrong war, at the wrong place, at the wrong time, and with the wrong enemy."[81]

The service chiefs extended the long rebuttal, each in his own area of expertise. General Collins of the army criticized MacArthur's troop handling, saying it had threatened execution of the strategy. Further, Collins directly charged MacArthur with insubordination by deploying American forces on the Yalu in violation of a JCS directive. Air force chief Vandenberg called MacArthur's proposed bombing of mainland China "pecking at the periphery," because all the assets of the United States Air Force would have been "a drop in the bucket" when employed against the vastness of the enemy's territory. Admiral Sherman, chief of naval operations, testified that MacArthur was overlooking the probability that the Soviets could, in a broader war, lend their potent Pacific submarine fleet to the Chinese. Moreover, he was convinced that a unilateral U.S. Navy blockade of the long Chinese coast would be ineffective. By the time they were finished, MacArthur's "soldiers versus civilians" narrative was in shreds.[82]

Public interest in the hearings and the controversy began to wane along with MacArthur's popularity. As senators wandered in and out of the committee room, they inevitably missed much of the testimony. As a result, witnesses fielded the same questions several times from various members. Moreover, such an approach to questioning left the transcripts with a disjointed feel—it was difficult to tease out a compelling story. Chairman Russell received high marks for his mature guidance of an unwieldy body over six weeks of testimony. Sensational hearings would not have been in his or the administration's interest. Russell slowly let the air out of the MacArthur balloon, and avoided an unpredictable explosion.

MacArthur spent much of the next year touring the country, giving speeches that extended his critique of the administration. The size and enthusiasm of the crowds that greeted him in April turned the head of a man who was ever seduced by adulation. Three million people lined his route in Chicago, and fifty thousand attended his speech at Soldier Field that night. Boston and Houston both turned out a half million for his motorcade. He crisscrossed the country several times and addressed dozens of crowds. He later said that "America took me to its heart with a roar that will never leave my ears."[83]

Wealthy supporters convinced MacArthur that he had an excellent chance of securing the 1952 GOP nomination. Conservative businessmen underwrote his travel expenses. As he toured the country his speeches became more overtly partisan, touching on domestic concerns as well as foreign policy. Crowds who had come to celebrate a storied general found themselves listening to a right-wing Republican. He settled on a strategy of attacking the Truman administration, and his language became sharper at each stop. By November in Seattle he was decrying "diplomatic blunders abroad and reckless spendthrift aims at home" and "graft and corruption over a broad front in our public service." He urged listeners "to reject the socialist policies covertly and by devious means being forced upon us, to stamp out Communist influence which has played so ill-famed a part in the past direction of our public administration." Some Seattle city fathers walked out of this speech, outraged at his abuse of their invitation. Later he railed against "the burden of taxation" imposed by "insidious forces" within the government. Such forces would "seek to convert us to a form of socialistic endeavor, leading directly to the path of Communist slavery." In March 1952 in Jackson, Mississippi, he directly charged the Truman administration with advancing policies that were "leading toward a Communist state with as dreadful certainty as though the leaders of the Kremlin were charting the course." His rhetoric had become full-throated militant McCarthyism. What was sad for MacArthur was that with every attack on Truman, the general expended a little bit more of the prestige he had built up over a half century of service.[84]

Worse yet, he delivered every attack on the president while wearing the uniform of a five-star general. He had not retired and was still drawing his generous salary. For more than a year in city after city, MacArthur appeared in a trim, dark "Ike jacket" adorned with the insignia of a general of the army, and publicly disparaged his commander in chief. In July he addressed the Massachusetts legislature so attired, inveighing against "insidious forces working from within" to threaten "our free institutions." He said he had been warned that speaking out against such forces would "bring down upon my head ruthless retaliation," but he would not be silent: "I find in existence a new and heretofore unknown and dangerous concept that the members of our armed forces owe primary allegiance or loyalty to those who temporarily exercise the authority of the executive branch of the government, rather than to the country and its Constitution which they are sworn to defend. No proposition could be more dangerous. None could cast greater doubt upon the integrity of the armed services."[85] MacArthur expressly arrogated the right to determine which of his "temporary" superiors merited his loyalty and, therefore, his obedience. Manifestly, Truman and Marshall had failed MacArthur's test. It was more than a right, but a duty to preserve the military profession from those who might destroy it. If those words had issued from the mouth of a Republican senator, they would have been outrageous. Coming from an army general in uniform they were chilling.

In July 1952 MacArthur gave the keynote address to the Republican National Convention in Chicago. Primary balloting had left him fourth in the delegate count, but in those days before stage-managed conventions, the unexpected could still happen. The general's wealthy handlers were banking on MacArthur's eloquence to stampede the delegates in his direction. It was not to be. Months on the stump had degraded, not enhanced, his oratorical skills. He had developed weird mannerisms, bouncing up and down on his toes and sharply gesticulating upward with his right hand. Moreover, his task was to bring together the disparate wings of the GOP, a job for which a year of red-meat rhetoric had left him ill-prepared. Perhaps he was uncomfortable appearing in mufti for the first time. The speech flopped. Another five-star general won the nomination and the election. Afterward, the old soldier truly did just fade away.[86]

The differences between the president and the general were myriad: the strategic importance of, and American policy toward, Formosa; limiting the war to Korea or widening it to threaten mainland China; determining the essential theater in the Cold War—Europe or the Far East; collective security versus unilateralism; negotiating peace or fighting to a total victory (or defeat). All of those issues share at least two traits. Each was vitally important to the United States, and each was beyond General MacArthur's purview. His views on those matters, if solicited by the JCS or the president, might have been interesting, insightful, and useful in the making of policy. But his opinions should never have been a matter of public record and certainly not a cause of controversy with the president and his administration. Yet they were.

Each of the principals in this drama deserves a share of the blame. MacArthur obviously knew better. Many times in correspondence with the JCS or in his Senate testimony, he acknowledged that certain matters were beyond "the competence of a theater commander." While he usually invoked such limitation on his authority when doing so shielded him from making unpleasant decisions or accepting responsibility for failure, his use of such phrases is proof that he knew his boundaries and that foreign policy and global strategy were not his province. Yet he issued policy communiqués with abandon.

Truman also bears some responsibility. From the beginning of his presidency he had watched "the right-hand man of God" with a wary eye. He knew that MacArthur was a prima donna who had been virtually autonomous for five years in the Philippines, had strode the southwest Pacific like a colossus during the Second World War, and had ruled Japan as proconsul for the past five years. He knew the size of MacArthur's ego, his habits of insubordination, his thirst for glory, and his unwillingness to brook interference. Yet Truman feared the political consequences of crossing an American hero, especially one with MacArthur's right-wing political connections. Throughout American history, relieving a senior commander has always been fraught with potential political consequences. A good rule of thumb for political-military relations is: when the president mistrusts or fears one of his senior commanders, that officer's relief is already overdue. Truman waited too long.

Truman's civilian advisers and the Joint Chiefs must also shoulder a measure of blame. Most of them knew MacArthur far better than the president. By their own accounts there were many times when they knew that MacArthur had gone too far with his public pronouncements. Yet they tiptoed around the issue of whether MacArthur had been technically or legally insubordinate in those statements. Time and again, they either overlooked his transgressions or handled them so gingerly as to remove the sting of rebuke. They conditioned MacArthur to believe that he could ignore their directions, exceed his authority, or stray beyond his "competence" with impunity. The Joint Chiefs of Staff and the secretary of defense were relatively new institutions of government, and Korea was their first wartime test, but the incumbents in those positions were old hands who should have better served their commander in chief.

Yet collected all together, the issues that divided them were not as important as a single conviction that Douglas MacArthur, Harry Truman, and his advisers shared: in wartime the president and leaders in Washington owe a large measure of deference to the commander in theater. They shared a flawed and antiquated misconception about the necessity of continuous negotiation. Truman believed that politicians should never interfere in military operations: "The commanders in the field have absolute control of the tactics and the strategy, and they always have." That misreading of history squares perfectly with MacArthur's view: "There should be no non-professional interference in the handling of troops in a campaign. You have professionals to do that job and they should be permitted to do it." The Joint Chiefs professed to share those convictions as traditional in American governance. Yet presidents have frequently breached this supposed wall between policy and strategy, sometimes to good effect, sometimes not. The time-honored tradition of political noninterference is a historical myth much treasured by some military professionals and their political supporters. However, the president is constitutionally responsible for every aspect of his government, foreign and domestic, military and civilian, in peace and in war. As commander in chief he can and must delegate many functions to subordinates, but he remains accountable to the electorate for all their actions. He may legally oversee any aspect of military affairs, from the selection of officers to the procurement of weapons to the tactical emplacement of machine guns if he so desires. How much he should involve himself is a matter of judgment, and should be based upon the president's assessment of his own abilities, his trust in his senior commanders and the military, and his estimate of the political and strategic environment in which he works.[87]

Truman's environment was unprecedented in American history. He presided over a superpower armed with atomic weapons, opposed by an equally powerful and implacable enemy that all believed was bent on destruction of the United States and its way of life. He was leader of the "free world," an alliance of capitalist democracies that Americans believed had to be persuaded, cajoled, mollified, and corralled to oppose the existential threat of communism. He led in the historic shadow of two world wars that had reaped carnage on hundreds of millions of people and the destruction of hundreds of billions of dollars in property and wealth, and almost all of that damage had been done before Truman himself had made the decision to employ the most awesome weapon mankind had ever seen. His tripartite charter was to protect his country and its allies, contain global communism, and prevent a third world war. Those imperatives were bound to come into conflict, and they did in Korea in the summer of 1950.

Every operational question during the Korean War had to be considered in light of possible Chinese and Soviet intervention. Therefore, every major decision, and many not so major, invited Truman and his advisers to delve into strategy and even theater operations. These decision points arrived with dizzying speed. MacArthur's tenure in the UN Command lasted just nine and a half months, but during that time the South Korean capital in Seoul and the boundary at the thirty-eighth parallel changed hands four times. The euphoria of imminent victory and the depression of defeat and evacuation thrice followed one another over a span of days rather than weeks. Consider the tactical and operational decisions, traditionally the province of military professionals, that had grand strategic and political implications: whether to send an American regiment into Korea in June 1950; the question of evacuating the Pusan perimeter; the Inchon operation; the first crossing of the thirty-eighth parallel; the deployment of American troops near the Manchurian frontier; the bombing of Yalu bridges; "hot pursuit" by American aircraft of enemy fighters into Chinese airspace; MacArthur's "Home for Christmas" counteroffensive; the question of evacuation in December 1950; the decision to cross the thirty-eighth parallel again in March 1951. Truman, Acheson, Secretaries Johnson and Marshall, and the Joint Chiefs played key roles in all these decisions and more. No "wall" between policy and strategy existed.

Likewise, it was only proper that MacArthur's views as theater commander should have carried great weight at all these turning points. Washington rightly solicited and deliberately considered his recommendations at each juncture. Yet, in deference to tradition and his heroic stature, they often deferred to his insistence when they ought to have trusted their own political and military judgments and broader strategic perspectives. Their habit of deferring, and his older habit of independent autonomy coupled with Olympian self-confidence, encouraged MacArthur to usurp the president's prerogatives in grand strategy and policy. If, like Grant, he had attempted to do so only within the councils of government, offering his strategic and political advice in private and graciously acceding to the broader competence of his superiors when decisions went against his counsel, the administration might have greatly benefited from his vast experience and his first-rate intellect. But time and again, and increasingly as the tide of war surged against him, MacArthur publicly dissented from his military superiors and his commander in chief, and he grew more vehement and self-absorbed with each communiqué. When he purposely undermined a purely political overture, the president's peace initiative to the Chinese, he arrogated a constitutional prerogative of the president, who rightly relieved him of command. When the president was preparing his speech announcing his relief of General MacArthur, Truman's staff urged him to say that he was acting with "the consent" of his military and civilian advisers. Although he had deliberately and scrupulously sought the counsel of leaders in all three branches of government, Truman refused. "I am taking this decision on my own responsibility as president of the United States. I want nobody to think I am sharing it with anybody else."[88] Truman's relief of MacArthur protected the constitutional principle of civilian control. In the long history of American political-military relations, that courageous decision stands in honor alongside Washington's quashing of the Newburgh Conspiracy and Lincoln's preservation of presidential supremacy.

The sacking of MacArthur was far from the final act in this tragedy. The Senate hearings and MacArthur's campaign against the president and for the 1952 GOP nomination completed his disgrace. Because the American people complacently worry so little about the place of their military within their government, the Russell Committee hearings were fraught with risk. It is a truism that politicians out of power give short shrift to the principle of civilian control. Both parties occasionally find it in their short-term interest to exploit controversy between the executive branch and the military. In the spring of 1951 the right wing of the Republican Party, led by Senators McCarthy and Nixon, Representative Martin, and others, saw an opening to paint the Truman administration and the Democratic Party as "soft on communism," incompetent in national security, dismissive of military professionalism and expertise, and, therefore, illegitimate as leaders of the American government. Their aim in the hearings, enthusiastically abetted by General MacArthur, was to show that the professional military was more than opposed to Truman's policies, that indeed our greatest military leaders feared those policies as threatening national survival. The national press decried the spectacle. During the deliberations, Walter Lippmann plaintively asked, "How can it have happened that we have sunk to the point where two parties are rallying around opposing generals?" The *Saturday Evening Post* expressed "doubt whether military leaders at any previous time in American history have figured so largely in nonmilitary affairs."[89] Their concerns gave voice to another novelty in American governance. World War II gave birth to a national security state in which every question of governance seemed to have existential ramifications. The beribboned and be-starred leaders of that war had come to exercise unprecedented influence in the councils of government. General of the Army Marshall had held three civilian positions in the postwar administration, including secretary of state and now secretary of defense. General of the Army Eisenhower was now supreme commander of Allied Powers in Europe and NATO. He was soon to be elected president. His wartime chief of staff, General Walter Bedell Smith, was CIA director. General of the Army Bradley was chairman of the Joint Chiefs of Staff. And of course, General of the Army MacArthur, recent holder of four commands in the Far East, was the lead actor in the current drama.

General Bradley was also concerned that the MacArthur controversy and the hearings might politicize the Joint Chiefs and the military. After he testified, Bradley expressed the rather naïve complaint that Democrats and Republicans had asked entirely different types of questions. He was disgusted with senators who "were trying to embarrass the president; they were not interested in the truth." Lippmann dolefully concluded that the hearing was "merely a culminating point of this most un-American and most unrepublican evolution of our affairs. . . . No civilian is regarded as having any authority or can get a respectful hearing, unless he has a general to speak up for him."[90] Of course, the military had been heavily political at earlier times in American history, but the professionalization of the officer corps over the previous century had done much to eradicate such partisanship. Bradley, along with the Joint Chiefs and Secretary Marshall, who had a storied career of apolitical military service, did much to blunt the GOP gambit. Their testimony showed that this was no clash between civilians and the military, still less a controversy between Democratic generals and Republican generals, but a case of insubordination by one theater commander jointly called to account by his military and civilian superiors. The professional military, more than any other institution of government except the president himself, had saved the principle of civilian control. General Eisenhower, former aide to General MacArthur and future president, applauded the example of his military colleagues during the hearings: "When the day comes that American soldiers can in war successfully defy the entire civil government then the American system will have come to an end."[91]

Through 1951 a solid 60 percent of Americans disapproved of Truman's decision to fire MacArthur. The president had other problems—corruption investigations, the "red scare," the stalemate in Korea—but the MacArthur controversy added to his political troubles. He decided not to run for reelection. Despite the personal and political cost, Truman was steadfast in his conviction of the rightness of his decision. He later wrote, "If I allowed him to defy the civil authorities in this manner, I myself would be violating my oath to uphold and defend the Constitution."[92]

The final act of this tragedy was MacArthur's self-disgrace. When he first arrived in San Francisco, the nation embraced him as a symbol of all that they hoped and all that they feared. He was a leader who seemed to have stood up to entrenched power and been wronged. MacArthur was an anticommunist general of impeccable credentials who seemed instinctively to know how to navigate the uncertain shoals of the Cold War. To a generation that had grown up under the inspiring leadership of Roosevelt and was now alienated by the nasal twang of a Missouri ward-heeler politician, MacArthur was the ideal of an eloquent patrician warrior born to lead. To a country scarred by two world wars and impatient with a limited conflict they seemed to be losing, MacArthur said, "There is no substitute for victory." Then, for a solid year he careened across America, soiling his uniform and besmirching his profession with vitriol directed against his commander in chief. In city after town, little by little, his rhetoric grew shriller, his audiences became smaller, and Americans learned once again, to their dismay, that all heroes have feet of clay.[93]

10

The Civil War was the American Iliad. World War II was the American Triumph. The Vietnam War was the American Tragedy. From 1961 to 1965 the United States mired itself in a civil war in Vietnam that it could never have won and should never have fought. The war was not in the nation's strategic interests. American allies around the world would have preferred that the United States not become involved. Congressional leaders and influential journalists urged two presidents to find a way out of the quagmire. America's South Vietnamese allies were politically feckless, militarily incompetent, and arrogantly dismissive of their own populace. Their counterparts in the North—nationalist before they were communist—were capable, organized, and ruthlessly committed to a lifelong struggle to reunite the Vietnamese people and impose their revolution. An overlay of the Manichean struggle between communist and capitalist superpowers complicated this civil war and raised the stakes on a global level. Yet the political and military leadership in the United States never fully grasped these realities. Unquestioned anticommunist ideology blinded American leaders to their folly, but dysfunctional political-military relations played a large role in America's descent into the morass.

After years of conflict with President Eisenhower, a fellow general who had come to dismiss their counsel, most senior military leaders had welcomed the Kennedy administration in 1961 with enthusiasm. High hopes, however, were soon dashed by miscommunication, policy disputes, and an overbearing secretary of defense, Robert McNamara. Kennedy came to mistrust the Joint Chiefs early in his term, and by the time of his assassination three years later, he scarcely bothered to solicit their views. His solution to this breach in political-military relations was to hire a politically congenial former general, Maxwell Taylor, to provide in-house military counsel. That choice essentially marginalized the JCS, the president's statutory military advisers. Kennedy's civilian assistants assumed the president's dismissive attitude toward the military chiefs, and often compounded the rift it had engendered. After Kennedy's death, Lyndon B. Johnson inherited these same advisers and their disposition to bypass the JCS. Undertaking an ambitious domestic agenda, LBJ gave less time and effort to the continuous negotiation. During his administration both the president and the military chiefs gave the appearance of consultation and of sharing candid professional advice, but in reality it was a superficial connection that reaped what it sowed.

Early in his presidency John F. Kennedy, with little foresight, codified a policy aim for the United States: to secure a free, independent, and non-communist South Vietnam. As good soldiers, the Joint Chiefs embraced that mission and sought to carry it out, although in their estimation the president was never willing to apply the ways and expend the means to accomplish his stated ends. The Joint Chiefs felt that Kennedy was unwilling to commit to a strategy or to provide the necessary resources that his policy seemed to demand.

The exception to that military consensus was Taylor. He joined the Kennedy administration with a policy doctrine of his own authorship called "flexible response." Kennedy's political advisers adopted its precepts and the theories that underpinned it, and together they eagerly applied them in Vietnam. As White House adviser and later as Joint Chiefs chairman, Taylor became the high priest of limited warfare, personally advising the president, usually to the exclusion and consternation of his military colleagues. He continued to urge limited warfare during the first years of Johnson's presidency. Even as he moved from the Pentagon to the embassy in Saigon, he insisted on a gradual course of increasing pressure on North Vietnam to arrest a deteriorating situation in the South. Johnson found Taylor's middle course suited to his political need to postpone hard decisions until after the 1964 election. Taylor's counsel was far more palatable than the "get in to win" or "get out" alternatives on offer from the service chiefs he had come to disdain. In early 1965, President Johnson made a fateful decision to begin bombing North Vietnam, a policy change that required the introduction of ground combat troops and Americanized an Asian civil war. Yet the foundation upon which this fateful decision rested was the flawed strategic thinking of one politically affable general, not the consensus of the Joint Chiefs. Taylor's doctrine gradually led the United States into another ground war in Asia, and America's first major strategic failure. Ten years of tragic loss ensued, in great part, from the early failures of political and military leaders to craft effective and attainable policy and strategy in Vietnam. America's prosecution of the war never recovered from these dismal beginnings.

At the end of the Korean War the military establishment occupied an increasingly ambiguous position within American government. The national security acts of the late 1940s had created a new Department of Defense and ratified the responsibilities of the Joint Chiefs of Staff. Those laws reflected the militarization of American foreign policy that had begun during World War II. They codified a new reality in American history, the national security state, wherein the answer to every diplomatic question came to have a significant if not dominant military component. Presidents soon promulgated orders through the National Security Council, rather than directly to the cabinet. The military establishment, accustomed to FDR's hands-on wartime leadership, became ever more responsive to presidential command. The four services—not just the army and the navy, for the air force was newly independent and the marine corps newly powerful—were behemoths in terms of prestige, manpower, budget share, and capability. They dwarfed both their prewar predecessors and the rest of the federal government, not least the Department of State. Indeed, it was difficult to determine where foreign policy left off and military affairs began. The rapid growth of atomic and then thermonuclear arsenals, capable of delivering greater and greater destruction at breathtaking speed over broader and broader swaths of the globe, compressed time for strategic decision making. A crisis might present leaders with global life-and-death dilemmas with minutes to decide and act, making consultation with allies and congressional leaders impossible. Controlling these weapons drastically changed the way presidents and generals thought about their roles with respect to one another, to the people and the state, and to allies and adversaries. The future was less predictable, more threatening, and swiftly changing.

Bedecked with battle laurels from World War II and Korea, military leaders enjoyed enormous respect. Former generals and admirals occupied positions of trust throughout the government. The service chiefs now answered to several masters: their own service secretaries, the JCS chairman, the secretary of defense, and, of course, the president. The national security acts gave the JCS a legal charter, but left the institution itself weak. MacArthur's partisanship and defiance of the president served mainly to educate the public on the need to control the generals lest they pose a threat. Walter Lippmann's lament about "two [political] parties rallying around opposing generals" captured the concerns of many Americans. As heads of large public enterprises, the chiefs often disagreed with one another over matters of national strategy and especially over the defense budget, which more than ever before became *the* index of institutional status. Such debate among professionals can be helpful, even illuminating, but during the 1950s, interservice rivalry often took on the trappings of institutional self-protection.[1]

Nothing bespoke military prestige so much as General of the Army Dwight D. Eisenhower's election to the presidency. Although he had never been politically active, his popularity was such that he might have claimed either party's nomination. During the campaign Ike purposely kept his policy positions ill-defined. He won the 1952 election in a walk, almost entirely on the strength of his wartime record as commanding general of Allied forces in Europe. Even before his inauguration Eisenhower put his prestige to work, traveling to Korea to find a way to break a two-year operational stasis and end the war. Through diplomacy and nuclear saber-rattling, he gained a truce that stopped the fighting. His stock had never been higher.

For a former army general, President Eisenhower chose a surprising path in national defense policy. Having seen enough of the destructiveness of war and believing that the nation's strength resided first in a sound economy buttressed by limited federal spending, Ike moved aggressively to trim the defense budget. His first budget submission cut Pentagon outlays by 20 percent. His "New Look" policy sought a radical restructuring, sharply reducing ground forces in favor of air power and nuclear capabilities, which could provide "more bang for the buck." The Eisenhower national security strategy called for "massive retaliation" with nuclear weapons against threats to American interests. The navy and air force vied over which service would benefit more from the New Look, both in budget share and strategic importance. The army found itself searching for relevance.[2]

Two army chiefs of staff came to grief opposing the new strategy. Matthew Ridgway, hero of World War II and Korea, squared off with Ike and his defense secretary, Charles C. "Engine Charlie" Wilson, and was not reappointed after a two-year term. Maxwell D. Taylor, the dashing and famous World War II commander of the 101st Airborne Division, succeeded him. Both chiefs—as well as their colleagues—aired their differences with the administration in testimony before congressional committees, a practice that Eisenhower called "legalized insubordination." Both men wrote books after leaving office, but Taylor's *The Uncertain Trumpet* had the greater impact. Published in 1959 near the end of Ike's second term, it lambasted the two choices inherent in massive retaliation, "the initiation of general nuclear war or compromise and retreat," calling instead for a diverse force structure that could offer the president a range of responses for various situations. The Taylor doctrine, which he dubbed "the Strategy of Flexible Response," quickly found an adherent in presidential candidate Senator John F. Kennedy, who was searching for ways to differentiate himself from the Eisenhower administration and GOP presidential nominee Vice President Richard Nixon. On the campaign trail, Kennedy invoked the names of Ridgway and Taylor as the sort of military experts whom he would call upon for advice, a clever means for a young nominee, short on national security credentials, to borrow credibility. Moreover, Kennedy pronounced *The Uncertain Trumpet* required reading for every American because it demonstrated how "we have not brought our conventional war capabilities into line with the necessities" of the global strategic dilemma.[3]

Another book came along at the end of the Eisenhower era that captured the new zeitgeist, at least among the Camelot cognoscenti. Thomas Schelling's *The Strategy of Conflict* offered an alternative to the Armageddon of massive retaliation. A Harvard professor of political economy, Schelling derided the nuclear superpower standoff as a "zero-sum" game, wherein a clear victory for one side balanced a disastrous loss for the other. He aimed at making war more complex, "non-zero-sum," whereby adversaries could bargain with one another to limit destruction and achieve solutions acceptable to both sides. What Schelling advocated was "coercive strategy," sending signals to the enemy through gradually increasing or decreasing pressure. War thus became a bargaining process between enemies, rather than simple kill-or-be-killed savagery. Schelling's thought meshed nicely with Taylor's "strategy of flexible response." The key, of course, was to ensure that enemies communicated well, that they understood one another and were able to interpret each other's signals effectively. Then, theoretically, they would respond in rational and predictable ways. Schelling was less forthcoming and insightful on what might happen should enemies misunderstand each other.[4]

By the end of his administration, Eisenhower was fed up with his highly politicized military advisers, calling their opposition "damn near treason." Eisenhower moved to curb the chiefs by reforming the Department of Defense. The Defense Reorganization Act of 1958 removed the JCS from the formal chain of command, so that they no longer exercised command over fleet and field forces, as Marshall and King had done in World War II. This reform did little to improve JCS decision making or harmony, but it greatly enhanced the authority of the civilian secretary of defense at the expense of senior military leaders. Now the JCS became simply advisers whom the president, the NSC, and secretary of defense could consult as they saw fit. Nonetheless, Eisenhower voiced his deepest fears when he warned in his farewell address of the dangers that a burgeoning military-industrial complex posed to the Republic.[5]

The Kennedy administration entered office with a volatile mixture of bravado and insecurity. On the one hand, they believed their own rhetoric: the torch truly had been passed to a new generation of leaders. Yet the Joint Chiefs who greeted the new president were Eisenhower holdovers—members of the World War II generation. Kennedy was well aware of Ike's troubles with the Joint Chiefs, so he and his principal advisers viewed them with suspicion from the outset. It was not lost on Kennedy that if the brass were willing to stand up to the conqueror of Europe, they would have little compunction about bucking a forty-three-year-old former navy lieutenant. The Kennedy team was aware of its inexperience in national security affairs and of the problems it was inheriting, not least of which was the real possibility of nuclear war. JFK named Ford Motor Company president Robert S. McNamara secretary of defense and charged him to tame the Defense Department. McNamara swept into the Pentagon with a brash, youthful cohort of systems analysts, management specialists, and defense intellectuals who became derisively known as the "whiz kids." With palpable arrogance and abiding faith in quantitative analysis and business management techniques, these men disdained military history, military experience, and military officers in equal measure. They blithely dismissed any argument based on evidence that could not be quantitatively measured—such as morale, combat power, or leadership—as hardly worth discussing. David Halberstam wrote that when McNamara later began trying to make sense of Vietnam he was "the quantifier trying to quantify the unquantifiable." One McNamara favorite, systems analysis director Alain Enthoven, suggested that a career in uniform was actually a hindrance "because it discourages seeing the larger picture." Indeed, he sniffed, the typical officer was no better qualified to be a "strategic planner than a . . . graduate of the Harvard Business School." During one meeting the thirty-year-old analyst impudently but accurately noted, "General, I have fought just as many nuclear wars as you have." With such men, McNamara gained control of the defense budget, the methods of vetting weapons systems, even the vocabulary for expressing the nature of strategic reality. Most of all, he tightly controlled the flow of information between the White House, his own office, and the military. Before long, he had the chiefs at war with one another and further muzzled them by curtailing their access to the press and Congress. Over time he replaced the old chiefs with men more to the president's liking, officers more likely to hew to the administration line, to learn the language of systems analysis and limited war. It took them four years, but by the time JFK's successor took office in his own right, McNamara and the whiz kids had largely brought the brass to heel.[6]

Two early encounters seemed to confirm JFK's worst fears about the military leadership. A few days after the inauguration a Rand Corporation analyst named Daniel Ellsberg briefed national security adviser McGeorge Bundy on the Joint Strategic Capabilities Plan (JSCP), the Joint Chiefs' intended nuclear response to any level of armed conflict with the Soviet Union.[7] Ellsberg told Bundy that no president or secretary of defense had ever seen the JSCP, which contained plans for dropping thousands of atomic and nuclear warheads—170 on Moscow alone—and destroying every major city from eastern Europe to China's Pacific coast. It was the military's codification of "massive retaliation." Worse, President Eisenhower had given written nuclear release authority to local military commanders in case of emergency. Bundy immediately called the Pentagon to ask for a copy of the JSCP. A general on the Joint Staff told him, "Oh, we never release that." Bundy clarified that he was calling on behalf of the president. The general still demurred, finally offering to present a briefing, but not to surrender a copy of the plan itself. Bundy was flabbergasted and appalled, but he never got a look at the actual JSCP. JFK got a briefing on the nuclear war plan that summer, after which he lamented to Secretary of State Dean Rusk, "And we call ourselves the human race." McNamara worked for years to gain control of the nuclear arsenal and to develop plans that resembled the administration's doctrine of "flexible response." Yet the episode only exacerbated the Kennedy administration's fears of rogue generals.[8]

The other test came in Cuba. Two and a half weeks before he left office, Eisenhower broke diplomatic relations with Castro's communist regime, leaving Kennedy, as one adviser put it, holding "a grenade with the pin pulled." Ike's CIA had been planning an invasion of Cuba and training anti-Castro Cuban expatriates for the task. The Kennedy administration, wary yet eager for an early chance to demonstrate its vigorous anticommunism, inherited those plans. The CIA briefed the president and pressed hard to follow through with the invasion, which called for no involvement of U.S. forces. Some in the State Department opposed the scheme as far too risky. Although the Joint Chiefs had analyzed the CIA's planning and found it slipshod, they muted their criticism, chary about knocking a paramilitary operation sponsored by the CIA. Kennedy reluctantly allowed the plans to proceed, but insisted that no American forces would take part. On April 17, 1961, less than two months into Kennedy's term, thirteen hundred Cuban exiles landed in the Bay of Pigs and found themselves surrounded by fifteen times as many Castro forces. The CIA and, finally, the JCS forcefully urged JFK to employ American air and naval power to save the expatriate brigade, but the president refused. Castro's forces made quick work of the exiles, and the invasion collapsed.[9]

The debacle humiliated the young president, who took personal responsibility and then fired the top two men in the CIA. Relations between Kennedy and his military advisers suffered a severe blow. Joint Chiefs chairman General Lyman Lemnitzer later accused JFK of "pulling out the rug," calling his unwillingness to employ U.S. troops at the Bay of Pigs "unbelievable, absolutely reprehensible, almost criminal." Air Force chief of staff General Curtis LeMay complained that the Joint Chiefs got all the blame, but "we didn't have a Goddamned thing to do with it." Kennedy fumed that "those sons of bitches with all the fruit salad just sat there nodding, saying it would work." He felt that both the CIA and the JCS had tried to manipulate him to take an unwise military action, and vowed never again to be "overawed by professional military advice." Kennedy and the chiefs felt betrayed by each other, and the memory of the Bay of Pigs would hang over every subsequent interaction between them. For the rest of his presidency, JFK would remain deeply suspicious of the Joint Chiefs.[10]

Smarting, the Kennedy administration was anxious to regain its footing. During the presidential transition, Eisenhower had briefed Kennedy on a communist insurgency in Laos, indicating that it was his primary national security concern. In 1954 Ike had pronounced his "domino theory," applying it specifically to Vietnam and Southeast Asia and more generally to the world. The domino theory, which in seven years had taken on the trappings of a papal bull, required the United States to stand firm against communist aggression lest the fall of one democracy allow an entire region to fall to the communists. Now Ike was warning his young successor that an insurgent victory in Laos might imperil all of Southeast Asia, and Kennedy could scarcely ignore him. In early March 1961 Kennedy employed his signature medium of television to speak to the nation on the situation in Laos. Brandishing a long presidential pointer at a large Laotian map, Kennedy convinced many Americans that he intended to intervene where he was pointing. Yet, two months later, the situation looked much different. Though General Lemnitzer vigorously supported such an intervention, recommendations from the service chiefs conflicted wildly, reinforcing administration skepticism about professional military expertise. McGeorge Bundy cross-examined Lemnitzer and forced him to admit that intervention into landlocked Laos would likely lead to general war and a massive and lengthy U.S. commitment. The president changed course and toned down his rhetoric. A few days later he picked up a stack of memos from Lemnitzer and said, "If it hadn't been for Cuba, we might be about to intervene in Laos. . . . I might have taken this advice seriously." Some conservative critics carped that Democrat Kennedy had given in to the communists, just like Truman in China, but in truth he paid no domestic political price.[11]

Soon after the Bay of Pigs debacle Kennedy called on Maxwell Taylor to investigate the failed operation. Taylor chaired a group whose final report sprayed blame around the government, from the CIA to the JCS to the NSC. Most worrisome, they found, relations between the Joint Chiefs and the president had reached a crisis. "My God," Taylor said to one Kennedy aide, "the bunch of advisers he inherited." Taylor counseled Kennedy to reinvigorate the political-military relationship and to reform the White House decision-making process. Kennedy asked the general how to put things with the chiefs on better terms. "By pure luck," Taylor later wrote, "I had a working paper of my own in my pocket which bore precisely on the subject." The president took the memo and "rushed off to the Pentagon" to talk with the Joint Chiefs. Referring to Taylor's memo, JFK told the skeptical group that he wanted their advice to "come to him directly and unfiltered." He thought of them, he said, "as more than military specialists and looked to them for help in fitting military requirements into the overall context of any situation." Their advice "could not and should not be purely military," as political, economic and other factors always impinged on national security decisions. They should make their "arguments for or against any course of action without fear or hesitation." The chiefs responded with "icy silence." Shortly thereafter, Kennedy recalled Taylor to active duty as a four-star general and appointed him military representative to the president, an entirely new position. Both men were at pains to describe Taylor's role as not supplanting the Joint Chiefs of Staff, certainly not a means through which to filter their counsel as the president's statutory military advisers. Yet with one appointment the president alienated himself from the JCS, who came to mistrust Taylor, and politicized and personalized his military advice in one ideologically compatible man. After his abortive fence-mending session with the Joint Chiefs, Kennedy rarely sought their counsel again. Taylor was preeminent, and the crisis in political-military relations only worsened.[12]

Taylor became Kennedy's general. During World War II he had infiltrated behind Axis lines to negotiate the surrender of the Italian government and later jumped into Normandy at the head of the 101st Airborne Division with a bottle of Irish whisky "prudentially stored" in his leg bag. Handsome, cerebral, urbane, and skillful with a tennis racket, he fit right in at Hyannisport. Robert Kennedy named a son after him. Fawning admirers suggested that Taylor was the kind of general that Harvard might have produced. Indeed, he had been a college president— superintendent of West Point—and was fluent in Spanish and French and conversant in Chinese and Japanese. Taylor was an inveterate self-promoter and cunningly lethal in bureaucratic close fights. Over the next few years he worked tirelessly to place himself at the center of the national security apparatus, ruthlessly displacing those who stood in his way. The chiefs were wary of him from the start, only partly because of the Bay of Pigs report. One of the chiefs said Taylor became "the military part of . . . Kennedy's mind" to the exclusion of all others. Taylor admitted that he had changed his mind about the ideal political-military relationship since his time in the Eisenhower administration:

> With the opportunity to observe the problems of a President at closer range, I have come to understand the importance of an intimate, easy relationship, born of friendship and mutual regard, between the President and the Chiefs. It is particularly important for

the Chairman [which he later became], who works more closely with the President and Secretary of Defense than do the service chiefs. The Chairman should be a true believer in the foreign policy and military strategy of the administration which he serves.[13]

It is small wonder that the Joint Chiefs saw Taylor as more of a Kennedy man than a military professional. They lost respect for a soldier who they thought had become a partisan politician. Over the next four years, Taylor hopped from one critical post to another, always taking care to eliminate or neuter the position he had just left, giving him greater influence and freedom to maneuver in the new job. He was the lone soldier among a small handful of civilian advisers who affected every decision that the JFK and LBJ administrations made on the road to disaster in Vietnam.[14]

Taylor made common cause with McNamara, even as the secretary and his whiz kids were infuriating the Pentagon brass with their business techniques, budgeting procedures, and weapons-buying regimen. In 1962 JFK transferred Lemnitzer to Europe to make way for Taylor to become chairman of the Joint Chiefs. Taylor recommended that Kennedy abolish his former position, military representative to the president. Kennedy approved, so that no White House general would be grading Taylor's work. Chairman Taylor then cemented his alliance with McNamara, who thought him "one of the wisest, most intelligent military men ever to serve." The service chiefs, who by statute gave their advice to the president through the chairman and the secretary of defense, came to believe that the two men filtered such counsel to suit their own designs. Over time, McNamara and Taylor replaced the old breed of flag officers in favor of a new crop that *Time* called "planners and thinkers, not heroes." In the business lexicon of the day, the new chiefs were "organization men." The top ranks of the military became less independent, less influential, and more and more thoroughly politicized.[15]

Taylor became chairman in October 1962, days before one of the most dangerous crises in world history. The fortnight of the Cuban Missile Crisis brought the United States and the Soviet Union within moments of nuclear Armageddon. The Kennedy team formed a crisis executive committee devoid of military advisers, except Taylor. The question before the committee, dubbed ExComm, was how to force the removal of Soviet missiles then being placed into operation in Cuba without risking a nuclear war. Growing over time to as many as seventy members, ExComm deliberated for days on end, discussing a wide range of solutions and reacting to hourly changes in the strategic situation. Yet by excluding the service chiefs it missed an opportunity for close coordination and understanding of military capabilities. When the president finally met with the service chiefs—in the Oval Office, away from the ExComm—they were ignorant of the substance of those days of political deliberations and possible complications. As a result, their bellicose recommendations were made in a political vacuum and reinforced administration prejudices of them as warmongers. Four days into the crisis ExComm was gravitating toward a "quarantine" of Cuba that would stop Soviet ships from delivering more missiles. At this point JFK wanted it on record that he had consulted the Joint Chiefs and that they had approved his decision. The chiefs wanted to invade Cuba, but McNamara and Taylor convinced them to shelve that recommendation. Instead, they demanded an air strike of some eight hundred sorties to destroy the missiles, which, after all, threatened the eastern half of the United States. With the rest of the Joint Chiefs present, Taylor backed away from the quarantine and endorsed the air strike. Air Force general Curtis LeMay, the histrionic World War II bomber commander who was the man most responsible for the destruction of Japan, was Kennedy's and Taylor's least favorite chief. The cigar-smoking pilot forcefully told the president that there was no alternative to an air offensive and compared the proposed quarantine to "the appeasement at Munich," a none-too-subtle allusion to the discredited isolationist stance of Kennedy's father, FDR's ambassador to Great Britain. LeMay added that America's allies and "a lot of our own citizens" would agree, implicitly threatening to take his dissent public. "In other words, you're in a pretty bad fix at the present time." Kennedy, angry and appalled that the chiefs were proposing an action that promised to start nuclear war, bristled, "What did you say?" LeMay repeated, "You're in a pretty bad fix," without appending a "Mr. President." The president gave a mirthless chuckle and said, "You're right there with me." Kennedy dismissed them from the Oval Office and never consulted them for the remainder of the crisis.

Kennedy did not listen to his chiefs, and the quarantine he promoted defused the tension. The Soviets agreed to withdraw their missiles in return for a secret deal to remove American missiles from Turkey. The administration received international kudos for its statesmanship in avoiding a nuclear war. For his part, McNamara derived a Schellingesque lesson from the episode: "There is no longer any such thing as strategy, only crisis management." The president gleaned another insight: the service chiefs were mad. "The first advice I'm going to give my successor is to watch the generals and to avoid feeling that just because they were military men their opinion[s] on military matters were worth a damn." JFK's mistrust was heartfelt, and he further marginalized the JCS, which, in the words of McGeorge Bundy, "only increased the difficulty of exercising his powers as commander in chief."[16]

Another Eisenhower legacy, a simmering conflict in Vietnam, afforded the administration yet another chance to prove its anticommunist bona fides. Vietnam had been almost continuously at war since World War II. The Vietnamese had thrown off the French colonial yoke at Dien Bien Phu in 1954, after which Ngo Dinh Diem, an anticommunist Catholic, seized power in the south. Nationalist and communist forces under Ho Chi Minh consolidated control in the north, governing from Hanoi. The Eisenhower administration had supported Diem when he refused to hold elections mandated by an international treaty in 1956, after which Diem's regime became increasingly repressive. Three years later Ho's government created the National Liberation Front (NLF) to support southern insurgents in a bid to overthrow Diem and reunite the country. By the time JFK took office, Diem's hold on the countryside was tenuous at best.[17]

At this remove, it is hard to see why an American president would have considered propping up a brutal, authoritarian oligarch like Diem to be in the national interest. Yet in 1961 the United States perceived itself to be in a life-or-death struggle with the Soviet Union, a Manichean conflict between capitalism and communism. Harry Truman had pronounced that containment of communism was the overarching imperative of American national security. Eisenhower had only intensified that focus with his domino theory. The Soviets reciprocated with their own bellicose rhetoric and provocative actions. The two sides agreed that any victory for the communists was a defeat for democracy, and vice versa—a "zero-sum" game. During the 1950s heyday of the execrable Senator Joseph McCarthy, a generation of savvy Asian experts—the State Department's "China hands"—were purged from government for the sin of having "lost" mainland China to Mao and the communists, as if it were theirs to lose. The few who survived this vetting were afraid to point out the differences both substantive and subtle among communist regimes in, say, North Vietnam or North Korea, or to explore carefully the apparent schism between Beijing and Moscow. Such dissent might have called into question the validity of the domino theory, and the strategic value of an American commitment to Vietnam. Yet the Kennedy brothers were veterans of the "red scares." Robert had served as special counsel on McCarthy's communist-baiting Senate committee. As senator from Massachusetts, John had been careful never to antagonize McCarthy, his colleague and fellow Irish Catholic, even though they were on opposite sides of the aisle. Both brothers knew how vulnerable their Democratic Party was to charges of being "soft on communism." They were unwilling to challenge anticommunist bromides in pursuit of more thoughtful policy, and the men they brought into government shared those blinders.[18]

In June 1961, hoping to defuse global tensions surrounding a crisis in Berlin, President Kennedy met Nikita Khrushchev in Vienna, only to receive a post–Bay of Pigs tongue-lashing from the bellicose Soviet leader. In a post-summit interview with James "Scotty" Reston of the *New York Times,* a discouraged Kennedy confessed that Khrushchev "thought anyone so young and inexperienced . . . had no guts. So he just beat the hell out of me. So I've got a terrible problem. If he thinks I'm inexperienced and have no guts, until we remove those ideas we won't get anywhere with him. So we have to act. . . . We have a problem in trying to make our power credible, and Vietnam looks like the place."[19] When the time came to determine Vietnam policy, there was little or no questioning of the containment doctrine or the domino theory, because such conversations were "soft" and not "tough." The debate skipped past the ends of global national security policy to the ways and means of military strategy in Vietnam.[20]

Less than two weeks after the Bay of Pigs fiasco, Kennedy presided over a day of "prolonged crisis meetings at the White House" focused on Vietnam. The president had initially been skeptical of American capacity to help the Diem regime, but in May 1961 he established a Vietnam task force to study how to proceed. JCS chairman Lemnitzer thought that the president "was ready to do anything within reason to save Southeast Asia." The qualifier in that phrase was important. Having been burned in Cuba, the chiefs were gun-shy about getting ahead of the president, fearing that he might "quibble for weeks and months." Warily, the Joint Chiefs proposed sending ground combat troops to Vietnam, but they carefully listed the risks of such a deployment. They believed that Kennedy's aim necessitated an aggressive strategy to confront the enemy, but they wanted to know how far the president was willing to go. In early May 1961 army general Charles Bonesteel represented the chiefs at a task force meeting. Pressed to defend the call for troops, Bonesteel said that the "central point" was to determine "how seriously are we to take the objective" of preventing a communist takeover of the South. If we are to take this seriously," Bonesteel argued, "we should recognize that it pose[s] a major requirement for very sizeable force commitments."

On May 11, 1961, the president approved National Security Action Memorandum (NSAM) 52, which clearly promulgated a U.S. objective "to prevent Communist domination of South Vietnam; to create . . . a viable and increasingly democratic society, and to initiate, on an accelerated basis, a series of mutually supporting actions of a military political, economic, psychological, and covert character to achieve this objective." The Joint Chiefs now had a mission from the commander in chief. The memo listed several actions, but was silent on the matter of combat troop deployments. They prodded him to match means to ends and send American combat forces to Vietnam. Kennedy approved sending four hundred special forces advisers to the South Vietnamese army, but he continued to reject the introduction of combat troops. Kennedy wanted to blunt the communist advance, but not at the cost of embroiling the United States in an Asian war.[21]

Taylor became Kennedy's military representative that summer and asked the Joint Chiefs for a plan to introduce troops into Vietnam. Before they could respond, he and State Department planner Walt Rostow drafted a "Goldilocks" memorandum for the president: three options, but only one correct choice. The first two proposals were meant for rejection—either an immediate offensive against North Vietnam or an immediate pullout and abandonment of the South. Taylor and Rostow's preferred option was deploying U.S. advisers to South Vietnam to help build "indigenous military, political, and economic strength" in order to contain the communist threat, all the while preparing to intervene with American combat forces if necessary. Following the Bay of Pigs and Laos, Kennedy was wary of military assessments and plans, even if they came from Max Taylor. Again, he refused to approve deployment of combat troops. Over the next several months advisers from various quarters in State, Defense, and the NSC, and even Vice President Johnson, pressed troop deployment recommendations on the reluctant president. In October 1961, Kennedy announced that he was sending Taylor and Rostow to Vietnam for an on-the-ground assessment. The next day press reports correctly speculated that the trip was meant to examine committing American combat forces in Vietnam. Indeed, before he left, Taylor reframed the issue: "The capital question is whether additional forces should be mobilized now or the limitation of our military capabilities in Southeast Asia accepted as a permanent fact."[22]

The situation Taylor and Rostow found was bleak. The NLF was gaining strength, and Diem's army was poorly trained and dispirited. The senior U.S. officer in Saigon asked for an American troop deployment, suggesting that recent flooding in the Mekong Delta could provide the pretext for a small "relief operation." His boss, Admiral Harry D. Felt, the commander in chief, Pacific Area (CINCPAC), vigorously opposed sending U.S. troops, which would look like the "reintroduction of [the] forces of white colonialism." Once in country, he warned, American combat forces would almost inevitably be drawn into battle with the NLF. He urged exploring any alternative that "will not kick off war with Communist China." After several days in Saigon, Taylor recommended forming a "limited partnership" with Diem—increased aid and a greater advisory role in exchange for political reform—as well as a six- to eight-thousand-man flood-control task force. Taylor later insisted in his memoirs that he "had no enthusiasm for the thought of using U.S. Army forces in ground combat in this guerrilla war." Yet Taylor's report to Kennedy concluded, "I do not believe that our program to save SVN will succeed without" troops. Asserting that "SVN is not an excessively difficult or unpleasant place to operate," Taylor outlined five purposes for the task force, including flood relief, self-defense combat operations, providing an emergency combat reserve for the ARVN, and acting as an advance party for additional American forces should they become necessary. The main goal was to show "the seriousness of the U.S. intent to resist a Communist takeover." Taylor admitted that "if the first contingent is not enough to accomplish the necessary results, it will be difficult to resist the pressure to reinforce." The term "mission creep" had not yet been coined, but Taylor warned that "there is no limit to our possible commitment (unless we attack the source in Hanoi)." Still, "the risks of backing into a major Asian war by way of SVN are present but not impressive."[23]

In November 1961, Robert McNamara still eyed Taylor warily as the man standing between him and the president. McNamara argued that Taylor's proposal "will not convince the other side (whether the shots are called from Moscow, Pieping [sic], or Hanoi) that we mean business." In fact, it would do little more than get them "increasingly mired down in an inconclusive struggle." If Taylor's report advised the president to raise the bet on Vietnam, McNamara recommended pushing in all his chips. In a rare moment of agreement with the Joint Chiefs, the defense secretary urged the president to commit "to the clear objective of preventing the fall of South Vietnam to Communism and that we support this commitment by the necessary military actions." He recommended that the United States send a bold signal in the form of 205,000 soldiers, or some six American divisions.[24]

Over the next few days the debate was vigorous. White House staffers, including McGeorge Bundy, sharply questioned McNamara's proposal to deploy 205,000 troops. Kennedy orchestrated press leaks knocking down the notion of troop deployments, denying that Taylor had advocated it and flatly asserting that the president was "strongly opposed" to such an idea. The day before the next NSC meeting, McNamara began to waver. It appears that JFK may have leaned on him through surrogates to change his advice so that the president would not have to disagree formally with his defense secretary.[25] Then, in a November 15, 1961, National Security Council meeting, Kennedy "expressed fear of becoming involved simultaneously on two fronts on opposite sides of the world," the other and more important being Western Europe. "He questioned the wisdom of involvement in Vietnam since the basis thereof is not completely clear." The domino theory notwithstanding, Kennedy was opposed to sending American troops to Vietnam. "I could even make a strong case," he argued, "against intervening in an area 10,000 miles away against 16,000 guerrillas with a native army of 200,000, where millions had been spent for years with no success." McNamara and Taylor both tried once more to advance their own plans, but the president's mind was made up. Tellingly, the president asked McNamara how he could support sending troops to Vietnam and not Cuba, giving the continuing communist domination there. General Lemnitzer butted in to say that "the JCS feel that even at this point [seven months after the Bay of Pigs] the United States should go into Cuba." The president passed over that comment, but said he would make no decisions on Vietnam immediately. Yet a few days later Kennedy signed NSAM 111, a directive that affirmed American commitment to South Vietnam, promised economic aid, and greatly increased the numbers of military advisers, but did not deploy ground formations. He explained to an aide his reluctance to commit combat soldiers: "The troops will march in; the bands will play; the crowds will cheer; and in four days everyone will have forgotten. Then we will be told we have to send in more troops. It's sort of like taking a drink. The effect wears off, and you have to take another." Nonetheless, under the "limited partnership" that Taylor recommended, Kennedy provided thousands more U.S. advisers "for insertion into the Governmental machinery of South Vietnam" and for "participation in the direction and control of South Vietnamese military operations," a level of interference in their affairs that the Saigon government quickly came to resent. Kennedy's analogy was an apt description of the incremental escalation that would take place in the years after his death. The United States had substantially increased its stake in South Vietnam's survival, and not necessarily in ways that most South Vietnamese appreciated. Moreover, the president left the door open to sending in combat troops later. McNamara and Taylor had each learned a lesson about dealing with this president; never again would either of them recommend to Kennedy the deployment of American combat troops to Vietnam.[26]

After Kennedy's decision, Vietnam policy receded into the background as the administration focused on superpower relations—growing tensions in Berlin, the Cuban Missile Crisis, and a limited test-ban treaty with the Soviet Union. The strategic concept for the United States in Vietnam was to assume a secondary role, assisting the Vietnamese in a counterinsurgency against the National Liberation Front, derisively called the Viet Cong or VC. The American mantra was that the conflict was a Vietnamese war and it was up to the South Vietnamese to win it. Nonetheless, the administration established a new four-star Military Assistance Command, Vietnam (MACV), to oversee American advisers. MACV drew up extensive plans for the Saigon government and military to implement with U.S. help, including the "strategic hamlet" program, a nationwide effort to separate the populace from the Viet Cong. For a while the idea seemed to work.[27]

Over the next year the number of advisers steadily increased, many of them special forces, the unconventional warfare experts whom Kennedy had favored with green berets and promoted as part of flexible response. With Taylor's acquiescence MACV suppressed realistic reporting from field advisers and rebuked or shunned those who persisted in holding "negative" views about South Vietnamese military capabilities. As a result, hardworking and dedicated officers closest to the fighting became cynical. One American adviser wryly noted that the ARVN was "equally proficient at attacking an open rice field with nothing in it and . . . at quickly by-passing any heavily wooded area that might possibly contain a few VC." *New York Times* reporter David Halberstam concluded that "the closer one gets to the actual contact level of the war, the farther one gets from official optimism." Taylor, in a September 1962 trip report that lauded the progress since his visit a year earlier, unwittingly ratified Halberstam's assessment: "The local Saigon press, particularly the American component, remains uninformed and often belligerently adverse to the programs of the U.S. and SVN Governments." He even joined in the suppression, canceling at the last minute a scheduled briefing to the Joint Chiefs from a "dissident" adviser, Lieutenant Colonel John Paul Vann, a man known to his peers as perhaps the most effective counterinsurgent in Vietnam. Bad news was unwelcome and therefore unheard at the highest levels of Taylor's Pentagon. Tellingly, McNamara returned from a mid-1962 trip to Vietnam saying, "Every quantitative measure shows that we're winning the war."[28]

By August 1963 some sixteen thousand American advisers were in South Vietnam at a cost of $1 million per day. Yet the United States was still not committed to war, in terms of actually fighting it, and the conflict there was not yet a daily preoccupation for the American government, its news media, or its people.[29] That was about to change. Although America was not yet committed to war, JFK was committed to a policy over which there had never been a serious debate: guaranteeing an independent noncommunist South Vietnam. Nor was there ever any serious consideration of trying to achieve it through diplomacy. Yet the president had committed American prestige in Vietnam before he had determined whether the objective was worth the price. The JCS thought him inexperienced or craven. He thought them mad and bellicose. By mid-1963 Kennedy scarcely bothered to consult them. Instead, JFK relied on Taylor, Bundy, McNamara, and McNamara's whiz kids in the Pentagon.

In the summer of 1963 the Diem regime was losing its grip—on the people, on its own government, on reality. The NLF routinely bested Army of the Republic of Vietnam (ARVN) troops and, therefore, effectively contested control of the countryside. It was an open secret that Diem's brother, Ngo Dinh Nhu—the real power in Saigon—was talking with Hanoi. In May Buddhist priests organized protests against the oppressive South Vietnamese regime that lasted through the spring and summer. Nhu coordinated a violent crackdown that became visible to the world when several monks immolated themselves. The government of South Vietnam seemed on the verge of collapse from within.[30]

Diem's shortcomings were well known in Washington, and discussions about getting rid of him had arisen in the past. Vice President Lyndon Johnson earthily summed up the problem: "Shit, man, he's the only boy we got out there." The mantra in American circles in Saigon was "Sink or Swim with Ngo Dinh Diem." Yet the new ambassador in Saigon, Henry Cabot Lodge, and some second-tier officials in State and the NSC feared that the Viet Cong might seize on the Buddhist uprising to overthrow Diem and form their own government. In late August 1963 these men concluded that the appropriate course was to push for Diem's removal. They took advantage of the absence of several cabinet principals, who were vacationing to escape the Washington heat, to gain JFK's acquiescence in a plan to encourage a military coup d'état. When McNamara and Taylor learned of the decision, they protested, but mainly on the grounds that the process was flawed and that the coup might backfire. The rest of the Joint Chiefs were also opposed, but by this time their demurrals scarcely registered with the Kennedy White House. There seems to have been little consideration that U.S. policy—maintaining a free, independent, noncommunist South Vietnam—might be undermined by such an undemocratic act.[31]

The events of August to November 1963 were not a point of no return on the road to war, but Diem's fecklessness, the NLF's strength, and pressure from allies and the press combined to present Kennedy an opportunity to disengage from a losing proposition. Instead, he committed to a coup, an extralegal interference in the affairs of an allied government that would only deepen American commitment and responsibility for the outcome of the Indochina conflict. JFK missed an opportunity to husband American blood and treasure in the interests of peace and more vital U.S interests around the world.[32]

On the first of November 1963 a cabal of South Vietnamese generals toppled the Diem regime, seizing the president and his brother, Ngo Dinh Nhu. Sometime during the next day, the two men were assassinated. American support for the overthrow was an open secret. Although JFK expressed shock at the killings, he had allowed the coup to proceed. Moreover, his policy was now a farce. The United States continued to support an independent, noncommunist South Vietnam, but it could not candidly use words such as "democracy" and "self-determination." A military junta under Major General Duong Van "Big" Minh assumed power in Saigon. The United States, now culpable, became more involved, more responsible, less able to extricate itself from the conflict in Vietnam.[33]

Three weeks after the Diem coup, President Kennedy was assassinated.

☆ ☆ ☆

Lyndon Johnson brought to the Oval Office the most complex congeries of personal qualities of any president in history. His intelligence was natural and formidable, but formally undeveloped. He possessed an uncanny ability to read people, to size them up, to find their wants and needs, to charm them or intimidate them, and ultimately to bend them to his will. He was a master political strategist, a trait that enabled him to win many elections in Texas and later to command the greatest majority in the history of presidential politics. He was also a political tactician par excellence, which made him the finest Senate majority leader in history, indeed the only great one. Yet he was insecure about his background— poor, rural, unrefined—his intellect, his appearance, and his destiny. Years later, George Ball, an adviser to both Kennedy and Johnson, said that LBJ did not suffer from a poor education; he suffered from the belief that he had a poor education.[34]

Johnson divided humanity into two camps. To superiors he could feign the most fawning obeisance. Of subordinates he demanded unquestioning loyalty and reflexive subservience. He spent his entire life in a relentless quest to conquer his superiors and turn them into his inferiors, for his ego could neither conceive of nor tolerate peers. Moreover, he was haunted by many fears, none of them more powerful than his fear of losing, his fear of failure, and his fear of humiliation. Following Kennedy's death, Lyndon Johnson's personal characteristics drove the United States toward a decisive commitment in Vietnam.

Succeeding JFK in the wake of a brutal assassination that the entire nation, indeed much of the world, seemed to experience in real time through television, aroused in LBJ two deep and conflicting beliefs. The first was fulfillment of his destiny—Johnson believed that he was intended to be president of the United States. Moreover, he would not just be president—he would be a great one, like his hero FDR. Becoming great demanded employing his talents to their fullest to achieve lasting, historic, societal change. From the moment he assumed office, Johnson strained every muscle, bone, and brain cell to become a great president. The second belief was that he was doomed to fail—the fates would never allow him to achieve his destiny. Johnson succeeded a man he knew to be his political inferior. Yet that man had beaten him in the 1960 presidential race—jumped over him in the only game Lyndon Johnson ever played or cared about: politics. And Johnson had leapt at the chance to become his running mate like a drowning man lunging at a life preserver. Now that young man lay dead, and Lyndon Johnson was an accidental president. In conversations over the next several months he used several derisive terms to describe his ascendancy: "illegal," "pretender," "naked," and "illegitimate." In the history of the presidency, no successor president has ever faced a shorter time—less than a year—than Johnson faced before the next election. Until he won the presidency in his own right, Lyndon Johnson saw himself as merely a caretaker of the Kennedy legacy. He was a trustee president, unless he could do something about it.[35]

Johnson immediately grasped that securing his election in 1964 meant establishing a legislative record that erased the public's sense—if it had such a sense—that he was a poor substitute for JFK. To do so, Johnson quietly established a purpose of reverent continuity. He deftly employed his predecessor's martyrdom for a massive legislative program, and then forcefully created legislative momentum in Congress to pass it. The results—the first civil rights act in American history that was worthy of the name, and a lean federal budget that redirected resources to the poor and disfranchised—were worthy of FDR's first hundred days.[36]

In his January 1964 State of the Union address, Johnson declared his ambition to become a great president in a single, unequivocal sentence: "This administration today, here and now, declares unconditional war on poverty in America." The speech was a tour de force. The nation was relieved and enthralled that Kennedy's successor was a forceful leader in his own right. The people were ready to follow. Few noticed that while declaring war on poverty, their new president said almost nothing about a real war halfway around the globe.[37]

In the days following the assassination, Johnson worked tirelessly to convince all of Kennedy's national security team to stay on—he needed to demonstrate continuity to the nation. Rusk, McNamara, and McGeorge Bundy agreed, and so did most of their staffs.[38] Keeping JFK's advisers meant maintaining Camelot's national security decision-making apparatus, which by late 1963 usually meant convening small, ad hoc meetings of the inner circle to discuss short-range execution—as in the weeks before the Diem coup—rather than debating the purpose and direction of policy. This regime was a far cry from the orderly routine that had characterized the Eisenhower administration, wherein standing subcommittees had made studied policy proposals to NSC principals. Retaining the Kennedy team also meant inheriting their prejudices against the military, including the now-ingrained habit of ignoring the generals. The Joint Chiefs, except Taylor, were all but excluded from decision making. When LBJ met with them, he did so to gain the appearance of consultation or their acquiescence in decisions already made.[39]

On Sunday LBJ held his first meeting on Vietnam with Bundy, McNamara, Rusk, and his undersecretary, George Ball, and CIA director John McCone. None of the Joint Chiefs was present. Ambassador Lodge was there to report on the situation since the coup. Johnson described himself as "a catfish" who had just "grabbed a big juicy worm with a right sharp hook in the middle of it." The hook was Vietnam, and LBJ was holding Lodge responsible. The coup, which Lodge had championed, had been a mistake. There had been "too much bickering" among the various U.S. agencies in Saigon, and Lodge had better stop it. The "main objective" was to "win the war," a pronouncement that elided the fact that the United States was not yet committed to war. The president ordered Lodge to return to Saigon and tell General Minh that "Lyndon Johnson intends to stand by our word." The message was clear: "I will not lose in Vietnam. . . . I am not going to be the president who saw Southeast Asia go the way China went." Later recalling his thinking during those first days in office, Johnson related his fears: "I knew that Harry Truman and Dean Acheson had lost their effectiveness from the day that the communists took over in China. I believed that the loss of China had played a large role in the rise of Joe McCarthy. And I knew that all these problems, taken together, were chickenshit compared to what might happen if we lost Vietnam."[40]

A few days later Johnson reaffirmed the Kennedy policy. Accepting MACV's overly optimistic predictions that the ARVN would be able to fight on its own within two years, he embraced a McNamara-Taylor withdrawal timetable with a first installment of one thousand troops to leave by the end of 1963. Furthermore, he ordered the military to begin planning operations against North Vietnam, although they had to maintain "the plausibility of denial." The U.S. Navy secretly dispatched so-called DeSoto patrols, destroyers equipped to eavesdrop and gather intelligence, into the Gulf of Tonkin well inside Hanoi's territorial waters, which the Democratic Republic of Vietnam (DRV) could not have failed to notice. South Vietnamese guerrillas also conducted raids into the North under the auspices of American Oplan (operations plan) 34A. In Laos, American advisers led South Vietnamese infantry against NLF infiltration routes, and U.S. aircraft conducted reconnaissance missions. The United States intended these operations to demonstrate American and South Vietnamese capability and resolve, but they also served to provoke the North Vietnamese.[41]

With that, the president hoped that he could postpone further decisions on Vietnam until after the 1964 election. He intended to turn his attention entirely toward domestic policy and electoral politics. It was not to be.[42]

As chief executive LBJ's overriding concern was maintaining the appearance of unity. Unlike his predecessor, he had no patience for intellectual discussions. He set a tone and established a decision-making process that stifled debate while pretending that it was occurring. He prized consensus among his advisers, but he absolutely demanded loyalty. Thus, once he had decided to stay the course in Southeast Asia, the main idea was not to let Vietnam get in the way of the domestic policy agenda, and, more important, to win the election.

Unfortunately for Johnson, the situation in Vietnam demanded attention. The Minh government was less competent and more lethargic than its predecessor. Minh himself was reported to be amenable to talks with Hanoi leading toward "neutrality," a concept that was intentionally ill-defined, but was anathema to the Johnson administration as the likely first step toward a communist takeover. Worse, despite continual glowing reports from MACV, Minh's writ extended little farther than the outskirts of Saigon. The National Liberation Front was making steady progress and generally owned the countryside after dark. Hanoi determined to step up its assistance to the NLF, hoping to win in the South before the United States decided to intervene. President Ho Chi Minh and his advisers were confident of victory so long as the United States did not commit to war, and they were willing to go to great lengths to see that it did not. At home, the *New York Times, U.S. News,* and Walter Lippmann pressed for a change in policy. Closer still, several of LBJ's longtime Senate colleagues—William Fulbright, chairman of the Foreign Relations Committee, Mike Mansfield, Johnson's handpicked successor as Senate majority leader and an Asian history expert, and Johnson's mentor, Richard Russell, chairman of the Armed Services Committee—were all beseeching the president to find a way out of Vietnam.[43] They did not reckon with LBJ's fears of failure and humiliation.

To gain a better understanding of the situation in Vietnam and to stop the momentum toward negotiations or "neutrality," LBJ dispatched Mc-Namara and Taylor to Saigon for another inspection tour in December 1963. The president had long admired McNamara. Sizing up the new Kennedy team in 1961, he had remarked that "the fellow from Ford with the Stacomb on his hair is the best of the lot." A quick study, McNamara had read his new boss's strengths and weaknesses accurately. LBJ expected unity and hated dissension, so McNamara and Taylor further tightened control over information going to and coming from the infamously disputatious Joint Chiefs. Taylor, now more than ever, would be the only soldier with clout in the administration. McNamara and Taylor found the situation in South Vietnam "very disturbing. Current trends, unless reversed in the next 2–3 months will lead to neutralization at best and more likely a communist-controlled state." CIA director McCone, who was also on the trip, reported that "there is no organized government in South Vietnam at this time." These assessments, more accurate than their forerunners, depicted a sharp fall in both military capability and political stability that had commenced with the Diem coup. Seven more coups d'état toppled South Vietnamese regimes in the coming year. The decline had to be arrested: Johnson had to act.[44]

McNamara had been leaning toward increasing pressure on North Vietnam before his trip. Now he recommended a program of covert action, including "a wide variety of sabotage and psychological operations against North Vietnam." He suggested targets that would "provide maximum pressure with minimum risk," which meant that the United States could still deny its involvement. On January 16, 1964, President Johnson approved part of McNamara's covert action plan, a decision that extended operations into North Vietnam—albeit with South Vietnamese forces—for the first time.[45]

The Joint Chiefs sensed a new direction. Kennedy had given them a mission to keep Vietnam independent and noncommunist, but neither the authority nor the means to carry it out. Now Lyndon Johnson refused to be the president who lost Vietnam. He had just approved tentative steps against the North, which was more than JFK had ever done. A week later the JCS presented McNamara a new plan for consideration. It began by restating domino-theory tenets as they applied to Southeast Asia. Furthermore, Vietnam represented the "first real test of our determination to defeat . . . communist wars of national liberation," which presented a challenge to the containment doctrine. Failure there, the Joint Chiefs argued, would call into question "U.S. durability, resolution, and trustworthiness" among allies and communist adversaries worldwide. Yet the current course reduced the United States to "fighting on the enemy's terms" because "we have obliged ourselves to labor under self-imposed restrictions," staying within South Vietnam and using only advisers but no American combat forces. The JCS argued it was time for the United States to take on a larger role. The author of flexible response, Taylor convinced his JCS colleagues to offer twelve progressively aggressive steps, beginning with empowering the American commander in Vietnam to take full control of the war (supplanting Ambassador Lodge and General Minh), helping the South Vietnamese with ground and air operations against the North, conducting American bombing raids against the North "under Vietnamese cover," and finally, if necessary, committing U.S. ground forces to combat in South and North Vietnam.[46] The proposal papered over important differences. The more bellicose chiefs were telling LBJ that if he would not be the president who lost Vietnam, these twelve measures were what he had to do to win. Taylor focused on the rungs on the ladder of escalation. The president did not respond to their proposal, at least not yet.

At the end of January 1964 the Minh government fell victim to yet another coup. Johnson was incensed: the Vietnam policy was hard enough to sell without the South Vietnamese playing musical chairs. Mansfield, Fulbright, Lippmann, and the *New York Times* were all telling him to get out. Johnson decided to send McNamara and Taylor to the region once again to show support for the new leader, General Nguyen Khanh, and to send a clear message to the Vietnamese: "No more of this coup shit." Of course, the success of a second coup in the span of three months made the political instability more acute and increased the likelihood of another overthrow.[47]

The problem was not just political instability at the top. The Khanh coup had undermined confidence in the United States among the South Vietnamese people. As a second regime fell with no visible sign of American support, many South Vietnamese began to suspect their ally's trustworthiness. Moreover, the Khanh regime was no more popular than its predecessor, and there was little support for the perpetual war the country had experienced. The CIA reported that the people were apathetic or leaning toward the NLF, a conclusion borne out by increasing insurgent control of the countryside. One CIA official was "shocked by the number of our people and of the military, even those whose job is always to say that we are winning, who feel that the tide is against us." French president Charles de Gaulle was pressing for neutralization, and other allies were beginning to listen. The second-ranking U.S. diplomat in Saigon concluded that de Gaulle was right: U.S. policy was either leading toward failure, meaning neutralization, or direct combat between the United States and the DRV.[48]

Worse still, none of these observers (or their superiors in Washington) was aware that the Central Committee of the Communist Party in Hanoi had just decided upon a major escalation of the war, committing the full resources of North Vietnam, including its regular army, to support the NLF, even if that meant a direct confrontation with American forces. Hanoi had decided that they could no longer prevent Americanization of the war. Thus, the chance to deter the DRV from a general war, on which much of American policy was predicated, had vanished, but the Americans did not know it.[49]

In preparation for his March trip McNamara formally asked the JCS for their advice: if there were to be a change in strategy from assisting and advising allies in a Vietnamese war, what should it be? Characteristically, the chiefs were divided. LeMay insisted on taking the war to enemy sanctuaries in Laos and Cambodia with both American and Vietnamese airpower: "We are swatting flies," he fumed, "when we ought to be going after the manure pile." U.S. Marine Corps commandant General Wallace M. Greene asked for a clear policy decision: "either to pull out of South Vietnam or to stay there and win. If the decision is to stay and win—which is the Marine Corps recommendation—this objective must be pursued with the full concentrated power of U.S. resources." Taylor, mistrusted as ever, forced a consensus position on the JCS that called for gradually extending the war through "a coordinated diplomatic, military, and psychological program," including direct military operations against the North. Those operations would begin with air attacks of two kinds, "a sudden blow for shock effect [and] another in the form of ascending order of severity with increasing U.S. participation," which would become known as graduated pressure. On March 4, 1964, the president invited the JCS to give him their views, the first of a few rare consultations between them and the commander in chief on Vietnam strategy. They made their individual recommendations, and Taylor presented the consensus. Johnson agreed on the need to increase pressure on Hanoi.

He certainly did not intend to lose South Vietnam, but neither did he want to take the nation into war before November.[50] Greene bluntly told the president that he would have to choose between withdrawal and escalation. The marine general made a record of Johnson's response:

> [The president] repeated again that the Congress and the country did not want war—that war at this time would have a tremendous effect on the approaching Presidential political campaign and might perhaps keep the Democrats from winning in November. He said that he thought it would be much better to keep out of any war until December; that would be after the election and whoever was going to be President could then go to Congress for a supporting and joint resolution, and . . . explain to [the people of the United States] why we had to risk the chances of another war by expanding our operations in Southeast Asia.[51]

Johnson returned to his office and repeated those thoughts in a phone call with McGeorge Bundy: "I just spent a lot of time with the Joint Chiefs. The net of it . . . is—they say get in or get out. And I told them, 'Let's try to find an amendment. . . .'"[52] These statements were among the clearest expositions of how heavily presidential politics weighed on Vietnam policy in 1964. They were also the first indications that LBJ would seek a congressional resolution before broadening the war.

Greene concluded that the president's decision to send McNamara and Taylor to Saigon for another inspection was a sham. LBJ had made a show of asking the secretary to test the Joint Chiefs' recommendations, but "the president . . . was indirectly telling General Taylor that he did not want him to return from SVN with a recommendation that the campaign there be expanded to include NVN." When Greene checked his assessment with Taylor, the chairman agreed that "his neck and the SecDef's neck were on the chopping block." McNamara and Taylor arrived in Saigon on March 8. They barnstormed the country with Khanh, stopping in one village after another in a futile attempt to boost the general's political support. They spoke to small crowds and posed for photos, Taylor on one side of Khanh and McNamara on the other, each holding one of the general's hands aloft in an awkward imitation of a victorious prizefighter. Strangely, the campaign did not seem to work. Further, the two Americans found that both the military and political situations in Vietnam had only worsened since their December trip. Nonetheless the secretary checked with the president before he made formal recommendations, cagily gauging how far LBJ was ready to go. Reflecting Johnson's concerns, their final report did not yet support bombing the North, but recommended that the JCS begin planning for quick retaliatory strikes on sensitive targets as well as a sustained and graduated bombing campaign. On March 17 Johnson convened the NSC, where he and McNamara performed a minuet in which the secretary presented the preapproved recommendations and the president accepted them with pleasure.[53]

The Joint Chiefs' advice had not been rejected outright—they were allowed to plan. In fact, however, the real planning was now being done by civilians in the White House, the State Department, and the Pentagon.[54]

Soon thereafter Johnson shook up the team in Saigon. Lodge resigned as ambassador, to be replaced by Maxwell Taylor, who was given full authority over all diplomatic *and military* affairs in Vietnam. Taylor and McNamara chose Army Chief of Staff Earle G. "Bus" Wheeler as the new chairman. So self-effacing that in his entire term he never corrected the president for calling him "Buzz," Wheeler could be relied upon as a pliable helpmate for McNamara. General William C. Westmoreland took over at MACV, where wishful thinking dressed up as reporting had finally shaken McNamara's confidence. Serving under the eminent and recently retired chairman of the Joint Chiefs now endowed with a new and extraordinary plenipotentiary as Johnson's envoy, Westmoreland effectively became Taylor's military deputy in Vietnam. Taylor continued to be the "general" on whom the president relied for military advice. The Joint Chiefs remained available for consultation when and if Johnson needed to say they had been consulted, but he knew that their advice would be to escalate.[55]

Conditions in Vietnam continued to deteriorate. Johnson made two telephone calls on May 27, 1964, that revealed his ambivalence, almost cognitive dissonance, on Vietnam. His confidant Senator "Dick" Russell gently tried to persuade the president to withdraw from the conflict. Johnson replied that his advisers—Rusk, McNamara, Bundy, etc.—were all telling him "we've got to show some power and some force." Russell, searching for solutions to "the worst damn mess I ever saw," offered a shrewd suggestion: "I'd get that same crowd that got rid of old Diem to get rid of these people and get some fellow in there that said he wished to hell we *would* get out. That would give us a good excuse for getting out." Johnson lamented the limitations of all his options, but revealed that withdrawal excited his greatest fears: "Well, they'd impeach a president though [*sic*] that would run out, wouldn't they?" Johnson admitted, "I just haven't got the nerve to do it [escalate in Vietnam], and I don't see any other way out of it." A few minutes later Johnson called McGeorge Bundy: "I don't think that we can fight them ten thousand miles away from home. . . . I don't think it's worth fighting for and don't think we can get out. It's just the biggest damned mess that I ever saw."[56]

Johnson might have found answers to such soul searching if he had possessed the self-assurance to take his military advisers into his confidence. Hard-headed analysis of politico-strategic conundrums was the Joint Chiefs' raison d'être. Yet with Taylor's departure, the Joint Chiefs were of two types: organization men who had been selected for their loyalty or cowed into submission by long exposure to McNamara (or both); and Greene and LeMay, who though frequently cantankerous would happily tell anyone exactly what they thought and damn the consequences. In short, they were a collection of military professionals who might have held a useful seminar on the pros and cons of going to war halfway around the world, if only someone had bothered to ask their candid opinions and honestly listened. Lyndon Johnson was not the sort of president to ask, and the chiefs had been long conditioned not to force their opinions on the commander in chief.

Nevertheless, in the spring and summer of 1964 Johnson was at the height of his powers. He passed a civil rights bill and sewed up his own nomination as president well in advance of the August convention. He was popular and seemed to be coasting to an election victory over the Republican nominee, Senator Barry Goldwater, whom the Johnson campaign lampooned as a reactionary and a warmonger.

In early August 1964 two incidents off the coast of North Vietnam allowed LBJ to gain a congressional resolution on Vietnam and with it enormous freedom of action. On August 2 local DRV commanders reacted to South Vietnamese guerrilla operations against coastal islands as well as a DeSoto patrol, the USS *Maddox,* in the Gulf of Tonkin. North Vietnamese patrol boats sped toward and shot at the *Maddox.* In response the United States deployed a second destroyer to the region, the USS *Turner Joy.* The two destroyers sailed in zigzag patterns near the site of the incident for two days—almost taunting the North Vietnamese. Then, on August 4 both vessels reported being under attack. However, a few hours later the *Maddox*'s commander revised his report, suggesting that nervous radar operators might have been overanxious. Johnson later griped, "Hell, those dumb, stupid sailors were just shooting at flying fish." Indeed, it is now clear that the second "attack" never occurred. By that time, however, following plans drawn for just such a scenario, the Johnson administration was well down the path of ordering a retaliatory strike on targets in North Vietnam, briefing the congressional leaders on the incidents and the U.S. response, and demanding a congressional resolution authorizing the president to take any steps he thought necessary to defend South Vietnam. LBJ, McNamara, and Rusk all spoke untruths to Congress or the press about the second incident, dismissing growing doubts within the navy and the Pentagon that it had occurred. Congress passed the Gulf of Tonkin resolution overwhelmingly, with only two dissenting votes in the Senate. LBJ later laughed about his new authority: the resolution was "like grandma's nightshirt; it covered everything." For the third time since World War II, the Congress had ceded its war-making powers to the chief executive, allowing the president to make war without a declaration of war. LBJ would later learn, however, that a vote of support for the president when American ships had been attacked was not necessarily a mandate to expand a war in Southeast Asia.[57]

Announcing the strikes against North Vietnam on the night of August 4, LBJ disingenuously insisted that he was only replying to acts of "open aggression on the high seas against the United States." He assured the nation that he understood "the risks of spreading conflict. We seek no wider war." Having responded decisively as commander in chief, Johnson pivoted to running for reelection as a man of peace. He limited DeSoto patrols and Oplan 34A raids into North Vietnam so as not to provoke another incident. His political campaign portrayed Johnson as a mature leader who would defend the country but not take it into a foreign war, unlike his extremist opponent. Johnson began drawing enthusiastic cheers by telling campaign crowds, "We don't want American boys to do the fighting for Asian boys." Sometimes, he qualified the line with "just for the moment" or "we are not going north and drop bombs at this stage of the game." Yet the public scarcely noticed such hedging. LBJ cruised to the broadest election victory since FDR's margin in 1936. Now he was president in his own right, no longer Jack Kennedy's caretaker. Now he could pursue his "war on poverty" and the even broader "Great Society," a name resonant of the "New Deal." He had a mandate to pursue new policies, especially concerning Vietnam. Most American allies, many influential Democrats, and an increasing number of editorial boards hoped that he would use his new lease on the presidency to wind down U.S. involvement in a civil war ten thousand miles away.[58]

On November 1, 1964, the Viet Cong attacked an airfield at Bien Hoa, destroying five B-57 jet bombers and damaging thirteen more, half the U.S. bomber force dispatched after the Gulf of Tonkin incident. Ambassador Taylor asked for a retaliatory strike against a MiG base in the North. The Joint Chiefs demanded a full-scale attack against ninety-four previously designated targets, along with the deployment of ground forces to protect U.S. bases. Not surprisingly the president refused to retaliate two days before the American election. Instead, he ordered William P. "Bill" Bundy, chief of the State Department's Far East desk, to conduct a thorough reexamination of U.S. policy in Vietnam.[59]

On Election Day 1964 "that other Bundy," as LBJ dubbed him, convened a group of eight officials from the CIA, State, Defense, and the Joint Staff. Over the next two months these men conducted the only comprehensive review of Vietnam policy until the aftermath of the 1968 Tet Offensive. The men of Bundy's group and the NSC principals to whom they reported all had long records in support of the American policy there, and therefore they all had personal stakes in the outcome. Nothing new emerged from the working group. The limited war options they developed resembled ideas that had been under consideration for months or years.[60]

Typically, Bundy's working group formulated three alternatives: the status quo; "fast/full squeeze," which would impose immediate, heavy pressure (meaning massive air bombardment) against North Vietnam to force their surrender; and graduated military pressure with options to increase or decrease as necessary to induce the North Vietnamese to capitulate. Over the next two weeks a consensus formed in support of graduated pressure, which was a form of Schelling's coercive strategy. Each of these options aimed at ending the war through successful negotiation to maintain an independent South Vietnam. Yet Bundy briefly floated a fourth option, a "fall-back" to disengage from the war. He based his argument on South Vietnamese political fragmentation that made success in the war unlikely under any scenario, as well as intelligence estimates that accurately described North Vietnamese and NLF resilience. "We have never thought that we could defend a government or a people that had ceased to care strongly about defending themselves or that were unable to maintain the fundamentals of government. And the overwhelming world impression is that these are lacking elements in South Viet-Nam." The JCS representative, Vice Admiral Lloyd Mustin, savaged such pessimism, invoking the commitment of "national prestige, credibility, and honor" to assert, "We have no further fall-back position in Southeast Asia." He ridiculed the notion that there was "some alternative to our holding South Viet-Nam. There is none." Mustin's attack killed the "fall-back" option. The working group's report explained "the need to consider a fall-back position" as merely meant "to assess the drawbacks associated with it." Thus, the working group never seriously considered a reevaluation of American policy in Vietnam.[61]

Far from advocating withdrawal from Southeast Asia, the Joint Chiefs preferred removing the constraints that limited-war thinking had thus far placed on U.S. efforts in Vietnam. They had no patience with graduated pressure, "sending signals" to the enemy rather than making war on him. While the chiefs seldom presented a united front, since March they had managed a somewhat durable consensus in favor of sustained bombing of the North. Mustin forcefully represented their views, demanding an end to "dallying and delaying." He proffered a fifth option called "hard knock," which called for "continu[ing] military pressures, if necessary, to the full limitations of what military actions can contribute." That vague formulation would have given the military a blank check when graduated pressure failed, as they believed it surely would (and eventually did). The working group considered "hard knock," but Mustin could not sway them, and they soon settled on graduated military pressure.[62]

None of the Joint Chiefs was present when the working group briefed LBJ on their three proposed options. The president seemed uncharacteristically disengaged. McGeorge Bundy noted the growing consensus for graduated pressure, and said that work would continue in that direction unless LBJ ordered otherwise. Johnson did not ask for more options and did not question George Ball, who was present, when McGeorge Bundy said that little work had been done on a "devil's advocate" memo that LBJ had asked him to write. The sixty-seven-page indictment of Vietnam policy was complete, but Ball said nothing to the president. When Johnson asked about the views of the absent Joint Chiefs, McNamara assured him that the JCS were "already deeply involved" and had been "working for weeks on this problem." A skeptical president told McNamara that he "could not face the congressional leadership on this kind of subject unless he had consulted with the relevant military people."[63]

Yet Maxwell Taylor was the only "relevant military" person for Johnson. Taylor flew back at the end of November 1964 to consult with the working group. As much as any JFK adviser and more than any other military officer, Taylor represented the continuity that LBJ coveted. As the father of "flexible response," a former chairman of the Joint Chiefs, and now the man on the spot in Saigon, Taylor's influence easily trumped that of his colleagues in the Pentagon. McNamara had sent Taylor copies of the Joint Chiefs' recommendations before he left Saigon. Taylor arrived in Washington on the twenty-sixth fully prepared; he dominated the final series of working group meetings. He enunciated three principles for U.S. policy: "do not enter into negotiations until the DRV is hurting"; never let Hanoi gain a victory "without having paid a disproportionate price"; and keep the South Vietnamese "in the forefront of the combat and the negotiations." Since his advocacy of a reprisal strike following the Bien Hoa attack, Taylor had shifted to support of sustained bombing. His thinking had changed in another way as well: he despaired of stable government in Saigon. South Vietnamese leaders were rapidly rotating through the top positions of government, and most seemed to favor negotiations with Hanoi. Taylor feared early National Assembly elections because they were likely to return a pro-neutrality majority. So dire was his assessment—he could not "foresee a stable and effective government under any name in anything like the near future"—that he advocated bombing the North even in the absence of political stability in the South. Stunningly, Taylor pushed for punishing North Vietnam regardless of the political situation in Saigon. His advocacy was critical in moving the working group and the president toward escalation of the war. Importantly, the working group's final report indicated that "the U.S. would seek to control any negotiations and would oppose any independent South Vietnamese efforts to negotiate." Any notion of self-determination was thus deleted from the U.S. policy goal of an "independent, non-Communist South Vietnam." America was about to take over the war.[64]

Taylor's advocacy pushed the working group toward a combination of the status quo and graduated pressure. A draft NSAM posited a two-phase escalation, which to the Joint Chiefs' consternation said nothing about a "hard knock." In the first phase armed reconnaissance strikes would target infiltration routes through Laos and allow for retaliation for attacks against bases in South Vietnam. The second phase would commence "graduated military pressure" against the ninety-four approved targets in North Vietnam. JCS chairman Wheeler was allowed to attend a final meeting with LBJ on December 1, 1964, but it was too late. The president approved the working group's two-phase recommendation. He then allowed Wheeler to make a presentation of the Joint Chiefs' position, which seemed to agree with many of the NSAM's points, especially the chairman's statement of the geopolitical stakes and the need for clear objectives. LBJ then dramatically said that if the situation did not improve, "I'll be talking with you, General." That was the extent of consultation between the president and the Joint Chiefs on the single most important decision of America's war in Vietnam.[65]

Johnson's memorandum approving the new policy made it "a matter of the highest importance that the substance of this position should not become public except as I specifically direct." The president personally charged his senior officers of government to restrict knowledge of his decisions "as narrowly as possible to those who have an immediate working need to know." In a *New York Times* interview a week later, LBJ flatly denied any change in policy or intention to escalate U.S. involvement in Vietnam.[66]

After Johnson's December 1964 decision the situation continued to deteriorate in Vietnam. Taylor had given up on the South Vietnamese government, and his relations with them became so strained that they considered expelling him from the country. On Christmas Day the Viet Cong bombed an American officers' quarters in Saigon, killing two and wounding fifty. Strains arose among the Americans in Saigon. The CIA recommended Taylor's recall. Westmoreland asked for as many as seventy-five thousand troops, a request that Taylor vetoed. Khanh staged another coup on January 27, prompting McGeorge Bundy and Robert McNamara to warn LBJ that the United States had reached "a fork in the road" with respect to Vietnam. Now, they argued, was either the time to negotiate and withdraw with what dignity they could salvage, or to implement Phase 2 and escalate the war. Furthermore, while Johnson's December directive had said that "we will not go further until there is a stable government," Bundy and McNamara now concluded that "no one has much hope that there is going to be a stable government while we sit still." The two men recommended commencing sustained bombing of North Vietnam immediately and regardless of political conditions in Saigon. Johnson agreed: "Stable government or no stable government, we'll do what we have to do." He ordered the resumption of DeSoto patrols and dispatched Bundy to inspect the situation in Vietnam, another instance of presenting an appearance of deliberation when decisions had already been made.[67]

Although Bundy had been overseeing U.S. policy in Vietnam for four years, he made his first visit to the country in early February 1965. He quickly confirmed that waiting on a stable government in Vietnam would be fruitless, for the country was in "a civil war within a civil war." In the early hours of February 7, NLF forces attacked a U.S. air base at Pleiku, killing 8 Americans and wounding 126 others. Bundy, Taylor, and General Westmoreland flew to the scene and viewed the carnage that was still strewn about the grounds. The national security adviser was visibly moved. Westmoreland later quipped that when Bundy "smelled a little gunpowder he developed a field marshal psychosis." One of Bundy's aides sensed that his boss had "caught religion on Vietnam." Bundy denied that Pleiku had changed his thinking, later manfully quipping that "Pleikus are like streetcars," meaning that once the decision had been made to prepare for reprisal strikes, it was only necessary to await a provocation that was sure to come along soon enough. Regardless, he immediately recommended reprisal bombing against the North, an action that Taylor and the JCS had advocated for months. LBJ convened the National Security Council, approved the recommendation, and Operation Flaming Dart commenced that same day.[68]

Bundy flew straight back to Washington, finished his report en route, and delivered it to Johnson late on February 7 (Washington time). "The situation in Vietnam is deteriorating," he argued, "and without new action defeat appears inevitable." The stakes were "extremely high," not least because the sense of American responsibility for conditions in Vietnam were "a fact of life which [was] palpable in the atmosphere." There was no meaningful prospect of "unloading the burden on the Vietnamese themselves," he asserted, quickly dispensing with four years of Kennedy-Johnson policy. Nor was there any chance for negotiating a withdrawal, which would amount to "surrender on the installment plan." Well aware of all the evidence against the efficacy of bombing alone, Bundy nevertheless recommended beginning reprisal air strikes immediately, knowing that doing so would likely trigger the sustained bombing campaign of

Phase 2. Bundy emphasized the need to be flexible in the level of reprisal in accord with Viet Cong responses, in order "to keep before Hanoi the carrot of our desisting as well as the stick of continual pressure." In a perfect exposition of game theory, Bundy declared, "The object would not be to 'win' an air war against Hanoi, but rather to influence the course of the struggle in the South." He cautioned that this policy would take a long time to work and admitted that the odds of success were one in four, yet "even if it fails, the policy will be worth it. At a minimum it will damp down the charge that we did not do all that we could have done." If Bundy's recommendation was hardly a stirring call to arms, it was a fitting tribute to the flexible response doctrine Taylor had brought to government four years earlier.[69]

The next morning LBJ convened the NSC once again. Johnson had sent his national security adviser to Vietnam to provide cover for his decision to escalate the war, and Bundy's report more than fit the bill. Johnson approved commencing Phase 2 bombing as soon as possible, but he refused to announce a change in policy. He ordered the NSC not to mention his decision to the press. After Bundy briefed him on his report, LBJ asked, "How many copies are there?" When Bundy said that several had been distributed, Johnson barked, "Get them back!"[70]

Over the next several weeks, the Johnson administration deceived members of Congress, the media, and the American people. On February 13, 1965, Johnson formally approved a massive bombing campaign that became known as Rolling Thunder. Four days later, despite entreaties from his top advisers to declare and define the new strategy for the American people, LBJ publicly said, "We seek no wider war." Of course, such a significant change in American war aims could not be kept secret. The story leaked, and the "credibility gap" was born.[71]

As planning for the bombing campaign commenced, General Wheeler penned an anodyne memo to McNamara detailing initial movements. Writing in the third person, Wheeler ended with the following: "He believes, however, that as a further action to the measures proposed herein, the feasibility and desirability of additional deployments to the Western Pacific area once these forces are in position should be examined as a matter of priority. A follow-on study for this purpose has been initiated." Writing to a colleague a day earlier, NSC staffer James C. Thomson Jr. was much more straightforward: "Are we willing—and is the President willing—to face a ground war in Southeast Asia? . . . Are the American people willing to face a ground war in Vietnam?" Two weeks later, General Westmoreland requested a marine battalion to provide base security for American air forces at Da Nang. Ambassador Taylor warned that "once this policy [against U.S. combat troop deployments] is breached, it will be very difficult to hold the line." Yet he acquiesced.[72]

American involvement in Vietnam had been premised upon a dubious "domino theory." Now a real domino effect of troop deployments commenced in earnest. Rolling Thunder began on March 2, 1965. More aircraft in South Vietnam required better base security, which necessitated deployment of ground troops. The first two marine battalions waded ashore at Da Nang less than a week later. The administration refused to acknowledge this deployment and did not consult with Congress or the government in Saigon. To be effective, of course, base security cannot be static or passive; it requires local patrolling. Patrolling begets skirmishing with enemy forces, which tends to escalate over time. The DRV strengthened its ties to both Moscow and Beijing and began sending its own ground forces into South Vietnam. ARVN desertion rates and South Vietnamese political metastasis continued apace. Another military coup toppled the Saigon government in June. In three months American combat forces grew to fifty thousand, with thirty thousand more troops preparing to deploy. By the end of 1965—just nine months after the first two battalions arrived—American combat troops on the ground in Vietnam numbered 180,000 and climbing, with no end in sight.[73]

At the beginning of 1965 American entry into the Vietnam War was anything but a foregone conclusion. Indeed, the United States might have avoided direct ground combat and the escalating spiral of engagement that followed. Myriad advocates—in the press, among senior politicians, policy makers, and foreign governments—urged the administration to step back from Vietnam. Yet against all these pressures for peace, American leaders chose to go to war, believing that the loss of Southeast Asia to communism was at stake. By 1965 the president's civilian advisers were heavily invested in the Vietnam policy and its outcome. They had counseled against withdrawal so often that they were incapable of seriously reexamining their positions. Moreover, they were nonmilitary men giving military advice. The Kennedy-Johnson men deeply believed in flexible response and limited war theory, and were only too happy to fill the vacuum left by the marginalized Joint Chiefs. By the time Bill Bundy con-

vened the Vietnam working group in November 1964, no one—save the
Joint Chiefs themselves—thought it amiss that the JCS had only one representative on a war strategy panel. Like their principals, the deputies
and policy assistants had a four-year investment in Vietnam. It was only
natural that the working group arrived at another middle-way compromise, a strategy that carried the nation gradually into war.

By January 1965 the Joint Chiefs had grown accustomed to the roles
that they had taken on in 1961. Chastised by Eisenhower, shunned by
JFK, muzzled by McNamara, usurped by Taylor, manipulated by LBJ,
they were parochial, divided, and finally ineffectual. The organization itself was moribund. Their predecessors on the JCS, including Taylor, bore
much responsibility for their marginalization. By opposing Eisenhower
over strategic and budgetary decisions, they set themselves up as political
rivals rather than loyal subordinates to the commander in chief. Kennedy
was right to be dubious at first, and the chiefs confirmed his worst suspicions during the Bay of Pigs. Yet when Kennedy pronounced his policy
for Indochina, the chiefs signed on—believing they could not lose in Vietnam. They clung to that mission through two administrations, consistently pressing the presidents to devote the military power necessary to
make good on their political commitments. McNamara and Taylor
forced them to learn the language of flexible response and limited war,
and they became quite fluent, but they were never true believers. Some,
especially Curtis LeMay, were foils who proffered extreme positions that
made moderate compromises possible. Others offered lists of gradually
escalating options, fully expecting that the escalation would not be gradual. These soldiers knew that, once begun, war takes on a life of its own.
Yet their civilian superiors, long accustomed to ignoring or filtering their
professional counsel, failed to ask what might happen after the bombing
campaign began and ground troops were deployed. By 1965, if the Joint
Chiefs knew, they weren't saying in a manner that could be clearly
grasped. In that way, not much had changed since the Bay of Pigs: the JCS
were still soft-pedaling their advice, letting the civilians make the decisions and take the responsibility. They owed better service to the president
and the country. Rolling Thunder began, and the marines landed at Da
Nang, followed in the months and years to come by hundreds of thousands more troops.

For four years Maxwell Taylor stood at the center of Vietnam policy
making. As in-house military counsel for Kennedy, Taylor allowed the
president to dispense with his statutory advisers. When he moved to the

Pentagon, he teamed with Secretary of Defense McNamara to dominate national security policy. Taylor became personally close to the Kennedys and, by his own admission, a "true believer" in their agenda. He presented a stark contrast with both Marshall and MacArthur. Where Marshall had remained personally aloof from the president to maintain military objectivity, Taylor sacrificed both distance and professional perspective. Where MacArthur had been a political opponent of both Roosevelt and Truman, Taylor became a partisan ally of the Kennedys. He had his own agenda, flexible response, and he pursued it in many forms, but always as an administration loyalist first and as a military professional a distantly lagging second. In three key roles he enabled his presidents to marginalize the Joint Chiefs, either by magnifying their disagreements, forcing unsatisfactory consensus, or simply ignoring their views altogether. Taylor's interposition between the president and the Pentagon, and later his dominance as JCS chairman and ambassador to South Vietnam, prevented the Joint Chiefs from exercising the authority, independence, and responsibility of their offices. Moreover, the Joint Chiefs' suspicions of Taylor compounded their mistrust of both Kennedy and Johnson. In such an atmosphere the trust necessary for effective policy and strategy making could not exist.

Ironically, the talking paper that Taylor gave Kennedy to help restore his relations with the Joint Chiefs was an excellent summary of how to build a political-military partnership. The president should get his military advice "directly and unfiltered." The chiefs should make their "arguments for or against any course of action without fear or hesitation." And their advice "could not and should not be purely military," as political, economic, and other factors always impinge on national security decisions. Of course, the political-military dialogue in the Vietnam era never approached this ideal, and the policy process was poorer for it.

Yet, even if the reverse had been true, the United States might still have bungled its way into Vietnam, because almost all the principals, military and civilian, were equally wrong in their analyses of the problem and their prescriptions to solve it. Time and again these presidents and their advisers missed opportunities to reassess their policies, to examine their goals in light of the national interest, and to ask if achieving victory in Vietnam was worth the cost, or even possible, all in the face of strong and respected opposition in the United States and abroad. For all the mistrust, miscommunication, and outright lies that bedeviled the American road to war, nothing was so important as the failure of two presidents and their generals to comprehend that Vietnam constituted a peripheral, not a vital national interest, to appreciate the patience and implacability of the NLF and the DRV, to look squarely at the fecklessness and corruption of the South Vietnamese government, and therefore to understand the futility of committing American prestige, treasure, and blood to the war. By March 1965, the United States had entered into a war that could not be won, because it stemmed from an unattainable policy aim—a South Vietnam that was both independent and noncommunist. No strategy could have salvaged that essential policy mistake. Thus, every failure that followed over the next decade, including America's ultimate defeat, rested upon the dysfunctional political-military relations that initially misled the nation into tragedy in Vietnam.

11

POWELL'S DOCTRINE

A month before the 1992 presidential election, Chairman of the Joint Chiefs Colin L. Powell fired off an op-ed in response to a *New York Times* editorial comparing him to Civil War general George B. McClellan in his reluctance to use military force. Still basking in the public adulation that had been his since the 1991 Gulf War victory over Iraq, the general confidently rebutted the charge, recounting numerous deployments the armed forces had effectively carried out during the George H. W. Bush administration. Indeed, he attributed that record of success to the incumbent: "President Bush, more than any other recent president, understands the proper use of military force." The proper use required clear political and military objectives, and the employment of decisive means to achieve decisive results. The opposite approach, deploying force "imprecisely or out of frustration rather than clear analysis," was to be deplored. "So you bet I get nervous when so-called experts suggest that all we need is a little surgical bombing or a limited attack." Powell made it clear that a contemplated military intervention in the Balkans, then an issue in the presidential contest, presented the potential for just the sort of imprecise and limited mission that gave him pause.[1] Astute voters had no need to read between the lines to conclude that the nation's top military officer would be greatly relieved if they returned his current boss to the White House.

Yet the implied political endorsement was not the most audacious aspect of the essay. Rather, it was Powell, the personification of the military renaissance after the defeat in Vietnam, presuming to pass judgment on policy decisions. Such hubris was a long march past the early twentieth-century conception of policy and strategy as naturally separate spheres—the exclusive provinces of politicians in the former and generals in the latter. Indeed, it was quite a distance beyond MacArthur's pronouncement of his own brand of foreign policy in 1950. It outstripped Taylor's "flexible response," which was merely a new school of thought in national security. General Powell insisted on prescribing not only how policy makers should frame problems but how they should craft solutions. He even offered to evaluate their decision-making efforts. The standard of measurement had become known as the Powell Doctrine. And Colin Powell's prestige was such that his rating of an administration's national security policy paper truly mattered.

Powell had achieved such power at a unique moment in American history. The United States had just triumphed in a decades-long Cold War, for which the American military received a large share of the credit. From its nadir in the Vietnam debacle, the military profession had reformed and rebounded to its apogee—a bloodless victory over its Soviet foe followed by two rapid defeats of far less worthy enemies in Panama and Iraq. General Powell ascended to the chair of the Joint Chiefs just after Congress vested unprecedented power in that post. No longer first among equals, the JCS chairman was now legally superior to the service chiefs and principal military adviser to the secretary of defense and the president. Colin Powell filled the position fully. He was an extraordinarily able and well-prepared chairman. To his gifts of intellect, leadership, and charisma he added a worldview shaped in the jungles of Vietnam and the corridors of Washington. Almost two decades at the highest levels of government endowed him with political savvy, bureaucratic skill, and an unrivaled network of mentors and allies. Powell arrived as chairman alive to the possibilities the role afforded, not least of which was the chance to exorcise the ghosts of Vietnam. He intended to make the most of the opportunity.

America's retreat from Vietnam had punctured a number of cherished national myths. Always victorious, America had been defeated. Ever successful, the country had failed. A symbol of strength, the United States now appeared weak. And a nation that had long comforted itself in a vision of national exceptionalism based on moral superiority found itself deeply divided over whether the war should have been fought at all. The deepest fissures appeared between those who had supported the war and fought it and those who had opposed the war and chosen not to fight. A malaise followed in the 1970s that manifested itself in a president's disgrace and resignation over the Watergate fiasco, Middle Eastern oil embargoes, a faltering economy plagued by a new malady called stag-flation, and a hostage crisis in Iran that festered more than a year and managed to cripple the Carter presidency. America was in a state of moral and political decline.

The military began a painful period of recovery. Congress eliminated conscription at the end of the Vietnam War, ushering in an all-volunteer force for the first time since before World War II. This change seemed to break a long-standing compact between the people and the government—that military service was an obligation of citizenship. Army Chief of Staff Creighton W. Abrams responded by restructuring the army so that essential supporting components shifted to the reserves and national guard, effectively constraining future commanders in chief, who in time of war would presumably have to call up tens of thousands of citizen-soldiers and involve large swaths of the electorate in the prosecution of national security policy.

Although the services made strides in many areas, operational failures over several years pointed up continuing problems. Most notable were a U.S. hostage rescue disaster in the Iranian desert in 1980, and a 1983 bombing of an American barracks in Beirut. Also in 1983, the Pentagon struggled to coordinate a joint operation against a small, rogue force on the Caribbean island of Grenada. These episodes demonstrated the Defense Department's shortcoming in joint operations and interservice coordination. In response, mid-1980s defense reformers fought a long bureaucratic and legislative battle to shake up the Joint Chiefs of Staff. The fruit of their labor was the Goldwater-Nichols Act, which strengthened the chairman, gave him a deputy, and enlarged the Joint Staff and made it responsible to the chairman rather than to the Joint Chiefs as a body. Most important, the chairman became principal military adviser to the secretary of defense and the president and officially superior to the Joint Chiefs. No longer was he required to gain his colleagues' consensus—a process that had long produced watered-down proposals and "least common denominator" solutions—but could present his own views to his civilian superiors and the National Security Council.

Born into a middle-class, Jamaican immigrant family in the Bronx, Colin Powell attended City College of New York and found a niche in the Army ROTC detachment. Graduating in 1958, he took a commission in the infantry. He hid his intelligence behind a mask of canny common sense, his ambition behind a ready and affable grin. Powell served two tours in Vietnam and was wounded both times. The war shaped his worldview in two ways. First, he believed that a focus on quantitative measures of success, a "body count" mentality, had fostered an ethical disquiet in the U.S. Army. Powell determined to do what he could in ensuing years to reform the army's professional values and uplift its sense of mission. Yet Powell also harbored a deep resentment against the civilian officials and senior generals who had led the nation into Vietnam. Like many of his colleagues, he "vowed that when our turn came to call the shots, we would not quietly acquiesce in halfhearted warfare for half-baked reasons that the American people could not understand or support." Instead, he would insist that "war should be the politics of last resort." If civilian leaders opted for war, generals should challenge them to develop sound policy with clear objectives and get the people behind them. With a well-defined mission and popular support "we should mobilize the country's resources to fulfill that mission and then go in to win." These lessons formed the seeds of what would one day become the Powell Doctrine.[2]

After Vietnam, Powell began a meteoric rise through the army ranks to become the youngest chairman of the Joint Chiefs of Staff in history. Unlike his peers, he had relatively few and short assignments commanding and training soldiers—normally considered essential steps for a fast-moving officer—and instead spent most of his career in Washington. He went to graduate school at George Washington University, took a White House Fellowship in the Office of Management and Budget, and served as military assistant to several senior officials in the Pentagon. Powell became known as a master bureaucrat, a man who knew how to get things done inside the national security establishment. He was also adept at cultivating civilian and military patrons, both Republicans and Democrats, who always seemed anxious to assist the talented young officer. Powell himself later admitted that his career path aroused "the suspicion, sometimes in my own soul, that I was becoming more politician than soldier."[3]

Such self-doubt was both unusual and close to the mark. For an officer who professed to love the company of soldiers, Powell spent the bulk of the 1970s and 1980s in Washington. During a rare troop assignment in Colorado, Powell suffered a blemish to his unsullied armor, receiving a mediocre evaluation from his division commander. He reacted by inviting two higher-ranking army mentors to dinner at his home. Soon, his commander's career was on ice and Powell was safely back on the fast track. Powell's Washington-honed skills worked in the byzantine world of army politics as well.[4]

Just over a year later he returned to the Pentagon, this time as military assistant to Secretary of Defense Caspar Weinberger, architect of President Reagan's defense budget increases. Powell became Weinberger's horse holder, gatekeeper, note taker, and close adviser. The position amounted to a hands-on fellowship in national security policy making. When Powell arrived, Weinberger was feuding bitterly with Secretary of State George Shultz over the use of military force as a policy tool. Weinberger opposed sending U.S. forces into Lebanon as peacekeepers in an Arab-Israeli war, but Shultz persuaded President Reagan to order the deployment. In October 1983 a truck bomb rubbled an American barracks in Beirut, killing 241 servicemen.[5]

Frustrated and angry at this senseless loss of life, Weinberger began preparing a speech outlining principles to guide the employment of American force and to curb the adventurists at State. Powell assisted with the drafts, and fully supported the framework that his boss eventually worked out. Indeed, the principles Weinberger recommended aimed at treating many of the symptoms Powell had diagnosed in Vietnam. The Reagan White House insisted that Weinberger delay delivering his speech until after the presidential election. So in late November 1984 Weinberger went to Washington's National Press Club and promulgated six tests for policy makers to weigh before ordering troops overseas: "(1) Commit only if our or our allies' vital interests are at stake. (2) If we commit, do so with all the resources necessary to win. (3) Go in only with clear political and military objectives. (4) Be ready to change the commitment if the objectives change, since wars rarely stand still. (5) Only take on commitments that can gain the support of the American people and the Congress. (6) Commit U.S. forces only as a last resort." Exorcising the ghosts of Vietnam, Weinberger explicitly cautioned against a "gradualist incremental approach," and promised that the Reagan administration would "not allow our military forces to creep—or be drawn gradually—into a combat role" overseas. While he liked what he heard, Powell professed concern about the public airing of what became known as the Weinberger Doctrine, fearing that it would give America's enemies a template to guide their own actions. Yet a few years later he would eagerly embrace his own revised version.[6]

Powell stayed three years in the secretary's office while his peers were commanding divisions. During that time Weinberger tried to slow down nefarious arms transfers to Iran and operations in Central America that had been hatched at the National Security Council under Admiral John Poindexter and his energetic aide, U.S. Marine lieutenant colonel Oliver North. Powell became involved when he facilitated the transfer of over forty-five hundred TOW missiles to the CIA in what became an "arms for hostages" swap with Israel and Iran. By the time he left to take command of an army corps in Germany, the Iran-Contra scandal was starting to threaten the Reagan presidency.[7]

Powell was still settling into command when Frank Carlucci, a mentor from his White House Fellowship days, called and asked him to return to Washington. Iran-Contra had exploded, forcing President Reagan to fire Poindexter and North. Reagan tapped Carlucci to take over as national security adviser. Carlucci wanted Powell to become his deputy and to help clean up the NSC. Powell had already skipped division command, an almost unheard of gap in a corps commander's résumé. Now he felt that his military career would be ruined if he curtailed his current assignment. He extracted an extraordinary condition from Carlucci: the request would have to come from the commander in chief himself. Two days later Ronald Reagan called and asked Powell to come work in the NSC. After just five months in corps command, Powell was on his way back to Washington.[8]

Carlucci and Powell were hired to clean the Augean stable, and they took to the task with grim efficiency. They dismissed half the NSC staff, including Oliver North's entire office. Powell began a review of all covert intelligence operations and stopped those directed from inside the White House. He established an interagency deputies' group to work through issues and make recommendations to the president and the NSC. Finding Reagan disengaged, almost passive as a decision maker, Carlucci told Powell to begin the rather prosaic practice of taking notes during presidential meetings so as to have a record of discussion and decision. Slowly, a sense of order returned.[9]

In November 1987 Carlucci took over from Weinberger as secretary of defense. Powell filled Carlucci's former position. Now national security adviser in his own right, it was his duty to give policy advice to the commander in chief. Powell was in an uncomfortable position for a military officer, especially after the disaster of Admiral Poindexter's and Lieutenant Colonel North's criminal shenanigans. As the president's honest broker on the National Security Council, he refereed disputes among departments and cabinet officers, evaluated the counsel of his military superiors, including the chairman of the Joint Chiefs, and made sure that the president heard a properly diverse array of advice. He dealt with foreign leaders, including Mikhail Gorbachev, leader of the Soviet Union. And for the first time in his career, he found himself the subject of press coverage. He developed an open and engaging style with the media that helped him establish an attractive popular image. Washington pundits soon put him on the short list of potential running mates in the 1988 election, although nothing came of the talk. Instead, when President-elect Bush began his transition to power, he offered Powell his choice of two high-level posts: director of central intelligence and undersecretary of state. Powell declined, saying he preferred to return to the army, this time as a full general and commander of U.S. Forces Command. Yet as was now normal in Powell's career, he stayed only a few months in command of soldiers before Bush appointed him, the most junior four-star in the armed forces, as the youngest chairman of the Joint Chiefs in history. He was the first chairman selected since the passage of the Goldwater-Nichols Act, and thus the first to enjoy the new power and prestige of that office throughout his tenure.[10]

Powell's new boss was Secretary of Defense Richard B. Cheney, a balding former congressman from Wyoming with a long Washington résumé. The two men could hardly have been more different. Powell the general was gregarious and ideologically flexible. Dick Cheney the politician was famously short on people skills and perched on the far right wing of the Republican Party. Vietnam had been Powell's formative experience, a prism through which he saw foreign policy and the use of military force. Cheney had taken advantage of five draft deferments during the war, and coolly testified during his Senate confirmation hearing that he had "had other priorities during the Sixties than military service." Still, Cheney was an accomplished Washington operator. He had ridden Donald Rumsfeld's coattails into the Nixon and Ford administrations, succeeding his mentor as White House chief of staff when Rumsfeld commenced his first tour as secretary of defense. During that time Cheney worked closely with James A. Baker and national security adviser Brent Scowcroft. After Ford left office, Cheney won Wyoming's House seat and rapidly climbed the ladder of Republican leadership to become minority whip. In 1989 President Bush tapped Cheney for secretary of defense after the Senate blocked his first nominee, John Tower, because of character flaws. For all their differences and more than a bit of friction, Powell and Cheney made an effective team, largely because they were both experienced Washington hands who knew how to play the political game.[11]

The United States had been seeking an opportunity to arrest Manuel Noriega, Panama's dictator and chief drug runner. Two months into Powell's chairmanship Noriega's Panamanian Defense Forces (PDF) shot a U.S. Marine lieutenant and assaulted an American naval officer and his wife. These incidents provided a pretext to remove Noriega from power and install a democratic government. Powell worked with General Maxwell Thurman, commander of U.S. Southern Command, to develop plans to destroy the PDF and decapitate Noriega's regime. It was just the sort of operation the Weinberger Doctrine had prescribed, meeting all the tests. The Canal Zone was a vital national interest, American citizens had been attacked, the mission was clear, U.S. forces were quantitatively and qualitatively superior, Congress was behind the action, and the president was determined to win. Operation Just Cause was swift and efficient, and American casualties were light. A joint team worked together with a proficiency that spotlighted the gains the military profession had made in the years since Vietnam, Desert One, and Grenada. Noriega's government collapsed within hours of the initial assault, although it took a few weeks to capture the fleeing former dictator. Powell clearly established himself as not only principal military adviser to the president and secretary of defense, but, contrary to the explicit dictates of the Goldwater-Nichols Act, firmly ensconced himself in the operational chain of command as well. He controlled the flow of information in both directions, giving orders to Thurman and providing battlefield reports to Cheney and the White House. Glowing news accounts of his masterly orchestration of the operation all agreed that Powell's star was ascendant.[12]

The most significant national security issues of the Bush administration were the collapse of the Iron Curtain, the end of the Cold War, and the dissolution of the Soviet Union. Powell had gained a palpable sense of coming change as national security adviser in April 1988. In Moscow to plan for a Soviet-American summit, Powell had sat patiently as Gorbachev railed for forty-five minutes about the United States' failure to appreciate the historic reforms he was undertaking with *glasnost* and *perestroika*. Powell later recalled, "He was saying, in effect, that he was ending the Cold War. The battle between their ideology and ours was over, and they had lost. He looked directly at me, knowing I was a military man, and said with a twinkling eye, 'What are you going to do now that you've lost your best enemy?' " Powell realized that "all the old verities" that had governed his career had ended.[13]

With that sensibility Powell got well ahead of the Bush administration in thinking about post–Cold War national security policy. He knew that the defense budget would have to shrink, but "I was determined to have the Joint Chiefs drive the military strategy train . . . rather than having military reorganization schemes shoved down our throats" by think tanks, "self-styled freelance military experts," or even Cheney's policy staff. In fact, Powell drove the train himself without consulting the Joint Chiefs. In May 1990 he told the *Washington Post* that the Pentagon could reduce spending as much as 25 percent over the next five years, which was 15 percent less than the president's budget. Not for the first time or the last, Cheney upbraided the chairman for stepping past his bounds: "I need to know if you support the president. I need to be sure you're on the team." Chastened, Powell assured Cheney that he was loyal, but he continued to test the reins throughout his tenure as chairman, and he won this bureaucratic battle. Within a few months the White House announced a 25 percent reduction in defense spending.[14]

If the end of the Cold War was the most significant historical event of the Bush administration, the 1990–91 war in the Persian Gulf consumed most of its time and energy. Powell was central in both the policy and strategy debates. Four times during the planning and conduct of the war Powell inappropriately presumed a role in policy making, each of which tended to limit political options. First, after Iraqi troops overran Kuwait, he vigorously opposed the use of military force to do more than defend Saudi Arabia. Second, when the president later decided on a policy of liberating Kuwait, Powell insisted on an offensive capability of overwhelming strength, almost a doubling of the numbers of forces in theater. Then, when the ground war began, he almost immediately began advocating a cease-fire, although the mission had not yet been accomplished. At each juncture, Powell acted in accordance with the six restrictive tests of what increasingly became known as the Powell Doctrine. He insinuated himself into the chain of command through force of personality. He attempted, usually successfully, to be the sole conduit of information up and down the chain of command. President Bush, sensitive to the so-called "lessons of Vietnam" and determined not to emulate LBJ in picking bombing targets from the White House, enabled Powell by insisting that neither he himself nor his administration would meddle with military prerogatives. Although the president was more hands-on than he admitted, his preference for forbearance often left Powell free to meddle with theater commander H. Norman Schwarzkopf's prerogatives, such as bomb targeting and campaign planning. Finally, at the premature end of the ground war, Powell and Schwarzkopf monopolized planning for cease-fire talks, which they botched, with long-term strategic and political consequences.

On August 2, 1990, Saddam Hussein's massive army invaded the Emirate of Kuwait and overran it in four days. Although officials at CIA and the Defense Intelligence Agency had been warning of an attack for over a week, the administration, largely because of Powell's Vietnam-born aversion to using military force to "send signals," made a tepid response, which Saddam may have interpreted as a green light. On the afternoon of the invasion Cheney, Powell, and their staffs met to discuss the crisis. Cheney wanted a bold plan, either to eject the Iraqis from Kuwait or perhaps to topple the Saddam regime in Baghdad. "We need an objective," he said. Powell was dismissive: "The next few days Iraq will withdraw, but Saddam Hussein will put his puppet in. Everyone in the Arab world will be happy." Referring to the president he said, "I don't see the senior leadership taking us into armed conflict for the events of the last twenty-four hours. The American people do not want their young dying for $1.50 gallon oil [sic], and the Arabs are not happy about cutting their lines off." The group discussed the need for Saudi permission to put U.S. troops on their soil, but Powell again insisted on a show of national support before such a deployment. Growing irritated, Cheney reminded the group of their responsibilities to the president: "We are the only ones who can tell the president what to do. He will look to us. The others can't do it. So what do we do?" Powell responded, "We must start with policy and diplomatic overtures. We can't make a case for losing lives for Kuwait, but Saudi Arabia is different. I am opposed to dramatic action without the president having popular support." Finally, Cheney barked, "I want some options, General."

"Yes, Mr. Secretary," Powell said.[15]

This exchange demonstrated the principal weakness of the Powell Doctrine: it solved every problem for the military by restricting the actions of policy makers. Powell wanted a clear policy from the president that the American people would vigorously support. The Vietnam veteran could not imagine the electorate backing a war for a small country halfway around the world that few Americans could find on a map. Cheney felt that the president could not sell a plan of action to the country before he had chosen a course, and he needed his advisers to help him. Still, the altercation had taken place within the confines of Cheney's office, where spirited political-military discussion should occur.

The next day the National Security Council met to discuss an American response to the invasion. Bush had met with British prime minister Margaret Thatcher on August 2, and she had insisted that they stand together to expel Saddam from Kuwait. Bush was inclined to agree, but in the NSC he played his cards close to his vest. National security adviser Brent Scowcroft led off and framed the discussion by noting a consensus among them that the United States could not allow Iraq's aggression to go unchallenged. Deputy Secretary of State Lawrence Eagleburger forcefully argued for ejecting the Iraqi invasion. Cheney agreed, and asked Powell to review the military options, which included putting at least one hundred thousand troops on the Saudi-Kuwaiti border as quickly as possible. All present agreed to the troop deployment and on the need to seek Saudi permission for it. President Bush said, "We're committed to Saudi Arabia." Taking that limited statement as an opening, Powell asked whether "it was worth going to war to liberate Kuwait." Both Bush and Scowcroft looked startled, and Powell "detected a chill in the room." The NSC was not yet ready to have that discussion, and the policy question should not have come from the chairman of the Joint Chiefs. Yet Powell felt the ghosts of Vietnam in attendance, those of his predecessors who had failed to ask tough questions of their civilian masters: What is the policy? What is our purpose? What is the objective? The meeting broke up without any answers, although later that day the president seemed to commit himself to putting economic and diplomatic pressure on Iraq.[16]

After they returned to the Pentagon, Cheney upbraided the chairman again: "Colin, you're the chairman of the Joint Chiefs. You're not secretary of state. You're not the national security adviser anymore. And you're not secretary of defense. So stick to military matters." Powell knew that he had overstepped and that someone, perhaps Scowcroft, had talked to Cheney about it. Yet while he accepted the rebuke, he was not remorseful. He was doing what he thought the chairman should do, and what his 1960s predecessors had failed to do, with tragic results.[17]

The next day Generals Schwarzkopf and Powell flew to Camp David, the president's Maryland retreat, to brief the president and his advisers.

Schwarzkopf, the mountainous commanding general of Central Command (CENTCOM), had earned a couple of nicknames in thirty-odd years of service. One of them was "the Bear." Another was "Stormin' Norman." They both fit. Norm Schwarzkopf could be charming and intellectual one moment, crude and insecure the next. He could be cruel to subordinates, and his uncontrolled temper made his Riyadh headquarters a hostile work environment for the CENTCOM staff. "Under pressure," Powell later said in his memoirs, Schwarzkopf "was an active volcano." Over the next several months the two generals engaged in numerous "transoceanic shouting matches . . . full of barracks profanity." Yet they learned to work together to prosecute the war.[18]

That Saturday at Camp David Schwarzkopf struck exactly the right tone with his civilian superiors—articulate, measured, reassuring—giving them confidence in his professional competence and temperament. For that reason alone, the meeting was important. He told the president precisely what was needed to defend Saudi Arabia. "Now," he added, "if you want to eject the Iraqis and restore Kuwait" the bill would be significantly higher: hundreds of thousands of troops and eight months or a year to get that offensive capability in place. Bush was not yet ready to make that decision, but he dispatched Cheney and a high-level team to Riyadh to gain King Fahd's agreement to accept deployment of U.S. ground and air forces to defend Saudi Arabia against a possible Iraqi invasion from Kuwait.[19]

On Sunday President Bush flew back to the White House, hopped off his helicopter, and strode toward a waiting phalanx of reporters. A patrician Connecticut Yankee turned Texas oilman and politician, Bush always seemed slightly out of place. Rarely has a candidate for the presidency boasted a stronger résumé than George Bush did in 1988—congressman, head of the Republican National Committee, ambassador to the United Nations, CIA director, U.S. envoy to China, vice president—yet he suffered by comparison with Reagan, his charismatic predecessor, under whom he served loyally for two terms. He had been captain of the Yale baseball team and the navy's youngest torpedo pilot in the Pacific in World War II, a bona fide hero, yet the national media had tagged him a wimp during his national campaigns. He seemed to have something to prove. On this afternoon, after several questions about his intended response to Saddam's invasion, Bush leaned in, brandished a presidential index finger, and insisted, "This will not stand, this aggression against Kuwait."[20]

Without alerting his allies or advisers beforehand Bush had just announced a policy: Iraq would have to leave Kuwait. He had not yet decided on offensive military action, as economic and diplomatic pressures might be sufficient. Yet, he later recalled, "I never wavered from the position that I would do whatever it took to remove Iraq from Kuwait." Powell had lost his bid to restrict the mission to the defense of Saudi Arabia. Two days later the president announced a deployment of American forces to the Persian Gulf region.[21]

President Bush visited the Pentagon the following week for a briefing on the troop buildup. Powell showed the president a timeline. If the mission was to defend Saudi Arabia and allow sanctions to work, they could stop the flow of troops at the end of October. On the other hand, if Bush wanted an option for an offensive into Kuwait, Powell would need a decision by that same date to keep the buildup going. More ambitious missions, such as destroying the Iraqi military or toppling Saddam, would require more troops, more money, and more time. Regardless, the president would have to order a reserve call-up soon. "It's a major political decision," Powell told the president. He was not pressing Bush for decisions, just preparing him for when he would have to make them.[22]

On his way out Bush stopped at the Pentagon's River Entrance to thank the defense staff for its hard work during the crisis. The television cameras were rolling as he spoke about Saddam's use of poison gas against his own people and the brutal atrocities his soldiers were committing in Kuwait. "It is Saddam who lied to his Arab neighbors," Bush charged. "It is Saddam who invaded an Arab state. And it is he who now threatens the Arab nation." Powell worried that the paltry force in the Saudi desert did not match the president's fiery rhetoric.[23]

As the summer wore on Bush became increasingly impatient. Saddam was still in Kuwait. The buildup of forces was costing billions of dollars. The administration had put its domestic agenda on ice to devote its energies to holding together a fractious and restive anti-Saddam coalition comprising dozens of countries. Yet it had no idea how long the American people would support the mission. Moreover, angered and appalled at the savagery of Saddam's occupation, Bush feared that "unless something happens soon, there may not be a Kuwait." The president wanted action. He told his diary he was considering "speeding up the timetable."

At one point he told Powell, "Colin, these guys have never been seriously bombed." Some Arab allies were urging an air campaign: "They all tell me the same thing. We can knock 'em out in twenty-four hours." Powell and Schwarzkopf shared an infantryman's skepticism about the efficacy of air power. Precision munitions soon proved that an "accuracy revolution" had significantly enhanced air power's capabilities, but Powell was reluctant to put all his eggs in that basket. Air Force chief of staff Michael Dugan chose that inopportune moment to tell the *Washington Post* that "airpower is the only answer that's available to our country." He also suggested targeting Saddam and his family and disparaged the capacity of the American electorate to commit to war. Cheney quickly fired Dugan for undermining national strategy.[24]

Nonetheless, Powell worried that the president might be more in tune with Dugan than his administration's own strategy. On September 24, 1990, he took his concerns to Cheney, who offered to escort him to the Oval Office that afternoon. Powell was soon standing before Bush, Scowcroft, and White House chief of staff John Sununu. "Mr. President," Cheney said, "the chairman has some thoughts for you." Once again, Powell's thoughts were more about national policy than military strategy, and his intention was to limit American commitment. The chairman reminded the president of his two options. The first was offensive: "If you decide to go that route in October, we'll be ready to launch sometime in January." Powell recommended continuing the buildup to put that option in place. The other option was to continue the sanctions. They had a sufficient force in place to protect Saudi Arabia. Allowing the sanctions to work, strangling Iraq economically, would take time, but it might save lives. When Powell finished, the president thanked him: "That's useful. That's very interesting. It's good to consider all angles. But I really don't think we have time for sanctions to work." Bush was still weighing options, but his thinking was far more aggressive than Powell's, increasingly viewing the reversal of Saddam's aggression as a moral crusade.[25]

As the president moved toward ordering an offensive, Powell tried to buy time for sanctions. In early October he had insisted that the CENTCOM staff brief the JCS and the White House on their offensive plans, even though Schwarzkopf complained that he was not ready. The air campaign plan was mature, but not the ground plan. With only enough forces to defend Saudi Arabia, the ground planners had no options for an offensive except a frontal assault into the teeth of Iraqi defenses. Because of his reservations about the plan, Schwarzkopf wanted to brief the president personally, but Powell, acting more as commander than as military adviser, ordered him to remain in Riyadh and send his planners to present the briefing. After a dress rehearsal at the Pentagon, Powell told the air planners not to oversell their pitch, lest the president think that they "could knock 'em out" with air power alone. Powell was managing expectations.

During the briefing the next day the president asked the planners if they could conduct the air campaign, then wait a week or ten days to see if Saddam gave up. If that would work, then there would be no need for a massive buildup of ground forces. Powell took charge: "I have to tell you, Mr. President, that it will not meet your objectives. I cannot assure you that Iraqi ground forces will be out of Kuwait, just because we do an air campaign." Then, predictably, the frontal-assault, ground campaign briefing did not go well. Scowcroft thought the presentation was "unenthusiastic, delivered by people who didn't want to do the job." Powell explained that Schwarzkopf needed an additional corps to execute a credible plan, a holding action at the border accompanied by a left hook into Iraq and then western Kuwait. He hoped to dissuade the president from committing too soon, especially with air power alone. Further, Powell wanted to buy more time, not only for additional ground forces to deploy, but also to allow sanctions to achieve their purpose. By insisting that he needed another corps he succeeded all too well, as the briefing caused Bush "to realize we had a long way to go before the military was 'gung ho' and felt we had the means to accomplish our mission expeditiously, without impossible loss of life." Bush still thought the air campaign could work: "We can do it from the air. Our military is waffling and vacillating in terms of what we can do on the ground." By providing no other options for a ground offensive, Powell hoped to force his superiors into a decision to fight with overwhelming force, just as his doctrine would dictate. Like Bush, Cheney was not buying the plan. He quietly resolved to find other sources of military advice, setting up a planning cell in his own office headed by retired army general Dale Vesser.[26]

As Powell might have predicted, the meeting caused the president and the NSC to lose a measure of confidence in Schwarzkopf's generalship and to lean more heavily on Powell's own advice. Scowcroft's deputy, Robert M. Gates, quipped, "General McClellan lives." Powell had forced the CENTCOM commander to offer a weak plan that both knew to be inadequate. After the meeting, Powell decided to "shove the bayonet between his ribs." He called Riyadh and toyed with Schwarzkopf's temper: "You know, some people are saying we've got a McClellan out there."

Powell held the receiver away from his ear as Schwarzkopf screamed, "You tell me what son of a bitch said that! I'll show him the difference between Schwarzkopf and McClellan!" Powell admitted to feeling guilty, but he had goaded his subordinate into thinking more imaginatively about the offensive.[27] He had also taught him a lesson about Washington politics.

The NSC convened on October 30, 1990, to decide whether the mobilization should continue. Powell took charge and told them they were at a fork in the road—either commit additional forces now or begin rotating forces in and out of theater for the long haul. Secretary of State James Baker reported that sanctions had clearly done little to harm Iraq thus far. Powell had lost that gambit, but he was not through fighting. When Bush asked again about trying an air campaign alone, Powell was adamant: "Mr. President, I wish to God that I could assure you that air power alone could do it, but you can't take that chance." Preparing for an offensive, Schwarzkopf had asked Powell for two more army divisions, additional marines, Air Force wings, and another aircraft carrier. Astoundingly, Powell now more than doubled that request: more than an army corps, three more aircraft carriers, and a doubling of air forces and marines then in theater. He forced the president into a "put up or shut up" moment—give the military, meaning Powell, what it wanted, or take the risk of failure. Scowcroft gasped. He thought the troop list was "so large that one could speculate they [sic] were set forth by a command hoping their size would change [the president's] mind about pursuing a military option." Gates also wondered if Powell was trying "to dissuade the president from action." Powell later protested, "I was not gaming him. Anybody who has the ability to generate overwhelming force should do so. We bought it to fight wars. There was no other crisis. This was the obvious place to pile on. We were getting ready to win as quickly, as overwhelmingly, as we could." Whether Powell was gaming him or not, President Bush did not flinch. "I was determined not to haggle," he later recalled. Sounding a bit like LBJ in spite of himself, he wrote, "The important thing was to be able to get the job done without leaks about divided views on force requirements." Powell's gambit worked. The president approved the additional deployments. The NSC had not made a firm decision to attack, but the president believed they were heading toward war. Now they would have the necessary forces in place by mid-January and Powell would be able to fight, if necessary, on his own terms. The president postponed announcement of the buildup until after the midterm congressional elections a week hence.[28]

Powell had carried the day. Indeed, he had done what he had promised himself he would do if ever given the chance—he had laid out the stark choices to the political leadership. The size of his troop request—and it was his, more than Schwarzkopf's or, certainly, Cheney's—exemplified the essential difference between the Weinberger Doctrine and the Powell variant. Weinberger had called for "clearly defined objectives" and the forces needed to accomplish them "with the clear intention of winning." Weinberger called for reassessing and adjusting the relationship between objectives and forces continually. Powell was more succinct. He insisted on "overwhelming force." Instead of the gradual escalation he had lived through in Vietnam, Powell wanted certain victory. Scowcroft scoffed at the notion: "I was strongly opposed to the Powell Doctrine," he said later. "I thought it precluded using force unless we went all out. I thought it was nonsense." Still, at the end of October Powell had persuaded his civilian superiors to give him almost everything he wanted before going to war.[29]

The only thing missing was a clear mandate from the American people, expressed through their representatives in Congress. Bush and Scowcroft were dubious about the necessity of a congressional resolution, and Cheney was sure they did not need it. Baker was more concerned about keeping the coalition together, which he and the president did admirably. Thinking politically, Powell felt congressional approval essential—it was one of the six tenets of the Powell Doctrine. Yet he had to be careful about raising this issue, especially since Cheney was opposed. All the president's civilian advisers were concerned about taking a war powers resolution to a Democratic Congress. The congressional leadership had already expressed its private doubts about an offensive, preferring to give sanctions time to work. Congress had adjourned for the year, but the armed services committees held hearings in November and December. Former JCS chairman Admiral William J. Crowe testified, arguing that sanctions should be given time to bear fruit. Although Cheney had opposed seeking congressional approval in the NSC, he argued forcefully for a resolution after the president made a decision to seek one. Congress passed the Gulf War resolution a few days into the new term in January 1991.[30]

The air campaign commenced on January 17 after Saddam had passed up dozens of diplomatic opportunities to avoid war. Six weeks of precision bombing then punished Saddam's capital in Baghdad and his forces in Kuwait. Yet air power had not won the war. It had not "decapitated" the Baathist regime as its planners had hoped. Saddam was still alive, still in charge, and still in the war. His army in Kuwait, however, was in a pitiable state. Although the air commanders had not quite achieved their goal of knocking out one-half of Iraq's armor and artillery, they had destroyed the army's mobility and, just as important, its morale.[31]

The coalition ground forces had swollen to more than sixteen divisions arrayed along the northern Saudi border from the Persian Gulf to the town of Rafha over three hundred miles to the west. CENTCOM's plan called for U.S. Marines and Arab forces to fix the Iraqi defenses by attacking due north into Kuwait. The U.S. Army VII Corps and the British First Armoured Division were to execute an operational envelopment, a "left hook" that would have them attack north into Iraq, then turn east and assault Iraqi forces in Kuwait. The U.S. Army XVIII Airborne Corps and Sixth French Armored Division would swing wider still, attacking farther north and then east to stop and destroy Iraqi forces, especially the Republican Guard, as they retreated into Iraq.

The ground war started early on the morning of February 24 with a coalition assault into southern Kuwait that worked all too well. Instead of fixing the Iraqi defenses in place, the attack started a stampede. Iraqi soldiers surrendered in droves, while surviving Iraqi vehicles sped north toward the Basra Highway and home. Although the two "left-hook" corps did not know it yet, they were losing a race with the rapidly retreating Iraqi forces, whose long columns and billowing dust trails marked easy targets for American airmen.[32]

The next day Baghdad formally admitted the ongoing withdrawal, and Powell called Schwarzkopf to ask about the timing of a cease-fire. Schwarzkopf asked for another day or two. In turn, he pressed his commanders to shut the gate and trap Saddam's army. By the third day of the ground war, television reports were showing thousands of Iraqi tanks, trucks, and cars strung out and burning along the roads where coalition air forces had bombed them. The Basra Highway was gaining a new nickname, "the Highway of Death." Focused again on political as much as military matters, Powell feared that a media narrative focusing on American brutality might mar an overwhelming victory and with it the image of the armed forces. The chairman renewed his prodding for a cease-fire.[33]

The irony was that coalition forces were not destroying too many Iraqi vehicles, but too few. The military objective was to destroy Saddam's army, but a methodical attack by VII Corps allowed much of the Republican Guard to cross into Iraq. Further, a line drawn on the map to prevent friendly air forces from hitting coalition troops inadvertently protected many Iraqis as well. Kuwait was liberated, but the best of Saddam's army was still intact. Yet that fact was not immediately clear to Schwarzkopf or his superiors in Washington.[34]

Schwarzkopf, thinking he needed one more day to trap the Iraqi army, proposed a cease-fire for the evening of February 28. "Do you realize," he asked Powell, "if we go until tomorrow night that will be five days? The five-day war. Does that have a good ring to it?" The chairman agreed that it had the advantage of beating the Israelis' lightning-fast 1967 war by twenty-four hours. Schwarzkopf began making plans to deliver a televised end-of-the-war briefing. His forces would have to move fast.[35]

On the afternoon of February 27 President Bush convened an Oval Office meeting to take stock of the war. The president sat in his customary seat to the right of the fireplace. British Foreign Minister Douglas Hurd and a few of his senior advisers were there, along with Vice President Dan Quayle, Baker, Scowcroft, Sununu, and Gates. Secretary Baker reported that the Iraqis had just agreed to the terms of the prewar United Nations Security Council Resolution. That changed things considerably, and Bush asked that Cheney and Powell be invited into the Oval Office. When they were seated the president turned to them: "What do you need?" Cheney said that they had all but accomplished their objectives and could finish the campaign soon: "now or maybe tomorrow." Bush wanted to pin down a time to stop the war. Cheney offered to consult with General Schwarzkopf.[36]

Powell interrupted his boss, noting that he had just spoken to Schwarzkopf. Concerned about the potential political fallout from the "Highway of Death," Powell did not want to let this moment for decision pass. As was his custom, Powell spoke before a map without notes, engendering confidence as he gave the assembled leaders a command briefing, which included the erroneous report that the Republican Guard was almost destroyed. "We are at most twenty-four hours away. There are three thousand destroyed tanks. We are in the home stretch. Today or tomorrow by close of business," he told the president. "Norm and I would like to finish tomorrow, a five-day war."[37]

Bush surprised him. "If that's the case, why not end it today?" They thought they had accomplished their objectives and were in danger of tarnishing a brilliant victory with television footage of unnecessary carnage. Powell ducked into the president's private study and called Schwar-zkopf. They discussed moving up the timeline. Schwarzkopf was amena-ble, but asked to talk with his subordinate commanders. He had just given his famous "mother of all briefings," where he announced that CENT-COM had accomplished its mission. "The gate is closed," he had inaccu-rately bragged. "There is no way out of here." A short time later the two generals spoke again and confirmed the cease-fire. All of Bush's advisers and the Joint Chiefs concurred. Sununu suggested ending the war pre-cisely at midnight, Washington time: "That'll make it the Hundred-Hour War." Once again, all agreed, although Scowcroft later admitted that the timing was "too cute by half."[38]

Of course, the gate was not closed, and the mission had not been accomplished. Kuwait was liberated, but much of Saddam's army had survived to fight again. The Iraqis escaped with over fourteen hundred armored personnel carriers, half its total complement, and 842 tanks, a quarter of the total. Moreover, the Republican Guard escaped with 365 of its top-of-the-line T-72 tanks, which meant that half of Saddam's elite armor got away. Schwarzkopf's control over his own forces was slipshod and his grasp of the military situation so weak that he designated a loca-tion for cease-fire talks, the small Iraqi town of Safwan, that the coalition did not control, an embarrassment that forced last-minute battlefield ma-neuvering to cover the mistake.[39]

As hostilities wound down, President Bush held Saddam personally responsible for the war and expressed his view that "the Iraqi people should put him aside." It was not to be. Before the talks Schwarzkopf an-nounced that he had no plans for marching to Baghdad, conceding a sig-nificant bargaining chip for nothing in return. He drafted his own terms for the cease-fire talks, which Powell quickly approved. Events were mov-ing too quickly for the Pentagon and State Department bureaucracies to react. As a result, lamented one senior Bush official, "Norm went in un-instructed." In fact, "the generals made an effort not to be guided. It [the cease-fire] was treated as something that was basically a military deci-sion, not one to be micromanaged." That laissez-faire attitude was a long way from Lincoln's oversight of Grant in similar circumstances. When Schwarzkopf arrived at Safwan to meet with two Iraqi generals, he was full of bravado: "This isn't a negotiation. I don't plan to give them any-thing. I'm here to tell them exactly what we expect them to do." Yet Schwarzkopf told them to do almost nothing beyond releasing coalition prisoners. He failed to grasp the leverage he wielded with several divisions positioned over a large swath of southeastern Iraq. He might have traded that territory, which included the vast Rumaila oil field, for the surrender of the thousands of armored vehicles still limping toward Baghdad. He might have insisted on gaining intelligence on the locations of suspected Iraqi nuclear and chemical facilities and an inspections regime to monitor them. He might have demanded that Saddam reach a political settlement with his Kurd and Shiite citizens. Instead, he conveyed to his counterparts that the United States military was in a hurry to leave southwest Asia and take its forces home. He assured them that the coalition had no intention of occupying Iraqi territory. Sensing opportunity, the Iraqi negotiators asked permission to use their helicopters over their own airspace. Schwarzkopf readily assented, seeming to mimic Grant at Appomattox, who had magnanimously allowed Lee's soldiers to retain their horses as they returned home to their farms. Yet armed helicopters are not horses, and the Iraqi army had no interest in agriculture. Saddam used his warbirds in a brutal crackdown on the Shiite and Kurdish peoples as he brutally reestablished his authority in the wake of crushing defeat. Powell and Schwarzkopf had usurped civilian authority with disastrous long-term results.[40]

For a time, Desert Storm seemed a complete triumph. Bush and his team received high marks from the American people for winning the war with minimal casualties, restoring order, and bringing the troops home. The president was grateful that the legacy of Vietnam could finally be put to rest.[41]

General Powell gained national acclaim for his leadership and his doctrine. Parades feted him in Washington, Chicago, and Manhattan's "Canyon of Heroes." He threw out the first pitch of the New York Yankees' 1991 season. Once again, pundits mentioned him as a potential Bush running mate in the approaching 1992 election. Well-placed Democrats likewise dangled the second spot on their ticket, but Powell preferred to remain in uniform and would not consider running against Bush.[42]

In May 1991 *Washington Post* reporter Bob Woodward published *The Commanders,* an account of Operation Just Cause and the road to war in Iraq. The book peered inside high-level policy and politics, a view gleaned from interviews with many of the players. Yet Woodward's reportorial method included granting anonymity to his sources, calling his accuracy into question and giving rise to suspicions that those officials who talked to him got more favorable treatment than those who refused. *The Commanders* depicted Powell as a reluctant warrior who fretted about the military naïveté of his civilian masters and a prudent statesman dismayed by the administration's haphazard policy-making processes. Indeed, Powell later admitted that he had twice met with Woodward and spoken to him by telephone several more times. Many concluded that Powell had been burnishing his own image at the expense of his administration colleagues. Yet Bush never doubted his chairman. When the *Post* began publishing excerpts of the book, the president told Powell not to "pay attention to all that crap. . . . Don't let them get under your skin." He nominated Powell for a second term as chairman a few weeks later.[43]

Although publication of *The Commanders* gave Powell some uneasy days in Washington, his standing in the country soared. National polls showed that 80 percent of Americans viewed him favorably, a rating higher than any contemporary politician. Senate Democrats who had opposed a successful and popular war now tried to score political points from Woodward's revelation that Powell had also argued for allowing sanctions to work. Sam Nunn, chairman of the Senate Armed Services Committee, sent Powell a long list of questions prior to his confirmation hearing, hinting at an investigation into the possibility that he had shared classified information with Woodward. Powell betrayed some irritation at the Friday hearing, saying he had "no second thoughts . . . no conscience problems" about talking to Woodward. Nunn decided to call another session on Monday before allowing a committee vote on Powell's confirmation. Then Nunn and ranking Republican John Warner sent another batch of questions to the general's Pentagon office. Powell exploded in rage, throwing the papers across the room. His staff tried to help, drafting answers for his approval, but Powell threw their work in the trash. He wrote a terse reply saying he had nothing more to say. Nunn and Warner warned Cheney that no senior officer had ever refused to answer questions from Congress, but Powell would not budge. Needless to say, the Monday hearing was tense, and it did not help matters that Powell's term was set to expire at midnight. The first time a senator mentioned *The Commanders*, citing Woodward's claim that the Pentagon had underestimated Saddam's intention to invade Kuwait and had failed to prepare for it, Powell barked an interruption: "That's absolutely wrong, Senator."

Malcolm Wallop of Wyoming continued, "Well, that's what the book—"

Powell yelled again: "I don't care what the book said, Senator."[44]

Such indecorum in a senior officer testifying before Congress was rare and contemptuous. Powell's refusal to answer congressional questions might have been grounds to hold up his confirmation or even to deny it. Furthermore, senators rarely reward verbal insolence from any witness. Yet the committee could read the polls: four of five Americans revered Powell. That afternoon they unanimously recommended approval of his nomination, and the Senate followed suit without a dissenting vote. No one dared stand in Colin Powell's way.[45]

Despite Powell's barely veiled endorsement in his *New York Times* op-ed, George Bush lost the 1992 election to Arkansas governor Bill Clinton, who had all but ignored foreign affairs during the campaign, instead focusing "like a laser beam" on the economy. Clinton benefited from an explicit endorsement from Powell's predecessor, retired admiral Crowe, and a platoon of other retired flag officers who helped inoculate the candidate from his Vietnam-era draft deferments and his youthful expression of "loathing" for the military. Crowe became American ambassador to the Court of St. James's for his trouble. From their first meeting, Clinton and Powell, both disarming charmers, got on quite well. The president-elect treated Powell with the respect due his office, his service, and his achievements, but also recognized him as a potential political rival. Clinton asked Powell's advice on his selection of a secretary of defense, although he didn't follow it. Powell, knowing how closely he was associated with the Reagan and Bush administrations, offered to step down quietly if Clinton preferred his own chairman. Clinton demurred. Powell also warned the president-elect that following through on his campaign promise to lift the military's gay ban would be a heavy lift, and advised him to take some time before attempting it.[46]

Five days after Clinton's inauguration, Powell and the Joint Chiefs sat across a table from the president in the Roosevelt Room of the White House. After a perfunctory review of the strategic situation, they opened a discussion on lifting the gay ban. Powell benignly asked each of the Joint Chiefs to speak, and one by one they weighed in heavily against any change, warning the new president not to risk the hard-won proficiency that the military had just displayed in Iraq by destroying its order and discipline. Although they listened respectfully to the president, wrote White House spokesman George Stephanopoulos, "they weren't there to be persuaded." Conservative members of Congress were against lifting the ban and were looking forward to dealing the new Democratic administration a quick defeat. The chiefs, wrote Stephanopoulos, "had the congressional troops they needed to fortify their position. Their message was clear: Keeping this promise will cost you the military. Fight us, and you'll lose—and it won't be pretty." Powell offered a compromise. Openly gay soldiers would still be separated, but the services would stop asking about sexual orientation upon enlistment. Over the next several months, conservatives and liberals faced off in a bitter "culture wars" campaign that wounded the administration before it had a chance to gain momentum. Powell had to fend off printed reports that he was threatening to resign over the issue. Other rumors had the Joint Chiefs contemplating mass resignation. Nine months later, after divisive congressional hearings, President Clinton tried to frame a new policy, "don't ask, don't tell," as a compromise. Yet most observers—Democrats, Republicans, the Pentagon, the gay rights community, and the media—saw it as a presidential capitulation to the military brass and its conservative allies. The new president had been rolled.[47]

Clinton's national security advisers enjoyed nothing like the stature of the Bush team, and Powell figuratively towered over them. "Part of the problem," recalled United Nations ambassador Madeleine Albright, "was that we were all new and Powell seemed like the grownup." She was unnerved by "the hero of the Western world" with his "chest full of medals." Veteran diplomat Richard Holbrooke said, "He regarded the new team as children. And the new team regarded him with awe." Powell was appalled at the lack of discipline in the new National Security Council. Meetings had no agendas, nor even seating charts. They resembled "graduate-student bull sessions" in which "backbencher" note takers felt free to argue with the national security adviser. When discussions turned to overseas deployments, Powell did not back off the sentiments he expressed in his 1992 op-ed. He tutored the Clinton NSC on the tenets of the Powell Doctrine—and the press now always called it the Powell Doctrine, although he never did—for which Albright had no more patience than Scowcroft. "He replied consistent with his commitment to the doctrine of overwhelming force," Albright recalled of a discussion about Bosnia, "saying it would take tens of thousands of troops, cost billions of dollars, probably result in numerous casualties, and require long and open-ended commitment of U.S. forces. Time and again he led us up the hill of possibilities and dropped us off on the other side with the practical equivalent of 'No can do.'" It was in one such session that Albright asked, "What's the point of having this superb military that you're always talking about if we can't use it?" It was a good question, but Powell said it almost gave him an "aneurysm." In his mind, Powell was demanding answers to questions his Vietnam-era predecessors had failed to ask. Clinton's advisers thought Powell's answer was always "a half million troops. What is the question?" For his part, Clinton was chary about bucking the advice of the hero of Desert Storm, who effectively wielded a veto over military operations. The president postponed intervening in Somalia until Powell gave a lukewarm endorsement, and refused to send troops to Bosnia until long after Powell's retirement.[48]

Powell closed more than thirty-five years of service at the end of September 1993. He was an American hero, one of the most admired men in the country. *U.S. News* put his face on its cover over the caption "Colin Powell: Superstar, From the Pentagon to the White House?"[49] No one believed they had heard the end of the Powell story.

Nonetheless, Powell decided to tell it. He hired a ghostwriter and set to work on a memoir. It was a measure of Powell's celebrity that, in an era when political and military autobiographies seldom fared well in bookstores, *My American Journey* sold more than a million copies. Powell promoted the book on a nationwide tour that resembled nothing so much as a presidential campaign. At least three "Draft Powell" committees started up, and polls indicated that the general would be highly competitive if not the front-runner for the Republican nomination. However, he had not declared a partisan affiliation, and Democrats were also wooing him to join their party, perhaps to become the standard bearer after Clinton left office. For almost a year Powell connected with audiences, consulted with advisers, and considered his options. Then, in November 1995, he ended the speculation, announcing that he was a Republican but ruling out a presidential run, saying politics was "a calling that I do not yet hear." He later endorsed Senator Robert J. Dole in the 1996 race.[50] Four years later, he again supported the GOP nominee, and subsequently became secretary of state in the George W. Bush administration.

The phenomenon that was General Colin Powell, chairman of the Joint Chiefs of Staff, emerged from a unique confluence of historical events. The first was the Cold War era, which demanded an extraordinarily large and unprecedentedly sustained commitment of national treasure and manpower to strategic defense. America's military forces remained in a high state of readiness for half a century. Leading those forces were three generations of professional officers who saw warfare as their calling and preparation for war as their duty and livelihood. Never before had so many Americans devoted themselves to national defense with such intensity for so long. Colin Powell was of the second of those generations.

As young men they suffered through the only strategic loss in the history of American arms. The Vietnam experience seared them. They mourned the loss of comrades and recoiled at the taste of defeat. Almost all recognized that the military had lost something vital but intangible in the war, its moral-ethical center. Those who stayed in the service knew that the institution had to reform, to regain its professional integrity. That renaissance became the mission of their generation, and it encompassed myriad tasks, from restoring a sense of official honesty to demanding realistic combat training to rekindling an esprit de corps. While many sought to blame the loss in Vietnam on someone else—LBJ and McNamara, the war protesters, the media—the most thoughtful officers realized that their own military leaders had failed the profession. Powell was among that introspective lot, and he blamed his superiors for failing to speak truth to political power. Yet he overshot his diagnosis of the malady, concluding that an essential part of the problem was the unquestioned superiority of political authority over professional military judgment. He swore that, given the chance, he would never again allow civilians to ignore sound professional advice.

Powell's generation became aware of the need to prepare for whenever their moment might come. In the parlance of the day, they experienced a "consciousness raising," a collective realization of their need to understand more than the nuts and bolts of military tactics. They went to graduate school and served apprenticeships in the Pentagon. As Powell's predecessor as chairman put it, "Few officers these days made it into the higher ranks without a firm grasp of international relations, congressional politics, and public affairs."[51] And while some of the best officers served an occasional tour on the Joint Staff during a career of field assignments, Powell spent most of a quarter century in various agencies of the executive branch, learning the folkways of Washington politics like no officer of his generation.

The Powell phenomenon coincided with an epochal event, a turning point in history. The final component of this historical confluence was the end of the Cold War, presaged by the collapse of the Berlin Wall and completed by the dissolution of the Soviet Union. Ironically, it was the Marxist "end of history," but capitalism had triumphed over socialism, turning Marx's prediction on its head. It was an immensely satisfying moment for Powell and his generation, for the military they had worked so hard to reform now enjoyed a lion's share of the credit for vanquishing the Soviet foe. They were poised to exploit their newfound prestige. And more than any member of his exceptionally talented and experienced cohort of colleagues, Powell had been training his entire life for this moment.

By 1990 the era of military reform was complete. The armed forces had recapitalized and reequipped. Their training was superb. The problems of drugs, racial strife, and indiscipline were fading memories. The military profession had regained its confidence, its élan, and its integrity. Operation Desert Storm extended the denouement of the Cold War, allowing the American military to write a fitting coda to its bloodless victory over its "best enemy" with a convincing defeat of another foe.

Just as important, Powell enjoyed a partnership with a political leadership determined not to replicate the mistakes of Vietnam, and that especially meant not micromanaging the military. George H. W. Bush and his administration inherited the Reagan legacy of celebrating military service and martial competence. Bush aimed to put "the Vietnam syndrome" to rest, and Saddam's invasion of Kuwait provided an opportunity. This time, he intended, the politicians and the military would work together, not at cross-purposes.

Enter Powell, brilliant and eloquent, hardworking and disciplined, charming and savvy. He had the good fortune to become chairman just as Congress had vested that office with authority and responsibility no uniformed officer had wielded since Marshall. He became custodian of the military at its professional acme and—keenly aware that the laws of physics and the rules of politics both require inevitable decline once the body has reached its zenith—was not about to allow anyone or anything to tarnish its luster, on his watch. If that meant controlling the flow of information in every direction, no one in Washington was a craftier bureaucrat. If that meant insinuating himself into the chain of command even though Goldwater-Nichols proscribed it, one of Powell's (unpublished) "rules to live by" was "You never know what you can get away with until you try." If that meant circumscribing policy options for the White House, the former national security adviser knew how to frame an agenda. If it meant imposing on his superiors a set of strict tests for the employment of military force, Powell had a doctrine ready at hand, ghostwritten by himself, promulgated by a Reagan defense secretary, and carefully revised and further restricted to reflect the combat-instilled lessons of Powell's generation. If it meant opposing his civilian masters on the road to war until there was no choice but to obey, Powell was a reluctant warrior and proud of the title. And if it meant stopping that war before the mission was accomplished, well, that was better than risking a stain on the recovered honor of the armed forces.[52]

And if it meant wielding unprecedented political clout to frustrate fulfillment of an inexperienced president's campaign promise, to intimidate his team, and to exercise a military veto over national security policy, Colin Powell was well enough versed in Clausewitz to stand on its head the Prussian theorist's dictum that "strategy is an extension of politics by other means."

One historian has described Powell as the most powerful general since Marshall, the most popular since Eisenhower, and the most political since MacArthur. He further strengthened the newly potent office of the chairman to the point that it rivaled that of the secretary of defense and the presidency itself in national security matters, especially after Clinton came into office. The pendulum of power in the continuous negotiation swung well to the direction of the military. When Powell left the chairmanship in 1993 he was "the most trusted man in America," according to opinion polls. Second-guessing of the legacy of the Gulf War had not yet begun. Powell forestalled involvement in the pesky, small wars of the 1990s until after his departure. Thus, his legacy remained remarkably unsullied even after the military's professional prestige had descended well below its peak.[53]

The laws of physics and politics demand reaction proportionate to every stimulus. After Powell retired, a rebalancing was in order. President Clinton and later President George W. Bush learned to appoint more compliant, more controllable chairmen of the Joint Chiefs. Bush, indeed, came into office intending to redress the balance of the continuous negotiation in favor of the civilians, indeed to restore civilian control of the military. To help him with that task he selected two former secretaries of defense, Dick Cheney and Donald Rumsfeld, along with one other experienced Washington hand, Colin L. Powell.

12

RUMSFELD'S ASSUMPTIONS

Donald Rumsfeld was enjoying himself. As secretary of defense in the midst of two wars, he had become the Pentagon's public face, briefing the press almost daily and always on television. His sense of humor, his quaint expressions, and his feisty insistence on challenging reporters' assumptions had made him a media star. President George W. Bush, famous for bestowing nicknames, had dubbed him "Rumstud." Now, a few weeks after the 2003 invasion of Iraq, the television images from Baghdad showed Iraqis looting government buildings, hospitals, and museums. Rumsfeld tutored the press corps in the natural "untidiness" of any transition from repression to freedom. Moreover, the Iraqis were looting symbols of Saddam's regime; "one can understand the pent-up feelings that may result from decades of repression."

Yet on this day, when the progress of the war, which had seemed irrepressible just days earlier, appeared to be slipping away into anarchy, the journalists were not willing to be cowed or mollified. They kept asking about the plan to restore law and order in Iraq. General Richard B. Myers, chairman of the Joint Chiefs, stepped to the microphone to help. But Rumsfeld, remembering how General Colin Powell had seized the spotlight during the Gulf War, had determined early in his tenure that he would not be upstaged by the military. He quickly interrupted Myers: "The images you are seeing on television you are seeing over, and over, and over, and it's the same picture of some person walking out of some building with a vase, and you see it 20 times, and you think, "My goodness, were there that many vases?" (Laughter.) "Is it possible that there were that many vases in the whole country?" Once again with characteristic folksiness and wit, Rumsfeld had extricated himself from a tight spot by attacking the integrity of television news. Or so he thought. Yet the reporter persisted: "Do you think that the words 'anarchy' and 'lawlessness' are ill-chosen—"

"Absolutely!" Rumsfeld interjected, and turned his guns on the print media: "I picked up a newspaper today and I couldn't believe it. I read eight headlines that talked about chaos, violence, unrest. And it just was Henny Penny—'The sky is falling.' I've never seen anything like it!" Rumsfeld was beginning to lose some of his legendary cool. "Stuff happens!" he insisted.[1] Of course, the problem was that Rumsfeld did not have an adequate plan for controlling Iraq after the regime had fallen. He and most of the Bush administration had assumed that American troops would "be greeted as liberators" by a grateful Iraqi people. "Stuff happens!" soon became popular shorthand for the administration's inability to comprehend what it had wrought by choosing to invade Iraq without adequate plans to govern the country afterward. In two words Donald Rumsfeld had captured the arrogance and hubris that launched the greatest American national security failure since the Vietnam War.

The George W. Bush administration came to power with a view of the United States as a global hegemon. Its spokesmen insisted on moving past the Cold War doctrines of containment and deterrence. They actively disowned the weak half-measures of the Clinton years, which had bogged America down in what they saw as pointless efforts at "nation building." Instead, they argued, America would not be shy about employing its military prowess in pursuit of national security, and sometimes that might mean confronting rogue states that threatened international order. The terrorist attacks of 2001 had given them a casus belli to put their intentions into practice.

George W. Bush was a national security neophyte sitting atop an administration full of experienced policy hands. He empowered Dick Cheney to become the most influential vice president in history, especially in foreign affairs. Cheney, together with Rumsfeld, formed a rivalry against Secretary of State Colin Powell for dominance of national security policy. Soon after 9/11, with Cheney's approval and assistance, Rumsfeld drove a bellicose policy toward Iraq leading to an invasion in early 2003.

Yet Rumsfeld wanted not only to defeat Iraq, but to do so using novel and untested strategies to inaugurate a new era in warfare, one in which speed, stealth, precision munitions, and smart, networked weapons systems would obviate the need for ponderous, heavy relics of the industrial age. He took on those whom he saw as defense traditionalists, including most of the Pentagon bureaucracy and the leadership of the United States Army. And he made common cause with a general of limited ability and vaulting ambition, the commander of Central Command, Tommy Franks. Together, they monopolized the political-military dialogue and largely marginalized the Joint Chiefs of Staff. Rumsfeld made a number of dubious assumptions about the coming campaign that Franks was unable or unwilling to contest. Along with most of the Bush administration, Rumsfeld overestimated and oversold the need for war with Iraq. Simultaneously he underestimated the difficulty of accomplishing the tasks the administration set for itself. The strategy Rumsfeld and Franks forged overpromised and under-delivered, and the upshot was a rapid and apparently successful initial invasion that was, in fact, merely a prelude to eight bloody years of indecisive war. The events of 2003 serve as an object lesson in folly, when the principal actors on both sides of the political-military nexus failed to understand the making of strategy. Their failures largely stemmed from Rumsfeld's assumptions.

George W. Bush emerged in 1999 as the GOP's presumptive favorite for the 2000 presidential nomination. Party elders aiming to avoid a bitter primary fight compromised on Bush, whose advantages included a scandal-free governorship and universal name recognition inherited from his father. During the campaign he came across as affable and manly, if a bit shallow, even incurious, and clearly unlettered in foreign affairs. The election was the closest in decades, and Bush narrowly lost the popular vote to Vice President Gore. Yet a controversial recount to determine the winner of Florida's decisive electoral votes ended up in the Supreme Court. Five weeks after Election Day, the court sided with Bush by a 5–4 decision. Half the country saw his election as tainted if not illegitimate. The inexperienced new president would assume office with considerable liabilities.

Dick Cheney had briefly considered a run for president himself after stepping down as defense secretary. Unable to attract attention or campaign donations, he left politics to become chief executive officer of Halliburton, a worldwide manufacturing and consulting firm. When Bush secured the 2000 nomination, he asked Cheney to chair the selection process for a running mate. Cheney's formative political experiences had come in the White House under Nixon and Ford. He had watched as Congress aggressively stripped power from the presidency in the wake of the Vietnam War and Watergate. He spent much of his career attempting to win back executive authority, buttressing his beliefs in a legal theory called the "unitary executive." With that foundation and subsequent experience in congressional leadership and the first Bush administration, Cheney had a lot to teach George W. about running the government and what he needed in a vice president. Among the lessons was a caution about the potential for rivalry between president and vice president, especially if the latter aimed to succeed the former. After weeks of vetting dozens of hopefuls, Bush decided that the best choice was sitting at his elbow. Cheney had no presidential ambitions. Indeed, for a politician he was unnaturally shy of publicity and almost dismissive of those who sought popularity. Bush put Cheney on the ticket. By their mutual agreement Dick Cheney became a dominant presence in national security affairs.

During the awkward interregnum between Election Day and the Supreme Court decision, Cheney quietly began working on the presidential transition. He knew the levers of executive power as well as anyone in Washington, and he quickly assembled lists of prospective appointees for positions throughout the government. While Bush was focused on the recount, Cheney began planning to place his own acolytes from three decades of public life at every level of the executive branch. After the election decision, time was so short until their inauguration that Bush could do little more than thank Cheney for his hard work staffing the administration.[2]

The first cabinet pick was a foregone conclusion. Colin Powell had endorsed the ticket, and Bush had promised to name him secretary of state. Powell would not have been Cheney's choice. Powell's memoir and the published histories of the Gulf War had only widened the rift between the two men. Yet Cheney understood politics. The president-elect needed Powell's popularity and gravitas more than ever. Bush named Powell secretary of state on December 15, 2000, just a few days after he won election. The televised press conference illustrated how much the inexperienced Texas governor needed a firm hand on the tiller. Powell answered question after question with mastery and aplomb. Many observers noted that the secretary was better fitted to his role than the president-elect to his. Indeed, Bush seemed to shrink as he fidgeted behind Powell. Glowering nearby stood Cheney, perhaps remembering the many times Powell had upstaged him while they shared power at the Pentagon. By some accounts, Powell's star in the administration crossed its zenith that day.[3]

Cheney moved quickly to counterbalance Powell's power. He asked his old mentor, Donald Rumsfeld, to interview with Bush for secretary of defense. As they discussed what lay ahead for the Pentagon, the two men hit it off. Bush wanted to make good on a campaign promise to "transform" the military, and he gave the mission to Rumsfeld. They agreed that America's unparalleled military strength granted an opportunity to "skip a generation of technology," procuring modern weapons systems that were lighter, more agile, and more deployable than the forces of the Cold War. The two men also agreed on the need for a robust ballistic missile defense program, an initiative that Rumsfeld had long championed. At a press conference just after Christmas, Bush introduced Rumsfeld, saying, "He's going to be a great secretary of defense, again." The president-elect publicly charged him "to challenge the status quo inside the Pentagon." Rumsfeld had his mission: "It is clearly not a time at the Pentagon for presiding or calibrating modestly."[4]

Paul Wolfowitz, a Cheney loyalist and intellectual guru of the neoconservatives, a group of national security hawks who had spent a decade plotting to finish the unfinished war against Saddam Hussein, joined Rumsfeld as deputy secretary. Most secretaries handle policy issues, delegating day-to-day running of the Pentagon to their deputies. Rumsfeld reversed the roles. He gave Wolfowitz a long policy leash, but kept the reins of bureaucracy in his own hands, believing that was the best way to "challenge the status quo."

Powell appointed his old friend and former Pentagon colleague Richard Armitage as his deputy. A gravelly voiced, plain-speaking, weight-lifting navy SEAL veteran of three tours in Vietnam, Armitage had little regard for "chickenhawks," an epithet to describe policy makers who championed the use of military force without the benefit of firsthand knowledge of combat. The term applied to most "neocons," including Cheney, Rumsfeld, and Wolfowitz, to name only the most prominent. Powell and Armitage were cautious about the use of force, but the neoconservatives considered military power America's most useful foreign policy tool. Thus two Vietnam veterans with extensive military and national security experience led the State Department, while the neocons steered at Defense. Before long, personal antipathies would widen the rift of these philosophical differences. Cheney, who might have refereed this contest, made no bones about favoring the neocons. From the very beginning, the Bush administration was less a "team of rivals" than a pair of rival teams.[5]

Rumsfeld had the short, compact build of the college wrestler he once was. After graduating from Princeton, he served a peacetime stint as a navy pilot, then returned home to his native Chicago and beat long odds to win a seat in Congress. After three terms he joined the Nixon administration's domestic policy team. Nixon made him ambassador to NATO just as Watergate was beginning to brew, so Rumsfeld avoided the taint of scandal. President Ford named him White House chief of staff and later secretary of defense in a cabinet shake-up. After Ford's election defeat, Rumsfeld became a corporate executive and made a fortune as chief executive officer of G. D. Searle, a pharmaceutical company. He served from time to time on government commissions or as a presidential envoy. He briefly explored a presidential run in 1988, but lost to Vice President George H. W. Bush, a lifelong and sometimes bitter rival. Because of that family history, the younger Bush's decision to appoint him was quite a surprise. Yet in 2001, Rumsfeld made history as both the youngest secretary of defense and the oldest.[6]

A fascinating blend of intellect, personality, and character made Rumsfeld one of the most consequential defense secretaries in the history of the office. Rumsfeld was blunt, ebullient, abrasive, charming, and confrontational. He had an incisive mind, logical and disciplined. He took pride in cutting to the crux of a problem, usually through a ruthless examination of assumptions and first principles. His prose was taut; he worked to make every word count. Rumsfeld insisted on managing the department through his outbox, and terse memos that came to be known as "snowflakes" were his medium. Shortly after his arrival, a blizzard of snowflakes began swirling through the Pentagon, making appointments, issuing directives, questioning procedures, and demanding information. If they seemed disruptive to bureaucratic order, that was Rumsfeld's precise intent. His staff tracked the outgoing memos, pestered their recipients, and made sure the secretary received prompt answers. Rumsfeld soon had the bureaucracy fighting to regain its balance.[7]

The snowflake was one of many tools that Rumsfeld employed to assert control over people, meetings, and information. He bridled under any form of procedural restraint, but demanded that his own preferred methods be followed to the letter. By his own admission he peppered Bush adviser Condoleezza Rice with a flurry of memos criticizing her management of the National Security Council. He often insisted that meeting participants—senior generals, White House assistants—refrain from taking notes. If he used briefing materials in a presentation, he insisted on retrieving every copy at the end of the meeting. He always sought to control the record of what he and others had said, and to make sure that no one else could provide evidence to dispute his version. Clearly, his concern was not to engender trust.[8]

At his most audacious, Rumsfeld demanded sovereignty over knowledge itself. In press conferences and congressional testimony he frequently mused upon "known knowns," sometimes called facts; "known unknowns," or understood gaps in one's knowledge; and scariest of all, "unknown unknowns," gaps in one's knowledge of which one is unaware. These epistemological categories are useful as a philosophical typology, but Rumsfeld took the exercise quite a bit further. He insisted upon defining what was and was not knowable. Once the secretary of defense had determined the limits of what could and could not be known, he established an unchallengeable dominance over professional advice, strategic discussion, and even thought.[9]

Charged by the president to transform the military, Rumsfeld insisted on challenging military assumptions—attempts to fill the gaps of the unknowns—that drove contingency planning. "If we get the assumptions right," he believed, "the strategy, tactics and details follow logically." He sometimes joked that "a trained ape can do the rest." That assertion set great store by high-level guesswork and disdained the tedious work of strategic planning, the bread and butter of the military profession. Contingency planning in the modern Pentagon is a perpetual cycle of thinking about how to respond to potential crises. How likely is a given scenario? How dangerous is it? Would we need to respond? How quickly? What policy aims would we pursue? What forces would be necessary? How would we use those forces to achieve our aims? Rumsfeld scoffed at the plans he inherited, which tended to respond to potential crises by building up massive forces to wield overwhelming power, a legacy of the Powell Doctrine. Instead he wanted light, agile, high-tech forces to move quickly to trouble spots, dispatch enemies, and redeploy just as fast. He spent a great deal of time reviewing contingency plans, throwing out assumptions that he thought exaggerated difficulties, and sending the planners back to the drawing board. An old military nostrum enjoins soldiers to "hope for the best case and plan for the worst." Rumsfeld decided time and again to assume the best case and plan for it. He disdained Clintonian nation-building as in the cases of Haiti, Bosnia, and Somalia as wasteful, ineffective, and purposeless, and he refused to countenance the notion that the Bush administration would ever allow itself to become involved in it.[10]

For Rumsfeld, "challenging the status quo" also meant reestablishing civilian control of the military. Like many conservatives, he believed that the generals and admirals, starting with Colin Powell, had dominated President Clinton and his administration. Rumsfeld viewed the holdover Joint Chiefs of Staff as "Clinton generals." When JCS chairman General Hugh Shelton tried to assure him of the chiefs' loyalty, Rumsfeld rebuffed him. He told Shelton that the Joint Staff was too large and that the chairman had no need for public affairs and legislative liaison staffs separate from the secretary's. He even challenged Shelton's statutory right to advise the president and the National Security Council, insisting that all military advice come through him. Shelton stood his ground before the onslaught, but he learned quickly that Rumsfeld viewed him and the Joint Chiefs as a rival political faction rather than as loyal subordinates and professional advisers. Rumsfeld made sure that Shelton and his successor, air force general Richard Myers, were not in the operational chain of command, as Colin Powell had been.[11]

The hectoring style he often used in press conferences he also employed in meetings with senior officers. During one meeting with the Joint Chiefs he upbraided army chief of staff Eric K. Shinseki in front of several junior officers, waving his hand and demanding, "Are you getting this yet? Are you getting this yet?"[12] At a January 2003 press conference, Rumsfeld responded to the assertion "that you tend to ride roughshod over your military leadership":

> I have received on occasion from people, military and civilian, work that I was not impressed with. . . . And there have been times when I've sent things back six, seven times. Why? Well, because it strikes me that it's terribly important that we do things well and we do them right. . . . The Constitution calls for civilian control of this department. And I'm a civilian. . . . This place is accomplishing enormous things. . . . And it doesn't happen by standing around with your finger in your ear hoping everyone thinks that that's nice.[13]

When it came time to plan for and execute actual military operations, the Joint Chiefs would find that Rumsfeld put little stock in their advice.

Many Bush appointees, Paul Wolfowitz foremost among them, came into office hoping to redeem what they viewed as the 1991 failure to conquer Iraq and overthrow Saddam Hussein. For the neoconservatives, the logic was simple. For decades the Middle East had been a vital national interest of the United States. For most of that time, American policy had futilely focused on finding a solution to the intractable Israeli-Palestinian conflict as a means of pacifying the entire region. The neocons believed Saddam's ruthless regime was a far greater threat to Middle Eastern stability. Moreover, with its insuperable military might, the United States had a moral obligation to finish what it had started in 1991. Destroy the Baathist dictatorship in Iraq and allow a democratic government to replace it, they asserted, and the rest of the Middle East would follow suit, no longer a menace to the United States or Israel.[14]

The Middle East was the sole agenda item at the new administration's initial NSC meeting in January 2001. Powell spoke first and argued that an upsurge in violence between Israel and the Palestinians was the most urgent matter in the region. Cheney and Rumsfeld both disagreed, advising the president to take a hands-off approach to what they saw as an intractable problem. National security adviser Condoleezza Rice then steered the discussion toward Iraq. Referring to the policy inherited from the Clinton administration, she said, "We have a regime change policy that isn't really regime change." Rumsfeld argued that since the UN sanctions regimen was not working, the United States should consider scrapping it. He was concerned about Iraq's weapons of mass destruction and wanted to take more aggressive measures to deal with them. Bush instructed Powell to devise more effective sanctions and Rumsfeld to explore what more could be done with air patrols enforcing the "no-fly" zone over Iraq. Shortly thereafter, the president approved both their recommendations. Just over a month after this first NSC meeting, American and British planes attacked twenty Iraqi air defense command and control sites, some of them on the outskirts of Baghdad. The pilots were only complying with Rumsfeld-approved protocols when they attacked, but high-level miscommunication left the secretary of defense and the president out of the loop. Both were surprised to learn of the attacks from televised news reports.

The administration took face-saving pains to describe the sorties as routine and no change in policy. Still, the new team was obviously ready to adopt a more bellicose posture toward Saddam Hussein.[15]

For the next several months the Bush administration turned its collective attention toward domestic matters, the tax cuts and social issues that had held pride of place in the campaign. Rumsfeld led the Pentagon through the Quadrennial Defense Review (QDR), an extensive exercise in defining strategic roles and missions for the armed forces and apportioning resources for the long-term future. Mandated by law every four years, the QDR was an all-important event for the services and an opportunity for the administration to put its stamp on defense policy. Rumsfeld intended to do just that. He had definite ideas about the future of warfare. He had voiced his commitment to "transformation," which connoted a network-centric approach to war, emphasizing precision-strike weaponry, information-age intelligence, and ballistic missile defense.

The army would have only a limited role in Rumsfeld's high-tech vision of future war. When it became apparent that Rumsfeld might seek to cut as many as four army divisions from the force structure, Shinseki insisted on an opportunity to refute the arguments with evidence of the need for a larger rather than a smaller army. The debate took place out of the public eye, and inasmuch as no divisions were cut, the army's view prevailed in the final report to the president and Congress; but the victory was pyrrhic. Rumsfeld was furious at losing an important transformation opportunity. He concluded that much of the Defense Department, especially the army, were hidebound and resistant to change.[16]

Shortly thereafter, Rumsfeld spoke at a Pentagon "town hall" meeting to several hundred Department of Defense employees:

> The topic today is an adversary that poses a threat, a serious threat, to the security of the United States of America. From a single capital, it attempts to impose its demands across time zones, continents, oceans, and beyond. With brutal inconsistency, it stifles free thought, and crushes new ideas. It disrupts the defense of the United States and places the lives of men and women in uniform at risk. . . . You may think I'm describing one of the last decrepit dictators of the world. But their day, too, is almost past, and they cannot match the strength and size of this adversary. The adversary's closer to home. It's the Pentagon bureaucracy.

Rumsfeld went on to attack cumbersome accounting processes, outdated business practices, incompatible information technologies, and institutional inertia. He was declaring war on his own department. The date was September 10, 2001.[17]

The next morning, Osama bin Laden launched an attack of his own. Nineteen al Qaeda hijackers commandeered four jetliners and crashed into the World Trade Center, the Pentagon, and the Pennsylvania countryside.[18] Almost immediately Rumsfeld began contemplating ways to strike Iraq, even though evidence quickly emerged that al Qaeda was responsible. He urged the president to think broadly about the U.S. response, to focus not just on al Qaeda but on all states that sponsored terrorism. Both Bush and Rumsfeld ordered aides to search the available intelligence to find a link between 9/11 and Saddam Hussein. Over the next several days Wolfowitz became the Pentagon's strongest proponent for attacking Iraq. Powell was adamantly opposed, noting that building a coalition against terrorism depended on keeping the focus on those who had attacked the United States. Powell won that argument, for the moment, as Bush decided to strike al Qaeda and its ally, the Taliban government of Afghanistan. Yet the president also asked the Pentagon to reexamine its contingency plans for Iraq so as to be ready to strike when the time was right.[19]

The U.S. Army's favorite novel, Anton Myrer's *Once an Eagle,* spans the two world wars and ends in Vietnam, extolling martial honor and duty, while portraying the military as a flawed but noble institution. Myrer narrates an epic (if somewhat simplistic) struggle between two main characters who embody courage and sacrifice on the one hand and ruthless, striving ambition on the other. The commander of Central Command (CENTCOM), army general Tommy Franks, a lanky, laconic son of the Plains and former enlisted man, seemed the modern incarnation of Sam Damon, Myrer's courageous and self-effacing hero. Yet soldiers who worked with Franks over his long career saw Damon's opposite, the conniving, deceitful Courtney Massengale. A legendary self-promoter, Franks was a bully to his subordinates and, like most bullies, a sycophant within earshot of his superiors. Given to vulgar profanity and vapid jargon, Franks was no one's intellectual, which was just fine with him. During the planning for the retaliatory war in Afghanistan, Franks had neither the mental agility nor the strength of character to resist Donald Rumsfeld, which was just fine with the secretary.[20]

With no contingency plans on the shelf, Franks scrambled to put together a strategy for attacking Afghanistan. His first offer was a powerful force package that would have taken months to assemble and deploy. Rumsfeld quickly rejected such traditional thinking and demanded a plan with forces that were lighter, fewer, and faster. Franks complied, and less than a month after the 9/11 attacks, special operations forces were on the ground and assisting Afghan tribal forces. Special forces teams, some riding horseback with their allies, controlled air strikes with sophisticated communications and global positioning systems. By early December Afghan fighters, supported by a mere four thousand U.S. troops, defeated the Taliban and drove them over the Pakistani border. Rumsfeld felt vindicated, not just in Afghanistan, but in his conception of a transformed military: heavy, lumbering tanks and artillery were obsolete, and special operations and precision-strike air power were the wave of the future. Those who advocated overwhelming superiority of combat power in operational planning, such as Powell and many in the army, now seemed hopeless traditionalists.

Overlooked in that analysis, of course, was the failure to achieve President Bush's goal of taking Osama bin Laden "dead or alive." In mid-December U.S. troops intercepted a radio transmission from bin Laden and located him and fifteen hundred al Qaeda fighters at Tora Bora in the rugged mountains of eastern Afghanistan. Yet air power, Afghan troops, and U.S. light infantry and special forces were not enough to seal bin Laden inside his cave complex, and he escaped into Pakistan to direct operations against Western infidels for another decade. At the same time, Rumsfeld's aversion to nation building left newly installed Afghan president Hamid Karzai largely on his own to establish his governmental writ. The United States turned its attentions elsewhere early in 2002.[21]

☆ ☆ ☆

The Sunday after 9/11, Vice President Cheney made a rare television appearance on NBC's *Meet the Press*. He subtly initiated the administration's effort to sell the American people on a war against Iraq. He averred that the United States would have to "go after those nations and organizations and people that lend support to these terrorist operators." That definition was much broader than al Qaeda, the Taliban, and Afghanistan, certainly broad enough to include Iraq without saying so outright. Cheney confided that most operations would be "sort of on the dark side, if you will . . . quietly, without any discussion, using sources and methods that are available to our intelligence agencies." Five days after 9/11, those words from the vice president of the United States seemed at once comforting and chilling.[22]

The 9/11 attacks had severely discredited U.S. intelligence agencies. If they had missed the signs of 9/11, what else were they missing? In coordination with Cheney, Rumsfeld quickly established an in-house intelligence analysis shop reporting to Undersecretary for Policy Douglas Feith, innocuously named the Office of Special Plans (OSP). Feith challenged intelligence agencies' conclusions with deductive logic: "build a hypothesis, and then see if the data supported the hypothesis." From its inception OSP constructed two working hypotheses: (1) that Saddam Hussein's regime was involved with al Qaeda and 9/11, and (2) that Iraq possessed weapons of mass destruction. Both Cheney's staff and Wolfowitz showed intense interest in the papers OSP produced. Rumsfeld, however, kept an arm's length from Feith and his counter-analysts. He often manifested a canny caution about enterprises that later became controversial.[23]

After bin Laden's escape, the administration saw a need to regain its momentum. Having no military plans at the ready, it employed new phrases that accentuated the novelty of this dangerous era. The first was "the war on terror," sometimes called "the global war on terror." The Bush team might have declared war on al Qaeda and the Taliban, but the neocons had already determined that bringing down Iraq had to be part of the solution to the 9/11 problem. Those who questioned the notion of waging war against terrorism, itself a method of war as old as humanity, were scorned as living in a "pre-9/11 world." Still, the war on terror chased an elusive enemy that has yet to be defined. Another phrase was "weapons of mass destruction," almost immediately reduced to the abbreviation "WMD," which then became ubiquitous. WMD encompassed the disparate categories of nuclear, biological, and chemical weapons. Chemical weapons are deadly, but their effects have a short range and usually dissipate quickly. Biological weapons are even more terrifying, but notoriously difficult to deploy. Nuclear weapons run the gamut from small "suitcase bombs" to massive flotillas of intercontinental bombers and missiles that can destroy humanity in minutes. WMD comprises and thereby fudges those categories. Saddam used chemical weapons against his own people in 1992. Reminding the American public of that atrocity became scarier by labeling it as a use of WMD, so that credulous listeners might conflate dangerous chemical weapons with an existential nuclear threat. Further, they might fear that he still possessed nuclear weapons and was prepared to use them again. It was even more effective rhetorically to combine the threats of terrorism and WMD. As bad as 9/11 had been, how much more damage might terrorists with WMD have done? And while building such weapons might be beyond the resources of a terrorist group, it was possible that rogue states with WMD might provide them to terrorists in a mutually beneficial deal.[24]

In his January 2002 State of the Union address, Bush made a stunning departure from decades of American foreign policy, promising that he would prevent "regimes that sponsor terror from threatening America or our friends and allies with weapons of mass destruction." He asserted that three countries—North Korea, Iran, and Iraq, whom he labeled "an axis of evil"—simply by seeking to possess WMD, posed "a grave and growing danger." Bush promised to work to deny their attempts to acquire these weapons, but "time is not on our side. I will not wait on events, while dangers gather. I will not stand by, as peril draws closer and closer. The United States of America will not permit the world's most dangerous regimes to threaten us with the world's most destructive weapons."[25] Gone was the rhetoric of diplomacy, containment, or deterrence. Bush insisted that the 9/11 attacks had fundamentally altered the game, and he claimed the right to go to war at a time of his choosing to prevent future harm to America, its allies, and its interests. National security adviser Condoleezza Rice explained that "the fall of the Berlin Wall and the fall of the World Trade Center were the bookends of a long transition period." National security professionals had been searching for "an overarching, explanatory theory." The attacks on 9/11 had provided the catalyst for new thinking: "America faces an existential threat to our security" as grave as any in its history.[26]

Four months later President Bush articulated the new framework in a commencement speech at West Point. Reminding the graduating cadets of his State of the Union theme, he said, "We are in a conflict between good and evil. And America will call evil by its name." This was a new time with new dangers. Old strategies would not work against these fundamentally different enemies: "For much of the last century America's defense relied on the cold war doctrines of deterrence and containment. . . . But new threats also require new thinking." He told the cadets to be ready to take "pre-emptive action" to protect the nation. "If we wait for threats to fully materialize we will have waited too long. . . . We must take the battle to the enemy, disrupt his plans, and confront the worst threats before they emerge."[27]

The more thoughtful cadets listening that day must have wondered if their commander in chief had just changed the laws of war. Their compulsory courses in law, philosophy, and military history had taught them that, according to moral codes dating back to St. Augustine and St. Thomas Aquinas, nations may go to war for only two reasons. The first is in self-defense. The United Nations Charter, whose drafting the United States had led, codifies the right of any nation to defend itself and its interests when attacked. A nation may also go to war preemptively, if the threat of military action against it is so imminent, potentially destructive, and substantive (in terms of both capability and intention) that an attack is virtually certain. For example, either the United States or the Soviet Union might have launched a nuclear strike against the other any number of times during the Cold War while remaining comfortably within the legal confines of preemptive war, but both sides refrained. Preventive war, however, going to war against an enemy that may pose a threat in the undefined future, is specifically prohibited by the UN Charter, international law, and just-war theory. In his West Point address Bush speciously asserted that the threat posed by twenty-first-century terrorists outstripped the potential for nuclear Armageddon that had been the world's daily dread for almost a half-century of Cold War. Then, before anyone had a chance to object, he discarded two millennia of rational thought and dressed up preventive war as preemptive war. He declared it moral and called it the "Bush Doctrine."

Tommy Franks ruefully described planning the war with Iraq as "an iterative process."[28] By that he meant that he would propose a force package, Rumsfeld would complain that it was too large, and Franks would return to his staff and berate them to draw up plans calling for fewer troops. Franks would then return to Rumsfeld with a smaller force package, and the dance would begin again. It was a process of give, on Franks's part, and take, on Rumsfeld's, that began soon after 9/11, long before the public was aware that Iraq was a potential U.S. target. It continued through 2002 until the invasion of Iraq in March 2003. Throughout, Rumsfeld drove the process with a small set of unchallengeable assumptions. Invading Iraq and toppling the Iraqi government would not require an enormous ground force because of the prowess of American air power and the weakness of Saddam's army. Rumsfeld was enamored of "shock and awe," a theory that posited hundreds of precise, conventional munitions rapidly delivered against an array of carefully selected targets could destroy "the adversary's will, perception, and understanding." The enemy's civilian population would quickly see the futility of resistance and capitulate. Large ground invasion forces would be unnecessary. The only times such a strategy had been attempted were at Hiroshima and Nagasaki, examples that did not give Rumsfeld pause as he pushed "shock and awe" on Franks.[29] A second assumption was that Saddam possessed weapons of mass destruction, which was a principal reason to invade, but which did not impinge on force planning. Third, after the invasion succeeded, as Rumsfeld knew it would, others—the United Nations, Arab allies, the State Department, the Iraqis themselves—would be responsible for rebuilding Iraq, because the United States was no longer in the nation-building business. Rumsfeld's assumptions would sow the seeds for another eight years of frustrating, often demoralizing war, with tens of thousands of American casualties and hundreds of thousands of Iraqis killed and wounded and millions more displaced.

Just after Christmas 2001, General Franks flew to the president's Texas home to brief him on progress in Afghanistan and plans for Iraq. Other NSC members joined in by video-teleconference. Franks had commanded Third Army, CENTCOM's land force headquarters, before he moved up to CENTCOM. In the former capacity he had been closely involved in contingency planning for a second war with Iraq. The plan he had helped write called for as many as four hundred thousand troops and an occupation that might last ten years. Rumsfeld blanched when he received his first briefing on that plan. Afghanistan had proven that such old thinking was obsolete. He sent Franks back to the drawing board. From November 2001 until CENTCOM kicked off the offensive in March 2003 Rumsfeld continually prodded, wheedled, questioned, and challenged Franks and his staff to be more innovative, which always meant fewer forces and shorter timelines. In just the month since their first discussion of the Iraq plan, Franks whittled the numbers down to a total invasion force of 275,000 troops. Yet when Franks briefed that plan to Bush at Crawford, Rumsfeld interrupted from his vacation home in New Mexico, "Mr. President, we are still working through the number. The number Tom is giving you is soft." Powell chimed in, telling Franks to make sure he had enough to accomplish the mission, but as secretary of state he could only push so far.[30]

Over the next few weeks the beleaguered CENTCOM staff wrote a new plan called "Generated Start." Deployments would begin within thirty days of a presidential order, with an initial ground force of 145,000 troops arriving in theater over the following two months. That force would kick off the attack, while another 130,000 troops would continue to flow in. Rumsfeld was still not satisfied. He relentlessly pressed Franks to lighten the ground component and speed up the deployment.[31]

He was also pressing CENTCOM to be ready to attack as soon as that spring of 2002. Franks's planners feared that attacking too soon would likely incur unnecessary casualties and take longer to finish the job. Still, in May Franks briefed the president again, this time offering another plan called "Running Start," which responded to Rumsfeld's prodding. It posited an air campaign that could commence rapidly and keep the Iraqis occupied while ground forces deployed. Its length and intensity could vary with conditions. The ground forces would commence their attack soon after arriving in Kuwait, perhaps with as few as two thousand troops initially and probably not more than two divisions. The CENTCOM staff and Franks's subordinate commanders considered Running Start too risky. The president did not commit to either plan, but he seemed less concerned about the size of the force than Rumsfeld.[32]

Two weeks later Bush traveled to Europe to begin forming a coalition against Saddam. At a Berlin press conference with his German counterpart the president harped on the dangers of Iraqi WMD, but denied that he had decided upon war: "I told the Chancellor that I have no war plans on my desk, which is the truth." The claim was probably true in a physical sense, as Bush's Oval Office desk was likely cleared when he left town. In every other way, it was patently false, for Bush was now mulling two war plans. A few days later, Franks lied more boldly, saying he did not know how many troops would be required to invade Iraq, "because my boss has not yet asked me to put together a plan to do that."[33] At that point, Franks's staff had been planning an invasion of Iraq for seven months.

Throughout the planning process Rumsfeld and Franks formed a closed loop. The new JCS chairman, air force general Richard Myers, was not in the operational chain as Colin Powell had been. Many observers saw him as Rumsfeld's sidekick. Moreover, Franks took on Rumsfeld's disdain for the Joint Chiefs, openly chafing at having to consult with them. He considered them parochial, intent on making sure their services were well represented in CENTCOM's force package, rather than trying to find the best way to prosecute two wars. Referring to their legal authority under the U.S. Code, Franks colorfully and collectively described them as "Title Ten Mother Fuckers."[34] The chain of command ran from Bush through Rumsfeld to Franks, with Cheney's hidden hand somewhere in the background. The Joint Chiefs wielded as little clout as their predecessors in the Kennedy and Johnson administrations.

In early August 2002 Franks held a planning conference with his commanders, telling them that they should be on alert to commence operations against Iraq at any moment. He stated that the goal for such an offensive would be regime change. CENTCOM would destroy the Iraqi power base, its WMD, and its conventional ability to threaten its neighbors. They would maintain Iraq's territorial integrity and assist in establishing a provisional government, although the plan assumed that the State Department would soon take the lead on political issues.[35]

To fulfill those tasks Franks's planners split the difference between Generated Start and Running Start, developing a plan called "the Hybrid." It took advantage of quiet deployments to Kuwait that had already occurred. A sixteen-day air campaign would cover a short mobilization and movement of some twenty thousand soldiers and marines, who would commence the ground assault. Reinforcements would flow in over four more months.[36]

In late August 2002 President Bush signed a secret document designating objectives for the war with Iraq. The broad goals were to eliminate Iraq's WMD and other threats to regional stability, liberate the Iraqi people from tyranny, and prevent the regime from supporting global terrorism. Saddam would have to be deposed, and the United States would help the freed Iraqis "build a society based on moderation, pluralism, and democracy." American forces would secure Iraq's WMD, stop any interference from Iran and Syria, and prevent disruptions of the international oil market. For good measure, the United States would help Iraqis write a new constitution that enshrined civil rights, including freedom of speech and worship and equal treatment of women.[37]

Thus, both the military strategy and national policy envisioned sweeping aims for an invasion of Iraq. Coalition forces would depose Saddam Hussein, free the Iraqi people, and ensure that no regime remnants could aid international terrorists. The coalition would find and secure WMD. It would secure Iraq from external threats and prevent Iraq from threatening its neighbors. The global oil market would proceed unmolested. And the free Iraqi people would soon enjoy the blessings of democracy and the rule of law. These aims extended into a Clintonian policy realm that the Bush administration had professed to despise—nation building.

It falls to operational planners to translate political and strategic aims into mission orders that troops can execute. Planners follow a number of steps that can seem mind-numbing to the uninitiated, among them delineating mission tasks and assigning troops to accomplish those tasks. Tasks fall into two types: specified and implied. The paragraph above generally describes the specified tasks for the invasion of Iraq. Planners earn their paychecks by ferreting out implied tasks. In other words, they ask themselves, given what we have explicitly been told to do, what else do we have to do to accomplish those specific missions? For example, in order to decapitate the Iraqi government, it was necessary to seize and secure Baghdad. Taking Baghdad, given a start line in Kuwait, meant attacking and building momentum to defeat the Iraqi army. Keeping those forces moving, in turn, required generating the logistical capacity to support them. Tellingly, Rumsfeld was quite willing to assume away the difficulties of generating operational momentum and its logistical support. Finding Iraqi WMD and securing them were next on the list of priorities. Then, assuming success in the first part of the operation, there were numerous security tasks: sealing the Iraqi borders from within and without; guarding Iraq's oil fields, and establishing control over the vast expanse of Iraqi territory and Iraq's many cities. Then, having disrupted the polity and the economy, it follows that thousands or hundreds of thousands of displaced persons would need protection, shelter, food, water, and medical attention. Thus a successful invasion would create an obligation for an enormous humanitarian mission. Finally, both the military and policy aims looked toward helping the Iraqi people establish a stable, constitutional government.

Having identified all essential tasks, planners then have to determine how many and what kinds of soldiers and equipment are necessary to accomplish them. Some units might be used for sequential mission tasks, such as defeating the Iraqi army, seizing Baghdad, and securing Baghdad. Soldiers of the invasion force could later secure other Iraqi cities, but they would need augmentation to seal Iraq's lengthy borders with Jordan, Syria, and Iran. Still more units would be needed to guard Iraq's extensive oil fields. Moreover, those same troops would not be available to find and identify WMD. Further, the soldiers needed and qualified to identify

WMD were not the same as the troops needed to guard them. The former have more esoteric skills and would need to move from one suspected WMD site to the next, rather than remaining at the first site for the mundane task of security.

The planners at the ground force headquarters one level below CENTCOM grew increasingly alarmed with each iteration of Franks's plan. They had been allocated no forces to search for WMD, let alone a force to guard weapons sites once they had been found. With no help from CENTCOM or the Pentagon, they scoured available intelligence (some of it years old) and identified 946 potential WMD sites, which created a tall order. After repeatedly asking for augmentation, the land force command received an artillery brigade to search for WMD just a month before the invasion. Beyond that, the other tasks included only those necessary to complete the invasion and consolidate it in its immediate aftermath. Pentagon and CENTCOM planners gave little attention to humanitarian operations or the complexities of reestablishing Iraqi government, which they called "Phase IV" of the operation. Indeed, Franks was openly dismissive of Phase IV requirements, telling the Joint Chiefs, "You pay attention to the day after, and I'll pay attention to the day of."[38]

The problem was not that no one was thinking about the day after. In August 2002 the NSC established a steering group to coordinate the interagency process working on Iraq, specifically the postwar phase. The State Department's Future of Iraq Project studied the challenges in detail and compiled a thirteen-volume report. The Council on Foreign Relations and the James A. Baker III Institute for Public Policy at Rice University combined to write a report on the postwar environment, as did the Center for Strategic and International Studies. A team at the Army War College wrote a pamphlet outlining 135 tasks to be accomplished after the invasion, warning that the potential of "winning the war and losing the peace in Iraq is real and serious." Veteran congressman and defense expert Ike Skelton made much the same argument in a personal letter to the president. Later, Bush administration officials repeatedly asserted that the postconflict challenges were not predictable. In fact, the problems were not only predictable, but widely predicted. In October Rumsfeld grew agitated at the number of chefs in the kitchen and asked the president to give him the lead on postwar planning. Still both Rumsfeld and Franks ignored the critics and refused to pay attention to Phase IV until it was too late. Both accepted early intelligence assumptions that the Iraqi army would remain intact and be recalled to help with reconstruction, that government ministries, including the police forces, would continue to function, that Iraq's infrastructure was modern and would remain intact, and that the Baath Party would be incapable of mounting a threat to stability. Rumsfeld, inveterate challenger of assumptions, never questioned these best-case guesses and allowed them to drive planning for the war. His aversion to nation building clouded his judgment. Most tragically, he never imagined the possibility of an insurgency.[39]

Powell continued to have concerns about the plan, especially as it pertained to the invasion's aftermath. He saw a tendency in the Pentagon to assume that his State Department would walk in and tidy up the mess. In early August, Powell took his concerns to the president and Condoleezza Rice. He warned the president about the "Pottery Barn rule," facetiously named after the retail chain famous for its fragile merchandise: if you break it, you own it. Yet Powell's admonition was more direct: the war would break Iraq and its government, and the United States would own the country and its 24 million people, like it or not. Powell asked Bush to gain international support for the war through another United Nations resolution. Cheney and Rumsfeld disagreed, but the president sided with Powell.[40]

The diplomatic maneuvers that followed gave CENTCOM breathing room, at least a few months before the war would start. Despite Rumsfeld's transformation preferences, the military had time to deploy a large ground force, so both Running Start and the Hybrid became unnecessary. The ground commander, army lieutenant general David McKiernan, asked Franks and Rumsfeld for two corps, a force essentially the same size as that envisioned in Generated Start.

On October 10, 2002, by a vote of 296–133, the House of Representatives authorized the president to use armed force "to defend the United States against the continuing threat posed by Iraq." Just after midnight the Senate followed suit, 77–23. Midterm elections were less than a month away, and there was little debate in either chamber. Almost all Republicans supported the president. No congressional Democrat with national ambitions dared to buck him. The votes were, with one exception, Congress's only significant intrusion into the administration's plans to go to war with Iraq.[41]

In late November, Franks sent Rumsfeld a request to deploy some three hundred thousand troops over the next few months, which his staff jokingly dubbed "the Mother of All Deployment Orders." Rumsfeld balked. Then, at the end of December, Rumsfeld agreed to General

McKiernan's request for two corps, but he insisted upon maintaining tight control over the flow of units into the theater of war through his approval or disapproval of deployment orders. That demand was to cause all manner of confusion, frustration, and chaos.[42]

The services coordinate overseas deployments with a complex database called the Time-Phased Force Deployment List (TPFDL, pronounced "tip-fiddle"), which is meant to synchronize the logistical demands of deploying units with the operational needs of commanders on the ground. Military staffs study and compose TPFDLs years in advance for many possible contingencies, to ensure that soldiers and their equipment arrive at seaports at the right times to avoid bottlenecks, that fuel trucks are on hand before tanks have to move, that ammunition resupplies and medical support are in place before the battle starts, and so on. Army planners and the CENTCOM staff were appalled when Rumsfeld delayed signing deployment orders, essentially invalidating the timing of the TPFDL, and refusing to deploy some logistical units at all.[43] They were rightly concerned that chaos might ensue and that deployed soldiers would go unsupported. Rumsfeld, having tried and failed to force on CENTCOM a minimalist operational plan, seized on the TPFDL as a means to pare the force to his liking.

The Joint Chiefs were understandably uncomfortable with these developments, but had little opportunity to affect them. Franks's secrecy and Rumsfeld's exclusivity prevented the services from providing expertise on force provision and sustainment. Moreover, Rumsfeld's insistence on controlling every detail exacerbated their concerns. In January 2003, President Bush met in the White House Cabinet Room with Cheney, Rumsfeld, Wolfowitz, the Joint Chiefs, and the combatant commanders. The purpose of the meeting was to review the war plan one final time and to gain the services' assurances that they could support it. The president began asking the assembled flag officers for their views, starting with General Shinseki. The army chief calmly offered seven specific concerns, focusing on the small size of the invading forces and the spare logistical capability to sustain them for the fight. The gist of his comments was not that the army was incapable of providing enough forces to support the plan; indeed, he was offering to do more. To one observer, the president seemed nonplussed, unsure of how to react. A long pause ensued. Bush asked no questions, and none of the other civilian or military leaders spoke up to address the general's reservations. Finally, the president quietly thanked Shinseki for his comments. Continuing around the room, every senior officer spoke, but no one else raised concerns about the war plan. The moment had passed. The meeting adjourned.[44]

A month later Senator Carl Levin also had serious doubts about the war plan, as did many in his party. Levin was ranking Democrat on the Senate Armed Services Committee and one of the Senate's most respected experts on national security issues. At a February 25, 2003, committee hearing, he asked Shinseki how many troops would be required to secure Iraq after a successful offensive. Despite the reservations he had aired with the president, Shinseki demurred, preferring to leave such an estimate to the combatant commander. Levin, a tenacious and effective interrogator, persisted: "How about a range?" Finally, drawing on his experience as Allied commander in the Balkans and historical analysis that his staff had provided, Shinseki answered that, given the geographic expanse of Iraq and its ethnic tensions,

> I would say that what's been mobilized to this point, something on the order of several hundred thousand soldiers, are probably, you know, a figure that would be required. We're talking about post-hostilities control over a piece of geography that's fairly significant, with the kinds of ethnic tensions that could lead to other problems. And so it takes a significant ground-force presence to maintain a safe and secure environment, to ensure that people are fed, that water is distributed, all the normal responsibilities that go along with administering a situation like this.[45]

Shinseki's number was intentionally vague, but his explanation for it, based on years of military experience, including his command in a remarkably similar situation, foreshadowed many of the challenges that U.S. forces would face in the coming months and years. Yet with that brief exchange, Levin placed Shinseki in a precarious position between executive and legislative branches engaged in a conflict over national security policy.

The administration might have let Shinseki's testimony pass without comment, or offered a bland "reasonable minds can differ" response. Instead three leading administration hawks chose to treat him publicly as if he were a political rival rather than a military subordinate. Two days later Wolfowitz testified before the House Armed Services Committee and called Shinseki's projection "outlandish" and "wildly off the mark." He reasoned that "it is hard to conceive that it would take more forces to provide stability in post-Saddam Iraq than it would take to conduct the war itself and to secure the surrender of Saddam's security forces and his army—hard to imagine." Rumsfeld agreed, telling reporters that "the idea that it would take several hundred thousand U.S. forces I think is far off the mark." The following Sunday Vice President Cheney echoed those comments on *Meet the Press,* and predicted that American forces would be "greeted as liberators."[46] All three questioned Shinseki's professional judgment, each using more or less the same phrases, in three public venues. Shinseki refused further public comment on the matter, but the message was clear: the administration would not tolerate military dissent from its assumptions, much less its policy.

More important, Rumsfeld continued to question the necessity to deploy units large and small. Franks failed to confront the secretary. Some of Franks's subordinates believed that the subsequent loss of expected reinforcements from the deployment pipeline sowed the seeds of the subsequent insurgency.[47]

A few weeks later American, British, and a handful of other coalition forces invaded Iraq. The offensive went quite well, at first. Then a sandstorm stalled movement for a few days, and Iraqis in a few cities began greeting their liberators with guerrilla attacks on their long, vulnerable supply lines. In a moment of candor an army corps commander, Lieutenant General William S. Wallace, admitted that "the enemy we're fighting is a bit different than the one we war-gamed against because of these paramilitary forces." Rumsfeld, incensed at the implied criticism of U.S. strategy, remonstrated with Franks, who then threatened to relieve Wallace. In the middle of combat operations, General McKiernan had to fly from Kuwait back to Frank's headquarters in Qatar to calm him down and save Wallace's job. Back in Washington, Rumsfeld faced mounting criticism that his meddling with the plan and the TPFDL had left the invasion force too small. He dodged responsibility for the war plan: "I keep getting credit for it in the press, but the truth is I would be happy to take credit for it, but I can't. It was not my plan. It was General Franks's plan, and it was a plan that evolved over a sustained period of time, which I am convinced is an excellent plan." He insisted that Franks and his commanders had received everything they had requested. At the same time, CENTCOM deputy commander John Abizaid was demanding that the Pentagon follow through on its promise to deploy two more army divisions, the First Armored and the First Cavalry. A few weeks later Rumsfeld and Franks agreed that the First Cavalry would not be needed.[48]

After the sandstorm the ground forces began moving again and seized Baghdad within a couple of weeks. Looting began the next day.

Rumsfeld refused to acknowledge the possibility that civil unrest in Iraq was anything more than "untidiness." He referred to those still fighting against coalition troops after the Iraqi army collapsed as "war criminals" or "dead-enders." When Jay Garner, the retired general designated to run the Pentagon's hastily assembled post-combat reconstruction team, arrived in Baghdad a couple of weeks behind the troops, he found seventeen of twenty-three government ministries ransacked, along with hospitals, schools, universities, hotels, and Saddam's palaces. The Iraqi oil ministry was intact because a U.S. Marine company had been assigned to guard it, but there were too few troops to secure all of Baghdad, much less the rest of Iraq. By failing to maintain order, the United States lost its prestige and dignity with the Iraqi people.[49]

After Baghdad fell both Rumsfeld and Franks seemed to disengage from the problems of Iraq. Franks flew into Baghdad for a victory lap about a week later. He toured the units on the ground, congratulated soldiers on their accomplishments, and flew out, never to return. With Garner in place, he had no interest in reconstruction, and expected McKiernan or Wallace to handle the military end of the occupation. As the "victor" in two wars, he intended to retire from the army as soon as possible. When General Myers called to say that he might have to put his plans on hold, perhaps to succeed Shinseki, Franks came unglued. "More than out of the question," he roared. "Not going home? Buttfuck me!" The only way he would consider becoming army chief of staff was with a fifth star as general of the army, a rank last held by leaders of World War II. Myers decided that, like a worn-out soldier at the end of a long march, Franks had "taken his pack off." Abizaid soon succeeded Franks, who retired, wrote his memoirs, and campaigned for Bush's reelection.[50]

Likewise, Rumsfeld seemed to back away from the occupation, which he hoped would be short, uneventful, and successful. Yet those hopes were already growing dimmer. Less than a month after Jay Garner arrived in Baghdad, Bush and Rumsfeld replaced him with L. Paul "Jerry" Bremer III, a former diplomat with no executive, military, or Middle Eastern experience. Garner agreed to stay on through a transition period, but left after three days when it became clear that Bremer did not want his help. In short order Bremer made two fateful decisions that almost all the studies of the post-invasion phase had warned against. Four days after he arrived, Bremer decreed that members of Saddam's Baath Party would be ineligible to serve in the new Iraqi government. With a signature he wiped out the top three or four layers of Iraqi bureaucracy, sacking the people who knew how to run the country. One week later, Bremer disbanded the Iraqi army, which occupation planners had been counting on to help re-establish order. These ill-considered and poorly coordinated choices disfranchised tens of thousands of competent bureaucrats and hundreds of thousands of trained soldiers, stripping them at once of identity, income, and dignity. Rather than partners, these aggrieved Baathists and soldiers became a fecund recruiting pool for a nascent insurgency. Most of them were already well armed. For those who were not, a ready supply of weapons was near at hand. Although coalition forces had yet to find any Iraqi WMD, millions of small arms lay about the country in hundreds of weapons caches abandoned by Saddam's defeated army. Yet the occupying coalition was stretched too thin to locate and secure these arsenals. Thus, while weapons of mass destruction posed no problem, weapons of small destruction soon empowered an insurgency and a civil war. Both eventualities flowed from flawed assumptions.[51]

On the first of May 2003 President Bush boarded a U.S. Navy S-3B Viking, took off from the coast of Southern California, and landed on the deck of the USS *Abraham Lincoln*. He climbed out of the cockpit garbed for the benefit of television cameras in a regulation navy flight suit, perhaps hoping to evoke memories of the Vietnam-era Texas Air National Guard pilot he had once and briefly been. Later, he addressed the crew in a speech broadcast around the globe. Standing on the flight deck before a gleaming red, white, and blue banner emblazoned "Mission Accomplished," Bush proclaimed the end of major combat operations: "In the battle of Iraq, the United States and our allies have prevailed." The proclamation was premature.[52]

Eager to grasp victory and sensitive to his father's political legacy, Bush was vulnerable to those who knew how to play on his inadequacies and insecurities. Cheney and Rumsfeld were masters of the art. Still, after 9/11 Bush decided to retaliate against al Qaeda and the Taliban first, forcing the Iraq hawks in his administration to wait. Yet within a few months, after the Taliban had been deposed, but not defeated, Bush was persuaded by his vice president, his secretary of defense, and other aides to shift his focus away from the terrorists who had attacked America and those who harbored them and to turn on Iraq, which had done neither. He credulously watched and listened as they built a case against Saddam Hussein. To be sure, the dictator's evil and perfidy toward his own people were never in doubt. Yet Cheney, Rumsfeld, Wolfowitz, Feith, and others too numerous to mention determined that Iraq was harboring terrorists, that it possessed WMD and was building more, that it presented a threat to its neighbors, and that it might assist terrorists in attacking America again. Then they deductively sifted through mountains of contrary evidence, seizing on uncorroborated assertions and the claims of impeachable witnesses to buttress that dubious case. By the summer of 2002 the president's Iraq hawks had persuaded him to become leader of their cause, and he never again wavered on the course to war.

Dick Cheney's tentacles reached deep into the Department of Defense and other agencies of the executive branch, but he had little direct contact with the military. Instead, his power and influence stemmed from his mastery of bureaucratic processes, his ruthless determination to drive his agenda, the unprecedented extent of the portfolio Bush had delegated to him, and his proximity to the president. In NSC meetings Cheney rarely spoke, but he was usually the last adviser in the Oval Office before the president made a decision. Cheney had determined before he entered the vice presidency that his major regret in life was to have left Saddam Hussein in power in 1991. Once again in executive power, he aimed to rectify that mistake, and he assertively guided his protégé president toward that goal.

Tommy Franks's bullying and bluster were a façade meant to cover an appalling weakness of character and dearth of professional competence. He railed against the Joint Chiefs as turf-conscious, parochial bureaucrats. A more confident commander might have enlisted their assistance in mustering strategic arguments against Rumsfeld's political schemes. Likewise, Franks brooked no dissent from his subordinate commanders or his overworked and long-suffering staff. He had a tendency to "shoot the messenger." In such a climate of command, bearers of bad tidings or even thoughtful alternatives became scarce. Ultimately, Franks stood alone with Rumsfeld with neither the wit nor the spleen to resist his blandishments.

Rumsfeld's Pentagon felt much like Franks's headquarters: dissidents beware. Early in his tenure Rumsfeld began interviewing candidates for every three- and four-star position in the armed forces. As secretary, he had a right to do so, and some have argued that he properly felt a responsibility to give personal attention to improving the quality of top military commanders. Yet many had the sense that selected candidates had to pass an ideological test by evincing a willingness to toe the Rumsfeld party line. The flip side of that coin showed in the treatment of General Shinseki and other army generals who seemed to be in his camp. Military leaders faced a choice: accept Rumsfeld's assertions about a novel form of warfare even if they contradicted a lifetime of experience and hard-won professional judgment, or be sidelined as a dinosaur. Rumsfeld's senior aides took on the attitudes of the boss, manifesting a sneering disdain for the professional military that all but precluded a productive exchange of views. Aside from Shinseki, the JCS hardly asserted itself to demand answers to strategic or operational questions, and ultimately found itself largely irrelevant to the continuous negotiation. Rumsfeld was alone with his acolytes and Tommy Franks, none of whom had the slightest notion of turning a policy of regime change in Iraq into a viable strategy.[53]

Neither Rumsfeld nor Franks seems to have thought through the imperatives of those two words: regime change. The Bush neocon partisans mounted a concerted effort to lay the groundwork for war. They started with Saddam's manifest evil, then asserted his ties to al Qaeda and the "grave and gathering threat" of his WMD. Sifting through mountains of contrary evidence, Feith and his "analysts" painstakingly gleaned the dubious kernels that buttressed their hypotheses. The neocons then packaged that spare bushel into speeches, opinion pieces, and a national intelligence estimate to sell Congress, the American people, and a doubting world on the need to rid Iraq of its tyrant. In an ironic twist, it fell to Colin Powell to spend a large measure of his long-husbanded credibility as a reluctant warrior in making the final case for deposing Saddam Hussein.

Having magnified Saddam into a twenty-first-century Hitler, the Bush administration watched credulously as Rumsfeld minimized the difficulty of overthrowing him. He and Franks—alone making strategy—focused exclusively on the task of decapitating Iraq's government. Yet overthrow was not the game. The mission was regime *change,* a charge far more complicated than decapitation. Rumsfeld and Franks made assumptions to build a force to rid Iraq of Saddam. American and coalition troops accomplished that aim with alacrity. Yet changing the government demanded a host of subsequent missions: securing the cities, the WMD, the oil fields, and the borders; providing water, food, and medicine to refugees; policing the country and helping the Iraqis themselves to restore order; and most important, assisting a new and legitimate government in taking control. The inattention to establishing legitimate government was the most heartbreaking failure in this fiasco of strategy.

At bottom, the invasion of Iraq was an object lesson in the failure of those at the political-military nexus to take responsibility for their decision making. Both Franks and Rumsfeld effectively went AWOL after the fall of Baghdad. But their greater failures occurred much earlier. Tommy Franks had been promoted into a position that he did not merit. To intellectual laziness and strategic incompetence he added weakness of character and bankruptcy of judgment. Yet the climate he established with peers and subordinates guaranteed that he would never get the help he desperately needed to follow the logic of mission analysis, to challenge the best-case assumption that CENTCOM could defeat Saddam's army, depose the Baathist regime, and be greeted as liberators by a grateful Iraqi populace.

Rumsfeld suffered many of the same maladies, but his sins were graver than Franks's. Donald Rumsfeld thought clearly, carefully categorizing his understanding and, more important, recognizing his lack of knowledge when it existed and rendering it all in incisive prose. Unlike Franks, Rumsfeld possessed the capacity to challenge assumptions. Yet his dogmatic adherence to transformation and a single-minded conviction that Saddam had to go blinded him to strategic realities. He domineered the Pentagon, the Joint Chiefs, Franks, and CENTCOM, forcing them all to accept his assumptions, with baleful consequences for strategic planning. Then, when those plans met the reality of "untidiness," Rumsfeld dodged responsibility for the consequences. He disavowed his role in planning the invasion, insisting that the plan was Franks's brainchild. Rumsfeld denied manipulating the TPFDL; that had been a CENTCOM change. When it became apparent that there were no WMD in Iraq, Rumsfeld insisted that all the intelligence said otherwise, conveniently forgetting his role in cherry-picking that intelligence. As Iraqi looters and "dead-enders" began to take on the appearance of insurgents, Rumsfeld rejected the demonstrable and contrary facts that many in positions to know had predicted post-invasion problems. And when Jerry Bremer dismantled and cashiered the Iraqi government and army, Rumsfeld disowned him, denying that Bremer even reported to him, much less that he himself had any connection to those fateful decisions.[54] Rumsfeld refused to take responsibility for these failures of strategy, of imagination, of judgment, that set the United States on the road to eight years of bitter war.

Let us return once more to examine Trumbull's *General George Washington Resigning His Commission*. Washington stands before a chair, one a little larger than all the rest and draped with a cloak—the throne will go unoccupied. Returning his commission, Washington becomes not Caesar but Cincinnatus, forsaking command, the military life, and a potential claim on executive, perhaps dictatorial, power. Like Cincinnatus, Washington has sheathed his sword and will return to the plow at his Mount Vernon estate. So, too, will his army. The negotiation between political and military leaders seems to have ended in tranquil and lasting peace.

The Trumbull canvas and its seven companions in the Capitol Rotunda express American ideals, but little nuance. For example, two other paintings depict Burgoyne's defeat at Saratoga and Cornwallis's surrender at Yorktown—unalloyed American triumphs. But none commemorates Lee's surrender to Grant. That moment of national reconciliation was equally significant for American history, but it would have evoked bitter memories of slavery and civil war as well. Trumbull might have chosen to paint Washington standing before his officers in the Temple of Virtue quashing the Newburgh Conspiracy, but such a rendering would have highlighted the officer-led uprising that made the meeting necessary. Ambiguity is not the stuff of national tropes. In nearly two centuries since Trumbull painted his memorial no one has sought to replace it with an image of Polk and Scott, Lincoln and McClellan, or Truman and MacArthur. No, far better for the purposes of mythmaking to remember a scene perpetuating a national aspiration—political-military harmony.

Myths are foundation stones of institutional identity. Storybook lessons of heroic deeds fill the treasured annals of cultures, nations, and religions. Perhaps they are even necessary for helping the young to understand their membership in a broad society.

Adult education and mature understanding, however, demand more complex history. The animating purpose of this book has been to offer correctives to any number of myths about political-military relations in America. The concord Trumbull depicted is rare, and rarer still in wartime relations between presidents and generals. Tension is natural. Conflict is ubiquitous. To the extent that these stresses foster informed decision making, they can be productive. But frequently, American political-military relations have been so strained that both policy and strategy have suffered. Some causes of the stress are structural, codified in the Constitution and in legislation governing the armed services. Yet the tensions have become more profound and less constructive over the past six decades. After the Allied victory in the Second World War, the United States gained a preeminent role in world affairs. The presidency assumed greater power and prestige both at home and abroad. The combination of nuclear capabilities and bipolar rivalry with the Soviet Union brought about an age of limited war, at least for the superpowers themselves. The need to maintain a nuclear arsenal and ready surface forces led to rapid growth of the U.S. military establishment and the size of defense budgets, both absolutely and as a proportion of federal spending. Expanding budgets spurred competition among the services and bureaucratic and political efforts to gain larger shares of those outlays. Each of these developments magnified the significance of defense and security issues. As a consequence of their enhanced status in World War II and the constant small wars of the twentieth century, military leaders took on more prominent roles in national affairs. At the same time, presidents and their civilian advisers began to demand tighter control of national security and the military muscle to ensure it. Political-military strains inevitably increased. These conditions are likely to persist well into the future, and heightened political-military stresses are likely to persist as well. Continuous negotiation has become an enduring fact of the political-military relationship.

Although managing these difficulties should be a high priority among all concerned, participants on both sides of the relationship are handicapped by their own institutional cultures. Civilian policy makers often have little acquaintance with the military, its mentality, and its methods. If they have any experience, it was usually gained briefly and at an early stage, before a long career in civil life and politics. Thus, they may be politically astute but quite ignorant of the military as a dynamic institution and as an influence on national policy. Senior military officers, who have at least three decades of military experience in progressively more responsible positions, similarly have limited familiarity with the political arena. They are militarily expert, but often far less aware of political motives and maneuvers. Thus, in this most important of relationships, the stage is set for a clash of orientations and dispositions.

Among Samuel Huntington's seminal contributions in *The Soldier and the State* was his ideal model for the management of such conflicts. Writing in the first decade of the Cold War, Huntington posited a form of political-military relations that he called "objective civilian control," which divorced the military from political life in exchange for maintaining its professional autonomy. Huntington argued that such a division maximized military professionalism, and hence national security, by erecting a wall between policy and strategy that neither general nor politician should breach.[1]

Theoretical abstractions, such as the concepts of absolute zero or the speed of light, are useful means of comparing reality to the ideal, thereby measuring phenomena in the real world. Seen as a concept, objective civilian control has much to recommend it. Ideally, professional soldiers would remain unequivocally subordinate to their political masters, who would, in turn, develop clear, unambiguous policy goals prior to a forthright declaration of war. Then soldiers would prosecute war to its successful conclusion unfettered by political interference. Upon the achievement of peace, civilians would resume their supremacy.[2]

Yet reality intrudes. The wall that Huntington would erect between the soldier and the state is the boundary between air and water. On a quiet day, the separation is easy to observe. But on a stormy and turbulent sea, the most experienced sailor would be hard-pressed to say where the sky ended and the water began. The physical properties of liquid and gas are fundamentally different. Yet when conditions are roiled and fraught, passing from one medium to the other is effortless, sometimes unnoticed. In the real world of necessity, there is continuous negotiation between political and military leaders. Soldiers sometimes stray into the realm of policy making, while civilian leaders involve themselves in professional military matters, such as operational planning and even battlefield decisions. No wall stands between political and military matters in practice, especially in the turbulent times of war.[3]

Huntington contrasts his ideal of objective civilian control with an unhealthy condition he calls subjective civilian control. In the latter, civilian groups compete to maximize their access to and power over the military. Such control has historically been achieved when government institutions, political parties, or social classes manage to monopolize control of the military, generally at the expense of other civilian groups. Huntington argues that subjective control decreases military security in the state because it compromises military professionalism "by civilianizing the military" and "making them the mirror of the state." Thus, subjective control, regardless of the form it takes, is the worst possible outcome for national security, except, perhaps, no control at all.[4]

Yet the rub is that political conflict over control of the military comports with human reality and the U.S. Constitution. Huntington's model of objective civilian control neglects the complexity fostered by the dual control of the military—the Constitution divides civilian control of the military between the executive and legislative branches of government—the president and Congress. The framers intended for the two branches to check one another, so that balance would occur not by conformity but by compromise among competing interests, and liberty was more likely to be protected. Although congressional influence over political-military relations has been waning since the nineteenth century—witness the absence of a congressional declaration of war since 1941—Congress controls the purse, which enables the nation to raise and support armed forces. The president is commander in chief and appoints the civilian and military officers of the armed forces, subject to the advice and consent of the Senate. Thus, while the president and secretary of defense top the military chain of command, officers owe fealty to the legislative branch as well.

The essential flaw in Huntington's theoretical wall is that it divorces the responsibilities for national security policy and strategy. This bifurcation demands too little both of military professionals and of their civilian superiors, both of whom can and should maintain a shared, but not equivalent, responsibility for sound policy and effective strategy, their interaction and their execution. Officers swear to defend the Constitution; so do civilian officials, and the Constitution makes them both accountable to the people to provide for the common defense. Contrary to Huntington's assertions about objective control, admitting that both sides shoulder parts of this responsibility does no violence to military professionalism.

Soldiers and politicians alike should understand that in the continuous negotiation between the two, both parties will regularly cross the fine boundary between their respective duties. As Clausewitz put it, "At the highest level the art of war turns into policy. . . . The assertion that a major military development, or the plan for one, should be a matter for *purely military* opinion is unacceptable and can be damaging. Nor indeed is it sensible to summon soldiers, as many governments do when they are planning a war, and ask them for *purely military advice.*"[5] Like Huntington, Clausewitz described a theoretical abstraction, "absolute war," as a means of measuring and describing "real war," as it happens in an imperfect world. Clausewitz's fundamental theoretical insight, that "war is merely the continuation of policy by other means," is meant to show the political limitations on war. It also pithily describes why objective civilian control of the military is impossible to achieve.

We can improve upon Huntington's objective and subjective types of civilian control of the military by placing them, as he did not, in dialectic form. Objective control is preferable, but unattainable. Perfect subjective control can lead to military tyranny. The solution in a healthy democracy lies somewhere in the negotiation between them. The synthesis of their opposition results in shared responsibility for the development and execution of national security policy.

The idea of constant and continuous negotiation resists hard-and-fast rules. Changes in historical circumstances and national institutions require that the bargaining begin again with each new political-military relationship. History, of course, will bequeath its share of practices and outcomes to the participants, and the interplay of personalities will be unpredictable. Human interaction is at the crux of every discussion, and it is subject to innumerable factors. Thus, while it may be impossible to establish lasting norms, perhaps we can employ a metaphor to help set parameters.

The president is captain of the ship of state. He may be an expert sailor or a nautical novice, but he remains the captain. He may choose to delegate navigation, propulsion, steering, even the defense of the ship, but he cannot delegate responsibility for the ship itself. Neither can his lieutenants presume to make important decisions for the captain, such as the ship's mission and its ultimate destination. If invited to opine on those topics, they are welcome to offer advice, but only as long and as far as the captain chooses to listen. They can and should advise on the best methods for carrying out the captain's wishes. Indeed, that is the reason the captain employs them, for he cannot do everything himself. For example, an expert navigator may suggest that because of currents and prevailing winds the optimal course between one port and another may not be a straight line. An astute captain will appreciate such advice and act on it. But he may decide to trust his own judgment and choose to plot his own course, for it is his prerogative to decide and to act.

It is incumbent upon the officers of the ship to earn the captain's trust through expert and ethical practice. The military profession must do likewise. Each military adviser must earn each president's trust, and that of his advisers and the Congress, in the same way. Finding the right balance in a given circumstance will require the civilian leaders and military commanders to negotiate with each other in good faith. But that negotiation should not mask the responsibility and the authority—indeed the duty—of civilian leaders to prescribe where the boundaries will lie and who their military leaders will be.

Generals have to trust in the American electoral process to have rendered the appropriate verdict on the political leadership needed in their own time. They must respect the legitimacy of political leadership to govern and to decide. To do so, in the words of their commissioning oath, is "to support and defend the Constitution." They must respect the competence of the president and his civilian advisers to craft effective policy. Generals are obligated to support that policy, whatever it is and wherever it leads, so long as the orders they receive are legal and moral.

They may be asked, and often are, to give their candid advice not just on how to execute policy but on what that policy should be. They should not shy away from giving either type of counsel. But even when they believe the president's policy to be flawed, it is incumbent upon generals to obey and support to the best of their abilities, to help the captain to maneuver the ship of state.

Presidents do not have to trust their generals, but the most successful wartime presidents learn to do so. The military services may not provide the right general at the beginning of a war. History shows that they often do not. Presidents need to heed their instincts, as Lincoln learned to do. He divined a lesson for future presidents: to think of one's generals as implements, potentially useful tools but certainly replaceable. Generals may not like to admit it, but they are expendable. In a military as large and professionally trained as ours, another talented officer is always waiting in the wings. Presidents can rest assured that the right officer will come along; he just may not be the one the services provide initially. The best officer for one situation may be completely unsuited for leadership in another if the president decides to change his political or strategic aims.

Presidents would do well to value the political-military relationship so highly that they are prepared to be ruthless to achieve an effective one. Generals should be replaced without remorse when the reciprocal give-and-take seems to be breaking down. If the "auger [is] too dull to take

374

hold," as Lincoln said, find another auger. Likewise, a military adviser ought to value the negotiation to the point of self-abnegation, being ready to step aside if he discerns that he is not the best adviser at this time for this president. Witness the example of General Stanley McChrystal, who, after a magazine article quoted him making disparaging remarks about the Obama administration, requested his own relief. He determined that he had lost the president's trust and could no longer command effectively in Afghanistan. He was right. It does the client—the nation as a whole—no good for a president to harbor mistrust in a general. It is far worse for the president or his advisers to begin to think of a general or the Joint Chiefs as political rivals, as several administrations have done to their chagrin. The rule of thumb derived from Truman's experience is that when a president has come to mistrust or fear a general, his sacking is long overdue.

Any human relationship must rest in part upon some degree of trust. It need not be perfect, but some level of trust, even between bitter enemies, must exist before earnest negotiation can begin. Perhaps no president has ever trusted a military leader as Wilson trusted Pershing. The general's portfolio was comprehensive, his authority "supreme," and his success unalloyed. Conversely, few presidents have been as niggardly with trust as Polk in his dealings with Taylor and Scott. Nonetheless, both generals enjoyed operational and strategic success, and Polk won his controversial war in astonishingly short time.

In the least effective relationships—Lincoln-McClellan and Truman-MacArthur—a lack of trust clearly hampered both policy and strategy. In the most effective relationships—Lincoln-Grant and Roosevelt-Marshall—the generals gradually earned trust with proven ability and demonstrated trustworthiness, and U.S. forces followed those political and military leaders to triumphant victories.

☆ ☆ ☆

We, as a body politic, can do our part to improve political-military relations. We can hold our leaders accountable for their decisions and the actions they pursue. We can attempt to promote an understanding of the intermeshing of strategy and policy that Clausewitz articulated by understanding that participants on each side of the continuous negotiation may stray into the other's realm. Generals will be called upon to give more than military advice, just as statesmen may delve into operational or even tactical matters. But practitioners on both sides should stray only as far as their own competence will allow, and most importantly, as far as they are willing to accept responsibility for their actions. Can a general accept responsibility for a policy outcome? No, only elected leaders can do that. Should a president make operational decisions? The answer to that question depends a great deal upon the particular president and his particular generals, their skills, their experiences, and the level of trust the president has in his military advisers. But it is his prerogative to decide.

We can and should view the military profession as an integral part of society. The military comes from society. It serves and protects society. It is and should be open to everyone in American society who can meet its exacting standards of entry and performance. There is an unfortunate tendency on the part of some in the military and some who presume to speak for it to denigrate American civilian society as undisciplined, immoral, or corrupt, and to set the military profession above and apart from it as morally superior. Such professional arrogance is both illogical and dangerous.[6] Illogical because such polemicists tend to impute to the military profession values that it does not profess for itself, and dangerous because military-cultural elitism can undermine the fundamental definition of a professional soldier as a servant of society. As Sir John Hackett noted, contra Huntington: "What a society gets in its armed forces is exactly what it asks for, no more and no less. What it asks for tends to be a reflection of what it is. When a country looks at its fighting forces it is looking in a mirror; if the mirror is a true one the face that it sees there will be its own."[7]

An ethos of nonpartisanship in a partisan world is challenging to pursue, but it protects the profession and enhances the trust that obtains in the best examples of the negotiation between soldiers and statesmen. Professional military education should promote nonpartisanship as a bedrock value of an officer corps serving a democratic republic. This is not to say that officers should have no political opinions or, as some have suggested, that they should not vote. Service to country does not entail the loss of citizenship. But no hint of political partisanship should ever impinge on an officer's performance of duty. Equating professionalism with any ideology or party is dangerous, both to the military and to society, as the history of Nazi Germany or any number of totalitarian regimes and failed states will attest. Professional credibility both inside and outside the institution derives from the oath of office, professional expertise, and a steadfast adherence to institutional values. This emphasis on nonpartisan integrity is especially valuable in the political world, where the temptations for encouraging partisanship are strongest. Politics in Washington is tough, partisan business, and officers at the political-military boundary, more than all others, need to uphold a nonpartisan military. Most civilians respect the professional military, partly because of its non-partisanship, and professionals must protect and nurture that standing.

Today, the problem plaguing a nonpartisan military is not in the officer corps itself, but in a small but vocal percentage of retired flag officers who have endorsed presidential candidates and allied themselves with their policies. The problem began in 1988, when retired marine commandant P. X. Kelley endorsed Vice President Bush. Since then, the floodgates have opened. In 1992 Admiral and former chairman of the Joint Chiefs William Crowe and twenty-one other flag officers endorsed Governor Clinton, which, in view of his lack of Vietnam service, gave the governor a significant boost against President Bush, a bona fide World War II hero. Four years later in a losing effort against President Clinton, Senator Bob Dole enthusiastically sought and received several military endorsements, including that of the recently retired chairman of the Joint Chiefs, Colin Powell. By 2000, the Gore and Bush campaigns engaged in a race for retired flag officers, a contest that Bush won with more than eighty military endorsements, led again by General Powell, who subsequently became President Bush's first secretary of state.

In 2004 former chairman of the Joint Chiefs General John Shalikashvili appeared onstage at the Democratic National Convention with twelve retired flag officers and gave his support to John Kerry. Not to be outdone, the Republican convention paraded a similar formation headed by recently retired CENTCOM commander Tommy Franks to endorse President Bush. In 2008 more than one hundred retired generals and admirals publicly endorsed Senators Obama, Clinton, or McCain. Powell bucked the GOP and supported Senator Obama. After that election Joint Chiefs chairman Mike Mullen became the first high-ranking active duty officer to call for an end to such endorsements.

Prior to the 2012 elections, JCS chairman Martin E. Dempsey echoed his predecessor's admonition: "In my judgment," he said, "we must continue to be thoughtful about how our actions and opinions reflect on the profession beyond active service. Former and retired service members, especially generals and admirals, are connected to military service for life. When the title or uniform is used for partisan purposes, it can erode the trust relationship. We must all be conscious of this, or we risk adversely affecting the very profession to which we dedicated most of our adult lives."

Unfortunately, too many retired flag officers ignored General Dempsey's advice. Admiral John B. Nathman, flanked by some thirty military retirees, spoke in support of President Obama's reelection bid at the Democratic National Convention. In October 2012 the Romney campaign countered with an announcement that some three hundred retired flag officers, led once again by Tommy Franks, had agreed to endorse the former governor. A few days later Colin Powell endorsed President Obama, just as he had done in 2008. Thus, the phenomenon has continued to grow, despite the admonitions of two sitting JCS chairmen and numerous students of civil-military relations.

In October 2012 the Center for a New American Security released a report on the issue of retired military officers' endorsements, which, they found, "can diminish the perception of the military as a nonpartisan institution serving the nation and increase the perception of the military as just another interest group serving its own bureaucratic and political interests." The higher the rank of the endorsing veteran, the more he can be perceived as speaking on behalf of the institution and the more his endorsement tends to damage the perception of a nonpartisan military. Generally speaking, no one would notice if a sergeant or a colonel announced his endorsement, although veterans' groups can have a negative impact. In general, the CNAS report finds that retired flag officer endorsements have little impact on voters, implying that they are surely not worth the damage they can do.[8]

If retired officers want to engage in political advocacy, including criticism of current policy or serving officials, or endorsements of political candidates, they should as a matter of professional responsibility distance themselves from the armed services, explicitly stating that they are speaking for themselves alone. If they do not, the Joint Chiefs of Staff should take steps to curb their activity, first through private persuasion and then, if needed, by publicly shunning and disavowing such behavior as harmful to the profession. We should not include in these sanctions retired officers who choose to run for office themselves. Inevitably, suffering the slings and arrows of campaigning and taking positions far afield from military matters will separate them from their former colleagues soon enough.

☆ ☆ ☆

Perhaps it is time to revisit the National Security Acts of 1947 and 1949 and the Goldwater-Nichols Act of 1986 to restructure the Joint Chiefs of Staff. Specifically, the service chiefs should be relieved of their duties as advisers to the president and secretary of defense. The conflation of those roles is a long-standing conflict of interest and an unintended legacy of FDR's ad hoc arrangements. Their roles as force providers and uniformed heads of the armed services are full-time responsibilities. The role of military adviser adds another duty that often conflicts with their obligations to their services. Sometimes, when critics have suggested that the chiefs have been parochial in their military advice, they have been correct. Each service wants to ensure that its representation in the conflict of the day will protect its relevance for tomorrow.

The Joint Chiefs of Staff should be disbanded in favor of a National Military Council of five to seven senior flag officers and led by a four-star chairman. This group would carry out the advisory responsibilities currently held by the Joint Chiefs, but the incumbents would serve on the NMC as their sole duty. The Joint Staff would remain in being and report to the chairman of the NMC. Members of the council would not be in the chain of command, and would report only to the secretary of defense and the president. The chairman would represent them on the National Security Council, or the president could require them all to be present, as he or she sees fit.

Members of the NMC would serve renewable two-year terms. To be eligible for service on the council, one would have to be a four-star officer who had served as a unified or combined commander or as a service chief. Upon leaving the council, members would not return to their services, but retire from the military. While on the council, members would be encouraged to take a joint view, to leave their service allegiances and prejudices aside. Having no other responsibilities but the national interest should assist them in assuming this attitude.

☆ ☆ ☆

The continuous negotiation between the president and the generals and the decisions that emanate from it are critical in the lives of every American. They will continue profoundly to affect the lives of our children and our posterity. The costs of ineffective and counterproductive political-military relations, especially over the past six decades, have been astounding and maddening, because they might well have been avoided had the principals given more attention to constructive negotiation and had the body politic been more attentive. May the dozen cases explored here enlighten the electorate as to the nature and significance of relations between presidents and generals, so that it will be better able to hold them accountable for their actions.

How might a modern-day Trumbull compose his canvas to depict the continuous negotiation? If he intends to perpetuate national myths, he ought to lay down his brushes and simply admire Trumbull's work. But if he aims at educating the American public by showing them the relationship in all its intricacy, he might start with a portrait of the NMC chairman telling impatient members of the Senate Armed Services Committee that he prefers to keep his advice to the president on the administration's national security policy private. Or he might depict the CENTCOM commander standing before an imposing map briefing the president and his advisers on a forthcoming operation. He might show the president chairing a heated discussion in the National Security Council, where a general and the secretary of state debate the utility of armed force. Having sketched and discarded these ideas, he might contact a film director to assist him with the project, having realized that a static portrait cannot capture the complexity of the continuous negotiation, where no debate is ever final, where the wall between policy and strategy does not exist, and where the high-level interactions of human beings faced with life-and-death decisions never cease.

INTRODUCTION

1. The other three paintings depict the discovery of the Mississippi, Pocahontas's baptism, and Burgoyne's surrender at Saratoga, emphasizing other nineteenth-century American values and totems, respectively: exploration and national expansion, Christian piety and evangelism, and military victory over the British.

I. GEORGE WASHINGTON AND THE CONTINENTAL CONGRESS

1. John Ferling, *The Ascent of George Washington: The Hidden Political Genius of an American Icon* (New York: Bloomsbury Press, 2009), 80; James Thomas Flexner, *George Washington in the American Revolution, 1775–1783* (Boston: Little, Brown, 1967), 11–15; George Washington to George William Fairfax, Philadelphia, May 31, 1775, in *The Papers of George Washington Digital Edition*, ed. Theodore J. Crackel (Charlottesville: University of Virginia Press, Rotunda, 2007), hereafter cited as *PGWDE*.

2. *Journals of the Continental Congress*, vol. 2, 76–78. Hereafter cited as *JCC*.

3. *JCC*, 2:78–89.

4. *JCC*, 2:89–90.

5. Joseph J. Ellis, *His Excellency: George Washington* (New York: Alfred A. Knopf, 2004), 68–71; Edmund Cody Burnett, *The Continental Congress* (New York: W. W. Norton, 1964), 76–77.

6. Don Higginbotham, *George Washington and the American Military Tradition* (Athens: University of Georgia Press, 1985), 33–38; Ferling, *Ascent*, 78–79, 86.

7. Higginbotham, *American Military Tradition*, 39–43.

8. Don Higginbotham, *The War of American Independence: Military Attitudes, Policies, and Practice, 1763–1789* (Boston: Northeastern University Press, 1983), 83–85; Burnett, *Continental Congress*, 75–77.

9. *JCC*, 2:91–92; Flexner, *George Washington*, 9.

10. *JCC*, 2:96.

11. Flexner, *George Washington*, 14–16.

12. Ellis, *His Excellency*, 71–77; Ferling, *Ascent*, xxi.

13. Ferling, *Ascent,* 87, 90; Flexner, *George Washington,* 14–16, 26; Address from the Massachusetts General Court to George Washington, March 28, 1776, *PGWDE; JCC,* 2;92.

14. George Washington to John Hancock, Camp at Cambridge, July 10–11, 1775, *PGWDE;* Flexner, *George Washington,* 37–38; Ellis, *His Excellency* 50; Fred Anderson, *A People's Army: Massachusetts Soldiers and Society in the Seven Years' War* (Chapel Hill: University of North Carolina Press, 1984), passim, and esp. 111–141.

15. George Washington to John Hancock, Camp at Cambridge, July 10–11, 1775, *PGWDE;* Ferling, *Ascent,* 97; Higginbotham, *American Military Tradition,* 51–53.

16. Anderson, *People's Army,* 65–141, 167–195; Higginbotham, *American Military Tradition,* 60–61.

17. George Washington to Lund Washington, Camp at Cambridge, August 20, 1775, *PGWDE;* Flexner, *George Washington,* 37–38; Ellis, *His Excellency,* 78.

18. George Washington to John Hancock, Camp at Cambridge, July 10–11, 1775, *PGWDE.*

19. Jonathan Trumbull Sr. to George Washington, Lebanon, Conn., September 15, 1775; George Washington to Jonathan Trumbull Sr., Camp at Cambridge, September 21, 1775; Jonathan Trumbull Sr. to George Washington, Lebanon, Conn., October 9, 1775; George Washington to Jonathan Trumbull Sr., Cambridge, December 2, 1775; Jonathan Trumbull Sr. to George Washington, Lebanon, Conn., December 7, 1775, all in *PGWDE.*

20. Higginbotham, *In the American Revolution,* 50–53; John Shy, *A People Numerous and Armed: Reflections on the Military Struggle for American Independence* (New York: Oxford University Press, 1976), 193–224.

21. Ferling, *Ascent,* 98–100; Higginbotham, *American Military Tradition,* 66–67; Abigail Adams to John Adams, Braintree, July 16, 1775, in *Adams Family Correspondence,* ed. L. H. Butterfield (Cambridge, MA: Belknap Press of Harvard University Press, 1963), 1:246; Address from the Massachusetts General Court to George Washington, March 28, 1776; George Washington, Address to the Massachusetts General Court, April 1, 1776, both *PGWDE.*

22. Proceedings of the Committee of Conference [with associated documents] and Minutes of the Conference, Cambridge, October 18–24, 1775; Council of War, Cambridge, October 18, 1775, both *PGWDE;* Burnett, *Continental Congress,* 114–115; Ira D. Gruber, *The Howe Brothers and the American Revolution* (New York: Atheneum, 1972), 82–84.

23. George Washington to Samuel Washington, Camp near the Falls at Trenton, December 18, 1776, *PGWDE.*

24. Gruber, *Howe Brothers,* 9–126; Ferling, *Ascent,* 104–120; Flexner, *George Washington,* 87–162, 167; Thomas Paine, *The American Crisis,* No. 1 (Philadelphia: Styner and Cist, 1776–1777), 1.

25. Ferling, *Ascent,* 114–115, 119–120; Flexner, *George Washington,* 156–160; David McCullough, *John Adams* (New York: Simon & Schuster, 2001), 153; *JCC,* 6:1027.

26. George Washington to John Hancock, Camp near the Falls at Trenton, December 20, 1776, *PGWDE;* Ferling, *Ascent,* 120–121; Flexner, *George Wash-*

ington, 163; Ron Chernow, *Washington: A Life* (New York: Penguin Press, 2010), 278.

27. James Kirby Martin and Mark Edward Lender, *A Respectable Army: The Military Origins of the Republic, 1763–1789* (Arlington Heights, IL: Harlan Davidson, 1982), 69–78; Ellis, *His Excellency,* 83; Higginbotham, *American Military Tradition,* 59–62; Flexner, *George Washington,* 67, 95.

28. George Washington to John Hancock, Camp near the Falls at Trenton, December 20, 1776, *PGWDE; JCC,* 6:1043–1046.

29. See David Hackett Fischer's *Washington's Crossing* (New York: Oxford University Press, 2004) for a brilliant exposition of this campaign.

30. Burnett, *Continental Congress,* 237–240, 248–258.

31. E. Wayne Carp, *To Starve the Army at Pleasure: Continental Army Administration and American Political Culture* (Chapel Hill: University of North Carolina Press, 1984), 31, 104; Higginbotham, *War of American Independence,* 233, 288–293.

32. Burnett, *Continental Congress,* 268–270; Flexner, *George Washington,* 238; John Adams to Abigail Adams, October 26, 1777, *Adams Family Papers: An Electronic Archive,* Mass. Historical Society, http://www.masshist.org/digitaladams/.

33. Ellis, *His Excellency,* 107–109, Charles Royster, *A Revolutionary People at War: The Continental Army and American Character, 1775–1783* (New York: W. W. Norton, 1979), 179–185.

34. Ferling, *Ascent,* 151–152; Flexner, *George Washington,* 240–244, 259; Higginbotham, *American Military Tradition,* 55–57; George Washington to Richard Henry Lee, Matuchen Hills, Philadelphia County, October 16, 1777, *PGWDE.*

35. Flexner, *George Washington,* 251–252; Burnett, *Continental Congress,* 271–275; Ferling, *Ascent,* 145–146; Royster, *Revolutionary People,* 184.

36. Ellis, *His Excellency,* 93; Ferling, *Ascent,* 151–153.

37. Gates had shown little political flair after his victory at Saratoga, suffering both Washington and Congress to wait more than a week for official word of his triumph. Gates, beginning to feel that he was equal and no longer subordinate to Washington, sent his chief word only after Washington sent a letter inquiring about Burgoyne's surrender. Further, Gates had signed a convention with Burgoyne, allowing his army to sail for Britain upon promise that none of its officers or soldiers would return to America. Of course, this agreement said nothing about the forces that Burgoyne's army might replace and leave free for deployment. Congress was distressed and at some pains for many months to abrogate the agreement. Burnett, *Continental Congress,* 260–268; Ferling, *Ascent,* 137–139; Flexner, *George Washington,* 253–257.

38. Henry Laurens to George Washington, York (Pa.), December 1, 1777; Circular to the General Officers of the Continental Army, December 3, 1777; from a Continental Congress Camp Committee, White Marsh (Pa.), December 10, 1777, all *PGWDE.* Another quandary for Washington and Congress coincided with the dispatch of diplomats abroad. European officers began to lobby American representatives for commissions in the Continental Army. To the extent that these men were skilled artillerymen or engineers—and that they spoke English—their services

were welcome. But American ministers abroad found that offering American commissions to recommended applicants was an effective means of currying favor with their counterparts. Members of Congress, whose responsibility it was to ratify commissions, soon described the flood of supplicants as an invasion, and the strain on Washington was equally great. Most of these foreign officers had little to offer in the way of leadership or technical expertise, although the Marquis de Lafayette, Colonel Thaddeus Kosciusko, and Baron von Steuben were notable exceptions. Some, having wrangled berths as general officers, were downright harmful. Among the most vexing was Philippe du Coudray of France. In June 1777 du Coudray arrived in Philadelphia with a coterie of eighteen officers and ten sergeants and an American diplomat's promise that he was to be commissioned a major general and assigned as chief of artillery for the Continental Army. His connections to the French Crown placed Congress in a difficult position. John Adams mused that it would be "impolitick, not to avail ourselves of him." Hearing of du Coudray's arrival, three American major generals, all of whom would have been subordinate in seniority to him, wrote to Congress threatening to resign if he were commissioned. Members of Congress were incensed at this breach of political-military decorum and moved toward granting du Coudray's request. That same day du Coudray trotted his horse onto a ferry to cross the Schuylkill River. The horse continued across the deck and into the water. As historian Thomas Flexner inimitably put it: "Having neglected the plebeian exercise of swimming, he drowned." Adams admitted that "this dispensation" had saved all of them a great deal of trouble. Burnett, *Continental Congress,* 240–244, Flexner, *George Washington,* 194–195; Higginbotham, *War of American Independence,* 215.

39. George Washington to Henry Laurens, Valley Forge, December 23, 1777, *PGWDE.*

40. To punctuate the point, the Board of War began consideration of a winter campaign into Canada without consulting Washington. Flexner, *George Washington,* 267–268; Ferling, *Ascent,* 152, 168–171. Ferling argues that Congress could not have been unaware of Washington's antipathy toward Conway when they appointed him.

41. George Washington to Brigadier General Thomas Conway, Whitemarsh (Pa.), c. November 5, 1777, *PGWDE.* The Conway-Gates letter, if it existed, has never been found.

42. Ferling, *Ascent,* 149, 157–159; Flexner, *George Washington,* 248–249, 257–265.

43. Flexner, *George Washington,* 266; Ferling, *Ascent,* 153–160.

44. Ferling, *Ascent,* 157–158; Flexner, *George Washington,* 264–268.

45. George Washington to Horatio Gates, Valley Forge, January 4, February 9, and February 24, 1778; Horatio Gates to George Washington, Albany, December 8, 1777, and York, January 23 and February 19, 1778, all *PGWDE;* Ferling, *Ascent,* 159–163.

46. Flexner, *George Washington,* 271–277; Ellis, *His Excellency,* 107.

47. Ferling, *Ascent,* 164–171.

48. Carp, *To Starve the Army,* 68–69, 72, 104.

49. Ibid., 171–187.

50. Ibid., 187; Martin and Lender, *Respectable Army*, 146–152, 158–165.

51. Carp, *To Starve the Army*, 191–204.

52. The nationalists rested their ideas for building a strong state on firm historical ground—around the turn of the century, Great Britain became a great power through the development of a rational system of taxation and debt service, administered by a competent and burgeoning bureaucracy for the purposes of a building an expansive foreign policy and a military state. See John Brewer, *The Sinews of Power: War, Money and the English State, 1688–1783* (New York: Alfred A. Knopf, 1989).

53. Carp, *To Starve the Army*, 204–208; Burnett, *Continental Congress*, 525; Flexner, *George Washington*, 472–475.

54. By July 1782, Rhode Island had become the lone holdout, and success seemed near. Over the next several months, however, the tiny state balked and finally refused to ratify. (Georgia, which had long been under British occupation and often unrepresented in Congress, had also not ratified the impost, but that was seen as politically insignificant. Rhode Island was the key.) A congressional delegation was en route to Providence to apply some political muscle when it learned that Virginia had rescinded its ratification. The impost was all but dead, and American finances were no closer to recovery than they had been eighteen months earlier. Morris threatened to resign by May if Congress did not find a way out of the impasse. Burnett, *Continental Congress*, 530–533.

55. Carp, *To Starve the Army*, 207–217; Burnett, *Continental Congress*, 525–528.

56. Richard H. Kohn, *Eagle and Sword: The Federalists and the Creation of the Military Establishment in America, 1783–1802* (New York: Free Press, 1975), 19; Ferling, *Ascent*, 227–229.

57. Kohn, *Eagle and Sword*, 20–23; Ferling, *Ascent*, 229–232; Flexner, *George Washington*, 488, 492–493.

58. Kohn, *Eagle and Sword*, 25–27; Gouverneur Morris to John Jay, quoted in Flexner, *George Washington*, 493.

59. Alexander Hamilton to George Washington, Philadelphia, April 8, 1783, in *The Papers of Alexander Hamilton*, ed. Harold C. Syrett, vol. 3, *1782–1786* (New York: Columbia University Press, 1962), 253–255.

60. Continental Congress Remarks on the Revenue and the Situation of the Army, Philadelphia, February 20, 1783, ibid., 3:263–265.

61. George Washington to Alexander Hamilton, Newburgh, March 4, 1783, in *The Writings of George Washington (from the Original Manuscript Series, 1745–1799)*, ed. John J. Fitzpatrick, vol. 26, *January 1, 1783–June 10, 1783* (Washington, DC: Government Printing Office, 1938), 185–188 (hereafter cited as *TWGW*); Flexner, *George Washington*, 502–503; Kohn, *Eagle and Sword*, 30.

62. Kohn, *Eagle and Sword*, 27.

63. Ibid., 29–30; Ferling, *Ascent*, 231; Flexner, *George Washington*, 503–505.

64. George Washington to Joseph Jones, Newburgh, March 12, 1783, *TWGW*, 26:213–216.

65. Kohn, *Eagle and Sword*, 30–31; Ellis, *His Excellency*, 142–144; Flexner, *George Washington*, 501–507 George Washington to the President of Congress,

Head Quarters, March 12, 1783, and George Washington to Joseph Jones, New-burgh, March 12, 1783, in *TWGW*, 26:211–216.

66. George Washington to Alexander Hamilton, Newburgh, March 12, 1783, *TWGW*, 26:216–218.

67. George Washington to the Officers of the Army, Headquarters, Newburgh, March 15, 1783, *TWGW*, 26:222–227.

68. Flexner, *George Washington*, 505–507.

69. George Washington to the Officers of the Army, Headquarters, Newburgh, March 15, 1783, *TWGW*, 26:222–227; Flexner, *George Washington*, 505–507.

70. Burnett, *Continental Congress*, 568–574.

71. Royster, *Revolutionary People*, 331–344; Henry Knox, Draft of Reply to the Newburgh Addresses, March 15, 1783, quoted in Royster, *Revolutionary People*, 336. Implementation of the impost was still dependent upon approval of the states.

72. Kohn, *Eagle and Sword*, 37–39.

73. "Sentiments on a Peace Establishment," Newburgh, May 2, 1783, *TWGW*, 26:374–398. The nationalists who came to the Continental Congress in 1780 would continue to pursue their goals. The "Sentiments" became their national defense program.

74. Alexander Hamilton to George Washington, Philadelphia, February 13, 1783, in *Papers of Alexander Hamilton*, 3:317–321.

75. Higginbotham, *American Military Tradition*, 105; Thomas Jefferson to George Washington, April 16, 1784, quoted in Kohn, *Eagle and Sword*, 39; Burnett, *Continental Congress*, 590–591; Flexner, *George Washington*, 526–527.

2. ADAMS, WASHINGTON, AND HAMILTON

1. Ron Chernow, *Alexander Hamilton* (New York: Penguin Press, 2004), 521–522, 622–625; David McCullough, *John Adams* (New York: Simon & Schuster, 2001), 549–550; John Adams to Benjamin Rush, Quincy, January 25, 1806, in *Old Family Letters* (Philadelphia: Press of J. B. Lippincott Co., 1892), 92.

2. McCullough, *John Adams*, 467–470; Chernow, *Alexander Hamilton*, 523.

3. Adams's *Thoughts on Government* (1776) influenced the framers of several state constitutions, and in 1780 he almost single-handedly drafted the Massachusetts Constitution.

4. Gordon S. Wood, *Revolutionary Characters: What Made the Founders Different* (New York: Penguin Press, 2006), 175–179; Joseph J. Ellis, *Founding Brothers: The Revolutionary Generation* (New York: Alfred A. Knopf, 2004), 164–166; Joseph J. Ellis, *Passionate Sage: The Character and Legacy of John Adams* (New York: W. W. Norton, 2001), 41–43, 47.

5. There are numerous works on Adams, although fewer biographies than a man of his stature deserves. Three of the best are David McCullough's *John Adams*, Joseph J. Ellis's *Passionate Sage*, and John Ferling's *John Adams: A Life* (New York: Holt, 1992). Ron Chernow provides an excellent sketch of Adams's character in *Alexander Hamilton*, 518–521. Benjamin Franklin to Robert R. Livingston, Passy, July 22, 1783, in *The Papers of Benjamin Franklin Digital Edition*, ed. Ellen

Cohn (Packard Humanities Institute, sponsored by the American Philosophical Society and Yale University), http://www.franklinpapers.org/franklin/.

6. James Thomas Flexner, *George Washington: Anguish and Farewell, 1793–1799* (Boston: Little, Brown, 1969), 248–251.

7. Chernow, *Alexander Hamilton,* 523; McCullough, *John Adams,* 469–471.

8. Ellis, *Passionate Sage,* 30.

9. Chernow, *Alexander Hamilton,* 523–524; McCullough, *John Adams,* 475, 488–489; Ellis, *Passionate Sage,* 28.

10. Chernow, *Alexander Hamilton,* 525, 558; McCullough, *John Adams,* 526; Ellis, *Founding Brothers,* 174.

11. *The Papers of Alexander Hamilton* (26 vols.), vol. 21, *April 1797–July 1798,* ed. Harold C. Syrett (New York: Columbia University Press, 1961–79), 193–194 (hereafter cited as *PAH,* 21); Ellis, *Passionate Sage,* 28; John Adams to Abigail Adams, January 9, 1797, and Abigail Adams to John Adams, January 28, 1797, both in *Adams Family Papers: An Electronic Archive,* Massachusetts Historical Society, http://www.masshist.org/digitaladams/.

12. I am indebted to Ron Chernow's excellent biography *Alexander Hamilton* for the sketch that follows.

13. Chernow, *Alexander Hamilton,* 232–233.

14. See *The Federalist,* Nos. 23–29.

15. Wood, *Revolutionary Characters,* 128–129, 132; Chernow, *Alexander Hamilton,* 294–308. For a seminal dissertation on how Great Britain became a great power through the development of a rational system of taxation and debt service, administered by a competent and burgeoning bureaucracy for the purposes of a building an expansive foreign policy and a military state, see John Brewer, *The Sinews of Power: War, Money and the English State, 1688–1783* (New York: Alfred A. Knopf, 1989).

16. Chernow, *Alexander Hamilton,* 524.

17. Ibid., 533–537; McCullough, *John Adams,* 480, 492–493.

18. Wood, *Revolutionary Characters,* 137–138. See also Joanne B. Freeman, *Affairs of Honor: National Politics in the New Republic* (New Haven, CT: Yale University Press, 2001).

19. Late in 1796 Washington recalled his minister to France, Republican James Monroe, who had taken a partisan view of his duties, undermined the administration, and failed to support the Jay Treaty in his dealing with the French. In his stead, the president dispatched Federalist Charles C. Pinckney to Paris in an attempt to restore amicable ties. The French Directory, the five-man council then in power in Paris, refused to accept Pinckney's credentials, betting that Thomas Jefferson would win the presidential election and that a Republican administration would be more favorable to French interests. They expelled Pinckney from France after Adams's election. James Thomas Flexner, *George Washington: Anguish and Farewell (1793–1799)* (Boston: Little, Brown, 1969), 285–291; Marvin R. Zahniser, *Charles Cotesworth Pinckney: Founding Father* (Chapel Hill: University of North Carolina Press, 1967), 136–148; Gordon S. Wood, *Empire of Liberty: A History of the Early Republic, 1789–1815* (New York: Oxford University Press, 2009), 196–199, 239–240; Richard H. Kohn, *Eagle and Sword: The Federalists and the Creation*

of the Military Establishment in America, 1783–1802 (New York: Free Press, 1975), 203–205; Ellis, *Founding Brothers*, 136–137; Chernow, *Alexander Hamilton*, 546–547; McCullough, *John Adams*, 477, 486–487.

20. Ellis, *Founding Brothers*, 162.

21. Ibid., 13–15, 142–143, 167–177; Chernow, *Alexander Hamilton*, 233; Kohn, *Eagle and Sword*, 195–197, 205, 214–218. Adams provided his foes plenty of evidence of his monarchism. *A Defence of the Constitutions of Government of the United States of America* advocated balancing the people's political desires against the moderating influence of the aristocracy on the fulcrum of an executive, which he alternately described as either a monarchy or an executive. In this he was badly out of step with the mainstream of American political thought. Wood, *Revolutionary Characters*, 184–202.

22. Wood, *Revolutionary Characters*, 181–182; Kohn, *Eagle and Sword*, 198–202, 217; Ellis, *Founding Brothers*, 46.

23. Alexander DeConde, *The Quasi-War: The Politics and Diplomacy of the Undeclared War with France, 1797–1801* (New York: Charles Scribner's Sons, 1966), 17, 28–30; Zahniser, *Charles Cotesworth Pinckney*, 136–149, 153–155; Chernow, *Alexander Hamilton*, 547–548; McCullough, *John Adams*, 477–478, 483–486; Kohn, *Eagle and Sword*, 208–209.

24. Chernow, *Alexander Hamilton*, 526–548; DeConde, *Quasi-War*, 26, 33; McCullough, *John Adams*, 491–493.

25. Speech of President John Adams, November 23, 1797, *American State Papers* 1, Foreign Relations vol. 1, 5th Congress, 2nd Session, No. 14; McCullough, *John Adams*, 491–494; Chernow, *Alexander Hamilton*, 526–545; Kohn, *Eagle and Sword*, 209–210; Thomas Jefferson to Edward Rutledge, Philadelphia, June 24, 1797, in *The Writings of Thomas Jefferson*, vol. 7, *1795–1801*, ed. Paul Leicester (New York: G. P. Putnam's Sons, 1896), 154–155.

26. The delegation was hampered from the outset by instructions—largely dictated by Hamilton to Secretary of State Pickering—that amounted to a list of American demands that offered the French nothing in return. Marshall and Pinckney were adamantly opposed to negotiating under the French-proposed preconditions. Elbridge Gerry undermined the delegation's unity by meeting with the agents and Talleyrand himself, showing that he was at least willing to discuss the proposals. However, he saw more clearly than his colleagues that the French had nothing to gain by a war with the United States at a time when they were preparing for war with Great Britain. Further French antagonism risked creating a real Anglo-American alliance. DeConde, *Quasi-War*, 30, 36–73; Zahniser, *Charles Cotesworth Pinckney*, 160–185.

27. Kohn, *Eagle and Sword*, 210–211; McCullough, *John Adams*, 495–499; Abigail Adams to Mary Cranch, Philadelphia, April 4, 1798, quoted in DeConde, *Quasi-War*, 71–73 and 400n; the *Gazette of the United States* drew bold lines through the body politic: "A friend to the present administration . . . is undoubtedly a true republican, a true patriot. . . . Whatever American opposes the administration is an anarchist, a jacobin and a traitor. . . . It is *Patriotism* to write in favor of government—it is sedition to write against it." John Fenno, the *Gazette*'s editor, stirred controversy over the next several months, reminding his readers of the Rev-

olutionary motto, "UNITE OR DIE." He exhorted patriots to be watchful for the "obedient engines of the enemy" in their midst. Fenno called on his readers to organize against the fifth column: "Let committees be appointed; funds raised; presses employed; let information be disseminated at cheap rates everywhere; let the ignorant be instructed; the wavering confirmed; the banditti watched, in their uprising and downlying." When treason was found, half-measures were worse than foolish, for "the man who will not unite with his own government and its friends . . . is a traitor, and ought to be immediately crushed; for . . . 'he that is not for us, is against us. . . .' It is safer to cut off a gangrened member, than to endanger the life of the body." *Gazette of the United States,* vol. 14, issue 1892, October 10, 1798, p. 1; *Gazette of the United States,* vol. 14, issue 1928, November 21, 1798, p. 3.

28. McCullough, *John Adams,* 499–501; Chernow, *Alexander Hamilton,* 555; DeConde, *Quasi-War,* 81–82, 90; Thomas Jefferson to John Taylor, June 4, 1798, in *The Papers of Thomas Jefferson Digital Edition,* ed. Barbara B. Oberg and J. Jefferson Looney (Charlottesville: University of Virginia Press, Rotunda, 2008).

29. Alexander Hamilton, "The Stand," in *PAH,* 21:381–387, 390–396, 402–408, 412–418, 418–432, 434–440, 441–447 (quotation on 432); Kohn, *Eagle and Sword,* 219–229; McCullough, *John Adams,* 499; DeConde, *Quasi-War,* 90; Chernow, *Alexander Hamilton,* 551–553, 577; Republicans accused the Federalists of "arming one part of the people to guard against the other." Virginia senator Stephens T. Mason charged "that there is no calculating how far they will go to attain their favorite object of crushing . . . Republicanism. Wood, *Revolutionary Characters,* 137.

30. Kohn, *Eagle and Sword,* 212–218; McCullough, *John Adams,* 504; Chernow, *Alexander Hamilton,* 549–550, 570–577.

31. DeConde, *Quasi-War,* 89, 102–108.

32. McCullough, *John Adams,* 494–495; Chernow, *Alexander Hamilton,* 523–525, 554; DeConde, *Quasi-War,* 18–19, 21–23, 64–67.

33. DeConde, *Quasi-War,* 19–23; Kohn, *Eagle and Sword,* 230. Alexander Hamilton to James McHenry, New York, March 22(?), 1797; Alexander Hamilton to Timothy Pickering, New York, March 29, 1797; Alexander Hamilton to Oliver Wolcott, New York, March 30, 1797, all in *PAH,* 21:556–557, 567–568, 574–575.

34. Kohn, *Eagle and Sword,* 219–231; Chernow, *Alexander Hamilton,* 553; DeConde, *Quasi-War,* 96; "John Adams to the Printers of the Boston Patriot," *Boston Patriot,* vol. 1, issue 28, June 6, 1809, p. 1.

35. Alexander Hamilton to George Washington, New York, May 19, 1798; George Washington to Alexander Hamilton, Mount Vernon, May 27, 1798; Alexander Hamilton to George Washington, New York, June 2, 1798, all in *The Papers of George Washington Digital Edition,* ed. Theodore J. Crackel (Charlottesville: University of Virginia Press, Rotunda, 2007), hereafter cited as *PGWDE.*

36. John Adams to George Washington, Philadelphia, June 22, 1798, *PGWDE.*

37. George Washington to John Adams, Mount Vernon, July 4, 1798, *PGWDE.* Washington made these same points at greater length and more detail to Secretary of War James McHenry on the same day: George Washington to James McHenry, Mount Vernon, July 4, 1798, *PGWDE.*

38. George Washington to James McHenry, Mount Vernon, July 5, 1798, *PGWDE*.

39. Washington produced such a list of officers and forwarded it to the president. George Washington, Suggestions for Military Appointments, Mount Vernon, July 14, 1798, *PGWDE*.

40. John Adams to George Washington, Philadelphia, July 7, 1798; Timothy Pickering to George Washington, Philadelphia, July 6, 1798; George Washington to Timothy Pickering, Mount Vernon, July 11, 1798; George Washington to John Adams, Mount Vernon, July 13, 1798; Suggestions for Military Appointments, Mount Vernon, July 14, 1798, all in *PGWDE*.

41. George Washington to Timothy Pickering, Mount Vernon, July 11, 1798; George Washington to Alexander Hamilton, Mount Vernon, July 14, 1798; George Washington, Suggestions for Military Appointments, Mount Vernon, July 14, 1798; George Washington to Henry Knox, Mount Vernon, July 16, 1798, all in *PGWDE*.

42. George Washington to Alexander Hamilton, Mount Vernon, July 14, 1798, and notes, *PGWDE*.

43. I am indebted to three principal sources for my interpretation of this confusion: (1) a letter from James McHenry to George Washington, Trenton, September 19, 1798, that details conversations and letters involving the president and the cabinet since the middle of July, in *PGWDE*; (2) extensive footnotes to a letter from George Washington to Alexander Hamilton, Mount Vernon, July 14, 1798, provided by the editors of *PGWDE*; and (3) extensive footnotes to the same Washington–Hamilton letter in *PAH*, 22:4–17.

44. Alexander Hamilton to Timothy Pickering, New York, July 17, 1798, *PAH*, 22:24; Henry Knox to James McHenry, Boston, August 5, 1798, *PAH*, 22:69–71; Alexander Hamilton to James McHenry, New York, September 8, 1798, *PAH*, 22:177; Alexander Hamilton to George Washington, Philadelphia, July 29, and New York, August 1, 1798; George Washington to Henry Knox, Mount Vernon, July 16, 1798; Henry Knox to George Washington, Boston, July 29, 1798; Henry Knox to George Washington, Boston, August 26, 1798, all in *PGWDE*.

45. John Adams to James McHenry, Quincy, August 29, 1798, in *The Works of John Adams, Second President of the United States, with a Life of the Author* by Charles Francis Adams, vol. 13 (Boston: Little, Brown & Co., 1854), 587–589 (hereafter cited as *WJA*). Adams said that if he could resign in favor of Washington, "I would do it immediately, and with the highest pleasure." However, "I never said I would hold the office, and be responsible for its exercise, while he should execute it."

46. Timothy Pickering to Alexander Hamilton, Philadelphia, July 16, 1798, *The Papers of Alexander Hamilton*, vol. 22, *July 1798–March 1799*, ed. Harold C. Syrett (New York: Columbia University Press, 1975), 22–23 (hereafter cited as *PAH*, 22); Timothy Pickering to George Washington (private), Trenton, September 1, 1798; George Washington to James McHenry, Mount Vernon, September 3, 1798; James McHenry to George Washington, Trenton, September 7, 1798; George Washington to Timothy Pickering (private), Mount Vernon, September 9, 1798; George Washington to James McHenry (private and confidential), Mount Vernon,

September 16, 1798, all in *PGWDE*. Washington quickly and curtly told McHenry that "if any change should take place in settling the relative Rank of the Majr Generals, I shall hope, & expect to be informed of it." McHenry confirmed what Pickering had confided to Washington, that "the president is determined to place Hamilton last and Knox first." With gathering anger, Washington told Pickering that he did not know what arrangements Knox might have with the president, but "I know that the President ought to Ponder well before he consents to a change in the arrangement." Then Washington wrote confidentially to McHenry that matters were coming to a head. He accused Adams of "forgetfulness of what *I* considered a compact," the conditions on which he had accepted the appointment. Ominously, Washington asserted that he might be forced "to return him my Commission." Washington was exceptionally displeased with McHenry, demanding to know how well the secretary had conveyed his concerns and conditions to the president after he returned from Mount Vernon in July. While this correspondence was ongoing, McHenry and Pickering were planning to send a joint cabinet letter to Adams insisting that he retain the order of precedence as Hamilton-Pinckney-Knox. They eventually decided that Secretary Wolcott alone should sign the letter, as he had not been involved in prior deliberations. They kept Washington informed of these deliberations. Timothy Pickering to George Washington (private), Trenton, September 13, 1798; Timothy Pickering to George Washington (confidential), Trenton, September 18, 1798; James McHenry to George Washington (confidential), Trenton, September 19, 1798, all in *PGWDE*.

47. Washington tried to reassure Adams, perhaps in answer to concerns Adams had expressed in his August 29 letter to McHenry, that he had no ambition "to increase the Powers of the Commander in Chief—or to lessen those of the President of the United States." George Washington to John Adams, Mount Vernon, September 25, 1798, *PGWDE*.

48. John Adams to George Washington, Quincy, October 9, 1798; Henry Knox to George Washington, Boston, November 4, 1798, both in *PGWDE*; Ellis, *Passionate Sage*, 45. Adams knew better about the behavior of general officers. While heading the Revolutionary Board of War and Ordnance, he had described Continental officers "Scrambling for Rank and Pay like Apes for Nuts."

49. Kohn, *Eagle and Sword*, 212, 257; John Adams to My Dear Philosopher and Friend [Benjamin Rush], November 11, 1807, in *The Spur of Fame: Dialogues of John Adams and Benjamin Rush, 1805–1813*, ed. John A. Schutz and Douglass Adair (San Marino, CA: Huntington Library, 1966), 97–99; Chernow, *Alexander Hamilton*, 503, 559; McCullough, *John Adams*, 502–503, 511–512.

50. George Washington, Suggestions for Military Appointments, Mount Vernon, July 14, 1798; George Washington to James McHenry, Mount Vernon, September 30, 1798, both in *PGWDE*; Alexander Hamilton to James McHenry, New York, August 1–2, 1798, *PAH*, 22:47; Alexander Hamilton to ____, New York, August 3, 1798, *PAH*, 22:48; Alexander Hamilton to James McHenry, New York, August 21, 1798, *PAH*, 22:87–146; George Washington to Alexander Hamilton, Philadelphia, November 12, 1798, *PAH*, 22:237–246; Candidates for Army Appointments from Connecticut, Delaware, Kentucky, Maryland, Tennessee, and Virginia, *PAH*, 22:270–313; James McHenry to Alexander Hamilton, War Department, January 21, 1799,

22:428–431; Alexander Hamilton to James McHenry, New York, February 6, 1799, *PAH*, 22:466–467; Kohn, *Eagle and Sword*, 243–244. In January McHenry explained to Hamilton why Federalist leaders in Congress had denied or delayed commissions for twenty-seven of those candidates. Eight of them, just short of 30 percent, were rejected for "anti-Federal," "anti-governmental," or "French" principles.

51. Kohn, *Eagle and Sword*, 237–243; George Washington to Alexander Hamilton, Mount Vernon, August 9, 1798, *PGWDE*; James McHenry to Alexander Hamilton, War Department, August 10, 1798, *PAH*, 22:66–68; Alexander Hamilton to George Washington, Philadelphia, July 29, and New York, August 1, 1798, *PGWDE*; George Washington to Alexander Hamilton, Mount Vernon, August 9, 1798, *PGWDE*; John Adams to James McHenry, Quincy, October 22, 1798, *WJA*, 8:612–613.

52. George Washington to James McHenry, Susquehanna, December 16, 1798, *PGWDE*; Kohn, *Eagle and Sword*, 243–246; Chernow, *Alexander Hamilton*, 562–566.

53. Chernow, *Alexander Hamilton*, 573–578; Wood, *Revolutionary Characters*, 138–139.

54. Kohn, *Eagle and Sword*, 251–252; Alexander Hamilton to Theodore Sedgwick, New York, February 2, 1799, *PAH*, 22:452–453; Alexander Hamilton to James McHenry, New York, March 18, 1799, *PAH*, 22:552–553; Thomas Jefferson to Thomas M. Randolph, February 2, 1800, in *The Writings of Thomas Jefferson*, ed. Paul Leicester Ford (New York: G. P. Putnam's Sons, 1892–1899). Hamilton was looking for an excuse to deploy the army in Virginia: "When a clever force has been collected let them be drawn towards Virginia for which there is an obvious pretext—and then let measures be taken to act upon the laws and put Virginia to the test of resistance."

55. Kohn, *Eagle and Sword*, 253; Stanley Elkins and Eric McKitrick, *The Age of Federalism* (New York: Oxford University Press, 1993), 616; Chernow, *Alexander Hamilton*, 565–568; Alexander Hamilton to Rufus King, New York, August 22, 1798, *PAH*, 22:154–155; Alexander Hamilton to Francisco de Miranda, New York, August 22, 1798, *PAH*, 22:155–156. Hamilton entrusted delivery of the Miranda letter to Rufus King, American minister in London, who was also in contact with Miranda, saying, "The command in this case would very naturally fall upon me and I hope I should disappoint no favourable anticipation." Hamilton's son, John, later annotated the Miranda letter as follows: "This and the following letter [to King] were copied by me on my birth day when I was six years old—the object being to preserve secrecy until circumstances shd warrant publicity." Alexander Hamilton to Harrison Gray Otis, New York, January 26, 1799, *PAH*, 22:552–553.

56. John Adams to Adrian Van der Kemp, Quincy, April 25, 1808, quoted in DeConde, *Quasi-War*, 112.

57. Elkins and McKitrick, *Age of Federalism*, 616–617; DeConde, *Quasi-War*, 171; Chernow, *Alexander Hamilton*, 568. Adams later remembered thinking that "this man is stark mad or I am." Adams told Otis that if Congress agreed to the Miranda-Hamilton folly, "it would produce an instantaneous insurrection of the whole nation from Georgia to New Hampshire."

58. Chernow, *Alexander Hamilton*, 593.

59. McCullough, *John Adams,* 503–504, 511, 516–517, 522. Dr. George Logan was a private citizen who traveled to Paris at his own expense in an attempt to maintain the peace. Although his efforts outraged the most extreme Federalists, Logan had talks with Talleyrand and returned home telling all who would listen that peace was still possible. Adams gave him an audience and listened to his views.

60. *WJA,* 9:161–162; Kohn, 249, 259; McCullough, *John Adams,* 523–524; Ellis, *Passionate Sage,* 34.

61. George Washington to Alexander Hamilton, Mount Vernon, March 25, 1799, *PGWDE;* Alexander Hamilton to James McHenry, New York, June 27, 1799, *PAH,* 23:227–228; Chernow, *Alexander Hamilton,* 595–600.

62. *WJA,* 9:254–255; Chernow, *Alexander Hamilton,* 595–597; McCullough, *John Adams,* 530–531.

63. Chernow, *Alexander Hamilton,* 600–602; McCullough, *John Adams,* 533–534, 539–540; Kohn, *Eagle and Sword,* 260–267.

64. Kohn, *Eagle and Sword,* 262–271; McCullough, *John Adams,* 538–539; Chernow, *Alexander Hamilton,* 622–623.

65. Alexander Hamilton, *A Letter from Alexander Hamilton, concerning the Public Conduct and Character of John Adams, Esq. President of the United States* (New York: printed for John Lang, by George F. Hopkins, 1800); Ellis, *Passionate Sage,* 22–23.

66. McCullough, *John Adams,* 463; Chernow, *Alexander Hamilton,* 522; Ellis, *Passionate Sage,* 28; John Adams to Benjamin Rush, September, 1807, in Schutz and Adair, *Spur of Fame,* 92–95; John Adams to Dr. Benjamin Rush, Quincy, November 11, 1806, in *Old Family Letters,* 118.

67. Ellis, *Passionate Sage,* 21.

68. John Adams to My Dear Philosopher and Friend [Benjamin Rush], November 11, 1807, in Schutz and Adair, *Spur of Fame,* 97–99.

69. Richard H. Kohn's concluding chapter in *Eagle and Sword,* "Politics, Militarism, and Institution-Forming in the New Nation," has greatly informed my understanding of the ramifications of this period. See pp. 277–303.

3. MR. MADISON'S WAR

1. Donald R. Hickey, *The War of 1812: A Forgotten Conflict,* bicentennial ed. (Urbana: University of Illinois Press, 2012), 22–24.

2. Allan R. Millett, Peter Maslowski, and William B. Feis, *For the Common Defense: A Military History of the United States from 1607 to 2012,* 3rd ed. (New York: Free Press, 2012), 92–94.

3. Hickey, *War of 1812,* 16–21.

4. Gordon S. Wood, *Empire of Liberty: A History of the Early Republic, 1783–1815* (Oxford: Oxford University Press, 2009), 659–664; George C. Herring, *From Colony to Superpower: U.S. Foreign Relations since 1776* (Oxford: Oxford University Press, 2008), 121–122.

5. Wood, *Empire of Liberty,* 666–669; Herring, *Colony to Superpower,* 124–127; Hickey, *War of 1812,* 29–39; David S. Heidler and Jeanne T. Heidler, *Henry Clay: The Essential American* (New York: Random House, 2010), 84–97.

6. Wood, *Empire of Liberty,* 670–672.

7. Ibid., 672–673; Alan Taylor, *The Civil War of 1812: American Citizens, British Subjects, Irish Rebels, and Indian Allies* (New York: Alfred A. Knopf, 2010), 411; James Madison, "War Message to Congress, 1 June 1812," in *The War of 1812: Writings from America's Second War of Independence* (cited hereafter as *Writings*), ed. Donald R. Hickey (New York: Library of America, 2013), 8; "U.S. House of Representatives, Committee on Foreign Relations, Report on the Causes and Reasons for War, 3 June 1812," ibid., 22.

8. Wood, *Empire of Liberty,* 660–661; Millett, Maslowski, and Feis, *Common Defense,* 96.

9. J. C. A. Stagg, *Mr. Madison's War: Politics, Diplomacy, and Warfare in the Early American Republic, 1783–1830* (Princeton, NJ: Princeton University Press, 1983), 77; Hickey, *War of 1812,* 66–68.

10. Hickey, *War of 1812,* 70; Wood, *Empire of Liberty,* 673.

11. Timothy D. Johnson, *Winfield Scott: The Quest for Military Glory* (Lawrence: University Press of Kansas, 1998), 9–17; Andro Linklater, *An Artist in Treason: the Extraordinary Double Life of General James Wilkinson* (New York: Walker, 2009); Winfield Scott, *Memoirs of Lieut.-General Scott, LL.D., Written by Himself* (New York: Sheldon and Co., 1864), 34–35.

12. Wood, *Empire of Liberty,* 674.

13. Hickey, *War of 1812,* 77–80.

14. Millett, Maslowski, and Feis, *Common Defense,* 96.

15. Heidler and Heidler, *Henry Clay,* 77; Hickey, *War of 1812,* 80–83.

16. Article I, Section 8, of the Constitution gives Congress the power "to provide for calling forth the Militia to execute the Laws of the Union, suppress Insurrections and repel Invasions." It is silent on the subject of whether militia may participate in foreign wars.

17. Taylor, *Civil War of 1812,* 182–190.

18. Wood, *Empire of Liberty,* 680.

19. Hickey, *War of 1812,* 89.

20. Ibid., 90–99; Wood, *Empire of Liberty,* 680–682.

21. Hickey, *War of 1812,* 100–105.

22. Ibid., 105–106; Stagg, *Mr. Madison's War,* 277–284.

23. Hickey, *War of 1812,* 123–145.

24. Taylor, *Civil War of 1812,* 269–277; Millett, Maslowski, and Feis, *Common Defense,* 96.

25. Hickey, *War of 1812,* 203–213; Wood *Empire of Liberty,* 690–692.

26. Hickey, *War of 1812,* 197–199; Wood, *Empire of Liberty,* 694, Taylor, *Civil War of 1812,* 407, 412–413, 417–419; Wayne E. Lee, "Plattsburgh 1814: Warring for Bargaining Chips," in *Between War and Peace: How America Ends Its Wars,* ed. Matthew Moten (New York: Free Press, 2011), 43–63.

27. Allan Millett, a military historian and student of the military profession, defines the following attributes of professions: "The occupation is a full-time and stable job, serving continuing societal needs; is regarded as a lifelong calling by the practitioners, who identify themselves personally with their job subculture; is organized to control performance standards and recruitment; requires formal, theoreti-

cal education; has a service orientation in which loyalty to standards of competence and loyalty to clients' needs are paramount; is granted a great deal of collective autonomy by the society it serves, presumably because the practitioners have proven their high ethical standards and trustworthiness. . . . The most salient characteristic of professions has been the accumulation and systematic exploitation of specialized knowledge applied to specialized problems." Allan R. Millett, *Military Professionalism and Officership in America* (Columbus: Mershon Center of the Ohio State University, 1977), 2.

28. Matthew Moten, *The Delafield Commission and the American Military Profession* (College Station: Texas A&M University Press, 2000), 39–42.

4. POLK AGAINST HIS GENERALS

1. Timothy D. Johnson, *A Gallant Little Army: The Mexico City Campaign* (Lawrence: University Press of Kansas, 2007), 263–265.

2. For example, army captain John C. Frémont led a band of frontiersmen west across the Sierra Nevada and, acting on his own authority, declared a revolution to establish an independent Bear Flag Republic in California. He waged battle on the Mexicans and fought with the U.S. Navy for operational control before a more senior army officer arrived to carry out the policy of the Polk administration. Similar confusion marked American operations in every theater.

3. For this brief biographical sketch I have relied on Walter R. Borneman's *Polk: The Man Who Transformed the Presidency and America* (New York: Random House, 2008). See also David A. Clary, *Eagles and Empire: The United States, Mexico, and the Struggle for a Continent* (New York: Bantam Books, 2009), 62–64.

4. Joseph Wheelan, *Invading Mexico: America's Continental Dream and the Mexican War, 1846–1848* (New York: Carroll and Graf, 2007), 59–60.

5. K. Jack Bauer's *Zachary Taylor: Soldier, Planter, Statesman of the Old Southwest* (Baton Rouge: Louisiana State University Press, 1985) is the finest biography of the soldier-president and the basis of this short biographical sketch. See also Clary, *Eagles and Empire,* 68–72; Allan Peskin, *Winfield Scott and the Profession of Arms* (Kent, OH: Kent State University Press, 2003), 135; Wheelan, *Invading Mexico,* 61–63. Taylor resigned his commission during an army reduction after the War of 1812, but returned to service a year later.

6. Winfield Scott, *Memoirs of Lieut.-General Scott, LL.D., Written by Himself* (New York: Sheldon & Co., 1864), 1:382–383.

7. Wheelan, *Invading Mexico,* 64–67.

8. Ibid., 71–76; Clary, *Eagles and Empire,* 81–84.

9. Wheelan, *Invading Mexico,* 85; Ulysses S. Grant, *Personal Memoirs of U.S. Grant,* ed. E. B. Long, introduction by William S. McFeely (New York: Da Capo, 1982), 30; Thomas Hart Benton, *Thirty Years View: Or, a History of the Working of the American Government for Thirty Years, from 1820 to 1850. . . .* 2 vols. (New York: D. Appleton and Co., 1854–56), 2:680.

10. Wheelan, *Invading Mexico,* 92–98; Clary, *Eagles and Empire,* 99–102; Bauer, *Taylor,* 149; Pres. James K. Polk, Message of May 11, 1846, in James D. Richardson, *A Compilation of the Messages and Papers of the Presidents: 1789–1908*

(published by the Bureau of National Literature and Art, 1908), 4:442 (cited hereafter as Richardson, *Messages and Papers*).

11. James K. Polk, *Polk: The Diary of a President, 1845 to 1849,* ed. Allan Nevins (New York: Longmans, Green and Co., 1952), entries dated May 13, 1846, May 30, 1846, pp. 90–92, 106–108.

12. Polk, *Diary,* entries dated May 13–14, 1846, pp. 90, 93–94.

13. Scott is the subject of three recent biographies. Allan Peskin's *Winfield Scott and the Profession of Arms* and Timothy D. Johnson's *Winfield Scott: The Quest for Military Glory* (Lawrence: University Press of Kansas, 1998) have different strengths and are both far superior to John S. D. Eisenhower's *Agent of Destiny: The Life and Times of General Winfield Scott* (New York: Free Press, 1997).

14. Martin Dugard, *The Training Ground: Grant, Lee, Sherman, and Davis in the Mexican War, 1846–1848* (New York: Little, Brown, 2008), 192; Pres. James K. Polk, First Annual Message, December 2, 1845, in Richardson, *Messages and Papers,* 4:413.

15. Polk, *Diary,* entry dated May 19 and 22, 1846, p. 100; Winfield Scott to R. P. Letchner, Washington, June 5, 1846, in *The Life of John Jay Crittenden: With Selections from His Correspondence and Speeches,* ed. Mrs. Chapman Coleman (Philadelphia: J. P. Lippincott and Co., 1873), 1:245; K. Jack Bauer, *The Mexican War, 1846–1848* (New York: Macmillan, 1974), 74–75; Peskin, *Winfield Scott,* 138–139; Clary, *Eagles and Empire,* 147–149.

16. Polk, *Diary,* entries dated May 14 and 19, 1846, pp. 93–94, 96–97.

17. Peskin, *Winfield Scott,* 139–140; Clary, *Eagles and Empire,* 129; Polk, *Diary,* entry dated May 21, 1846, pp. 99–100. Polk appointed thirteen volunteer generals during the war. All were loyal Democrats. Richard Bruce Winders, *Mr. Polk's Army: The American Military Experience in the Mexican War* (College Station: Texas A&M University Press, 1997), 32–49.

18. Winfield Scott to William L. Marcy, Headquarters of the Army, Washington, May 21, 1846, in *The New American State Papers: Military Affairs,* vol. 6, *Combat Operations,* ed. Benjamin F. Cooling (Wilmington, DE: Scholarly Resources Inc., 1979), 57–61.

19. Polk, *Diary,* entries dated May 23 and 25, 1846, pp. 100–104.

20. Winfield Scott to William L. Marcy, Headquarters of the Army, Washington, May 25, 1846, in *New American State Papers,* 6:75–77; Clary, *Eagles and Empire,* 148; Peskin, *Winfield Scott,* 141; Otis A. Singletary, *The Mexican War* (Chicago: University of Chicago Press, 1960), 119.

21. Bauer, *Taylor,* 171; William L. Marcy to Zachary Taylor, Washington, June 8, 1846, in *Messages of the President of the United States with the Correspondence, Therewith Communicated, between the Secretary of War and Other Officers of the Government on the Subject of the Mexican War* (Washington, DC: Wendell and Van Benthuysen, Printers, 1848), 324–325 (hereafter cited as *Mexican War Correspondence*); William L. Marcy to Zachary Taylor, Washington, July 9, 1846, in *Mexican War Correspondence,* 333–336.

22. Zachary Taylor to the Adjutant General, Matamoras, July 2, 1846; Zachary Taylor to James K. Polk, Matamoras, August 1, 1846, both in *Mexican War Correspondence,* 329–332, 336–339; Polk, *Diary,* entry dated September 5, 1846, pp. 143–145.

23. Borneman, *Polk*, 242–247; Clary, *Eagles and Empire*, 211.

24. Borneman, *Polk*, 246–247; Bauer, *Taylor*, 186–190.

25. Borneman, *Polk*, 246–249; Bauer, *Taylor*, 186–190; Polk, *Diary*, entry dated November 21, 1846, p. 174.

26. Peskin, *Winfield Scott*, 141–144; Robert W. Merry, *A Country of Vast Designs: James K. Polk, the Mexican War, and the Conquest of the American Continent* (New York: Simon & Schuster, 2009), 307; Polk, *Diary*, 170–171; Scott, *Memoirs*, 1:397–399.

27. Clary, *Eagles and Empire*, 148–149, 212, 214, 253; Polk, *Diary*, entries dated November 17 and November 18 and December 14, 19, 21, 24, 25, and 28, 1847, and January 23, 1848, pp. 169, 170, 171–172n, 175–176, 178–179, 190–191; Scott, *Memoirs*, 2:401, 402; Johnson, *Winfield Scott*, 161, 163.

28. Singletary, *Mexican War*, 112–113.

29. Winfield Scott to Zachary Taylor, New York, November 25, 1846, in *Mexican War Correspondence*, 373–374.

30. Bauer, *Taylor*, 192–214; Peskin, *Winfield Scott*, 146; Singletary, *Mexican War*, 113–116; Merry, *A Country of Vast Designs*, 352–354.

31. Peskin, *Winfield Scott*, 142–160; Clary, *Eagles and Empire*, 287–304.

32. Johnson, *Winfield Scott*, 157–158, 166–207.

33. Clary, *Eagles and Empire*, 307; Merry, *A Country of Vast Designs*, 360–361.

34. Johnson, *Winfield Scott*, 188–189; Merry, *A Country of Vast Designs*, 358, 361, 366–371; Clary, *Eagles and Empire*, 326; Winfield Scott to Nicholas P. Trist, Head-Quarters of the Army, Jalapa, May 7, 1847; Nicholas P. Trist to Winfield Scott, Bivouac at San Juan del Rio, May 9, 1847; Nicholas P. Trist to Winfield Scott, Jalapa, May 20, 1847, all in *Mexican War Correspondence*, 814–825.

35. Clary, *Eagles and Empire*, 327; Johnson, *Winfield Scott*, 195; Merry, *A Country of Vast Designs*, 371; Singletary, *Mexican War*, 123.

36. Merry, *A Country of Vast Designs*, 371–374; Johnson, *Winfield Scott*, 195–196.

37. Peskin, *Winfield Scott*, 183–184; Johnson, *Winfield Scott*, 201–202; Merry, *A Country of Vast Designs*, 384–386.

38. Johnson, *Winfield Scott*, 209; Merry, *A Country of Vast Designs*, 384–386; Clary, *Eagles and Empire*, 384–385, 399–401, 404, 406; Peskin, *Winfield Scott*, 195–197.

39. Clary, *Eagles and Empire*, 327, 406; Polk, *Diary*, entry dated January 3, 1848, p. 293.

40. Johnson, *Winfield Scott*, 210–211; Clary, *Eagles and Empire*, 191, 406; Peskin, *Winfield Scott*, 174, 197–198; Merry, *A Country of Vast Designs*, 363, 390–391.

41. Clary, *Eagles and Empire*, 406–408; Johnson, *Winfield Scott*, 211; Peskin, *Winfield Scott*, 174, 199; Merry, *A Country of Vast Designs*, 389–390, 407–409; Polk, *Diary*, entries dated December 30 and 31, 1847, January 1, 2, 3, 5, and 9, 1848, pp. 287–295; *The Diary of James K. Polk during His Presidency, 1845–1849*, ed. Milo M. Quaife (Chicago: A. C. McClurg & Co., 1910), entry dated July 13, 1848, 4:16–17.

42. Johnson, *Winfield Scott*, 210–211; George B. McClellan to John H. B. Mc-Clellan, Mexico City, February 22, 1848, in *The Mexican War Diary and Correspondence of George B. McClellan*, ed. Thomas W Cutrer (Baton Rouge: Louisiana State University Press, 2009), 141; Peskin, *Winfield Scott*, 199–203; Clary, *Eagles and Empire*, 191, 408; Merry, *A Country of Vast Designs*, 389, 399.

43. Clary, *Eagles and Empire*, 305; Bauer, *Taylor*, 314–327.

44. Peskin, *Winfield Scott*, 181, 191; Clary, *Eagles and Empire*, 416.

45. Winders, *Mr. Polk's Army*, 14.

46. Merry, *A Country of Vast Designs*, 401; Polk, *Diary*, 198.

47. Merry, *A Country of Vast Designs*, 411; Winders, *Mr. Polk's Army*, 14; Grant, *Memoirs*, 22–24.

5. LINCOLN'S LETTER TO HOOKER

1. Abraham Lincoln to Maj. Gen. Joseph Hooker, January 26, 1863, in *The War of the Rebellion: A Compilation of the Official Records of the Union and Confederate Armies*, 70 vols. in 128 parts (Washington, DC: Government Printing Office, 1880–1901), series 1, vol. 25, pt. 2, p. 4. (hereafter cited as, e.g., *OR*, I, 25, ii: 4.)

2. John M. Hay and John G. Nicolay, *Abraham Lincoln: A History*, 10 vols. (New York: Century Co., 1890), 6:175; Francis Fisher Browne, *The Every-Day Life of Abraham Lincoln* (New York: G. P. Putnam's Sons, the Knickerbocker Press, 1913), 417–418.

3. James M. McPherson, *Tried by War: Abraham Lincoln as Commander in Chief* (New York: Penguin Press, 2008), 10–19; Doris Kearns Goodwin, *Team of Rivals: The Political Genius of Abraham Lincoln* (New York: Simon & Schuster, 2005), 341–342.

4. McPherson, *Tried by War*, 17–18.

5. Ibid., 19.

6. Ibid., 21–23.

7. Ibid., 34–41.

8. The definitive McClellan biography is Stephen W. Sears, *George B. McClellan: The Young Napoleon* (New York: Ticknor & Fields, 1988). See pp. 1–49. For a revisionist view see Ethan S. Rafuse, *McClellan's War: The Failure of Moderation in the Struggle for the Union* (Bloomington: Indiana University Press, 2005). See also Matthew Moten, *The Delafield Commission and the American Military Profession* (College Station: Texas A&M University Press, 2000), 100–211.

9. Sears, *Young Napoleon*, 50–70.

10. George B. McClellan to Mary Ellen McClellan, Washington, July 27, 1861, July 30, 1861, and August 10, 1861, in George B. McClellan, *The Civil War Papers of George B. McClellan: Selected Correspondence, 1860–1865*, ed. Stephen W. Sears (New York: Ticknor & Fields, 1989), 70, 71, 81–82 (hereinafter cited as *McClellan Papers*).

11. George B. McClellan to Winfield Scott, Head Qtrs Dept of the Ohio, Beverly, Virginia, July 18, 1861; George B. McClellan to Mary Ellen McClellan, Washington, August 2, 1861, both in *Civil War Papers*, 60, 75.

12. George B. McClellan to Mary Ellen McClellan, Washington, August 8, 1861, in *McClellan Papers*, 81.

13. George McClellan to Abraham Lincoln, Memorandum for the Consideration of His Excellency the President, submitted at his request, Washington, August 2, 1861, in *McClellan Papers*, 71–75.

14. Joseph T. Glatthaar, *Partners in Command: The Relationships between Leaders in the Civil War* (New York: Free Press, 1994), 59–60; McPherson, *Tried by War*, 46; George McClellan to Winfield Scott, Head Quarters, Division of the Potomac, Washington, August 8, 1861, in *McClellan Papers*, 79–81.

15. Winfield Scott to Simon Cameron, Headquarters of the Army, Washington, August 8, 1861, *OR*, I, 11, iii: 4.

16. George McClellan to Abraham Lincoln, Washington, August 10, 1861; Winfield Scott to Simon Cameron, Headquarters of the Army, Washington, August 12, 1861, both *OR*, I, 11, iii: 4–6; George B. McClellan to Mary Ellen McClellan, Washington, August 15 and 16, 1861, in *McClellan Papers*, 84–86; McPherson, *Tried by War*, 46–47.

17. George B. McClellan to Mary Ellen McClellan, Washington, August 16, 1861, and August 19, 1861; George McClellan to Simon Cameron, Washington, September 13, 1861, all in *McClellan Papers*, 85, 87, 100; Glatthaar, *Partners in Command*, 61; McPherson, *Tried by War*, 47, 49.

18. George B. McClellan to Mary Ellen McClellan, Washington, October 11, 1861, and August 19, 1861, both in *McClellan Papers*, 106–107; Glatthaar, *Partners in Command*, 61; McPherson, *Tried by War*, 48.

19. George B. McClellan to Mary Ellen McClellan, Lewinsville, October 19, 1861, George B. McClellan to Mary Ellen McClellan, Washington, October 26, 1861, both in *McClellan Papers*, 106–107; McPherson, *Tried by War*, 50.

20. McPherson, *Tried by War*, 50–51.

21. George McClellan to Simon Cameron, Washington, October 31, 1861, in *McClellan Papers*, 114–119.

22. Sears, *Young Napoleon*, 132–133; McPherson, *Tried by War*, 52–53; Glatthaar, *Partners in Command*, 63–64.

23. George B. McClellan to Mary Ellen McClellan, Washington, November 17, 1861, in *McClellan Papers*, 135; Glatthaar, *Partners in Command*, 64–65; McPherson, *Tried by War*, 2–4, 53; Goodwin, *Team of Rivals*, 152–153.

24. Abraham Lincoln, "Memorandum to George B. McClellan on Potomac Campaign," c. December 1, 1861, in *The Collected Works of Abraham Lincoln*, 9 vols., ed. Roy P. Basler (New Brunswick, NJ: Rutgers University Press, 1953–1955), 5:34–35 (hereafter cited as *Collected Works*); George McClellan to Abraham Lincoln, Washington, December 10, 1861, in *McClellan Papers*, 143, McPherson, *Tried by War*, 53–54.

25. Bruce Tap, *Over Lincoln's Shoulder: The Committee on the Conduct of the War* (Lawrence: University Press of Kansas, 1998), 103–107.

26. "General M. C. Meigs on the Conduct of the Civil War," *American Historical Review* 26, no. 2 (January 1921): 292; Irvin McDowell's notes of the meetings, in William Swinton, *Campaigns of the Army of the Potomac* (New York: Charles B. Richardson, 1886), 79–80.

27. "General M. C. Meigs," 292–293; McDowell's notes, in Swinton, *Campaigns*, 80–85; Sears, *Young Napoleon*, 140–141.

28. Sears, *Young Napoleon*, 142–143.

29. Abraham Lincoln to Simon Cameron, Executive Mansion, Washington, January 11, 1862; Edwin M. Stanton to Charles A. Dana, Washington, January 24, 1862, both in Charles A. Dana, *Recollections of the Civil War: With the Leaders at Washington and in the Field in the Sixties* (New York: D. Appleton & Co., 1899), 4–5; Abraham Lincoln, "President's General War Order No. 1," Executive Mansion, Washington, January 27, 1862; Abraham Lincoln, "President's Special War Order No. 1," Executive Mansion, Washington, January 31, 1862, both in *Collected Works,* 5:96–97, 111–112, 115; McPherson, *Tried by War,* 67–70; Glatthaar, *Partners in Command,* 68–69.

30. Abraham Lincoln to Don C. Buell, Washington, January 13, 1862, in *Collected Works,* 5:99; Henry W. Halleck to Abraham Lincoln, Headquarters Department of the Missouri, St. Louis, January 6, 1862 (endorsed by Lincoln, January 10, 1862), *OR,* I, 7, 532–533.

31. Henry W. Halleck to Abraham Lincoln, Headquarters Department of the Missouri, St. Louis, January 6, 1862 (endorsed by Lincoln, January 10, 1862), *OR,* I, 7, 532–533; McPherson, *Tried by War,* 69–73.

32. Abraham Lincoln to George B. McClellan, Executive Mansion, Washington, February 3, 1861, in *Collected Works,* 5:118–119.

33. George B. McClellan to Edwin M. Stanton, Headquarters of the Army, Washington, January 31 [February 3], 1862, *McClellan Papers,* 162–171.

34. Tap, *Over Lincoln's Shoulder,* 112–113.

35. President's General War Order No. 2, Executive Mansion, Washington, March 8, 1862; President's General War Order No. 3, Executive Mansion, Washington, March 8, 1862; President's War Order No. 3, Executive Mansion, Washington, March 11, 1862; Edwin M. Stanton to George B. McClellan, War Department, March 13, 1862, all in *OR,* I, 5, pp. 18, 50, 54, 56; McPherson, *Tried by War,* 78–80; Glatthaar, *Partners in Command,* 71.

36. George B. McClellan to Mary Ellen McClellan, near Yorktown, April 6, 1862, in *McClellan Papers,* 230.

37. Abraham Lincoln to George B. McClellan, Washington, April 9, 1862, *Collected Works,* 5:184–185.

38. Joseph E. Johnston to Robert E. Lee, Lee's Farm, Virginia, April 22, 1862, *OR,* I, 11, iii: 455–456.

39. George B. McClellan to Abraham Lincoln, Headquarters Army of the Potomac, Camp near New Bridge, May 26, 1862; George B. McClellan to Edwin M. Stanton, Headquarters Army of the Potomac, New Bridge, June 2, 7, 10, 1862; George B. McClellan to Edwin M. Stanton, Headquarters Army of the Potomac, Camp Lincoln, June 14, 15, 1862; George B. McClellan to Abraham Lincoln, Headquarters Army of the Potomac, Camp Lincoln, June 18, 20, 1862; George B. McClellan to Edwin M. Stanton, Headquarters Army of the Potomac, Camp Lincoln, June 25, 1862; George B. McClellan to Edwin M. Stanton, Headquarters Army of the Potomac, Savage Station, June 28, 1862, all in *McClellan Papers,* 277, 285–286, 291–292, 295–296, 299, 300, 302–303, 304, 309–310, 322–323.

40. Glatthaar, *Partners in Command,* 79–80.

41. George B. McClellan to Abraham Lincoln, Headquarters Army of the Potomac, Harrison's Bar, James River, July 4, 1862; George B. McClellan to Abraham Lincoln, Headquarters Army of the Potomac, Camp near Harrison's Landing, July 7, 1862, in *McClellan Papers,* 336–338, 344–345; Tap, *Over Lincoln's Shoulder,* 122–124; Glatthaar, *Partners in Command,* 80–82; Goodwin, *Team of Rivals,* 451.

42. Abraham Lincoln, Order Making Henry W. Halleck General-in-Chief, Executive Mansion, Washington, July 11, 1862, *Collected Works,* 5:312–313; Glatthaar, *Partners in Command,* 82–83.

43. McPherson, *Tried by War,* 114, 117–122; Glatthaar, *Partners in Command,* 83–84; Goodwin, *Team of Rivals,* 474–479.

44. Glatthaar, *Partners in Command,* 85–86; Abraham Lincoln to George B. McClellan, War Department, Washington, September 15, 1862, OR, I, 19, i: 53; Sears, *Young Napoleon,* 248–323; McPherson, *Tried by War,* 123–126.

45. George B. McClellan to Mary Ellen McClellan, Camp near Sharpsburg, September 18, 20, 1862, in *McClellan Papers,* 469, 473; McPherson, *Tried by War,* 126–132.

46. George B. McClellan to Samuel L. M. Barlow, Washington, November 8, 1861; George B. McClellan to William H. Aspinwall, Head-Quarters Army of the Potomac, Sharpsburg, September 26, 1862; George B. McClellan to Mary Ellen McClellan, Sharpsburg, September 25, 1862; George B. McClellan to Abraham Lincoln, Head-Quarters Army of the Potomac, Sharpsburg, October 7, 1862, all in *McClellan Papers,* 128, 481, 493–494.

47. Henry W. Halleck to George B. McClellan, Washington, October 6, 1862; Abraham Lincoln to George B. McClellan, Executive Mansion, Washington, October 13, 1862, both OR, I, 19, i: 10, 13–14; Baron Antoine Henri de Jomini, *The Art of War,* with an introduction by Charles Messinger (London: Greenhill Books, 1992), 70.

48. George B. McClellan to Henry W. Halleck, Headquarters Army of the Potomac, October 25, 1862, OR, I, 19, ii: 484–485; Montgomery C. Meigs to Edwin M. Stanton, Quartermaster-General's Office, Washington, October 25, 1862, OR, I, 19, i: 21–22; McPherson, *Tried by War,* 139–140.

49. Abraham Lincoln to George B. McClellan, War Department, Washington, October 24 [25], 1862, OR, I, 19, ii: 485.

50. McPherson, *Tried by War,* 140–141.

51. Ibid., 141.

52. T. Harry Williams, *Lincoln and His Generals* (New York: Vintage Books, 1952), 232.

6. LINCOLN AND GRANT

1. Ulysses S. Grant, *Personal Memoirs of U. S. Grant,* ed. E. B. Long, introduction William S. McFeely (New York: Da Capo, 1982), 127.

2. Abraham Lincoln to Ulysses S. Grant, Executive Mansion, Washington, July 13, 1863, in *The Collected Works of Abraham Lincoln,* 9 vols., ed. Roy P. Basler (New Brunswick, NJ: Rutgers University Press, 1953–1955), 6:326 (hereafter cited

as *Collected Works*); James M. McPherson, *Tried by War: Abraham Lincoln as Commander in Chief* (New York: Penguin Press, 2008), 186.

3. Joseph T. Glatthaar, *Partners in Command: The Relationships between Leaders in the Civil War* (New York: Free Press, 1994), 191–194; Brooks D. Simpson, *Ulysses S. Grant: Triumph over Adversity, 1822–1865* (Boston: Houghton Mifflin, 2000), 119–187.

4. Ulysses S. Grant to Elihu B. Washburne, Savanna, Tennessee, March 22, 1862, in Ulysses S. Grant, *Memoirs and Selected Letters: Personal Memoirs of U. S. Grant and Selected Letters, 1839–1865* (New York: Library of America, 1990), 990; Glatthaar, *Partners in Command*, 195–199; McPherson, *Tried by War*, 202; Simpson, *Triumph over Adversity*, 210–211.

5. Ulysses S. Grant to Henry W. Halleck, Headquarters Military Division of the Mississippi, Chattanooga, December 7, 1863, in *The War of the Rebellion: A Compilation of the Official Records of the Union and Confederate Armies*, 70 vols. in 128 parts (Washington, DC: Government Printing Office, 1880–1901), series 1, vol. 31, pt. 2, pp. 349–350 (hereafter cited as, e.g., *OR*, I, 31, ii: 349–350); Charles A. Dana to Ulysses S. Grant, Washington, December 21, 1863, *OR*, I, 31, iii: 457–458; Abraham Lincoln to Ulysses S. Grant, Executive Mansion, Washington, August 9, 1863, *OR*, I, 24, iii: 584; Henry W. Halleck to Ulysses S. Grant, Headquarters of the Army, Washington, January 8, 1863, *OR*, I, 32, ii: 40–42.

6. Matthew Moten, *The Delafield Commission and the American Military Profession* (College Station: Texas A&M University Press, 2000), 31–38, 54–72.

7. Ulysses S. Grant to Henry W. Halleck, Headquarters Military Division of the Mississippi, Nashville, January 19, 1864, *OR*, 1, 33: 394–395; Henry W. Halleck to Ulysses S. Grant, Washington, February 17, 1864, *OR*, I, 32, ii: 411–413; Glatthaar, *Partners in Command*, 201–205; Moten, *Delafield Commission*, 51.

8. Glatthaar, *Partners in Command*, 203–204; Michael Burlingame and John R. Turner Ettlinger, eds., *Inside Lincoln's White House: The Complete Civil War Diary of John Hay* (Carbondale: Southern Illinois University Press, 1997), 191–192, entry dated April 28, 1864.

9. McPherson, *Tried by War*, 211–212, Glatthaar, *Partners in Command*, 205–206, Simpson, *Triumph over Adversity*, 257–258.

10. Ulysses S. Grant to William T. Sherman, Headquarters Armies of the United States, Washington, April 4, 1864, *OR*, I, 32, iii: 245–246; Ulysses S. Grant to George G. Meade, Culpeper Court House, April 9, 1864, *OR*, I, 33, 827–829.

11. Ulysses S. Grant to William T. Sherman, Headquarters Armies of the United States, Washington, April 4, 1864, *OR*, I, 32, iii: 245–246.

12. Grant, *Personal Memoirs*, 362; William O. Stoddard, *Abraham Lincoln: The Man and the War President* (New York: Fords, Howard, & Hulbert, 1888), 425; McPherson, *Tried by War*, 214; Ulysses S. Grant to William T. Sherman, Headquarters Armies of the United States, Washington, April 4, 1864, *OR*, I, 32, iii: 245–246.

13. Stoddard, *Abraham Lincoln*, 424–425.

14. Abraham Lincoln to Ulysses S. Grant, Executive Mansion, Washington, April 30, 1864; Ulysses S. Grant to Abraham Lincoln, May 1, 1864; *Collected Works*, 7:324–325.

15. Ulysses S. Grant to Henry W. Halleck, Headquarters Armies of the United States, near Spotsylvania Court-House, May 11, 1864, *OR*, I, 36, ii: 627; McPherson, *Tried by War*, 219.

16. Simpson, *Triumph over Adversity*, 281–287; Glatthaar, *Partners in Command*, 210–212; McPherson, *Tried by War*, 216–225, 231–242.

17. McPherson, *Tried by War*, 216–217.

18. Ibid., 222–224.

19. Ulysses S. Grant to Henry W. Halleck, City Point, July 9, 1864; Abraham Lincoln to Ulysses S. Grant, Washington, July 10, 1864; Ulysses S. Grant to Abraham Lincoln, City Point, July 10, 1864; Abraham Lincoln to Ulysses S. Grant, Washington, July 11, 1864; Ulysses S. Grant to Henry W. Halleck, City Point, July 18, 1864; Henry W. Halleck to Ulysses S. Grant, Washington, July 19, 1864; Abraham Lincoln to Ulysses S. Grant, Washington, July 20, 1864; Henry W. Halleck to Ulysses S. Grant, Washington, July 21, 1864; Ulysses S. Grant to Henry W. Halleck, City Point, July 22, 1864; Henry W. Halleck to Ulysses S. Grant, Washington, July 23, 1864; Ulysses S. Grant to Henry W. Halleck, City Point, July 24, 1864; Ulysses S. Grant to Abraham Lincoln, City Point, July 25, 1864; Edwin M. Stanton to Ulysses S. Grant, Washington, July 26, 1864; Ulysses S. Grant to Edwin M. Stanton, City Point, July 26, 1864; Ulysses S. Grant to Henry W. Halleck, City Point, July 26, 1864; Edwin M. Stanton to Henry W. Halleck, Washington, July 27, 1864; Abraham Lincoln to Ulysses S. Grant, Washington, July 28, 1864, all in *OR*, I, 37, ii: 134, 155–156, 191, 374, 408, 413–414, 422, 426, 433–434, 444–445, 463, 492; Joseph T. Glatthaar, "U. S. Grant and the Union High Command during the 1864 Valley Campaign," in *The Shenandoah Valley Campaign of 1864*, ed. Gary W. Gallagher (Chapel Hill: University of North Carolina Press, 2006), 38–49.

20. Ulysses S. Grant to Henry W. Halleck, City Point, July 30, 1864, August 1, 1864, and August 2, 1864; Abraham Lincoln to Ulysses S. Grant, Washington, August 3, 1864; Ulysses S. Grant to Philip H. Sheridan, Washington, August 7, 1864, all *OR*, I, 37, ii: 558, 582; *OR*, I, 40, i: 17–18; and *OR*, I, 43, i: 719; Glatthaar, "Grant and the Union High Command," 49–52.

21. Henry W. Halleck to Ulysses S. Grant, Washington, August 11, 1864; Ulysses S. Grant to Henry W. Halleck, City Point, August 15, 1864; Abraham Lincoln to Ulysses S. Grant, Washington, August 17, 1864, all *OR*, I, 42, ii: 111–112, 193–194, 243.

22. William T. Sherman to Ulysses S. Grant, Atlanta, October 1, 1864; Henry W. Halleck to Ulysses S. Grant, Washington, October 2, 1864; Ulysses S. Grant to William T. Sherman, City Point, October 11, 1864; William T. Sherman to Ulysses Grant, Atlanta, October 11, 1864; Ulysses S. Grant to William T. Sherman, City Point, October 11, 1864; Edwin M. Stanton to Ulysses S. Grant, Washington, October 12, 1864; Ulysses S. Grant to William T. Sherman, City Point, October 12, 1864; Ulysses S. Grant to Edwin M. Stanton, City Point, October 13, 1864; Abraham Lincoln to William T. Sherman, Executive Mansion, Washington, December 26, 1864; all *OR*, I, 39, iii: 3, 25–26, 202, 222, 239, and *OR*, I, 44, 809.

23. Ulysses S. Grant to Edwin M. Stanton, City Point, March 3, 1865; Edwin M. Stanton to Ulysses S. Grant, Washington, March 3, 1865,; *OR*, I, 46, ii: 802–803.

24. Ulysses S. Grant to Abraham Lincoln, City Point, March 20, 1865; Abraham Lincoln to Ulysses S. Grant, Washington, March 2, 1865; Abraham Lincoln to Edwin M. Stanton, City Point, March 30, 1865; Edwin M. Stanton to Abraham Lincoln, War Department, Washington, March 31, 1865; Philip H. Sheridan to Ulysses S. Grant, Cavalry Headquarters, April 6, 1865, all *OR*, I, 46, iii: 50, 280, 332, 610; Abraham Lincoln to Ulysses S. Grant, City Point, April 7, 1865, *Collected Works*, 8:392; Glatthaar, *Partners in Command*, 221–223.

25. Carl von Clausewitz, *On War*, ed. and trans. Michael Howard and Peter Paret, introductory essays by Peter Paret, Michael Howard, and Bernard Brodie, commentary by Bernard Brodie (Princeton, NJ: Princeton University Press, 1976), 101–104.

26. Ibid., 105–112.

7. THE PERSHING PARADOX

1. Allan R. Millett, Peter Maslowski, and William B. Feis, *For the Common Defense: A Military History of the United States from 1607 to 2012*, 3rd ed. (New York: Free Press, 2012), 286–287.

2. Ibid., 292; Clayton E. Kahan, "Dodge Commission or Political Dodge? The Dodge Commission and Military Reform" (unpublished MA thesis, University of Houston, July 2003), concludes that the commission was a political whitewash that had no impact on the reforms that followed.

3. Elihu Root, "Extract from the Report of the Secretary of War for 1899," in *The Military and Colonial Policy of the United States*, ed. Robert Bacon and James B. Scott (Cambridge, MA: Harvard University Press, 1916), 350–359, 429.

4. Millett, Maslowski, and Feis, *Common Defense*, 282–285; Julian E. Zelizer, *Arsenal of Democracy: The Politics of National Security—from World War II to the War on Terrorism* (New York: Basic Books, 2010), 18.

5. Mark A. Stoler, *Allies and Adversaries: The Joint Chiefs of Staff, the Grand Alliance, and U.S. Strategy in World War II* (Chapel Hill: University of North Carolina Press, 2000), 1–2.

6. Ibid., 1–2.

7. Carl von Clausewitz, *On War*, ed. and trans. Michael Howard and Peter Paret, introductory essays by Peter Paret, Michael Howard, and Bernard Brodie, commentary by Bernard Brodie (Princeton, NJ: Princeton University Press, 1976), 87; Stoler, *Allies and Adversaries*, 1.

8. John Milton Cooper Jr., *Woodrow Wilson: A Biography* (New York: Alfred A. Knopf, 2009), 267–268, 247–248, 275–278, 297–298, 362–371, 370–374; George C. Herring, *From Colony to Superpower: U.S. Foreign Relations since 1776* (Oxford: Oxford University Press, 2008), 378–410; Frank E. Vandiver, *Black Jack: The Life and Times of John J. Pershing*, vol. 2 (College Station: Texas A&M University Press, 1977), 724.

9. Daniel R. Beaver, *Newton D. Baker and the American War Effort, 1917–1919* (Lincoln: University of Nebraska Press, 1966), 1, 8.

10. Donald Smythe, *Pershing: General of the Armies,* introduction by Spencer C. Tucker (Bloomington: University of Indiana Press, 2007; originally published 1986), 1–3.

11. Ibid.

12. Frederick Palmer, *Newton D. Baker: America at War,* vol. 1 (New York: Dodd, Mead & Co., 1931), 180.

13. Smythe, *Pershing,* 1–12; Vandiver, *Black Jack,* 2:675–696; Cooper, *Woodrow Wilson,* 401–402.

14. Millett, Maslowski, and Feis, *Common Defense,* 312; Smythe, *Pershing,* 35.

15. Millett, Maslowski, and Feis, *Common Defense,* 325.

16. Beaver, *Newton D. Baker,* 120–121; Smythe, *Pershing,* 70–72.

17. Beaver, *Newton D. Baker,* 120–128, Smythe, *Pershing,* 70–80.

18. Smythe, *Pershing,* 96–98, 105; Beaver, *Newton D. Baker,* 137–139.

19. Smythe, *Pershing,* 100–101; Beaver, *Newton D. Baker,* 129–133.

20. Smythe, *Pershing,* 102–104, 113–119; Beaver, *Newton D. Baker,* 134–147.

21. Smythe, *Pershing,* 133–137; Beaver, *Newton D. Baker,* 147–149.

22. Beaver, *Newton D. Baker,* 149–150.

23. Smythe, *Pershing,* 170.

24. Beaver, *Newton D. Baker,* 112–115; Smythe, *Pershing,* 77–78.

25. Cooper, *Woodrow Wilson,* 421–424, 428, 441–443. Wilson continued to expound on these principles in speeches throughout the year.

26. Cooper, *Woodrow Wilson,* 442–445; Beaver, *Newton D. Baker,* 199.

27. Beaver, *Newton D. Baker,* 188, 200–201.

28. Ibid., 201–203; Smythe, *Pershing,* 219–221.

29. Beaver, *Newton D. Baker,* 204–205; Smythe, *Pershing,* 220–221.

30. Smythe, *Pershing,* 221; Beaver, *Newton D. Baker,* 205.

31. Beaver, *Newton D. Baker,* 206–208: Smythe, *Pershing,* 222.

32. Russell F. Weigley, *History of the United States Army* (New York: Macmillan, 1967), 355–394; Edward M. Coffman, *The Regulars: The American Army, 1898–1941* (Cambridge, MA: The Belknap Press of Harvard University Press, 2004), 213.

33. Edward M. Coffman, "Greatest Unsung American General of the Great War," *MHQ: The Quarterly Journal of Military History,* Summer 2006: 16–21; Brian Neumann, "A Question of Authority: Reassessing the March-Pershing 'Feud' in the First World War," *Journal of Military History* 73, no. 4 (October 2009): 1117–1142.

34. Sir Alexander Morris Carr-Saunders and Paul Alexander Wilson, *The Professions* (Oxford: Clarendon Press, 1933), 3; Stoler, *Allies and Adversaries,* 1–3.

8. ROOSEVELT, MARSHALL, AND HOPKINS

1. Forrest C. Pogue, *George C. Marshall: Education of a General, 1880–1939,* foreword by General Omar N. Bradley (New York: Viking Press, 1963), 322–323; Kenneth S. Davis, *FDR: Into the Storm, 1937–1940; A History* (New York: Random House, 1993), 372–373.

2. George C. Herring, *From Colony to Superpower: U.S. Foreign Relations since 1776* (Oxford: Oxford University Press, 2008), 502–506.

3. Mark A. Stoler, "FDR and the Origins of the National Security Establishment," in *FDR's World: War, Peace, and Legacies,* ed. David B. Woolner, Warren F. Kimball, and David Reynolds (New York: Palgrave Macmillan, 2008), 66; Herring, *Colony to Superpower,* 506–512.

4. Herring, *Colony to Superpower,* 512–516.

5. Robert E. Sherwood, *Roosevelt and Hopkins: An Intimate History* (New York: Harper & Brothers, 1950), 100–101; Thomas Parrish, *Roosevelt and Marshall: Partners in Politics and War* (New York: William Morrow and Co., 1989), 92–94; Doris Kearns Goodwin, *No Ordinary Time: Franklin and Eleanor Roosevelt; The Home Front in World War II* (New York: Simon & Schuster, 1994), 87–89, 212–215.

6. Louis Morton, "Germany First: The Basic Concept of Allied Strategy in World War II," in *Command Decisions,* ed. Kent Roberts Greenfield (Washington, DC: United States Army Center of Military History, 2000), 11–20.

7. Ibid., 20–24.

8. Herring, *Colony to Superpower,* 517.

9. Ibid., 518.

10. Parrish, *Roosevelt and Marshall,* 91–92, 95–100; Sherwood, *Roosevelt and Hopkins,* 101; Pogue, *Education of a General,* 330; Davis, *FDR: Into the Storm,* 380–387.

11. Stoler, "FDR and the Origins," 66; Kent Roberts Greenfield, *American Strategy in World War II: A Reconsideration,* repr. ed. (Malabar, FL: Krieger Publishing, 1982), 76–77.

12. Herring, *Colony to Superpower,* 545; Stoler, "FDR and the Origins," 69–70; Mark A. Stoler, *Allies and Adversaries: The Joint Chiefs of Staff, the Grand Alliance, and U.S. Strategy in World War II* (Chapel Hill: University of North Carolina Press, 2000), 108; George C. Marshall, *Interviews and Reminiscences for Forrest C. Pogue,* 3rd ed., ed. Larry I. Bland (Lexington, VA: George C. Marshall Foundation, 1996), 623; Waldo Heinrichs, "FDR and the Admirals: Strategy and Statecraft," in *FDR and the U.S. Navy,* ed. Edward J. Marolda (New York: St. Martin's Press, 1998), 116–117; Greenfield, *American Strategy,* 77.

13. Stoler, *Allies and Adversaries,* 19–20, 26–28; Marshall, *Reminiscences,* 599.

14. Forrest C. Pogue, *George C. Marshall: Ordeal and Hope, 1939–1942* (New York: Viking Press, 1965), 22; Stoler, "FDR and the Origins," 69–74.

15. Pogue, *Ordeal and Hope,* 22–25.

16. Parrish, *Roosevelt and Marshall,* 126.

17. Pogue, *Ordeal and Hope,* 24–32; Marshall, *Reminiscences,* 433–434.

18. Pogue, *Ordeal and Hope,* 28; Stoler, "FDR and the Origins," 68; Parrish, *Roosevelt and Marshall,* 136–137.

19. Parrish, *Roosevelt and Marshall,* 136; Marshall, *Reminiscences,* 331–332.

20. Pogue, *Ordeal and Hope,* 22–24. In discussion of a tricky appropriations battle, Marshall laughed when he remembered that "some fool came up with the

statement that if they would let me handle it, I could put it right over and, of course, that just infuriated [FDR]." Marshall, *Reminiscences,* 331.

21. Russell F. Weigley, *History of the United States Army* (New York: Macmillan, 1967), 423–424; Pogue, *Ordeal and Hope,* 4, 18.

22. Herring, *Colony to Superpower,* 519–521.

23. Ibid., 520; Pogue, *Ordeal and Hope,* 39; Brian Waddell, *Toward the National Security State: Civil-Military Relations during World War II* (Westport, CT: Praeger Security International, 2008), 68; Davis, *FDR: Into the Storm,* 593–598.

24. Parrish, *Roosevelt and Marshall,* 133–134; Pogue, *Ordeal and Hope,* 30–32; Marshall, *Reminiscences,* 329–331. Marshall: "Recalling that a man has a great advantage, psychologically, when he stands looking down on a fellow, I took advantage, in a sense of the president's condition."

25. Pogue, *Ordeal and Hope,* 53; Parrish, *Roosevelt and Marshall,* 153–155; Herring, *Colony to Superpower,* 522; Marshall, *Reminiscences,* 263–264, 288, 289.

26. Stoler, *Allies and Adversaries,* 25–27; Stoler, "FDR and the Origins," 71.

27. Stoler, *Allies and Adversaries,* 29–37; Waddell, *National Security State,* 73; Pogue, *Ordeal and Hope,* 126.

28. Greenfield, *American Strategy,* 49–84.

29. Herring, *Colony to Superpower,* 523.

30. James MacGregor Burns, *Roosevelt: The Soldier of Freedom; 1940–1945* (New York: Francis Parkman Prize Edition, History Book Club, 2006; originally published in 1970), 24–25.

31. Ibid., 26.

32. Ibid., 27–29.

33. Ibid., 34–35.

34. Stoler, *Allies and Adversaries,* 37–39.

35. Pogue, *Ordeal and Hope,* 69.

36. Parrish, *Roosevelt and Marshall,* 171–173; Pogue, *Ordeal and Hope,* 70–71.

37. Pogue, *Ordeal and Hope,* 71–74.

38. Parrish, *Roosevelt and Marshall,* 173–181; Marshall, *Reminiscences,* 302–303.

39. Parrish, *Roosevelt and Marshall,* 184–194; Burns, *Roosevelt,* 125–131.

40. Pogue, *Ordeal and Hope,* 178–189; Herring, *Colony to Superpower,* 529–535; Parrish, *Roosevelt and Marshall,* 203.

41. Stoler, *Allies and Adversaries,* 47–49.

42. Parrish, *Roosevelt and Marshall,* 203–204; Pogue, *Ordeal and Hope,* 72–79; Marshall, *Reminiscences,* 281–282.

43. Waddell, *National Security State,* 70; Pogue, *Ordeal and Hope,* 207.

44. Winston S. Churchill, *The Second World War,* vol. 3, *The Grand Alliance* (Boston: Houghton Mifflin, 1950), 604–609.

45. Forrest C. Pogue, *George C. Marshall: Organizer of Victory, 1943–1945* (New York: Viking Press, 1973), xi.

46. Burns, *Roosevelt,* 178–179, 185; Goodwin, *No Ordinary Time,* 305–310.

47. Stoler, *Allies and Adversaries,* 67–70.

48. Burns, *Roosevelt,* 179; Parrish, *Roosevelt and Marshall,* 212; Greenfield, *American Strategy,* 78–79. Greenfield also argues that keeping China in the war was a Roosevelt principle.

49. Marshall, *Reminiscences,* 599; Pogue, *Ordeal and Hope,* 263–264, 269–270; Parrish, *Roosevelt and Marshall,* 213–219; Goodwin, *No Ordinary Time,* 311.

50. Stoler, *Allies and Adversaries,* 67.

51. Pogue, *Ordeal and Hope,* 275–281; Burns, *Roosevelt,* 201; Parrish, *Roosevelt and Marshall,* 221–225; Marshall, *Reminiscences,* 357–358, 594–595, 600–601; Sherwood, *Roosevelt and Hopkins,* 456–457, 607.

52. Pogue, *Ordeal and Hope,* 282–284; Parrish, *Roosevelt and Marshall,* 226–229.

53. Pogue, *Ordeal and Hope,* 286–287; Sherwood, *Roosevelt and Hopkins,* 470–472.

54. Pogue, *Ordeal and Hope,* 288; Marshall, *Reminiscences,* 593.

55. Pogue, *Ordeal and Hope,* 212, 289–301; Parrish, *Roosevelt and Marshall,* 245–248; Waddell, *National Security State,* 43–45, 76; Stoler, *Allies and Adversaries,* 64–67.

56. Eric Larrabee, *Commander in Chief: Franklin Delano Roosevelt, His Lieutenants, and Their War* (New York: Harper & Row, 1987), 153–157; Stoler, *Allies and Adversaries,* 69; Parrish, *Roosevelt and Marshall,* 248–249; Marshall, *Reminiscences,* 434–435, 593, 599.

57. Marshall, *Reminiscences,* 430–432, 623; Parrish, *Roosevelt and Marshall,* 249–252.

58. Pogue, *Ordeal and Hope,* 304–306; Marshall, *Reminiscences,* 599.

59. Pogue, *Ordeal and Hope,* 302–320; Parrish, *Roosevelt and Marshall,* 266–276; Sherwood, *Roosevelt and Hopkins,* 523–543.

60. Parrish, *Roosevelt and Marshall,* 276–279; Pogue, *Ordeal and Hope,* 326–327; Stoler, *Allies and Adversaries,* 70.

61. Pogue, *Ordeal and Hope,* 326–327.

62. Ibid., 327–329.

63. Marshall, *Reminiscences,* 590. Marshall continued: "It was difficult because the Navy was pulling everything toward the Pacific, and that's where the Marines were, and they got a lot of publicity. The president's tendency to shift and handle things loosely and be influenced, particularly by the British, was one of our great problems." Parrish, *Roosevelt and Marshall,* 285–286.

64. Pogue, *Ordeal and Hope,* 332–333; Parrish, *Roosevelt and Marshall,* 286–287.

65. Stoler, *Allies and Adversaries,* 70.

66. Henry L. Stimson and McGeorge Bundy, *On Active Service in Peace and War* (New York: Harper and Bros., 1948), 424; Parrish, *Roosevelt and Marshall,* 289; Stoler, *Allies and Adversaries,* 79–85; Pogue, *Ordeal and Hope,* 340–341.

67. Stoler, *Allies and Adversaries,* 79, 84.

68. Larrabee, *Commander in Chief,* 136.

69. Pogue, *Ordeal and Hope,* 341–343.

70. Pogue, *Ordeal and Hope,* 343–347; Stoler, *Allies and Adversaries,* 89–90.

71. Marshall, *Reminiscences, 599*, 622; Stoler, "FDR and the Origins, 75; Davis, *FDR: Into the Storm*, 13.

72. Stoler, *Allies and Adversaries*, 89–97. These deliberations went forward within the context of a real concern for a potentially imminent Soviet collapse on the eastern front, which would have caused a complete reevaluation of Allied strategy. Of course, that collapse never occurred.

73. Stoler, *Allies and Adversaries*, 97–100.

74. Ibid., 103; Waddell, *National Security State*, 83–84; Parrish, *Roosevelt and Marshall*, 322–326.

75. Stoler, *Allies and Adversaries*, 103–107, 119–121; Waddell, *National Security State*, 84.

76. Stoler, *Allies and Adversaries*, 160–164.

77. Parrish, *Roosevelt and Marshall*, 365.

78. Sherwood, *Roosevelt and Hopkins*, 802–803; Marshall, *Reminiscences*, 343–344; Parrish, *Roosevelt and Marshall*, 363–369, 381–384, 415–417.

79. Sherwood, *Roosevelt and Hopkins*, 100–101.

80. Marshall, *Reminiscences*, 414–415; Stoler, "FDR and the Origins," 68.

81. Greenfield, *American Strategy*, 76–77.

82. Waddell, *National Security State*, 87–89.

9. EXIT MACARTHUR

1. D. Clayton James, *The Years of MacArthur*, vol. 3, *Triumph and Disaster, 1945–1964* (Boston: Houghton Mifflin, 1985), 612–616; William Manchester, *American Caesar: Douglas MacArthur, 1880–1964* (Boston: Little, Brown, 1978), 657–661.

2. Michael D. Pearlman, *Truman and MacArthur: Policy, Politics, and the Hunger for Honor and Renown* (Bloomington: University of Indiana Press, 2008), 2.

3. Manchester, *American Caesar*, 13–16, 29–38; Pearlman, *Truman and MacArthur*, 3–4.

4. Manchester, *American Caesar*, 149–156.

5. William E. Leuchtenberg, *Franklin D. Roosevelt and the New Deal* (New York: Harper & Row, 1963), 96; Pearlman, *Truman and MacArthur*, 5.

6. D. Clayton James with Anne Sharp Wells, *Refighting the Last War: Command and Crisis in Korea, 1950–1953* (New York: Free Press, 1993), 36–43; Richard H. Rovere and Arthur Schlesinger Jr., *The MacArthur Controversy and American Foreign Policy* (New York: Farrar, Straus and Giroux, 1965), 92.

7. James, *Refighting the Last War*, 40.

8. David McCullough, *Truman* (New York: Simon & Schuster, 1992), 792–794; Pearlman, *Truman and MacArthur*, 17–18; James, *Refighting the Last War*, 16.

9. Pearlman, *Truman and MacArthur*, xviii, 22–23.

10. Ibid., 13.

11. James, *Refighting the Last War*, 23; McCullough, *Truman*, 792.

12. Pearlman, *Truman and MacArthur*, 13; James, *Refighting the Last War*, 23.

13. Manchester, *American Caesar*, 538–542; Rovere and Schlesinger, *MacArthur Controversy*, 123–124; Dean Acheson, *Present at the Creation: My Years in*

the State Department (New York: W. W. Norton, 1969), 354–358; James, *Refighting the Last War*, 134.

14. Manchester, *American Caesar*, 540; Pearlman, *Truman and MacArthur*, 67.

15. James Reston, "As a U.N. General, M'Arthur Faces New Tasks: Besides Running a War, He Must Please Washington, Other Capitals," *New York Times*, July 9, 1950, E3; James, *Years of MacArthur*, 436–438; James, *Refighting the Last War*, 35–38; Pearlman, *Truman and MacArthur*, 67.

16. I will use Formosa, as that was the name contemporaries used during the Korean War.

17. James, *Years of MacArthur*, 407–410.

18. Reston, "As a U.N. General," E3; James, *Years of MacArthur*, 438–441; Pearlman, *Truman and MacArthur*, 67–68; James, *Refighting the Last War*, 32–33.

19. Pearlman, *Truman and MacArthur*, 29; Manchester, *American Caesar*, 549–550.

20. James, *Years of MacArthur*, 452–453.

21. Manchester, *American Caesar*, 562–567; Pearlman, *Truman and MacArthur*, 74–77.

22. James, *Years of MacArthur*, 452–454.

23. Pearlman, *Truman and MacArthur*, 79–83; James, *Years of MacArthur*, 456–457.

24. James, *Years of MacArthur*, 457–458; Manchester, *American Caesar*, 567.

25. Manchester, *American Caesar*, 567; James, *Years of MacArthur*, 458.

26. Manchester, *American Caesar*, 568; Pearlman, *Truman and MacArthur*, 94, 96.

27. McCullough, *Truman*, 796–797; James, *Years of MacArthur*, 461–464; Omar N. Bradley and Clay Blair, *A General's Life: An Autobiography of General of the Army Omar N. Bradley* (New York: Simon & Schuster, 1983), 551; Manchester, *American Caesar*, 569–571; Pearlman, *Truman and MacArthur*, 95–98.

28. James, *Years of MacArthur*, 462–463.

29. Robert Debs Heinl, *Victory at High Tide: The Inchon-Seoul Campaign* (Philadelphia: J. B. Lippincott, 1968), 10.

30. James, *Refighting the Last War*, 166–169; Bradley and Blair, *General's Life*, 544, 555; Manchester, *American Caesar*, 574–577.

31. James, *Refighting the Last War*, 49; Pearlman, *Truman and MacArthur*, 106.

32. James, *Years of MacArthur*, 482; Bradley and Blair, *General's Life*, 557; Pearlman, *Truman and MacArthur*, 105.

33. James, *Years of MacArthur*, 486–489; Manchester, *American Caesar*, 583–585.

34. "Text of the Truman-MacArthur Wake Island Conference Document," in Rovere and Schlesinger, *MacArthur Controversy*, 275–285; Acheson, *Present at the Creation*, 456; Manchester, *American Caesar*, 588–596; McCullough, *Truman*, 800–801; James, *Years of MacArthur*, 500–510. The JCS soon sent MacArthur the stenographer's transcript of the meeting. He made no emendations, although his political supporters later protested the "secret" recording.

35. McCullough, *Truman*, 800–808; Bradley and Blair, *General's Life*, 576; James, *Years of MacArthur*, 510–517; Manchester, *American Caesar*, 592–596; Acheson, *Present at the Creation*, 456.

36. Manchester, *American Caesar*, 599–600; Forrest C. Pogue, *George C. Marshall: Statesman, 1945–1959* (New York: Viking, 1987), 458; Pearlman, *Truman and MacArthur*, 119–120.

37. Manchester, *American Caesar*, 585–587.

38. James, *Years of MacArthur*, 518–522; Bradley and Blair, *General's Life*, 584–585.

39. James, *Years of MacArthur*, 518–522; Bradley and Blair, *General's Life*, 580.

40. Bradley and Blair, *General's Life*, 587.

41. Ibid., 581, 590; James, *Years of MacArthur*, 522–523.

42. James, *Years of MacArthur*, 524–525.

43. Bradley and Blair, *General's Life*, 591–594; Pearlman, *Truman and MacArthur*, 122; James, *Years of MacArthur*, 525–530.

44. Manchester, *American Caesar*, 604–606.

45. James, *Years of MacArthur*, 532–536.

46. Ibid., 536–537.

47. Ibid., 540–542; Rovere and Schlesinger, *MacArthur Controversy*, 154–155; Manchester, *American Caesar*, 613–615.

48. McCullough, *Truman*, 822–823; Rovere and Schlesinger, *MacArthur Controversy*, 11; Acheson, *Present at the Creation*, 475; Matthew B. Ridgway, *The Korean War: How We Met the Challenge* (New York: Doubleday, 1967), 61–62.

49. Ridgway, *Korean War*, 62; McCullough, *Truman*, 823; Manchester, *American Caesar*, 619.

50. McCullough, *Truman*, 820–822.

51. James, *Years of MacArthur*, 550–551; Pearlman, *Truman and MacArthur*, 139.

52. Acheson, *Present at the Creation*, 514–517; Pogue, *George C. Marshall*, 474–475; Bradley and Blair, *General's Life*, 618–622 (italics are Bradley's).

53. James, *Refighting the Last War*, 49–50, 55–56; Manchester, *American Caesar*, 625; Bradley and Blair, *General's Life*, 622–623.

54. Manchester, *American Caesar*, 611, 620–621; James, *Years of MacArthur*, 571–577; Ridgway, *Korean War*, 109–110; Pearlman, *Truman and MacArthur*, 159.

55. James, *Years of MacArthur*, 584–585.

56. Ibid., 581–584; Rovere and Schlesinger, *MacArthur Controversy*, 167–168.

57. James, *Years of MacArthur*, 586–587; Manchester, *American Caesar*, 635; McCullough, *Truman*, 837–838; Pogue, *George C. Marshall*, 479.

58. McCullough, *Truman*, 835–837; Bradley and Blair, *General's Life*, 627; James, *Years of MacArthur*, 587–589; Acheson, *Present at the Creation*, 518–519.

59. James, *Years of MacArthur*, 588; Pearlman, *Truman and MacArthur*, 193.

60. James, *Years of MacArthur*, 589–590.

61. Manchester, *American Caesar*, 638–640; James, *Years of MacArthur*, 590–591.

62. James, *Years of MacArthur*, 591–594; McCullough, *Truman*, 839.

63. Bradley and Blair, *General's Life*, 633. Bradley eventually accepted Truman's nomination for a second two-year term as chairman of the Joint Chiefs of Staff.

64. Bradley and Blair, *General's Life*, 634–635; James, *Years of MacArthur*, 594–595.

65. James, *Years of MacArthur*, 596; Bradley and Blair, *General's Life*, 635–636.

66. Manchester, *American Caesar*, 643–645; McCullough, *Truman*, 841–843.

67. Bradley and Blair, *General's Life*, 637; Rovere and Schlesinger, *MacArthur Controversy*, 249; McCullough, *Truman*, 843–845; Manchester, *American Caesar*, 648–649.

68. Manchester, *American Caesar*, 650–651; McCullough, *Truman*, 847.

69. James, *Years of MacArthur*, 607–608; Manchester, *American Caesar*, 649–650; Pearlman, *Truman and MacArthur*, 195; McCullough, *Truman*, 846–847.

70. Pearlman, *Truman and MacArthur*, 192; James, *Years of MacArthur*, 611–612; Manchester, *American Caesar*, 656–657.

71. Douglas MacArthur, Address to a Joint Meeting of Congress, April 19, 1951; James, *Years of MacArthur*, 612–617; Manchester, *American Caesar*, 657–664.

72. Manchester, *American Caesar*, 663.

73. Ibid., 664.

74. Pearlman, *Truman and MacArthur*, 188, 192, 212.

75. James, *Years of MacArthur*, 626–629; Manchester, *American Caesar*, 666.

76. James, *Years of MacArthur*, 630; Manchester, *American Caesar*, 631.

77. Manchester, *American Caesar*, 667; James, *Years of MacArthur*, 631; Rovere and Schlesinger, *MacArthur Controversy*, 226.

78. James, *Years of MacArthur*, 629–630.

79. Ibid., 631.

80. Pearlman, *Truman and MacArthur*, 211; James, *Years of MacArthur*, 623, 632–633.

81. Bradley and Blair, *General's Life*, 640; Pearlman, *Truman and MacArthur*, 212; James, *Years of MacArthur*, 634.

82. James, *Years of MacArthur*, 634; Rovere and Schlesinger, *MacArthur Controversy*, 191; James, *Years of MacArthur*, 632–633.

83. Manchester, *American Caesar*, 678–681.

84. James, *Years of MacArthur*, 642–645; Manchester, *American Caesar*, 679–684.

85. James, *Years of MacArthur*, 643–644; Douglas MacArthur, "Address before the Massachusetts Legislature in Boston, 25 July 1951," in Rovere and Schlesinger, *MacArthur Controversy*, 336–344.

86. James, *Years of MacArthur*, 650–652.

87. Pearlman, *Truman and MacArthur*, xviii, 23; James, *Years of MacArthur*, 631.

88. Pearlman, *Truman and MacArthur*, 194.

89. Ibid., 186.

90. Ibid., 213.

91. Ibid., 246.
92. Manchester, *American Caesar,* 631.
93. Ibid., 683.

10. TAYLOR'S THEORY

1. Richard H. Kohn, "Out of Control: The Crisis in Civil-Military Relations," *National Interest,* Spring 1994, 4–5; George C. Herring, *LBJ and Vietnam: A Different Kind of War* (Austin: University of Texas Press, 1994), 25–27; Jack Shulimson, *The Joint Chiefs of Staff and the War in Vietnam, 1960–1968,* part 1 (Washington, DC: Office of Joint History, Office of the Chairman of the Joint Chiefs of Staff, 2011), 2–5; Robert Buzzanco, *Masters of War: Military Dissent and Politics in the Vietnam Era* (Cambridge: Cambridge University Press, 1996), 5–6, 12–16.

2. Buzzanco, *Masters of War,* 17; Andrew J. Bacevich, *The Pentomic Era: The U.S. Army between Korea and Vietnam* (Washington, DC: National Defense University, 1986).

3. Herring, *LBJ and Vietnam,* 26; Matthew B. Ridgway, *Soldier: The Memoirs of Matthew B. Ridgway,* as told to Harold H. Martin (New York: Harper Bros., 1959); Maxwell D. Taylor, *The Uncertain Trumpet* (New York: Harper Bros., 1959), 5–6; Buzzanco, *Masters of War,* 17–20; H. R. McMaster, *Dereliction of Duty: Lyndon Johnson, Robert McNamara, the Joint Chiefs of Staff, and the Lies That Led to Vietnam* (New York: HarperCollins, 1997), 10–11; Maxwell D. Taylor, *Swords and Plowshares* (New York: W. W. Norton, 1972), 179–180.

4. Fred M. Kaplan, *The Wizards of Armageddon* (New York: Simon & Schuster, 1983), 330–332; Thomas C. Schelling, *The Strategy of Conflict* (Cambridge, MA: Harvard University Press, 1960).

5. Herring, *LBJ and Vietnam,* 27; Shulimson, *Joint Chiefs,* 5; Buzzanco, *Masters of War,* 18, 36–78. A reporter suggested to one general that his congressional testimony had probably helped the Democrats more than their own campaign speeches. The officer deadpanned, "You get the idea, don't you."

6. Buzzanco, *Masters of War,* 16–20, 75–79; Herring, *LBJ and Vietnam,* 30, 40; David Halberstam, *The Best and the Brightest* (New York: Random House, 1969), 274; McMaster, *Dereliction of Duty,* 5, 18–22; Kaplan, *Wizards of Armageddon,* 254.

7. Ellsberg would later gain fame as the leaker of the Pentagon Papers and a principal victim of "dirty tricks" by the Watergate "plumbers' unit." After he left government service, Ellsberg became an inveterate antinuclear activist.

8. Kai Bird, *The Color of Truth: McGeorge Bundy and William Bundy, Brothers in Arms; A Biography* (New York: Simon & Schuster, 1998), 208–210; Kaplan, *Wizards of Armageddon,* 263–285; Lawrence S. Kaplan, Ronald D. Landa, and Edward J. Drea, *History of the Office of the Secretary of Defense,* vol. 5, *The McNamara Ascendancy, 1961–1965* (Washington, DC: Historical Office, Office of the Secretary of Defense, 2006), 316–321 (cited hereafter as Kaplan et al., *McNamara Ascendancy*). Steven L. Rearden, *Council of War: A History of the Joint Chiefs of Staff, 1942–1991* (Washington, DC: Joint History Office, NDU Press, 2012), 218.

9. Mark Perry, *Four Stars* (Boston: Houghton Mifflin, 1989), 97–106; Rearden, *Council of War*, 214; Bird, *Color of Truth*, 193–201; Gordon M. Goldstein, *Lessons in Disaster: McGeorge Bundy and the Path to War in Vietnam* (New York: Henry Holt, 2008), 35–40.

10. Goldstein, *Lessons in Disaster*, 40–43; Richard Reeves, *President Kennedy: Profile of Power* (New York: Touchstone, 1993), 103; Robert A. Caro, *The Years of Lyndon Johnson: The Passage of Power* (New York: Alfred A. Knopf, 2012), 183; Herring, *LBJ and Vietnam*, 28; Buzzanco, *Masters of War*, 86.

11. John Prados, *Vietnam: The History of an Unwinnable War* (Lawrence: University Press of Kansas, 2009), 29, 66–67; Bird, *Color of Truth*, 201–202; Goldstein, *Lessons in Disaster*, 44–48.

12. Buzzanco, *Masters of War*, 84–86; Taylor, *Swords and Plowshares*, 187–189; David Halberstam, *Best and the Brightest*, 40; McMaster, *Dereliction of Duty*, 11–17; Bird, *Color of Truth*, 197–198; Perry, *Four Stars*, 115; Lawrence Freedman, *Kennedy's Wars: Berlin, Cuba, Laos, and Vietnam* (New York: Oxford University Press, 2000), 145–146.

13. Taylor, *Swords and Plowshares*, 252.

14. Ibid., 56–84; Halberstam, *Best and the Brightest*, 40, 123; Buzzanco, *Masters of War*, 99; Perry, *Four Stars*, 111–118.

15. Taylor, *Swords and Plowshares*, 252–254; McMaster, *Dereliction of Duty*, 22–23; Herring, *LBJ and Vietnam*, 29.

16. Bird, *Color of Truth*, 226–240; McMaster, *Dereliction of Duty*, 24–30; Herring, *LBJ and Vietnam*, 39; Rearden, *Council of War*, 228–231, 233. The account of the Oval Office meeting between Kennedy and the chiefs is based on Robert Dallek, *An Unfinished Life: John F. Kennedy, 1917–1963* (New York: Little, Brown, 2003), 554–555. When the chiefs left his office, Kennedy asked his aide, Kenny O'Donnell, "Can you imagine LeMay saying a thing like that? These brass hats have one great advantage in their favor. If we listen to them, and do what they want us to do, none of us will be alive later to tell them that they were wrong."

17. Buzzanco, *Masters of War*, 25–79; Prados, *Vietnam*, 26–61; Bird, *Color of Truth*, 202; Goldstein, *Lessons in Disaster*, 48–51.

18. Halberstam, *Best and the Brightest*, 12, 97, 103–105, 117–120; Kaplan, *Wizards of Armageddon*, 331; Robert S. McNamara, James G. Blight, and Robert K. Brigham, with Thomas J. Biersteker and Herbert Y. Schandler, *Argument without End: In Search of Answers to the Tragedy of Vietnam* (New York: PublicAffairs, 1999), 161–164, 177–180, 195–202.

19. Halberstam, *Best and the Brightest*, 76.

20. Leslie H. Gelb and Richard K. Betts, *The Irony of Vietnam: The System Worked* (New York: Brookings Institution), 72–73.

21. Bird, *Color of Truth*, 202; Goldstein, *Lessons in Disaster*, 52–54; Gelb and Betts, *Irony of Vietnam*, 72; Buzzanco, *Masters of War*, 92–99; Rearden, *Council of War*, 281; *Foreign Relations of the United States, 1961–1963*, vol. 1, *Vietnam 1961*, ed. Ronald D. Landa and Charles S. Sampson (Washington, DC: Government Printing Office, 1988), 74–134; Bonesteel's comments on pp. 118–119; NSAM 52 on pp. 132–133 (cited hereafter as *FRUS, Vietnam 1961*).

22. Goldstein, *Lessons in Disaster,* 55–58; Buzzanco, *Masters of War,* 104–108; Kaplan et al., *McNamara Ascendancy,* 270.

23. *FRUS, Vietnam 1961,* 380–738; Goldstein, *Lessons in Disaster,* 58–63; Gelb and Betts, *Irony of Vietnam,* 74–76. Taylor, *Swords and Plowshares,* 225–245; Kaplan et al., *McNamara Ascendancy,* 271–272.

24. *FRUS, Vietnam 1961,* 532–534, 538–540, 543–544, 559–566; Undersecretary of State George Ball warned President Kennedy on November 7, 1961, that "to commit American forces to South Vietnam would . . . be a tragic error. . . . 'Within five years we'll have three hundred thousand men in the paddies and jungles and never find them again.'" JFK replied with asperity, "George, you're just crazier than hell. That just isn't going to happen." *FRUS, Vietnam 1961,* 547–548; Gelb and Betts, *Irony of Vietnam,* 76; Goldstein, *Lessons in Disaster,* 59–61. Dean Rusk was content to follow McNamara's lead on Vietnam policy so long as military solutions were on offer. Only when it came time to negotiate a treaty—meaning dictate terms of Hanoi's surrender—State would step to the fore. Rusk was a throwback to Cordell Hull in this regard. Frederik Logevall, *Choosing War: The Lost Chance for Peace and the Escalation of War in Vietnam* (Berkeley: University of California Press, 1999), 36.

25. *FRUS, Vietnam 1961,* 569–582, 586, 588–607; Gelb and Betts, *Irony of Vietnam,* 76–78. McNamara has written about this episode on at least two occasions. In his Vietnam memoir, *In Retrospect,* he says that over "the next couple of days I dug deeper into the Vietnam problem. . . . I realized that seconding the Taylor-Rostow memo had been a bad idea." This statement is disingenuous, as he had done far more than simply agree. He had recommended a commitment that Hanoi would have seen as waging general war. Robert S. McNamara with Brian VanDeMark, *In Retrospect: The Tragedy and Lessons of Vietnam* (New York: Times Books, 1995), 38–39. In *Argument without End,* McNamara relates that between his first memo and the Kennedy demurral, Ambassador-at-Large Averell Harriman gave Kennedy a recommendation to seek negotiations through the 1954 Geneva Accords process. McNamara records JFK's reaction, but does not say whether he was aware of the proposal at the time. McNamara et al., *Argument without End,* 106–108. Perhaps the best analysis remains that of the Pentagon Papers editors: "Three days later McNamara joined Rusk in a quite different recommendation, and one obviously more to the President's liking (and, in the nature of such things, quite possibly drawn up to the President's specifications)." *Final Report, OSD Vietnam Task Force,* dated January 15, 1969, Part IV-B-1, Kennedy Commitments and Programs, 1961, 158 (hereafter cited as, e.g., *Pentagon Papers,* IV-B-1, 158).

26. Buzzanco, *Masters of War,* 111; *FRUS, Vietnam 1961,* 607–610, 656–657; Goldstein, *Lessons in Disaster,* 59–66; Michael H. Hunt, *Lyndon Johnson's War: Americas' Cold War Crusade in Vietnam, 1945–1968* (New York: Hill & Wang, 1996), 57–60. Kaplan et al., *McNamara Ascendancy,* 273–274.

27. *FRUS, Vietnam 1961,* 1–12; Kaplan et al., *McNamara Ascendancy,* 277–280. The United States was also supplying new technologies to fight the war—helicopters, napalm, and defoliants.

28. *Foreign Relations of the United States, 1961–1963,* vol. 2, *Vietnam 1962,* ed. David M. Baehler and Charles S. Sampson (Washington, DC: Government Printing Office, 1990), 660–663 (hereafter cited as *FRUS, Vietnam 1962*). Buzzanco, *Masters of War,* 117–143; Kaplan et al., *McNamara Ascendancy,* 277–284; Halberstam, *Best and the Brightest,* 179–188, 200–205, 247–250; Prados, *Vietnam,* 67–74. Like Taylor, Harkins was a true believer in the mission, and his optimism blinded him to problems. "There is no doubt we are on the winning side," he told McNamara.

29. Logevall, *Choosing War,* 2–4.

30. Kaplan et al., *McNamara Ascendancy,* 283–285. No one knew at the time whether Ho's government was taking the peace overtures seriously; Prados, *Vietnam,* 74–76. In late August 1963 French involvement helped changed the trajectory of the conflict. In Paris, French president Charles de Gaulle called for "all of Vietnam"—the United States insisted that there were two Vietnams, North and South—to come together to solve problems "for the country as a whole." Despite the French defeat in its colonial war a decade earlier, French opinion and French policy still resonated in Vietnam. De Gaulle, victorious leader of the Free French in World War II, spoke with the credibility of a deliverer when he reminded listeners that the French understood and shared "the hardships of the Vietnamese people." He expressed French support for Vietnam and his hope that the Vietnamese would soon be able to act "independent of outside influences, in peace and unity." De Gaulle's language was vague, and he did not name the United States, but his statement was an indictment of American policy, and it opened the door to bilateral or multilateral talks to resolve the crisis and reunify Vietnam. The announcement sent shock waves through Washington. Logevall, *Choosing War,* 2–36.

31. "October 29, 1963: President Kennedy Meets with His National Security Council on the Question of Supporting a Coup in South Vietnam," in John Prados, *The White House Tapes: Eavesdropping on the President* (New York: New Press, 2003), 92–150; Logevall, *Choosing War,* 3, 44, 62–63; Goldstein, *Lessons in Disaster,* 78. Buzzanco, *Masters of War,* 98, 146; *Pentagon Papers,* IV-B-1, 102–103; Kaplan et al., *McNamara Ascendancy,* 288–289; Logevall, *Choosing War,* 48–51. It is worth noting that in 1963 Americans were far less punctilious about the propriety of interceding in the sovereign affairs of foreign states than they would become in the 1970s. McNamara and Taylor visited Vietnam in September, continuing to find "great progress" with the training of the RVNAF, and recommended that the United States could begin withdrawing troops by the end of 1963 in anticipation of victory within two years. Yet for the first time McNamara began to doubt MACV's rosy reporting. He was especially skeptical of Harkins's estimate that the Diem regime controlled 80 percent of the population. "Prove me wrong," he challenged Harkins.

32. Quoted in Logevall, *Choosing War,* 38–39. Buzzanco, *Masters of War,* 143; Logevall, *Choosing War,* 6–10, 16–20, 37–39, 55–58, 62–74. The Diem regime was weak, corrupt, out of touch, and unworthy of American support. The Soviet Union and Great Britain, brokers of the 1954 Geneva Accords partitioning Vietnam, seemed amenable to reprising those roles. Although most of the American media supported the administration, key opinion makers were beginning to recog-

nize a strategic inflection point. The *New Republic,* a liberal bastion firmly in the Kennedy political base, openly questioned the domino theory and argued that the United States should look to a nonaligned Vietnam. *U.S. News & World Report* and the *New York Times* began raising cogent questions about the premises of American policy. And a few days after de Gaulle's announcement, Walter Lippmann, the dean of American foreign policy columnists, syndicated in almost two hundred U.S. newspapers, warned that ignoring the French president's pronouncement might lead the United States into "a protracted and indecisive war of attrition." Two days later he declared, "The price of a military victory in the Vietnamese war is higher than American vital interests can justify." Furthermore, Lippmann argued, the limited nature of the U.S. commitment thus far showed that the administration recognized Vietnam was "an important secondary . . . not a primary vital interest." Despite Democratic bugaboos about being labeled soft on communism, Kennedy had a chance to get out of Vietnam. In 1959 Eisenhower had "lost Cuba" and suffered no criticism. Kennedy had disengaged from Laos with no political ill effects. Moreover, in the summer of 1963 most Americans could not have pointed to Vietnam on a globe. Publicly Kennedy was steadfast in backing South Vietnam: "In my opinion, for us to withdraw would mean a collapse not only of South Vietnam, but of Southeast Asia. So we are going to stay there." Off the record, the president was candidly skeptical: "We don't have a prayer of staying in Vietnam. Those people hate us. They are going to throw our asses out of there at almost any point. But I can't give up a piece of territory like that to the Communists and then get the people to reelect me." Yet with his formidable political and media skills, Kennedy still had the option reducing the American presence and deflecting public attention until the British, the Soviets, the French, and the Vietnamese solved the problem in Vietnam.

33. Goldstein, *Lessons in Disaster,* 84–91.

34. Halberstam, *Best and the Brightest,* 306.

35. Caro, *Passage of Power,* 339–345.

36. There are many treatments of the Johnson life and presidency, including Johnson's own *The Vantage Point: Perspective of the Presidency, 1963–1969* (New York: Holt, Rinehart, and Winston, 1971); Robert Dallek's two-volume biography, *Lyndon Johnson and His Times: Lone Star Rising* (New York: Oxford University Press, 1991) and *Flawed Giant, 1961–1973* (New York: Oxford University Press, 1998); and Ronnie Dugger's *The Politician: The Life and Times of Lyndon Johnson: The Drive for Power; From the Frontier to Master of the Senate* (New York: W. W. Norton, 1982). The portrait of LBJ above owes a great debt to the masterly and seminal works, four volumes to date, of Robert A. Caro, *The Years of Lyndon Johnson* (New York: Alfred A. Knopf): *The Path to Power* (1982), *Means of Ascent* (1990), *Master of the Senate* (2002), and *The Passage of Power* (2011).

37. Caro, *Passage of Power,* 545–548.

38. Ibid., 344–345, 351–353, 365–366, 409–414.

39. McMaster, *Dereliction of Duty,* 41, 49–50; Logevall, *Choosing War,* 79.

40. Logevall, *Choosing War,* 75–77, Caro, *Passage of Power,* 401–402.

41. *Pentagon Papers,* IV-C-1, 1–4; Kaplan, *Wizards of Armageddon,* 500–501; Logevall, *Choosing War,* 171.

42. Graham A. Cosmas, *The Joint Chiefs of Staff and the War in Vietnam, 1960–1968*, part 2 (Washington, DC: Office of Joint History, Office of the Chairman of the Joint Chiefs of Staff, 2012), 6–10; Caro, *Passage of Power,* 401–403.

43. Logevall, *Choosing War,* 80–83; Michael R. Beschloss, ed., *Taking Charge: The Johnson White House Tapes, 1963–1964* (New York: Simon & Schuster, 1997), 88, 95; Halberstam, *Best and the Brightest,* 179–180.

44. *Pentagon Papers,* IV-C-1, U.S. Programs in South Vietnam, November 1963–April 1965: NSAM 273—NSAM 288—Honolulu, ii–iii, 17–24; Halberstam, *Best and the Brightest,* 41, 183–188, 200–205, 249, 256; McMaster, *Dereliction of Duty,* 48, 57–58; Logevall, *Choosing War,* 89–90; Kaplan et al., *McNamara Ascendancy,* 498–502; Prados, *Vietnam,* 80–82; Rearden, *Council of War,* 282.

45. Kaplan et al., *McNamara Ascendancy,* 501–502; David Kaiser, *American Tragedy: Kennedy, Johnson, and the Origins of the Vietnam War* (Cambridge, MA: The Belknap Press of the Harvard University Press, 2000), 293–294.

46. Cosmas, *Joint Chiefs,* 16–19; FRUS, *Vietnam 1964,* 35; *Pentagon Papers,* IV-C-1, 37–40.

47. Kaplan et al., *McNamara Ascendancy,* 502–504; Halberstam, *Best and the Brightest,* 351–353.

48. Logevall, *Choosing War,* 111–122; Cosmas, *Joint Chiefs,* 21–23.

49. McNamara et al., *Argument without End,* 180–184.

50. Rearden, *Council of War,* 282–283; FRUS, *Vietnam 1964,* 97–99, 110–120, 129–130; Cosmas, *Joint Chiefs,* 25–30, Kaplan et al., *McNamara Ascendancy,* 505–507.

51. Kaiser, *American Tragedy,* 304.

52. Beschloss, *Taking Charge,* 266–267.

53. FRUS, *Vietnam 1964,* 130–134, 142–167, 170–173; Kaplan, *Wizards of Armageddon,* 507–510; Halberstam, *Best and the Brightest,* 353–354.

54. Historian John Prados argues that in the spring of 1964 the Johnson administration secretly began working to develop a political-military plan called "the scenario," which would allow it to prepare both the United States and South Vietnam for American forces to take a more direct role in the conflict. Prados, *Vietnam,* 83, 96–100. A series of documents from NSC, State, and Defense officials as well as the embassy in Saigon gives credence to this theory. While the language within these papers is often cryptic, often referring to earlier conversations without detailing them, taken together the papers indicate that civilian staffers within the Johnson administration were taking an active role in contingency planning both military and political. FRUS, *Vietnam 1964,* 93–96, 206–214, 225–229, 232–233, 242–243, 248–253, 271–272. One of these documents, dated March 31, 1964, specifically mentions plans for the president to ask Congress for a resolution authorizing direct U.S. attacks against North Vietnam. See FRUS, *Vietnam 1964,* 212.

55. FRUS, *Vietnam 1964,* 200; Logevall, *Choosing War,* 164–165.

56. Beschloss, *Taking Charge,* 363–373. Bundy acknowledged that going to war was a big decision and that he was not sure what he would do in the president's position, but he sympathized with "the difficulty your own people have in—I'm not talking about Dean Rusk or Bob McNamara or me—but people who are at second remove [such as George Ball and Bundy's brother Bill, assistant secretary of

state for Far Eastern affairs], who just find it very hard to be firm if they're not absolutely clear what your decision is. And yet you *must* safeguard that decision." Bundy had encapsulated one of the keys to presidential leadership—knowing when to decide. The two men acknowledged that while most of the public favored current policy, the poll numbers fell off sharply when the questions turned to sending troops to war.

57. Kaplan et al., *McNamara Ascendancy,* 517–524; Prados, *Vietnam,* 83, 96–100; Kaiser, *American Tragedy,* 326–340; Logevall, *Choosing War,* 196–205. The Korean conflict and the Quemoy-Matsu crisis were the other two occasions.

58. Logevall, *Choosing War,* 237–238, 253–254.

59. *Pentagon Papers,* IV-C-2c, 3–5; Kaiser, *American Tragedy,* 353.

60. *Pentagon Papers,* IV-C-2c, viii–xii, 5–6; Logevall, *Choosing War,* 255–257; Herbert Y. Schandler, *The Unmaking of a President: Lyndon Johnson and Vietnam* (Princeton, NJ: Princeton University Press, 1977), 8–9.

61. *Pentagon Papers,* IV-C-2c, 18–31; Logevall, *Choosing War,* 258–259.

62. *Pentagon Papers,* IV-C-2c, 15–17, 31–35; Cosmas, *Joint Chiefs,* 155–169; McMaster, *Dereliction of Duty,* 181–188; Logevall, *Choosing War,* 256.

63. *FRUS, Vietnam 1964,* 914–916. In response to LBJ's request that he play "devil's advocate," Undersecretary of State George Ball had recently written a sixty-seven-page memorandum that surveyed the dreary political and military situations in Vietnam, the place of Vietnam in the nation's global foreign policy, and the attitudes of American allies and adversaries. The outlook for American policy in Vietnam was bleak; the status quo was not working. The South Vietnamese government was corrupt, the army ineffective, and the people either apathetic or hostile to the regime. Two recent war games had shown that a bombing campaign against the North would only strengthen Hanoi's resolve while doing nothing to help in the South. Ball counseled strongly against engaging in a game of tit-for-tat escalation with Hanoi, which Taylor advocated, because each "move passes the option to the other side," thereby surrendering the initiative. He warned of actions that would be difficult to control, such as deploying ground combat forces, for "once on the tiger's back we cannot be sure of picking the place to dismount." Ball recommended telling the South Vietnamese that the United States would "continue the struggle" if they were willing to "achieve a unity of purpose" by establishing a stable government and committing to the war effort. Saigon would likely take that statement as a warning and begin negotiations with the NLF, which would "permit a political settlement without direct U.S. military involvement." Ball knew that his conclusions were unpalatable to the administration. Indeed, McNamara was said to view this and all subsequent Ball memos as he would "poisonous snakes." Yet the paper was such a cogent argument for negotiation and withdrawal that Bill Bundy found it necessary to counter its "heresies" point by point. Nevertheless Bundy found himself accepting many of Ball's conclusions, conceding, for example, that the loss of Vietnam "could be made bearable" because "the domino theory is much too pat." Still, he recommended that the United States step up its military involvement in order to strengthen its bargaining position for the talks to come. Rusk and McNamara, fearing the force of Ball's logic, suppressed his memo. LBJ never saw it until months later, after irrevocable decisions had been made.

George Ball, "A Light That Failed," *Atlantic Monthly*, July 1972, 33–49; Kaiser, *American Tragedy*, 349–353; Logevall, *Choosing War*, 243–248.

64. *Pentagon Papers*, IV-C-2c, 42–58; Cosmas, *Joint Chiefs*, 170–176; *FRUS, Vietnam 1964*, 948–957; McNamara et al. *Argument without End*, 169–170; Logevall, *Choosing War*, 261–269.

65. *FRUS, Vietnam 1964*, 964–978; Logevall, *Choosing War*, 269–270; McMaster, *Dereliction of Duty*, 191–193.

66. *Pentagon Papers*, IV-C-2c, 54–58; Kaiser, *American Tragedy*, 384–391.

67. *Foreign Relations of the United States, 1964–1968*, vol. 2, *Vietnam January–June 1965*, ed. David C. Humphrey, Ronald D. Landa, and Louis J. Smith (Washington, DC: Government Printing Office, 1996), 12–28, 93–95 (hereafter cited as *FRUS, Vietnam January–June 1965*). Kaiser, *American Tragedy*, 392–393; Logevall, *Choosing War*, 316–319; Goldstein, *Lessons in Disaster*, 152–154.

68. *FRUS, Vietnam January–June 1965*, 155–172; Kaiser, *American Tragedy*, 394, 398; Logevall, *Choosing War*, 320–325; Goldstein, *Lessons in Disaster*, 155–156; Andrew Preston, *The War Council: McGeorge Bundy, the NSC, and Vietnam* (Cambridge, MA: Harvard University Press, 2006), 175–176.

69. *FRUS, Vietnam January–June 1965*, 166–185; Logevall, *Choosing War*, 328–330; Goldstein, *Lessons in Disaster*, 156–158; Kaiser, 399–400.

70. Logevall, *Choosing War*, 330.

71. Ibid., 330–352; Kaiser, *American Tragedy*, 400–401. The *New York Herald Tribune* coined the phrase "credibility gap" in March 1965 to explain the growing distance between LBJ's Vietnam policy and the realities on the ground. Senator Fulbright used the phrase repeatedly in his Foreign Relations Committee hearings on the war. "Credibility gap" became part of the American lexicon.

72. *FRUS, Vietnam January–June 1965*, 228–229, 240–243; 347–349, 351.

73. Logevall, *Choosing War*, 362–368, 373; McMaster, *Dereliction of Duty*, 288.

II. POWELL'S DOCTRINE

1. Colin L. Powell, "Why Generals Get Nervous," *New York Times*, October 8, 1992, A35.

2. Colin L. Powell with Joseph E. Persico, *My American Journey* (New York: Random House, 1995), 144–149.

3. Powell, *My American Journey*, 260; Karen DeYoung, *Soldier: The Life of Colin Powell* (New York: Alfred A. Knopf, 2006), 110–124.

4. DeYoung, *Soldier*, 125–134.

5. Ibid., 134–141.

6. Ibid., 141–142; Powell, *My American Journey*, 302–303.

7. DeYoung, *Soldier*, 147–154; Powell, *My American Journey*, 304–315.

8. DeYoung, *Soldier*, 146–150; Powell, *My American Journey*, 316–331.

9. DeYoung, *Soldier*, 156–162.

10. Ibid., 162–180.

11. Ibid., 177–179, 190–191; Bob Woodward, *The Commanders* (New York: Simon & Schuster, 1991), 60–66.

12. DeYoung, *Soldier*, 182–184; Woodward, *Commanders*, 83–196; James R. Locher III, *Victory on the Potomac: The Goldwater-Nichols Act Unifies the Pentagon* (College Station: Texas A&M Press, 2002), 440.

13. Powell, *My American Journey*, 374–375.

14. DeYoung, *Soldier*, 188–191; Powell, *My American Journey*, 437–440, 454–455; Michael R. Gordon and Bernard E. Trainor, *The Generals' War: The Inside Story of the Conflict in the Gulf* (Boston: Little, Brown, 1995), 25.

15. Gordon and Trainor, *Generals' War*, 14–18, 23–29, 33–34.

16. George Bush and Brent Scowcroft, *A World Transformed* (New York: Alfred A. Knopf, 1998), 317–324; DeYoung, *Soldier*, 194–195; Powell, *My American Journey*, 462–465.

17. DeYoung, *Soldier*, 195; Powell, *My American Journey*, 465–466.

18. Powell, *My American Journey*, 492; Gordon and Trainor, *Generals' War*, 40–42, 66; Woodward, *Commanders*, 208–209, 298.

19. Powell, *My American Journey*, 466; Bush and Scowcroft, *World Transformed*, 327–335; Gordon and Trainor, *Generals' War*, 48–49.

20. Powell, *My American Journey*, 466–467; Bush and Scowcroft, *World Transformed*, 332–333.

21. Bush and Scowcroft, *World Transformed*, 332–333; Gordon and Trainor, *Generals' War*, 49–53.

22. Powell, *My American Journey*, 469–470.

23. Woodward, *Commanders*, 281–282; Powell, *My American Journey*, 470–471.

24. Powell, *My American Journey*, 476–478; Bush and Scowcroft, *World Transformed*, 372–374.

25. Powell, *My American Journey*, 478–480; DeYoung, *Soldier*, 196–198; Bush and Scowcroft, *World Transformed*, 374–375.

26. Gordon and Trainor, *Generals' War*, 128–145; Bush and Scowcroft, *World Transformed*, 380–383; Steven L. Rearden, *Council of War: A History of the Joint Chiefs of Staff, 1942–1991* (Washington, DC: NDU Press, 2012), 512, 515–516.

27. Powell, *My American Journey*, 485.

28. Gordon and Trainor, *Generals' War*, 153–155; Powell, *My American Journey*, 487–489; Rearden, *Council of War*, 517–518; Bush and Scowcroft, *World Transformed*, 389–396.

29. Rearden, *Council of War*, 484.

30. Bush and Scowcroft, *World Transformed*, 388–391, 396–398, 400–402, 416–419, 421–423, 425–429, 436–439, 443–446; Woodward, *Commanders*, 35–39, 331–362.

31. Gordon and Trainor, *Generals' War*, 331.

32. Ibid., 355–399.

33. Ibid., 395–406; H. Norman Schwarzkopf, *It Doesn't Take a Hero* (New York: Linda Grey Bantam Books, 1992), 468–469.

34. Gordon and Trainor, *Generals' War*, 362–387, 411–414, 424.

35. Ibid., 405; Powell, *My American Journey*, 519–520; Schwarzkopf, *Doesn't Take a Hero*, 469.

36. Gordon and Trainor, *Generals' War*, vii–x, 413–415.

37. Ibid., 415.

38. Powell, *My American Journey,* 520–524; Schwarzkopf, *Doesn't Take a Hero,* 469; DeYoung, *Soldier,* 207–208; Bush and Scowcroft, *World Transformed,* 485–487.

39. Gordon and Trainor, *Generals' War,* 429, 439–443; Schwarzkopf, *Doesn't Take a Hero,* 472–478.

40. Gordon and Trainor, *Generals' War,* 443–450. The authors do not name the senior Bush official. Schwarzkopf, *Doesn't Take a Hero,* 481–491; Andrew J. Bacevich, "The United States in Iraq: Terminating an Interminable War," in *Between War and Peace: How America Ends Its Wars,* ed. Matthew Moten (New York: Free Press, 2011), 308–310.

41. Bush and Scowcroft, *World Transformed,* 486.

42. DeYoung, *Soldier,* 209–210, 219–222.

43. Ibid., 213–216; Powell, *My American Journey,* 535–536; Woodward, *Commanders,* passim and 46–47,53–54, 146–153, 236–241, 261–262, 281, 298–303, 318–319, 344–345.

44. DeYoung, *Soldier,* 217–219.

45. Ibid., 219.

46. Powell, *My American Journey,* 561–564; Richard H. Kohn, "The Erosion of Civilian Control of the Military in the United States Today," *Naval War College Review 55,* no. 3 (Summer 2002): 10.

47. George Stephanopoulos, *All Too Human: A Political Education* (Boston: Little, Brown, 1999), 122–129; DeYoung, *Soldier,* 230–234; Powell, *My American Journey,* 570–574; Andrew J. Bacevich, "Elusive Bargain: The Pattern of U.S. Civil-Military Relations since World War II," in *The Long War: A New History of U.S. National Security Policy since World War II,* ed. Andrew J. Bacevich (New York: Columbia University Press, 2007), 247–249.

48. Stephanopoulos, *All Too Human,* 159, 163, 165; DeYoung, *Soldier,* 234–236; Powell, *My American Journey,* 575–577; Madeleine Albright, *Madam Secretary* (New York: Miramax Books, 2003), 181–182.

49. *U.S. News & World Report,* September 20, 1993, cover and 48–59.

50. David Halberstam, *War in a Time of Peace: Bush, Clinton, and the Generals* (New York: Scribner, 2001), 237–238; DeYoung, *Soldier,* 240–284; Dan Balz, "Powell Passes Up 1996 Presidential Race," *Washington Post,* November 9, 1995, A1, A14.

51. William J. Crowe Jr., *The Line of Fire: From Washington to the Gulf, the Politics and Battles of the New Military* (New York: Simon & Schuster, 1993), 23.

52. DeYoung, *Soldier,* 180–181.

53. Richard H. Kohn, "Out of Control: The Crisis in Civil-Military Relations," *National Interest,* Spring 1994, 9; DeYoung, *Soldier,* 4.

12. RUMSFELD'S ASSUMPTIONS

1. Secretary of Defense Donald Rumsfeld and General Richard B. Myers, "Department of Defense News Briefing, 11 April 2003," in Thomas R. Mockaitis, *The Iraq War: A Documentary and Reference Guide* (Santa Barbara, CA: Greenwood,

2012), 145–151; Bradley Graham, *By His Own Rules: The Ambitions, Successes, and Ultimate Failures of Donald Rumsfeld* (New York: PublicAffairs, 2009), 308–310.

2. Barton Gellman, *Angler: The Cheney Vice Presidency* (New York: Penguin Press, 2008), 31–57; James Mann, *Rise of the Vulcans: The History of Bush's War Cabinet* (New York: Viking, 2004), 262–275; Graham, *By His Own Rules*, 202–205.

3. Gellman, *Angler*, 36–37; Mann, *Vulcans*, 264–266.

4. Mann, *Vulcans*, 268–270; Graham, *By His Own Rules*, 202–204; Michael R. Gordon and General Bernard E. Trainor, *Cobra II: The Inside Story of the Invasion and Occupation of Iraq* (New York: Pantheon Books, 2006), 6–8.

5. Karen DeYoung, *Soldier: The Life of Colin Powell* (New York: Alfred A. Knopf, 2006), 135–136, 298–302; Mann, *Vulcans*, 271–276.

6. The best Rumsfeld biographical sources are his own memoir, *Known and Unknown* (New York: Sentinel, 2011) and Bradley Graham's *By His Own Rules*.

7. Graham, *By His Own Rules*, 214–217.

8. Gordon and Trainor, *Cobra II*, 148.

9. Rumsfeld, *Known and Unknown*, xiii–xv; Graham, *By His Own Rules*, 271–273.

10. Graham, *By His Own Rules*, 230, 271–274.

11. Gordon and Trainor, *Cobra II*, 7; Graham, *By His Own Rules*, 205–207, 241–253.

12. Thomas E. Ricks, "Rumsfeld on High Wire of Defense Reform: Military Brass, Conservative Lawmakers Are among Secretive Review's Unexpected Critics," *Washington Post*, May 20, 2001, A01; Vernon Loeb and Thomas E. Ricks, "Rumsfeld's Style, Goals Strain Ties in Pentagon," *Washington Post*, October 16, 2002; Dave Moniz, "Rumsfeld's Abrasive Style Sparks Conflict," *USA Today*, December 10, 2002; Seymour M. Hersh, "Annals of National Security: Offense and Defense; The Battle between Rumsfeld and the Pentagon," *New Yorker*, April 7, 2003; Dave Moniz and John Diamond, "Rumsfeld Is Perched at 'Pinnacle of Power,' " *USA Today*, May 1, 2003, 10.

13. Ricks, "Rumsfeld on High Wire"; Department of Defense News Briefing, Secretary Rumsfeld and General Myers, January 29, 2003, accessed at http://www.defenselink.mil/transcripts/transcript.aspx?transcriptid=1349.

14. Thomas E. Ricks, *Fiasco: The American Military Adventure in Iraq* (New York: Penguin Press, 2006), 6–24; Mann, *Vulcans*, 235–238.

15. DeYoung, *Soldier*, 314–318; Lloyd C. Gardner, *The Long Road to Baghdad: A History of U.S. Foreign Policy from the 1970s to the Present* (New York: New Press, 2008), 124–125.

16. Rumsfeld outlined his thinking in several congressional committee appearances. See, for example, "Prepared Testimony of U.S. Secretary of Defense Donald H. Rumsfeld, Senate Armed Services Committee Hearing on Defense Strategy Review," June 21, 2001. Ricks, "Rumsfeld on High Wire"; Peter Boyer, "A Different War: Is the Army Becoming Irrelevant?" *New Yorker*, July 1, 2002, 63–65; Ricks, *Fiasco*, 68–70.

17. Graham, *By His Own Rules*, 277–280.

18. The fourth plane crashed near Shanksville, Pennsylvania, after passengers attempted to retake control.

19. Graham, *By His Own Rules*, 285–291; Gardner, *Long Road to Baghdad*, 128–129; Mann, *Vulcans*, 300–302; Gordon and Trainor, *Cobra II*, 10–21; De-Young, *Soldier*, 348–353.

20. Anton Myrer, *Once an Eagle* (New York: HarperTorch, 1986); Gordon and Trainor, *Cobra II*, 24, 107, 112; Ricks, *Fiasco*, 33–34, 39–41.

21. Peter Boyer, "The New War Machine," *New Yorker*, April 7, 2003; Mann, *Vulcans*, 308–309; Graham, *By His Own Rules*, 304–308, 313–315.

22. Mann, *Vulcans*, 296–297; Gardner, *Long Road to Baghdad*, 129–130.

23. Graham, *By His Own Rules*, 338–339; Gardner, *Long Road to Baghdad*, 131–132; Gellman, *Angler*, 222–226.

24. Mann, *Vulcans*, 315–317.

25. George W. Bush, "State of the Union 2002," excerpt in Mockaitis, *Iraq War*, 6–7.

26. Gardner, *Long Road to Baghdad*, 140.

27. George W. Bush, "Commencement Address at West Point, 31 May 2002," accessed at http://www.nytimes.com/2002/06/01/international/02PTEX-WEB.html ?pagewanted=all.

28. Gordon and Trainor, *Cobra II*, 25.

29. Gardner, *Long Road to Baghdad*, 164–166.

30. Gordon and Trainor, *Cobra II*, 26–32; Graham, *By His Own Rules*, 326–328.

31. Gordon and Trainor, *Cobra II*, 36–37; Graham, *By His Own Rules*, 328.

32. Gordon and Trainor, *Cobra II*, 48–54.

33. Ibid., 51–52.

34. Ibid., 46–48; Graham, *By His Own Rules*, 356–361; Ricks, *Fiasco*, 89–90; Tommy Franks with Malcolm McConnell, *American Soldier* (New York: Regan Books, 2004), 207–208, 274–278; 440–441; General (retired) Richard B. Myers, former chairman, Joint Chiefs of Staff, interview with author, November 13, 2007. General Myers noted that General Franks met the Joint Chiefs on several occasions, but did not seem to understand their roles other than as providers of forces for his operations.

35. Gordon and Trainor, *Cobra II*, 66–68.

36. Ibid., 66–68.

37. Ibid., 72–73.

38. Ricks, *Fiasco*, 42–43; Franks, *American Soldier*, 441; Gordon and Trainor, *Cobra II*, 74–77, 80–83; Graham, *By His Own Rules*, 348–354.

39. Graham, *By His Own Rules*, 349–355, 380–382; Ricks, *Fiasco*, 59–60; Conrad C. Crane and W. Andrew Terrill, *Reconstructing Iraq: Insights, Challenges, and Missions for Military Forces in a Post-Conflict Scenario* (Carlisle, PA: Strategic Studies Institute, U.S. Army War College, February 2003).

40. Gordon and Trainor, *Cobra II*, 70–71.

41. Ibid., 130–131; Ricks, *Fiasco*, 61–63.

42. Graham, *By His Own Rules*, 362–363; Gordon and Trainor, *Cobra II*, 86–95.

43. Graham, *By His Own Rules*, 362–365; Gordon and Trainor, *Cobra II*, 95–102; Myers interview with author, November 13, 2007. General Myers noted that he had to pay inordinately close attention to the TPFDL, presiding over weekly meetings between CENTCOM and Transportation Command to resolve differences. Hersh, "Annals of National Security."

44. James Fallows, "Blind into Baghdad," *Atlantic*, January–February 2004, 53–64; Gordon and Trainor, *Cobra II*, 95–102; Ricks, *Fiasco*, 71, 73–74; Myers interview, November 13, 2007; Dr. Kori Schake, director for defense strategy and requirements on the National Security Council during President Bush's first term, interview with author, February 15, 2007. General Myers described this meeting as "positive" and not "contentious." Schake, the observer mentioned, was also present at the January 30, 2003, meeting in the Cabinet Room.

45. Matthew Moten, "A Broken Dialogue: Rumsfeld, Shinseki, and Civil-Military Tension," in *American Civil-Military Relations: The Soldier and the State in a New Era*, ed. Suzanne C. Nielsen and Don M. Snider (Baltimore: Johns Hopkins University Press, 2009), 42–71; "U.S. Senate Armed Services Committee Hearing on FY 2004 Defense Authorization," transcript, February 25, 2003; Gordon and Trainor, *Cobra II*, 102, notes 522–523; George Packer, *The Assassins' Gate: America in Iraq* (New York: Farrar, Straus and Giroux, 2005), 114; Ricks, *Fiasco*, 96–97.

46. Eric Schmitt, "Pentagon Contradicts General on Iraq Occupation Force's Size," *New York Times*, February 28, 2003; Bob Woodward, *State of Denial: Bush at War, Part III* (New York: Simon & Schuster, 2006), 151; Gordon and Trainor, *Cobra II*, 102–103, 486; Ricks, *Fiasco*, 96–100; Packer, *Assassins' Gate*, 114.

47. Ricks, *Fiasco*, 120–123.

48. Ibid., 120–127; Gordon and Trainor, *Cobra II*, 311–314, 317–318; Graham, *By His Own Rules*, 394–397.

49. Graham, *By His Own Rules*, 396–397.

50. Michael R. Gordon and General Bernard E. Trainor, *The Endgame: The Inside Story of the Struggle for Iraq, from George W. Bush to Barack Obama* (New York: Pantheon Books, 2012), 12.

51. Graham, *By His Own Rules*, 398–403; Ricks, *Fiasco*, 158–167.

52. Ricks, *Fiasco*, 145; Gardner, *Long Road to Baghdad*, 173–176.

53. Graham, *By His Own Rules*, 275–277.

54. Gordon and Trainor, *Cobra II*, 317–318; Graham, *By His Own Rules*, 391–394, 400–411; Ricks, *Fiasco*, 147–155, 166–171, 179–191.

CONCLUSION

1. Samuel P. Huntington, *The Soldier and the State: The Theory and Politics of Civil-Military Relations* (Cambridge, MA: Belknap Press of Harvard University Press, 1957), 80–97, quotation p. 84. For a discussion of the influence of this idea on the military profession see Eliot Cohen, *Supreme Command: Soldiers, Statesmen, and Leadership in Wartime* (New York: Free Press, 2002), 225–248.

2. In fairness to Huntington, he does not describe such a wall directly. Some may criticize my interpretation here as a caricature. Indeed, Huntington acknowledges

that, because of our constitutional system, objective civilian control is difficult to achieve and that it has occurred in the United States only rarely, when the military was relatively weak and officers themselves reduced their political power and influence. Huntington, 189–192, 260–263. He also details moral, legal, and operational reasons why officers might disobey their civilian superiors. Ibid., 70–79. Yet he clearly prefers objective civilian control as an ideal type: "The antithesis of objective civilian control is military participation in politics. . . . The essence of objective civilian control is the recognition of an autonomous military professionalism." Ibid., 83.

3. Clausewitz used a water metaphor to describe friction in war: "Action in war is like movement in a resistant element. Just as the simplest and most natural of movements, walking, cannot easily be performed in water, so in war it is difficult for normal efforts to achieve even moderate results. A genuine theorist is like a swimming teacher." Carl von Clausewitz, On War, ed. and trans. Michael Howard and Peter Paret, introductory essays by Peter Paret, Michael Howard, and Bernard Brodie, commentary by Bernard Brodie (Princeton, NJ: Princeton University Press, 1976), 120.

4. Huntington, Soldier and the State, 80–85, quotation, p. 83.

5. Clausewitz, On War, 607–608. Emphasis in the original.

6. Huntington, Soldier and the State, 59–79, 464–466. For a typical example of the genre see John Hillen, "Must US Military Culture Reform?" Parameters 29, no. 3 (Autumn 1999): 9–23. Hillen describes American culture in the 1990s as "narcissistic, morally relativist, self-indulgent, hedonistic, consumerist, individualistic, victim-centered, nihilistic, and soft" (p. 18).

7. Sir John Hackett, The Profession of Arms (Washington, DC: U.S. Army Center of Military History, 1986), 34. Originally the 1962 Lee Knowles Lectures at Trinity College, Cambridge.

8. Peter Feaver, James Golby, and Kyle Dropp, Military Campaigns: Veterans' Endorsements and Presidential Elections (Washington, DC: Center for a New American Security, 2012). The history and figures above come from this study.